The Americans with Disabilities Act and the Emerging Workforce

Employment of People with Mental Retardation

Peter David Blanck, Ph.D., J.D.

David Braddock
Editor, Books and Research Monographs
AAMR
American Association on Mental Retardation

Printed in the United States of America.

Published by
American Association on Mental Retardation
444 North Capitol Street, NW
Suite 846
Washington, DC 20001-1570

The points of view expressed herein are those of the author and do not necessarily represent the official policy or opinion of the American Association on Mental Retardation. Publication does not imply endorsement by the editor, the association, or its individual members.

Library of Congress Cataloging-in-Publication Data

Blanck, Peter David, 1957-
The Americans with Disabilities Act and the emerging work force: employment of people with mental retardation / Peter David Blanck; book and research monograph editor, David Braddock.
p. cm.
Includes index.
ISBN 0-940898-52-7
1. Mentally handicapped—Employment—United States. 2. Mentally handicapped—Employment—Law and legislation—United States.
3. United States. Americans with Disabilities Act of 1990.
I. Braddock, David L. II. Title.
HV3005.B55 1998
331.5'94'0973—dc21 98-10269
CIP

Table of Contents—Summary

Table of Contents—Detailed

Foreword

Paul Steven Miller, Esq.[1]

The ADA and the Emerging Workforce of Persons with Mental Retardation

This year marks the eighth anniversary of the enactment of the Americans with Disabilities Act (ADA), a law intended to remove barriers, both physical *and* attitudinal, that prevent people with mental and physical disabilities from participating fully in all aspects of community life. Title I of the ADA prohibits discrimination against people with disabilities in employment.

The passage of the ADA marked a significant step in the integration of people with disabilities into the mainstream of society. Following the civil rights movement of the 1960s, people with disabilities in general, and people with mental retardation in particular, remained without legal redress for employment discrimination. In the area of employment, in 1973 Congress passed Title V of the Rehabilitation Act, prohibiting federal government agencies and businesses that receive federal funds from discriminating against qualified workers with disabilities. However, it was not until the passage of the ADA in 1990 that individuals with disabilities were provided with the federal protection from discrimination in all forms of public and private employment.

This book is the first major treatment of the application of the ADA to persons with mental retardation in the employment context. The importance of the book to the community of persons with mental retardation and their families, employers, lawyers, researchers, and policy makers is evident in its extensive empirical research and legal analysis of ADA disability law and policy. The book is a tool to aid in understanding the importance of the antidiscrimination protections set forth in the ADA by persons with mental retardation, their families, advocates, and employers.

This book comes at an important time in the evolution of the ADA. On one hand, people with mental retardation and their advocates are only just beginning to utilize the employment provisions of the ADA to protect their civil rights in the workplace. This marks an important shift in thinking about the employment of persons with mental retardation, from being recipients of "charity" and corporate "generosity" when employed in the workplace, to being respected as contributing and productive employees with the full panoply of rights that other employees possess.

On the other hand, the book appears at a time when civil rights, particularly disability civil rights, have been demonized and trivialized, caricatured and sound bited, making the legal and political climate for these issues very difficult.

ADA Support and Then Backlash

In 1990 President Bush signed the ADA with overwhelming bipartisan support. The American public, in testimony before Congress and in responses to surveys such as the Harris poll, strongly supported the Act (*see Chapter VI*). The political climate, however, has since changed. Today, a significant backlash against the disability rights movement is threatening to undermine many of the civil rights gains achieved over the last 30 years, including the passage of the ADA.

---

[1] B.A., University of Pennsylvania, 1983; J.D. Harvard Law School, 1986.

One recurring theme in the backlash against the disability rights movement has been criticism of the ADA's enforcement. A major contribution of the book is its comprehensive review illustrating that virtually all of the criticism to date has been either anecdotal or not supported by careful empirical study (*see Chapter I*).

Critics of the ADA contend that the law's employment provisions have failed to increase the number of persons with disabilities in the workforce. The media asserts that the excessive costs of litigation and the provision of workplace accommodations required by ADA Title I will result in small employers being driven out of business.

Critics portray the ADA as a cumbersome law and an endless source of frivolous legal claims. Some claim that now nearly everyone claims to be "disabled" and thereby protected by the law. Others contend that the law is being abused by people who are not disabled, but who want to take advantage of companies that would rather settle than incur the costs of litigating an ADA lawsuit, even a meritless one.

The Need for Facts and the Present Book

Contrary to the criticisms leveled against the ADA, a look at the facts presented in this book tell a different story. As described in several chapters in the book, recent surveys show that 800,000 additional Americans with severe disabilities have obtained employment since 1994, the date the ADA employment provisions began to apply to businesses with 15 or more employees (*see Chapters XIII and XIV*).

Small and large employers have supported the implementation of the ADA (*see research findings presented in Chapter XI*). The costs of workplace accommodations often are far outweighed by their benefits to qualified workers, to employers, and to society (*see findings presented Chapter IV*). In addition, these benefits have been realized without the avalanche of litigation predicted by critics of Act implementation (*see Chapter XV*).

An estimated $200 billion a year in governmental expenditures support people with disabilities. By prohibiting workplace discrimination against individuals with disabilities and requiring the infrastructure changes necessary to increase physical accessibility, the ADA has made it possible for many individuals with disabilities who have had to rely on public assistance in the form of Medicaid, Social Security Disability Insurance, and Supplemental Security Income to have enhanced prospects of obtaining and maintaining employment (*see Chapter XVI*). Enabling individuals with disabilities to escape what Professor Blanck has called "the black hole of segregation" (*see Chapters XI and XII*) and to become productive members of society by facilitating their entry into the workforce is one of the major public policy goals of the ADA (*see Chapter XVI*).

In addition to an increase in employment among severely disabled individuals, a significant number of individuals with "nonvisible" disabilities seeking employment have benefited from the ADA's prohibition on preoffer disability-related inquiries and medical exams (*see Chapters II and III*). Prior to the ADA, qualified job applicants were no doubt excluded from the workforce when a prospective employer would learn from their job application that they had a disability. Such questions are now illegal under the ADA until after a job offer has been made (*see Chapter XV*).

Given the ADA's relatively short life, criticism of the Act's potential for increasing the employment of disabled individuals is inappropriate, and this is particularly true when most criticism is made without hard facts. Five years after the passage of the Civil Rights Act of 1964, no one would have argued that the landmark legislation should be repealed simply because the number of women and people of color employed had not significantly increased. As with race and gender discrimination, there are many things that impact the employment of people with disabilities.

ADA Enforcement and Persons with Mental Retardation

From the time the Equal Employment Opportunity Commission (EEOC) began enforcing the employment title of the ADA, it has received more than 80,000 charges of employment discrimination based on disability (*see Chapter V*). Of these charges, *less than one half of one percent* involved charging parties who identified mental retardation as their disability. Yet over 80 percent of these charges brought by persons with mental retardation have been resolved successfully by the EEOC. The trends illustrate, however, that people with mental retardation are not, for the most part, using the ADA aggressively to assert their civil rights.

Part of the reason for the small number of EEOC charges involving discrimination against persons with mental retardation is that it can be administratively difficult for any person to file a charge with the EEOC. The EEOC, however, is increasingly proactive in supporting and enforcing claims of ADA employment discrimination (*see Chapter V*). My hope is that the EEOC will work collaboratively with organizations such as the American Association on Mental Retardation, The ARC, the national and state Protection & Advocacy, and People First to address discrimination against people with mental retardation administratively, through informal dispute resolution, and in the courts (*see Chapter XV*).

The Future of the ADA

The ADA is a civil rights statute *in place* to protect people who want to work, not those who want to be malingerers. The message of the ADA is about independence, empowerment, and integration. A careful look at the facts studied and compiled in this book rebuts the critics' contentions that the ADA is an extreme law, that the law does not make business sense, and that it will open the courts to a flood of frivolous litigation by unqualified workers with mental retardation and other disabilities.

Civil rights laws like the ADA are based on a simple concept—qualified people in the workplace, whether they are racial minorities, women, older workers, religious minorities, people with physical or mental disabilities, or *people with mental retardation*—should be hired, promoted, and judged on their ability and merit, not on stereotypes, bias, or paternalistic notions (*see Chapter XI* discussing survey of employers of persons with mental retardation). The goal of the ADA is to keep good workers in their jobs and in the workforce. It is the antithesis of a give-away program.

This book and Professor Blanck's research model and findings support the view that the message of the ADA is about independence, self-advocacy, community integration, inclusion in society, and empowerment. This is what the ADA stands for and what must be the standards for business today. This is what I believe must be the commitment of all of us.

Preface

As our society approaches the next millennium, critical questions about the nature and composition of the emerging workforce of the 21st century come to the fore.

Will our increasingly diversified and aging workforce include millions of qualified persons with disabilities?

What will be the characteristics, capabilities, and qualifications of this workforce?

What types of training and job supports will be available to employees of this emerging workforce?

What qualifications will be needed to attain and retain competitive employment?

How will the dramatic changes that have occurred in the last quarter of the 20th century in areas such as disability law, public policy, and assistive technology shape the emerging workforce of the next century?

This book describes an ongoing empirical investigation of many of these issues for the emerging workforce that includes persons with mental retardation. Its focus is on how employment integration and economic growth may occur and continue to be documented in areas related to disability law and policy

Disability law and policy has evolved dramatically over the past 25 years, culminating in the passage of the Americans with Disabilities Act of 1990 (ADA). In March 1998 the United States Supreme Court heard its first case of interpretation of the ADA. The importance of this and other ADA cases is discussed throughout the book, with analysis of their implications for the thousands of people with mental retardation and developmental disabilities and for the millions with other disabilities.

The book is divided into five parts, summarized as follows:

Part I. An overview of the present empirical investigation and its major findings (Chapter I);

Part II. Analysis of the developing law surrounding interpretation of the employment provisions of the ADA and its implications for persons with mental retardation (Chapters II - VI);

Part III. Discussion of the process of the empirical investigation and its research framework and model (Chapters VII - VIII);

Part IV. Description of the findings of the investigation (Chapters IX - XI); and

Part V. Review of the implications of the findings for researchers, employers, policy makers, and the disability community (Chapters XII - XVII).

These areas are examined so that readers may have a base from which to assess implementation of disability law and related policy initiatives. The areas of study reflect the recent paradigm shift in disability policy and law toward individual and civil rights, equal participation in the democratic process, empowerment and self-determination.

The book is meant to be a resource to legal scholars, health professionals in multiple disciplines involved in the delivery of services to persons with mental retardation, policy makers, social science researchers, legal practitioners, employers, and members of the disability community. It is formatted in the style of legal scholarship and incorporates footnotes in the body of the work that contain parenthetical information that supplements the text. It contains a table of legal cases cited in the book and a subject index to facilitate use of the book by nonlawyers.

The investigation described in this book is the result of the collaboration of many people. The author gratefully acknowledges support from the Oklahoma Developmental Disabilities Services Division through a contract with the Oklahoma State University, the Annenberg Washington Program, the University of Iowa College of Law Foundation, and Iowa Creative Employment Opportunities (CEO).

Many people provided important comments and reviews on earlier drafts; among them I thank James Arenson, David Baldus, Marjorie Baldwin, Dennis Bean, Leigh Bienen, Heidi Berven, Marca Bristo, Barbara Broffitt, David Braddock, Scott Burris, Steve Burton, Bill Buss, Tom Chirikos, Dennis Coll, James Conroy, Robert Dinerstein, David Fram, Stanley Herr, Andrew Imparato, Ken Kress, Ted Kastner, Joe Lakis, Marc Linder, Mollie Marti, Arlene

Mayerson, Paul Miller, Newton Minow, Lawrence Paradis, Alan Reich, Robert Rosenthal, Michael Saks, Len Sandler, Pat Steele, Kathy Tinker, Jeanne Thobro, Rud Turnbull, James Weinstein, Steve Willborn, and Sidney Wolinsky. Although the views expressed in the book are my own, this work would not have been possible without the important collaboration with those listed above and with others undoubtedly I have failed to mention.

Finally, this work is dedicated with love to my wife, Wendy, and our four children—Jason, Daniel, Albert, and Caroline—who will be stakeholders in the emerging workforce of the next century.

—Peter David Blanck, Ph.D., J.D.
Iowa City, March 1998

PART I:

Overview and Organization of the Volume

CHAPTER I

Overview of the Volume

Today, America welcomes into the mainstream of life all our fellow citizens with disabilities...And now I sign legislation which takes a sledgehammer to another wall, one which for too many generations separated Americans with disabilities from the freedom they could glimpse, but not grasp...Let the shameful wall of exclusion finally come tumbling down.

President George Bush, ADA Signing Ceremony, July 26, 1990[1]

1.1 Introduction

In the past 25 years, disability law and policy, as reflected most directly by the passage of the Americans with Disabilities Act of 1990 (ADA),[2] has undergone a dramatic shift toward the equal employment of persons with disabilities. Title I of the ADA, embodying the law's employment provisions, is playing a central role in enhancing the labor force participation of qualified persons with disabilities and in reducing their dependence on governmental entitlement programs.[3] Despite advancements, critics argue that there is little definitive evidence that disability law and policy have resulted in larger numbers of qualified persons with disabilities participating in the workplace.[4]

This book addresses these concerns through an ongoing investigation of employment integration and economic opportunity during the initial

[1] President George Bush, Remarks on Signing the Americans with Disabilities Act of 1990, July 26, 1990, *in* Bernard D. Reams, Jr., Peter J. McGovern, & Jon S. Schultz, 1 **Disability Law in the United States: A Legislative History of the Americans with Disabilities Act of 1990, Public L. No. 101–336,** at 1164–65 (1992).

[2] 42 U.S.C. § § 12101–12113 (1993). *See* **infra Appendix A** for the text of the ADA.

[3] *See* Peter David Blanck, The Economics of the Employment Provisions of the Americans with Disabilities Act: Part I—Workplace Accommodations, 46 **DePaul L. Rev.** 877–914 (1997) (discussing the economics of Title I implementation).

[4] Sherwin Rosen, Disability Accommodation and the Labor Market, *in* **Disability and Work: Incentives, Rights, and Opportunities,** at 18, 22 (Carolyn L. Weaver ed., 1991) [**hereinafter Disability and Work**].

period of ADA Title I implementation.[5] Begun in 1989 the investigation follows the lives of more than 5,000 adults and children with mental retardation.[6] It collects empirical information on the participants' backgrounds, employment opportunities, economic growth, health status, self-advocacy involvement, and other measures.

The term "empirical" is used to denote a systematic attempt to gather scientifically quantitative and qualitative information, through the use of questionnaire, survey, interview, and observational data collection techniques. The information collected illuminates issues related to individual inclusion and empowerment as central goals in the ADA and other related laws, such as the Rehabilitation Act of 1973 and its amendments in 1986 and 1992.[7]

Information on the quality of the work lives of persons with disabilities is lacking.[8] The promise of the ADA and related laws to integrate into society millions of Americans[9] makes this lack of information troubling.[10] In the last quarter of this century, dramatic positive changes have occurred in public attitudes and behavior toward individuals with disabilities in employment, governmental services, telecommunications, and public accommodations.[11]

The changes in disability law and policy are not being documented and communicated adequately.[12] Documentation is necessary to

---

[5] Earlier parts of this series include: Peter David Blanck, Employment Integration, Economic Opportunity, and the Americans with Disabilities Act: Empirical Study from 1990–1993, 79(4) **Iowa L. Rev.** 853–923 (1994) [**hereinafter Employment Integration**]; Peter David Blanck & Mollie W. Marti, Attitudes, Behavior, and the Employment Provisions of the Americans with Disabilities Act, 42 **Vill. L. Rev.** 345–408 (1997) [**hereinafter Attitudes and the ADA**] (discussing 1995 findings from the present investigation); Peter David Blanck, **The Americans with Disabilities Act: Putting the Employment Provisions to Work**, White Paper of the Annenberg Washington Program (1993) [**hereinafter Annenberg White Paper**] (discussing earlier findings and the need for communication to effectuate ADA implementation); Peter David Blanck, Empirical Study of the Employment Provisions of the Americans with Disabilities Act: Methods, Preliminary Findings and Implications, 22 **N.M. L. Rev.** 119 (1992) [**hereinafter Empirical Study**] (discussing baseline findings and methodological issues); Peter David Blanck, On Integrating Persons with Mental Retardation: The ADA and ADR, 22 **N.M. L. Rev.** 259 (1992) [**hereinafter ADA and ADR**] (discussing alternative dispute resolution and the ADA); Peter David Blanck, The Emerging Work Force: Empirical Study of the Americans with Disabilities Act, 16 **J. Corp. L.** 693 (1991) [**hereinafter Emerging Work Force**] (discussing findings and Civil Rights Act of 1991).

[6] This project is an evaluation of a social experiment in the sense of Campbell's influential article, Reforms as Experiments, which suggests that a new program's effectiveness is determined on a trial and error basis. Donald T. Campbell, Reforms as Experiments, 24 **Am. Psychologist** 409 (1967); *see also* James W. Conroy & Valerie J. Bradley, **The Pennhurst Longitudinal Study** 86 (1985) (providing analysis of a long-term study of the lives of people with mental retardation).

[7] **Pub. L.** 99-506. *See also* the Developmental Disabilities Assistance and Bill of Rights Act of 1984, **Pub. L.** 98-527.

[8] For an overview of how the ADA applies to persons with mental disabilities, *see* **Attitudes and the ADA, supra Ch. I § 1.1** (discussing hidden disabilities); Bonnie Milstein, et al., The Americans with Disabilities Act: A Breathtaking Promise for People with Mental Disabilities, 24 **Clearinghouse Rev.** 1240 (1991) (same).

[9] Jack McNeil, U.S. Bureau of the Census, Current Population Reports, **Americans with Disabilities: 1991–1992, Data from the Survey of Income and Program Participation** 5 (Pub. No. P70-33, 1993) (presenting data on the disability status of noninstitutionalized persons in the United States); Jane West, The Evolution of Disability Rights, *in* **Implementing the Americans with Disabilities Act: Rights and Responsibilities of All Americans,** 3 (Lawrence O. Gostin & Henry A. Beyer, eds., 1993) [**hereinafter Rights and Responsibilities**] (noting that the ADA seeks to establish full participation and independent living as national goals for persons with disabilities).

[10] For a review, see Jane West, Introduction—Implementing the Act: Where We Begin, 69 **Milbank Q.** 1, 3–6 (1994) (concluding that the limited data on persons with disabilities often raises more questions than they answer); National Academy of Social Insurance, **Preliminary Status Report of the Disability Policy Panel** 135 (1994) (calling for data to evaluate the prevalence of disability in the American population).

[11] Peter David Blanck, **Communications Technology for Everyone: Implications for the Classroom and Beyond,** White Paper of the Annenberg Washington Program (1994) (discussing the integral role that technology has played and continues to play in improving the lives of persons with disabilities).

[12] For a review of the literature, *see* **Integrated Employment: Current Status and Future Directions,** American Association on Mental Retardation (William E. Kiernan & Robert L. Schalock, eds., 1997) [**hereinafter Integrated Employment**].

address the growing attitudinal backlash against disability law and policy implementation.[13] Critics of the ADA, such as House Majority Leader Dick Armey, have stated that the law should be rewritten to protect only people with "genuine" disabilities.[14]

In his book *No Pity,* Joseph Shapiro has articulated the challenges ahead:

> Never has the world of disabled people changed so fast. Rapid advances in technology, new civil rights protections, a generation of better-educated disabled students out of "mainstreamed" classrooms, a new group consciousness, and political activism mean more disabled people are seeking jobs and greater daily participation in American life. But prejudice, society's low expectations, and an antiquated welfare and social service system frustrate these burgeoning attempts at independence. As a result, the new aspirations of people with disabilities have gone unnoticed and misunderstood by mainstream America.[15]

1.2 Substituting Hard Data for Myths About Disability

The empirical investigation described in this book is part of an effort to substitute information for the prevalent myths and misconceptions about persons with disabilities, particularly in the realm of employment.[16] Professor Jack McNeil estimates that people with disabilities make up 20 percent of the total U.S. population, excluding persons living in nursing homes or other institutions.[17]

According to McNeil's 1997 report, *Americans with Disabilities,* which is based on U.S. Census Bureau data collected between October 1994 and January 1995, approximately 54 million Americans reported some level of disability.[18] Approximately 26 million people described their disability as severe.[19] Approximately 500,000 children between the ages of 6 and 14 were reported to have a developmental disability (including the condition of mental retardation). Roughly 60 percent of these children, many of whom will be in the workforce of the next century, reported needing personal assistance in daily life activities.

The findings from Census Bureau data form a backdrop against which the empirical results of the present study of persons with mental retardation may be discussed and examined. According to the most recent census results, the employment rate for people ages 21 to 64 without a disability was 82 percent and 77 percent for those with nonsevere disabilities. In comparison, only 26 percent of those with severe disabilities were employed. Among the 6 million individuals reported to have a mental disability—including mental retardation, learning disability, or other mental or emotional conditions—the employment rate was somewhat higher, at 41 percent.

The presence of a disability also is associated with lower earnings. The median monthly

---

[13] Paul Steven Miller, The Americans with Disabilities Act in Texas: The EEOC's Continuing Efforts in Enforcement, 34 **Hous. L. Rev.** 777, 778 (1997) (discussing the backlash against the disability rights movement); Kathi Wolfe, Bashing the Disabled: The New Hate Crime, **The Progressive,** at 24 (Nov. 1995) (same).

[14] *See* Anna Macias & Catalina Camia, Disabilities Act Needs Revision, Armey Says, **Dallas Morning News,** at A30 (Apr. 19, 1995) (Armey stating that "ADA in its current state is a disaster" and "gold diggers" are using the law's protections).

[15] Joseph P. Shapiro, **No Pity: People with Disabilities Forging a New Civil Rights Movement,** at 4 (1993) (discussing societal and self-perceptions of persons with disabilities).

[16] Peter David Blanck, ed., **Employment, Disability, and the Americans with Disabilities Act: Issues in Law, Public Policy, and Research,** Northwestern Univ. Press *(forthcoming* 1999) (reviewing multidisciplinary approaches to studying ADA implementation); ADA Watch Year One: A Report to the President and the Congress on Progress, *in* National Council on Disability, **Implementing the Americans with Disabilities Act** 3 (1993) [**hereinafter ADA Watch**] (reflecting early experiences in implementing ADA); Bureau of National Affairs, **Sensitivity to People with Disabilities: Training Managers to Comply with the Americans with Disabilities Act** 8 (1991) [**hereinafter BNA Report**] (noting that some see employers' fears about the cost of ADA compliance as "a smoke screen for the fear of the unknown").

[17] McNeil, **supra Ch. I § 1.1**, at 3

[18] Jack McNeil, **Americans with Disabilities: 1994–95.** U.S. Census Bureau—Household Economic Studies Current Population Reports, P70-61 (Sept. 16, 1997) (defining disability to include a person with mental retardation or another developmental disability).

[19] *Id.* (the Census Bureau defines a person with a severe disability as one who is completely unable to perform a major functional activity or who needs personal assistance).

earnings were $2,190 for men ages 21 to 64 without disabilities and $1,470 for comparable women. For those with nonsevere disabilities, the median monthly earnings were $1,857 for men and $1,200 for women. For those with severe disabilities, the median monthly earnings dropped substantially to $1,262 for men and $1,000 for women.

Thus, the presence of a disability is related to a lower likelihood of being employed, and, when employed, to a substantially lower level of income. Chapter XVI of this book examines the relation of disability to individual incentives and barriers to work. One important barrier identified is that people with disabilities who want to work are less likely to have affordable private health insurance available to them, as compared to those without disabilities.[20]

1.3 Communicating Information About Disability

Communicating information in the aggregate about people with disabilities is critical to effective ADA implementation. It is also instrumental to the future evaluation of employment integration and economic opportunity for all Americans.[21] Policy makers, employers, courts, and members of the disability community benefit from this information.[22]

In *Americans with Disabilities,* McNeil writes: "The passage of the Americans with Disabilities Act (ADA) brought with it an increased awareness of the need to monitor the situation of people with disabilities."[23] This need to inform stakeholders of the progress toward achieving equal employment opportunity for all qualified Americans is not unlike that faced after the landmark Supreme Court school desegregation decision in *Brown v. The Board of Education.*[24] After the Supreme Court's decision, extensive study was conducted on attitudes and behavior toward school desegregation policies. Scholars from many disciplines took up the challenge—social psychologists, political scientists, economists, and sociologists—examining the links between historically rooted prejudicial attitudes and social behavior.[25]

An analogous body of multidisciplinary research is needed of employment integration under ADA implementation. The passage of the ADA alone may have significantly changed biased attitudes toward persons with disabilities in American society. This may have resulted from the government's recognition of disabled persons' civil rights or in the acknowledgment of the prejudice and segregation historically faced by many qualified individuals with disabilities. Beyond these effects, practical knowledge of employment integration under ADA Title I is needed. Information is required on national, state, and local levels, based on study of disability law and policy.[26]

1.4 Three Central Goals of the Present Investigation

Employment integration during the initial stages of ADA implementation poses many challenges that may be addressed through the systematic

---

[20] *See* **infra Ch. XVI §§ 16.4–16.7** (discussing welfare and health care reform strategies and employment integration and economic opportunity for persons with disabilities).

[21] *See* Shapiro, **supra Ch. I § 1.1,** at 6–7 (*citing* national survey data regarding effect of disabled population on society as a whole); McNeil, **supra Ch. I § 1.1,** at 3 (same).

[22] Lauren B. Edelman, Legal Ambiguity and Symbolic Structure—Organizational Mediation of Civil-Rights Law, 97 **Am. J. Soc.** 1531, 1533 (1992) (noting empirical studies showing the mixed picture of the benefits of equal-employment and affirmative-action law).

[23] **Americans with Disabilities: 1994–95, supra Ch. I § 1.2** (arguing also that the most important source of periodic data on people with disabilities is the Survey of Income and Program Participation (SIPP)).

[24] 347 U.S. 483 (1954).

[25] *See* Charles Black, The Lawfulness of the Segregation Decisions, 69 **Yale L. J.** 421 (1960); Robert L. Crain & Rita E. Mahard, The Effect of Research Methodology on Desegregation-Achievement Studies: A Meta-analysis, 88 **Am. J. Soc.** 839–54 (1983) (reviewing 93 research studies).

[26] *See* William E. Kiernan, Dana S. Gilmore, & John Butterworth, Integrated Employment: Evolution of National Practices, *in* **Integrated Employment, supra Ch. I § 1.1,** at 17 (describing employment integration policies and practices).

[27] *See* Edelman, **supra Ch. I § 1.3,** at 1533 (study of employment law has shown that "those responsible for formulating, interpreting, and enforcing the law are part of the dominant class and that they use their authority to construct law in a way that preserves the status quo while giving the appearance of change.").

study of people with disabilities who grapple with the law on a daily basis.[27] The present investigation has three related goals:

1. to foster a meaningful dialogue about employment integration and economic opportunity for persons with mental retardation during ADA implementation;[28]
2. to raise awareness of the work capabilities and qualifications of people with mental retardation; and
3. to enhance the effective implementation of the ADA law and disability policy by providing information to improve communication about employment integration, welfare reform, health care reform, and related areas.

To date, the literature has not adequately addressed these issues. Although criticism of the ADA and disability policy by the press and academia is abundant, little effort has been devoted to communicating their importance to the future of American society. This book examines employment integration and economic opportunity during initial ADA implementation through study of a large sample of persons with mental retardation. The premise is that empirical research models are crucial to complement knowledge about individual civil rights in the area of disability law and policy.[29]

There is no denying that ADA implementation warrants such attention. It is the most comprehensive federal civil rights law addressing discrimination against people with disabilities in all aspects of their daily lives.[30] The Civil Rights Act of 1964[31] does not address discrimination on the basis of a disability. The Rehabilitation Act of 1973[32] prohibits discrimination against persons with disabilities by federal contractors and recipients of federal grants but does not apply to providers of public accommodations or to private-sector employers. The Individuals with Disabilities Education Act (IDEA)[33] is meant to ensure an equal and appropriate education to children and young adults with disabilities.

Unlike these prior laws, the ADA prohibits discrimination against persons with disabilities in employment, governmental and local services, public accommodations, insurance, telecommunications, and public transportation.[34] Given the breadth of the ADA, Senator Tom Harkin, a sponsor of the law, called it the "emancipation proclamation" for persons with disabilities.[35]

1.5 Overview of the Book

This book presents a research framework for examining the emerging issues in employment policy and law in general, and aspects of the employment provisions of the ADA in particular. It provides information about trends in employment integration under ADA Title I through the collection and analysis of information from

---

[28] *See* Francine S. Hall & Elizabeth L. Hall, The ADA: Going Beyond the Law, 8 **Acad. Mgmt. Exec. J**. 17 (1994) (presenting a model for communicating information about the ADA); Deborah A. Pape & Vilia M. Tarvydas, Responsible and Responsive Rehabilitation Consultation on the ADA: The Importance of Training for Psychologists, 38 **Rehab. Psychol.** 117 (1993) (same).

[29] *See* David M. Engel, Law, Culture, and Children with Disabilities: Educational Rights and the Construction of Difference, 1991 **Duke L. J.** 166, 180–203 (discussing the cultural context of law and a 1975 empirical study of Education for All Handicapped Children Act); Craig Haney, Psychology and Legal Change, 17 **Law & Hum. Behav.** 371, 382–83 (1993) (arguing for empirical and methodological creativity in addressing important social problems and change).

[30] *See* Elizabeth C. Morin, American with Disabilities 1990: Social Integration Through Employment, 40 **Cath. U. L. Rev.** 189, 201–02 (1990) (comparing the ADA with other legislation); West, **supra Ch. I § 1.1,** at xi, xvi (noting that "the [ADA] and most of its predecessor legislation is about rights—and rights are based on values, not knowledge").

[31] Title VII of the Civil Rights Act of 1964, 42 U.S.C. §§ 2000e–2000e-17.

[32] **Pub. L.** 93-112.

[33] **Pub. L.** 101-476. *See* **infra Ch. XVI § 16.8** (discussing 1997 amendments to IDEA).

[34] *See* Henry H. Perritt, Jr., **Americans with Disabilities Handbook** 1 (1990) (noting that Title I is the most significant labor and employment legislation in a decade); Robert L. Burgdorf, Jr., The Americans with Disabilities Act: Analysis and Implications of a Second-Generation Civil Rights Statute, 26 **Harv. Civil Rights Civil-Liberties Rev.** 413 (1991) (discussing "people first" emphasis of Act); Robert L. Burgdorf, Jr., **Disability Discrimination in Employment Law** (1995).

[35] Bonnie P. Tucker, The Americans with Disabilities Act: An Overview, **U. Ill. L. Rev.** 923 (1989) (quoting Senator Harkin's statement that the Act is the "emancipation proclamation" for Americans with disabilities).

people affected by the law, in part based on information "in their own voices." The book sets forth a research process and model of study by which aspects of the long-term effectiveness of disability policy and employment law may be measured.[36]

Legal scholars have described the import of the ADA in general.[37] The ADA's employment provisions have been the subject of considerable discussion.[38] During the 1990 Congressional debate, some employers attempted to limit the reach of Title I, in terms of the types of persons covered by the law and the remedies available under the law. Others opposed provisions in an early draft version of the ADA that allowed for jury trials in cases of employment discrimination and for compensatory and punitive damages when employers intentionally discriminate against workers with disabilities.[39] Employers in the small business sector have expressed concern over what they characterized as vague and undefined terms and obligations of the employment provisions of the ADA.[40]

As is the case with any new legislation, questions about ADA Title I implementation may be raised in terms of its impact on the citizens it is designed to serve and on those responsible for complying with and enforcing it. This is why the development of information relating to the implementation of the law in practice is crucial. Independent of the civil rights guaranteed by the ADA, this information helps to define the parameters of the law. It enables ADA stakeholders—persons with disabilities, employers, and others—to attempt proactive interpretations that make business sense and that transcend minimal compliance with the law.

1.6 Organization of the Book

The focus in this book is to explore aspects of employment integration and economic opportunity as they relate to ADA implementation from the perspectives of a group of persons with mental retardation who, in many cases, have physical disabilities.[41]

Part II (Chapters II–VI) sets forth the conceptual bases for the investigation and their relation to the legal provisions of ADA Title I's definition of discrimination and of disability. The chapters in this part describe the central provisions of Title I, including a "qualified" individual with a disability, "reasonable workplace accommodations," and "undue hardship." This part also examines how prior study of employment integration of persons with mental retardation has shaped the design of this research project.

Part III (Chapters VII–VIII) sets forth the research framework and model of study for the present investigation. It describes the collaborative research process and highlights the legal, methodological, and ethical issues in this research, including discussion of research logistics, ethical considerations, methods for data collection, and follow-up concerns. Part III also presents the research model or framework for the present empirical study. The research model is derived from prior studies of persons with disabilities.

Part IV (Chapters IX–XI) presents empirical findings from the research model. This part provides information that helps to disprove many of the myths or misconceptions about ADA implementation. A related goal is to further assess the law so that legal and policy questions may be addressed as to their impact on qualified persons with disabilities.[42] The information presented has a baseline component, in that it

---

[36] *See* Perritt, **supra Ch. I § 1.4,** at vii (arguing that it is essential that adequate information and data be developed about Title I implementation).

[37] *See* 22 **N.M. L. Rev.,** Symposium on the ADA (1992) (discussing legal significance of ADA).

[38] Perritt, **supra Ch. I § 1.4,** at 1 (Title I is the most significant employment legislation in a decade).

[39] *See* **The Americans with Disabilities Act: A Practical Legal Guide to Impact, Enforcement and Compliance, Bureau Nat'l Affairs Special Rep.** 35–36 (1990).

[40] *See* U.S. Small Business Administration, **Comments on Proposed EEOC Regulations for Title I of the ADA** (Apr. 29, 1991).

[41] *See* James W. Conroy, **The Hissom Outcomes Study,** Brief Rep. No. 1 (Dec. 1995), at 16 (finding that 41 percent of the focus class members in the Hissom litigation had physical disabilities).

[42] For a related analysis, *see* James Conroy, et al., 1990 Results of the CARC v. Thorne Longitudinal Study, **The Connecticut Applied Research Project,** Rep. No. 10 (Jan. 1991).

was gathered during and after the enactment of Title I in the years 1990 to 1992, and after its effective date during the years 1992 to 1996. The collection of longitudinal and cross-sectional data is an important step in the assessment of employment integration and in understanding the evolving definition of the employment provisions of the ADA.

Finally, Part V of the book (chapters XII–XVII) examines the implications of the investigation for future study and policy development. The investigation's findings are discussed in regard to recent legal and policy initiatives in areas such as health insurance and welfare reform. Several avenues for study are examined, including analysis of the emerging labor force of persons with mental retardation, the importance of workplace accommodations and supports, the analysis of corporate culture, the increasing use of medical and genetic testing in the workplace, and the economic costs and benefits of ADA implementation.

1.7 Overview of the Research Model

The empirical information described in this book is based on data collected on adults and children with mental retardation and other disabilities living in Oklahoma. Pilot testing of the investigation began in 1989. Formal data collection began in 1990, two and a half years before the July 26, 1992, effective date of Title I. This book presents analysis of information collected annually from 1990 to 1996.[43] The primary focus of the examination is on changes in the social and economic positions of the adult participants as indicators of progress made during Title I implementation.

There are two major types of outcome variables:

1. *employment integration*—defined as the degree of integration in an employment setting, and
2. *economic opportunity*—defined by various income level measures.

The analyses examine employment integration and economic opportunity for the adult participants before and during Title I implementation, during a time when other individual, legal, and policy factors changed dramatically.[44] They are meant to stimulate discussion of the issues and complement the case-by-case approach for monitoring ADA implementation and compliance followed by the Equal Employment Opportunity Commission (EEOC), the federal agency responsible for enforcing the law.[45]

The research model used in the study of employment integration and economic opportunity is presented as Figure 1.1.

Several factors in the model are used to predict employment integration and economic opportunity.[46] The predictor variables include measures of the participants' personal backgrounds, capabilities and qualifications, inclusion and empowerment in society, and self-reported perceptions of ADA implementation. The research model and its components illustrated in Figure 1.1 are described in detail in Part III of this book.

---

[43] *Cf.* Mitchell P. LaPlante, The Demographics of Disability, 69 **Milbank Q.** 55, 60–63 (1991) (discussing researchers' demographic estimates of persons with disabilities); Gerben DeJong & Raymond Lifchez, Physical Disability and Public Policy, **Sci. Am.,** 43 (June 1983) (stressing the need for longitudinal research by noting that "[m]ost surveys of health and disability provide only an instantaneous view of disability in the U.S."); Dean B. McFarlin, et al., Integrating the Disabled into the Work Force: A Survey of Fortune 500 Company Attitudes and Practices, 4 **Employee Resp. & Rts. J.** 107, 110 (1991) (describing results from surveys designed to test hiring practices for employees with disabilities and exposure to employees with disabilities).

[44] *See* Shapiro, **supra Ch. I § 1.1,** at 4. *Cf.* Wilma Randle, After a Year, ADA's Impact Is Barely Felt, **Chi. Trib.,** at 4-1 (July 26, 1993) (noting that the current unemployment figure for minorities with disabilities is approximately 90 percent).

[45] *See* Lisa A. Lavelle, The Duty to Accommodate: Will Title I of the Americans with Disabilities Act Emancipate Individuals with Disabilities Only to Disable Small Businesses?, 66 **Notre Dame L. Rev.** 1135, 1142 (1991) ("In drafting the ADA regulations, the EEOC used the Rehabilitation Act regulations and case law to establish parameters which they intended to serve as guidelines for the case by case inquiries that determinations under the ADA may require.").

[46] **CARF Standards Manual for Organizations Serving People with Disabilities** 162 (1993) [**hereinafter CARF Standards**] (defining integration as "[p]articipation in the mainstream of life"). Participation means that the individual has relationships with community members without disabilities and the individual has access to public resources.

Figure 1.1

Model of Employment Integration and Economic Opportunity

Capabilities & Qualifications		Personal Background
• Adaptive Skills • Health Status • Equipment/Accommodation Needs		• Age • Gender • Race

Employment Integration & Economic Opportunity
• Job Advancement • Monthly Income

Inclusion Factors	Legal Factors	Empowerment Factors
• Living Arrangement • Job/Life Satisfaction & Choice	• ADA Composite Title I Title II Title III	• Self-Advocacy • Family & Government Support • Job/Skill Educational Goals

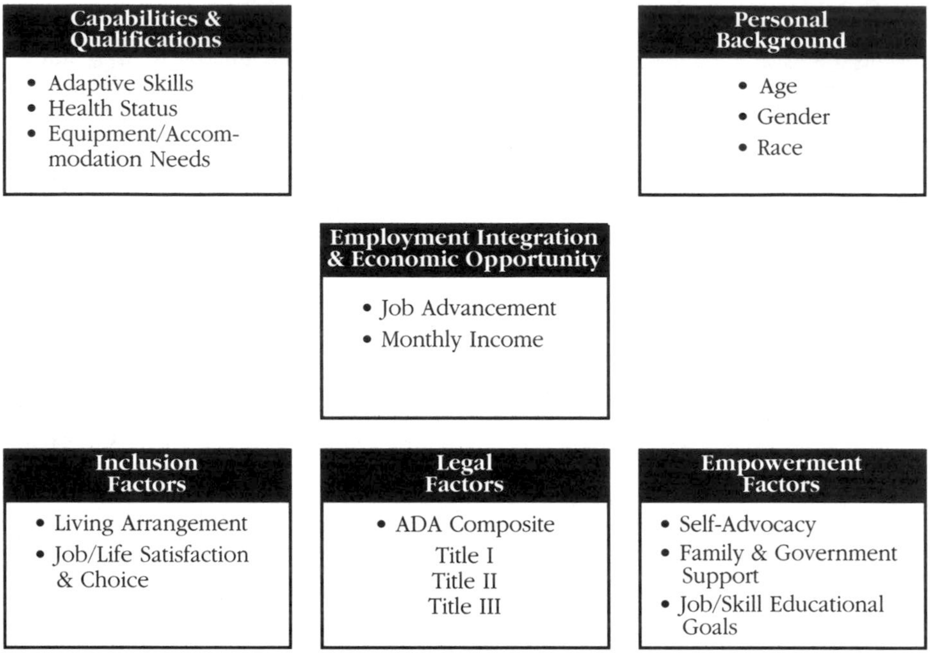

1.8 Summary: Five Core Findings from the Present Investigation

Five core findings of the investigation are presented in Part IV of this book and summarized below:

1. *Employment integration:* From 1990 to 1996 almost half of the participants (47 percent) remain in the same type of employment and almost half (44 percent) are engaged in more integrated employment settings, while almost one tenth (9 percent) regress into less integrated employment settings. Younger relative to older participants, and men relative to women, show substantial gains in integrated employment. Relative unemployment levels for all participants decline by 25 percent, dropping from 38 percent in 1990 to 13 percent in 1996. During the same period, the proportion of participants in competitive employment increases threefold—from 3 percent in 1990 to 9 percent in 1996.
2. *Economic opportunity:* From 1990 to 1996 the gross income of all participants rises significantly. Younger participants show substantial increases in earned income. Higher levels of job-related skills, greater independence in living, and more involvement in self-advocacy activities relate to higher earned income levels for these participants.
3. *Individual growth:* From 1990 to 1996 participants improve substantially in their capabilities and qualifications, level of inclusion and empowerment in society, and level of self-reported accessibility to society as defined by the ADA.
4. *Black hole effect:* Almost 80 percent of those participants not employed or employed in nonintegrated settings in 1990 remain in these settings in 1996. At the same time, less than half of the participants employed in integrated settings remain in these settings by 1996.
5. *Usefulness of the research model:* The explanatory power of the research model is substantial. The predictor measures in the model in combination and alone predict employment integration and economic opportunity.

The implications of the findings for future analysis of ADA implementation and disability law and policy are examined in the final part of this book.

PART II:

ADA Title I Provisions

CHAPTER II

ADA Title I and Persons with Mental Retardation: Definitions of Employment Discrimination and Disability

Senator Helms: *In the bill, the definition of "individuals with disabilities" includes anyone with a physical or mental impairment limiting one of life's major activities, and anyone regarded as having such an impairment.... Does the list of disabilities include... people with intelligence levels, as measured on standardized tests such as the IQ test, which are so far below standard average levels as to limit substantially one or more major life activities, but who do not have any identifiable mental disease?*

Senator Harkin: *It is my understanding that they would be covered in this bill.*

Congressional Debate on Proposed Bill, 1989[1]

2.1 Introduction

The ADA has made explicit the national commitment to the inclusion into the workforce of qualified persons with disabilities.[2] ADA Title I has heightened the awareness of employment discrimination facing persons with disabilities.[3] The law has created high expectations in the disability community for employment integration and labor force opportunities. As discussed in Chapter I, empirical study is one means for enhancing awareness of the employment-related issues facing persons with disabilities.[4]

This chapter begins with an overview of two

[1] U.S. Senate (Sept. 8, 1989), Debate on S. 933, statements of Sen. Helms and Sen. Harkin. **Cong. Rec.** S10765, 135.

[2] *See* Goldman, Right of Way: The Americans with Disabilities Act, 5(4) **Wash. Law.** Mar.–Apr., at 34, 40 (1991) (noting that the ADA is "landmark legislation that has raised the consciousness of persons with disabilities and their potential employers and service providers").

[3] In addition to ADA Title I's provisions, the employment rights of persons with mental retardation are set forth in the Developmental Disabilities Assistance and Bill of Rights Act. This Act states in its findings that as of 1990, there are more than 3 million persons with developmental disabilities in the United States, and that employers tend to be unaware of the capabilities and qualifications of these persons. *See* **Pub. L.** 101-496, § 101; § 101(a)(1); § 101(a)(8); **BNA Report, supra Ch. I § 1.5,** at 18–19 (Act provides funding for care and treatment for persons with severe long-term developmental disabilities).

[4] *Cf.* Michael J. Saks, Turning Practice in Progress: Better Lawyering Through Experimentation, 66 **Notre Dame L. Rev.** 801 (1991) (program of empirical investigation would rapidly accelerate knowledge of the legal system).

central aspects of ADA Title I interpretation: the definition of employment discrimination and the definition of disability. The chapter describes how development of the research model highlighted in Chapter I may be useful in furthering interpretation of the concepts of employment discrimination and disability as they apply to persons with mental retardation.

2.2 Types of Employment Discrimination Recognized Under Title I

ADA Title I prohibits covered entities from discriminating against a qualified person with a disability in any aspect of employment, including hiring, the provision of accommodations, advancement, medical testing, compensation, benefits, and training.[5] Title I covers business organizations with more than 15 employees.[6] Organizations covered by Title I include employment or temporary staffing agencies, labor organizations, and joint labor-management committees.[7]

There are several forms of employment discrimination that a charging party (that is, the plaintiff in an ADA lawsuit) may allege under ADA Title I. The major types of discrimination recognized by Title I are described in the law's Subchapter I, Section 12112, set forth in Appendix A to this book.

Discrimination by an employer (typically the defendant named in the lawsuit) against a qualified job applicant or employee with a disability because of that disability may be set forth in a claim of "disparate treatment."[8] Under this theory of discrimination, a plaintiff will claim the occurrence of unjustified employment discrimination on the basis of a "disability" covered by the law, as compared to the more favorable treatment of a similarly qualified employee without a disability.[9]

In explaining the theory of a disparate treatment claim, the EEOC provides that:

> Disparate treatment means, with respect to title I of the ADA, that an individual was treated differently on the basis of his or her disability. For example, disparate treatment has occurred where an employer excludes an employee with a severe facial disfigurement from staff meetings because the employer does not like to look at the employee. The individual is being treated differently because of the employer's attitude towards his or her perceived disability.[10]

In some circumstances, where there is no direct proof of discrimination, a charging party (that is, a job applicant or a current employee) may prove indirectly that an employer did not hire or fired a qualified worker because of his or her disability. This may occur in a situation where an employer makes an adverse employment decision on the basis of unjustified fears about the future performance of an individual with a disability.[11]

Discrimination under Title I may be found where an employer fails to provide a "reason-

---

[5] 29 C.F.R. § 1630.2(m) (1991). The Rehabilitation Act of 1973 was amended in 1992 to provide that the standards used to determine employment discrimination under that Act shall be the same as those applied under ADA Title I. *See* § 503 (b) of the Rehabilitation Act Amendments of 1992, **Pub. L.** 102-569; 29 U.S.C. 791 (g) (applying only to the nonaffirmative action employment sections of the Rehabilitation Act). *See also* **infra Ch. XVI § 16.8** (discussing 1992 Rehabilitation Act Amendments).

[6] 42 U.S.C. § 12111(5)(A) & (B) (Supp. Feb. 1991).

[7] 42 U.S.C. § 12111(2) (Supp. IV 1992).

[8] *See* Pamela S. Karlan & George Rutherglen, Disabilities, Discrimination, and Reasonable Accommodation, 46 **Duke L. J.** 1, 14 (1996) (discussing theories of discrimination under ADA Title I).

[9] *See Johnson v. Boardman Petroleum, Inc.*, 923 F. Supp. 1563 (S.D. Ga. 1996); 42 U.S.C. § 12112.

[10] 29 C.F.R. pt. 1630, app. § 1630.15(a). *See Monette v. Electronic Data Systems Corp.*, 90 F.3d 1173 (6th Cir. 1996) (discussing the burden-shifting framework in a disparate treatment claim in the disability context).

[11] *See Bultemeyer v. Fort Wayne Community Schools*, 100 F.3d 1281, 1283 (7th Cir. 1996) (discussing the McDonnell-Douglas burden-shifting test in Title I context using direct or indirect evidence of discrimination). Under the indirect method, plaintiff must raise a genuine issue of material fact as to each element of the ADA prima facie case. *See* **infra Ch. V § 5.2** (discussing prima facie ADA case). The evidentiary burden then shifts to the defendant to set forth a nondiscriminatory reason for its conduct. If the defendant satisfies its burden of proof, then the burden shifts back to the plaintiff to prove that the reasons proffered were pretextual or unworthy of belief. Demonstrating pretext gets the plaintiff "over the hurdle of summary judgment." *See Ingels v. Thiokol Corp.*, 42 F.3d 616, 622 n.3 (10th Cir. 1994).

able" workplace accommodation, such as job coaching supports or flexible scheduling, to a qualified person with a disability.[12] In addition, discrimination may be found where an employer forces a qualified worker with a disability to accept an "unreasonable" accommodation, such as to transfer to a new worksite location or to work alone. In one case decided in 1998 by the Seventh Circuit Court of Appeals, it was held that the forced reassignment of a qualified worker with bipolar disorder was an unreasonable workplace accommodation that resulted in the segregation of the employee in violation of the ADA.[13]

Under the failure to provide a reasonable accommodation theory of employment discrimination, there is no need for indirect proof or the legal burden shifting described above under the theory of discrimination based on disparate treatment. Similar to the implementation of Title VII of the Civil Rights Act of 1964, interpretation of concepts such as unjustified discrimination and reasonable accommodation are made on a case-by-case analysis.[14]

Chapter V discusses an example of a case involving two plaintiffs with mental retardation who claimed that their employer (in this case the *Hertz* rental car company) discriminated against them by failing to accommodate their known disabilities.[15] In the Hertz case, the plaintiffs argued unsuccessfully that the company violated the ADA by not allowing them the workplace accommodation of a job coach, who was to be retained by an outside agency at no cost to Hertz. The plaintiffs contended that *Hertz* could have "reasonably" accommodated their disabilities.

Discrimination under the ADA also includes denying equal employment opportunity to a qualified individual because of the known disability of a person with whom the qualified individual has a relationship or association.[16] A family relationship is the typical example used under the association provision of the ADA.[17] Discrimination under the ADA would be found where a job applicant discloses to the employer that her son has mental retardation, the applicant is qualified for the job, but the employer refuses to hire the applicant solely on the belief that she will have to miss work or frequently leave work early to care for her son.[18]

2.3 Study of Discrimination Recognized Under Title I

The goal of this and the following chapters is to examine the central terms of Title I, such as the law's antidiscrimination component. This analysis is warranted for several reasons.

First, many of the discretionary terms of Title I require interpretation so that future implementation of the law may be guided by accurate information.[19] Although this book focuses

---

[12] 42 U.S.C. § 12112(a) (Supp. IV 1992) (defining discrimination as "not making reasonable accommodations to the known physical or mental limitations of an otherwise qualified individual with a disability").

[13] *See Duda v. Board of Education of Franklin Park Public School District No. 84,* 133 F.3d 1054 (7th Cir. 1998) (citing 42 U.S.C. § 12112(b)(1), that the ADA includes "segregating" a job applicant or worker among its definitions of discrimination). *See* **also infra Ch. IV § 4.10** (discussing job reassignment as a workplace accommodation).

[14] *See* Edelman, **supra Ch. I § 1.3,** at 1536 (discussing the difficulty of defining discrimination under Title VII because of its ambiguous language); Kristin Bumiller, Victims in the Shadow of the Law: A Critique of Legal Protection, 12 **Signs: J. Women Culture & Soc'y** 421, 433 (1987) (discussing the need for individuals who suffer discrimination to assume the role of victim before filing a claim); Patricia DeMichele & Vicki Gottlich, Using Titles II and III of the Americans with Disabilities Act as Part of a Legal Services Practice, 27 **Clearinghouse Rev.** 1099–2000 (1996) (stating that the definition of discrimination depends on adequate description of comparison groups).

[15] *Hertz v. EEOC* is discussed **infra in Ch. V § 5.8.** *See also* **infra Appendices C and D** (presenting "friend of the court" briefs in the *EEOC v. Hertz* case).

[16] 42 U.S.C. § 12112(b)(4) (known as the "association provision").

[17] *See Den Hartog v. Wasatch Academy,* 129 F.3d 1076 (10th Cir. 1997) (discussing association provision of Title I and reviewing related cases).

[18] *Cf. Tyndall v. National Educ. Ctrs., Inc.,* 31 F.3d 209 (4th Cir. 1994) (finding for employer in case where mother of disabled son brought claim under association provision of ADA). *See also* **infra Ch. XVI § 16.7** (discussing barriers to work); **infra Ch. XV § 15.4** (discussing ADA discrimination on the basis of employment-related medical tests).

primarily on the role of empirical study in guiding ADA implementation, other political, legal, cultural, and social agenda contribute to the evolution of the law.[20] Many of these factors are discussed in the final part of this book.

Second, unlike the implementation of earlier disability-related laws, such as the Rehabilitation Act of 1973, Title I primarily regulates procedures for complying with the law, rather than mandating substantive or affirmative results for employment integration of persons with disabilities. Professor Lauren Edelman has commented that antidiscrimination employment laws such as the ADA allow organizations wide latitude toward compliance in ways that correspond to their business demands and norms.[21] Evaluation is needed of the ADA compliance strategies by large and small organizations in different business sectors. Chapter XI of this book describes the findings of our investigation of the attitudes toward employees with mental retardation in small, medium, and large organizations.

Third, the enforcement mechanisms of Title I, as described in later chapters, are guided by reliance on good faith compliance efforts by entities covered by the law. Compliance efforts are monitored by various federal agencies, such as the EEOC and the Justice Department. In the absence of strong enforcement mechanisms, attempts at proactive compliance are enhanced by informative data, rather than by retroactive and punitive judicial interpretations of the Act.[22] The value of empirical study, therefore, lies in its ability to assist in prospective interpretations and evaluations of ADA implementation and disability policy.

The following sections examine the legal and empirical foundations on which the statutory definition of "disability" under Title I rests, so that these bases may be assessed in the present investigation for the participating persons with mental retardation. This approach complements study of Title I concepts based on traditional case-by-case legal analysis.

2.4 ADA Title I: Definition of Disability and Persons with Mental Retardation

The scope of the definition of "disability" has been one of the most contentious aspects of ADA law, research and policy.[23] As suggested in the dialogue between Senators Helms and Harkin presented at the opening of this chapter, persons with mental retardation are covered generally, but not necessarily, under Title I's definition of disability.

Mental retardation has been held to be a "disability" in cases involving the definition of disability adopted by ADA.[24] According to a

---

[19] Bonnie P. Tucker, Section 504 of the Rehabilitation Act After Ten Years of Enforcement: The Past and the Future, 1989 **U. Ill. L. Rev.** 845, 877, 915 (1989) (arguing that failures of § 504 of the Rehabilitation Act are attributable to inadequate enforcement and lack of definition of the Act's key terms); Peter T. Killborn, Major Shift Likely as Law Bans Bias Toward Disabled, **N.Y. Times,** at § 1, 1 (July 12, 1992) ("Congress deliberately left central provisions of the [ADA] vague."); Mervyn Rothstein, For the Disabled, Some Progress, **N.Y. Times,** at § 2, 2 (Oct. 24, 1993) (stating that the ADA remains vague and that "critics charge that its vagueness can hinder enforcement").

[20] *See* Arlene Mayersen, The History of the ADA: A Movement Perspective, *in* **Rights and Responsibilities, supra Ch.1 § 1.1,** at 17 (describing the many divergent groups responsible for passage of the ADA); Sara D. Watson, A Study in Legislative Strategy: The Passage of the ADA, *in* **Rights and Responsibilities, supra Ch. I § 1.1,** at 25, 26–33 (describing the "evolution of the movement").

[21] Edelman, **supra Ch. I § 1.3,** at 1532 (reviewing compliance with the Civil Rights Act of 1964). *See also* Stephen L. Percy, Challenges and Dilemmas in Implementing Disability Rights Policies, 4 **J. Disability Pol'y Stud.** 41–63 (1993) (discussing potential economic and policy challenges in implementing the ADA).

[22] *See* Peter David Blanck, **Communicating the Americans with Disabilities Act: Transcending Compliance: A Case Report on Sears, Roebuck and Co.** (1994) [**hereinafter Sears I**] (discussing ADA compliance programs); Edelman, **supra Ch. I § 1.3,** at 1532 (identifying theory of interplay between organizations and their legal environments).

[23] The ADA's definition of disability is the same as used in the Rehabilitation Act of 1973, 29 U.S.C. 791–96 (1988). *See also* **People with Disabilities: Federal Programs Could Work Together More Efficiently to Promote Employment,** GAO Report, GAO/HEHS–96–126, at 4 (Sept. 1996).

1997 study by the President's Committee on the Employment of Persons with Disabilities, there are approximately 2.5 million persons with mental retardation, comprising 1 percent of the U.S. population.[25] Yet not all these individuals would be considered "disabled" for purposes of ADA analysis because of the individualized approach required to define whether an impairment rises to the level of a "disability" covered by the law.[26]

There are three general categories of persons with disabilities covered by ADA Title I law, encompassing a wide range of individuals. A person with a disability has:

1. "a physical or mental impairment that substantially limits that person in some major life activity" (referred to as the first prong of the definition of disability);
2. "a record of such a physical or mental impairment" (the second prong of the definition); or
3. is "regarded as having an impairment" (the third prong of the definition). [27]

Under the three-prong definition of disability, physical characteristics, such as hair color or left-handedness, and temporary conditions, are not covered disabilities, nor are an individual's economic, environmental, or cultural disadvantages. Negative but common personality traits—for instance, poor judgment or short temper—are not considered ADA disabilities.[28] In addition, expressly excluded in the statute from coverage are individuals who are pregnant, addicted to illegal drugs, or homosexual.[29]

For purposes of Title I analysis, many persons with mental retardation likely would be considered to have a "substantial" mental impairment that "limits a major life activity," such as the activities of learning, thinking, or working.[30] The diagnosis of mental retardation—or any impairment—may not *per se* qualify an individual as having a disability covered under the first prong of the definition, unless the impairment substantially limits a major life activity.

Many courts are finding that even serious impairments or conditions are not necessarily disabilities for purposes of ADA analysis. In a case decided in 1997, the United States Court of Appeals for the Ninth Circuit found that, despite the serious side effects from treatment for cancer, an employee who was able to perform his job duties was not "disabled" for purposes of ADA analysis.[31] Similarly, in a case decided in 1997 by the United States Court of Appeals for the Fourth Circuit, an employee with asymptomatic HIV disease was determined not "disabled" under the ADA.[32]

Other courts have concluded that individuals with serious asymptomatic conditions, such as

---

[24] *See Wilson v. State Insurance Fund,* 106 F.3d 414 (10th Cir.1997) (finding that plaintiff with mild mental retardation was an individual with a disability covered under Title I); **BNA Report, supra Ch. I § 1.5,** at 81–82 (covering mental retardation generally, educable mental retardation, and profound or severe mental retardation). But *See School Board of Nassau County, Florida v. Arline,* 480 U.S. 273 (1987) (concluding that fear of contacting tuberculosis—underlying physical illness—may not be a basis for terminating an employee).

[25] **Ability: The Bridge to the Future,** President's Committee on Employment of Persons with Disabilities, Educational Kit (July 1997).

[26] The National Council on Disability has four categories of disabilities that include (1) sensory, e.g., visual or hearing impairments, (2) cognitive, e.g., mental retardation or learning disabilities, (3) mental or emotional, e.g., mental illness, and (4) physical, e.g., deformity. *See also* **BNA Report, supra Ch. I § 1.5,** at 79, 83 (*citing* National Council of the Handicapped, Toward Independence, at 1, U.S. Gov. Printing Off.: Washington, D.C. (1986)—and citing cases identifying multiple disabilities, such as mental retardation and physical disability); Robert L. Burgdorf, Jr., **The Legal Rights of Handicapped Persons: Cases, Materials and Text,** at 31–46 (1980) (dividing disabilities into 10 categories).

[27] 42 U.S.C.S. § 12102(2) (Supp. Feb. 1991); 29 C.F.R. § 1630.2(g) (1991). Title III's public accommodation provisions protect individuals from discrimination "on the basis of disability." *See* **infra Ch. XVI § 16.3.**

[28] *See Mundo v. Sanus Health Polan of Greater New York,* 966 F. Supp. 171 (E.D.N.Y. 1997) (determining that ADA does not cover common personality traits).

[29] *See* Burgdorf, **supra Ch. I § 1.4,** at 145–46 (discussing other exceptions).

[30] *See* **infra Ch. III § 3.5** for discussion of the contrasting definition of "disability" under the ADA and under Social Security regulations. Some courts have judicially prohibited or "estopped" a charging party from bringing a Title I claim if the person subsequently declares him- or herself as totally disabled for purposes of receiving disability benefits.

[31] *See Innes v. Mechatronics, Inc.,* 120 F.3d 268 (9th Cir. 1997).

[32] *See Runnebaum v. Nationsbank of Md.,* 120 F.3d 156 (4th Cir. 1997) (en banc).

those with HIV disease, are disabled for purposes of ADA analysis. In *Abbott v. Bragdon,*[33] a case decided by the United States Court of Appeals for the First Circuit, the court found that HIV disease, whether symptomatic or asymptomatic, constitutes a disability under the ADA. In 1998 the United States Supreme Court will resolve the conflict of interpretation among the lower courts by reviewing *Bragdon v. Abbott,*[34] the first ADA case to be reviewed by the Court. The implications of this case for future ADA implementation are discussed in greater detail in Chapter XVI.

Overall, the trend in the case law has reflected a narrowing of the definition of disability, making it increasingly difficult for individuals even with serious and life threatening impairments to be covered by the law.[35] Professor Steven Locke has commented that "what was once touted as 'the most comprehensive civil rights legislation passed by Congress since the 1964 Civil Rights Act' has become increasingly narrowed to the point where it is in danger of becoming ineffective."[36]

2.5 The First Prong of the Definition of Disability

The first prong of the definition of disability is directed toward individuals with actual and substantial impairments or conditions—such as those with mental retardation, visual or hearing impairments, cancer, mental illness, physical paralysis or HIV disease—that affect a major life activity. It employs a functional definition of disability that is determined on a case-by-case basis.[37]

The first prong is based not only on the diagnosis of the impairment, but also on the effect of the impairment on the individual's life.[38] As mentioned, not all persons with mental retardation have a disability covered by the law. This is because their impairment may not substantially limit a major life activity, such as working or learning.[39] Thus, even an apparent or underlying genetic predisposition to illness or disease is not necessarily a disability covered by the law.[40]

Courts are split as to whether the "voluntariness" of a condition or impairment is relevant to the determination of a disability under the ADA. This issue may be raised in cases examining the relation of sexual promiscuity to subsequent HIV disease, smoking to the development of lung cancer, or riding a motorcycle without a helmet to brain damage from a motorcycle accident.[41]

Some courts have concluded that volition is not relevant to the statutory definition of disability.[42] In a 1997 decision that likely will have important consequences for persons with mental disabilities who take medications for their impairments, the Seventh Circuit U.S. Court of Appeals concluded that an individual is not covered under the ADA's definition of disability if, through his own fault, he fails to control an otherwise controllable illness (in this case,

---

[33] 107 F.3d 934, 939 (1st Cir. 1997) (holding that HIV-positive status, whether asymptomatic or symptomatic, is per se a disability under the Rehabilitation Act of 1973).

[34] The United States Supreme Court agreed to review the Abbott case on the issue of whether asymptomatic HIV disease constitutes a "disability" for purposes of ADA analysis, *Abbott v. Bragdon,* 107 F.3d 934, *cert. granted, Bragdon v. Abbott,* 118 S. Ct. 554 (1997) (the first case in which the Supreme Court has reviewed the implementation of the ADA).

[35] *See EEOC v. R.J. Gallagher Co.,* 959 F. Supp. 405 (S.D. Tex. 1997) (holding that being critically ill with cancer is not necessarily an ADA "disability").

[36] Steven S. Locke, The Incredible Shrinking Protected Class: Redefining the Scope of Disability Under the Americans with Disabilities Act, 68 **U. Colo. L. Rev.** 107–46, at 107 (1997) (quoting others).

[37] *See* Burgdorf, **supra Chap. I § 1.4,** at 129–30 (1995).

[38] 29 C.F.R. 403 (app. to pt. 1630) (providing commentary on § 1630.2(j)(1993). *Cf. Murphy v. United Parcel Service,* 1998 WL 105933 (10th Cir. 1998) (finding high blood pressure impairment that is controlled by medication not a covered disability).

[39] *See* **infra Ch. II § 2.9** (discussing case involving definition of major life activity for plaintiff with mental retardation).

[40] *See* **infra Ch. XV § 15.5** (discussion of genetic discrimination under the ADA).

[41] *See* EEOC Compliance Manual, § 902.2(e), at 14 (Mar. 14, 1995) (describing definition of disability under ADA).

[42] *See Cook v. Rhode Island Department of Mental Health,* 10 F.3d 17 (1st Cir. 1993) (concluding that underlying reason for plaintiff's obesity is not relevant to determination of disability under the ADA).

bipolar disorder) because of a decision not to take medication.[43]

Other issues involving the definition of disability under the ADA have included:[44]

1. the definition of a "major life activity," for instance, is reproduction a major life activity of females?
2. the relation of medication or other mitigating measures to the determination of whether a major life activity is "substantially limited," for instance, is a person with insulin-controlled diabetes disabled?
3. the nature and extent of a substantial limitation on working, for instance, as defined by an inability to work in a class of jobs or just a single job?

These and related issues are examined below and in later chapters in the book.

2.6 "Major Life Activity" Under the First Prong of the Definition of Disability

Under the first prong, disability is interpreted to mean that the individual is substantially limited in a "major life activity," for instance, in the ability to work.[45] Findings from the 1992 National Health Interview Survey show that 19 million working-age adults, roughly 12 percent of the population between the ages of 18 and 69, are restricted in the major life activity of working.[46] More than half of this group—10.9 million people—report that they are unable to work. Not all of these individuals necessarily would be covered by the ADA.

The ADA does not define the term "major life activity."[47] Courts are split on the issue of what constitutes a major life activity. Activities like walking, standing, learning, speaking, and working have been considered major life activities.[48] Other activities have been held not to be major life activities, such as lifting, interacting with others, or caring for others.[49] Most courts have concluded that an impairment does not have to affect an individual's ability to work for that individual to be covered under ADA Title I.

One of the central issues to be addressed by the United States Supreme Court in *Bragdon v. Abbott,*[50] the first ADA case to be reviewed by the Court, will be whether reproduction is a major life activity under the ADA. In *Bragdon* the First Circuit concluded that the plaintiff's HIV-positive status had a profound impact upon her ability to engage in reproduction, childbearing, and familial relations. According to the court, the touchstone for determining whether an activity is a "major life activity" under the ADA is its significance to an individual's daily life and day-to-day existence. The Supreme Court's analysis of the definition of a major life activity and disability under the ADA will have important ramifications for millions of Americans with asymptomatic and hidden impairments.

---

[43] *Van Stan v. Fancy Colours & Co.,* 125 F.3d 563 (7th Cir 1997). *See also Siefken v. Village of Arlington Heights,* 65 F.3d 664 (7th Cir. 1995) (finding that plaintiff's failure to monitor and control his controllable diabetes prevented recovery under the ADA).

[44] David K. Fram, **The Complete Guide to Resolving Complex ADA Workplace Questions,** at I-16–I-37 (3d ed., 1997) (providing a comprehensive review that is available from the National Law Institute).

[45] *See Gordon v. Hamm,* 100 F.3d 907 (11th Cir. 1996) (finding that while side effects of chemotherapy treatment may be an impairment, it may not substantially limit an individual to work in a class of jobs or in a broad range of jobs in various classes); *Weiler v. Household Finance Corp.,* 101 F.3d 519 (7th Cir. 1996) (holding that an individual does not have a covered disability when incapable of satisfying demands of particular job).

[46] *See* Steve Kaye, **Disability Watch: Status Report on the Condition of People with Disabilities,** Disability Rights Advocates and Disability Statistics Center, at 2 (1998) [**hereinafter Disability Watch**] (noting that more than half of this group—10.9 million people—report that they are unable to work). For extensive analysis of factors related to work limitation, *See* Mitchell P. LaPlante & D. Carlson, **Disability in the United States: Prevalence and Causes, 1992,** Disability Statistics Report No. 7: U.S. Dept. Ed., Nat'l Institute Disability Research (1996).

[47] *See Abbott v. Bragdon,* 107 F.3d 934, 939 (1st Cir. 1997).

[48] *See* EEOC Compliance Manual, 29 C.F.R. § 1630.2(i).

[49] *See Soileau v. Guilford of Maine,* 105 F.3d 12 (1st Cir. 1997) (interacting with others not a major life activity); *Krauel v. Iowa Methodist Medical Center,* 95 F.3d 674 (8th Cir. 1997) (caring for others not a major life activity).

[50] *Cert. granted,* 118 S. Ct. 554 (1997).

2.7 "Substantial Limitation" Under the First Prong of the Definition of Disability

The EEOC has found a "substantial limitation" resulting from an impairment in circumstances where an individual is unable to perform or is significantly restricted in performing a major life activity (for instance, in the areas of learning, thinking, breathing, walking, or talking) compared to an average person in the population.[51] The evaluation of a substantial limitation on a major life activity is determined by the nature and severity of the impairment, the duration of the impairment, and the permanent and long-term impact of the impairment.

Under the ADA, the individual with an impairment must prove that the condition is substantially limiting.[52] For persons with mental retardation, evidence of the Social Security Administration's determination of disability, receipt of governmental disability, or Medicaid benefits are not sufficient by themselves to establish a disability covered by the ADA.[53] Likewise, evidence of a hospital stay by itself may not be determinative of whether a person is substantially limited in a major life activity.[54]

Courts have held that temporary impairments do not qualify as disabilities under the ADA because they are not substantially limiting.[55] The permanency of the condition—for instance, as in the case of a severe developmental disability from birth—has been called "the touchstone" of a substantially limiting impairment.[56] Nevertheless, serious episodic but not continuous conditions—for instance, bipolar disorder and epilepsy—have been determined to be substantially limiting impairments.[57]

Some courts have examined whether the effects of medication, assistive devices, or prosthetics should be considered in determining whether there exists a substantial limitation on a major life activity. The EEOC has taken the position that the nature of the underlying impairment is determinative of a disability covered by the law, regardless of the availability of any mitigating measures.[58] A few courts have found that an impairment was not substantially limiting when controlled by medication—for instance, in cases involving individuals with diabetes or depression, and in circumstances where the individual performs well in employment.[59]

2.8 "Substantial Limitation" in Working

The first prong definition of disability does not mean that an individual covered by the law must work at the job of his choice.[60] Rather, to fall under the first prong definition, the individual's access to a particular labor market

---

[51] EEOC Compliance Manual, 29 C.F.R. § 1630.(j)(1)–(2).

[52] For a review, *see* Robert L. Burgdorf, Jr., "Substantially Limited" Protection from Disability Discrimination: The Special Treatment Model and Misconceptions of the Definition of Disability, 42 **Vill L. Rev.** 409–585 (1997) (reviewing cases).

[53] *See Robinson v. Neodata Services, Inc.*, 94 F.3d 499 (8th Cir. 1996) (finding Social Security Administration determination not preclusive on whether impairment covered by ADA); *Weiler v. Household Finance Corp.*, 101 F.3d 519 (7th Cir 1996) (impairment determined by Social Security disability system not dispositive of finding ADA disability).

[54] *See Burch v. Coca-Cola,* 101 F.3d 305 n.4 (5th Cir. 1997) (ADA requires individualized inquiry beyond existence of hospital stay).

[55] *See* Burgdorf, **supra Ch. II § 2.7,** at 469–88 (reviewing cases).

[56] *See Burch v. Coca-Cola,* **supra Ch. II § 2.7,** at n.4.

[57] EEOC Compliance Manual, § 902.4(d), at 34.

[58] *Id.* at 35–36; 28 C.F.R. Part 35, App. A, § 35.104 (U.S. Department of Justice regulations). *See also Matczak v. Frankford Candy and Chocolate Company,* 136 F.3d 933 (3d Cir. 1997) (finding that disabled individuals who control their disability with medication may still invoke the protections of the ADA); *Arnold v. United Parcel Service, Inc.*, 136 F.3d 854 (1st Cir. 1998) (same).

[59] *See, e.g., Schulter v. Industrial Coils, Inc.*, 928 F. Supp. 1437 (W.D. Wisc. 1996) (plaintiff with diabetes); *Wilking v. County of Ramsey,* 983 F. Supp. 848 (D. Minn. Fourth Div. 1997) (plaintiff with depression); *Fuller v. Iowa Department of Human Services,* 1998 Iowa Sup. LEXIS 50 (Iowa 1998) (same).

[60] *See Welsh v. City of Tulsa, Okla.*, 977 F.2d 1415, 1417 (10th Cir. 1992) (major life activity of working does not necessarily mean working at the job of one's choice); *Knapp v. Northwestern University,* 101 F.3d 473 (7th Cir. 1996), *cert. denied,* 117 S. Ct. 2454 (1997) (same); *Weiler v. Household Finance Corp.*, 101 F.3d 519 (7th Cir. 1996) (holding that an individual does not have a covered disability when incapable of working under a particular supervisor because of anxiety or stress related to job review).

must be substantially limited by the impairment or condition.[61]

Factors considered in determining whether an impairment substantially limits the major life activity of work, and therefore is a covered disability, include the individual's access to a geographic area, the number and type of jobs requiring similar training or skills (such as the class of jobs in the relevant labor market), and the number and type of jobs not requiring similar training and skills (such as the range of similar jobs in the relevant labor market).[62]

An individual's failure to qualify for one job in a labor market, even because of a substantial impairment or condition, does not mean that the individual has a covered disability for purposes of Title I analysis. A court must still assess whether the individual's impairment or condition creates a significant barrier to employment or to a particular labor market.[63] This "access to labor market" test suggests that in cases where an employer's failure to hire a job applicant with a degree of mental retardation forecloses that individual from working within a range of jobs in an industry or in a company, that individual may have a disability covered under the first prong of the statutory definition.[64]

Courts have found that an individual is not substantially limited in working in cases where mental impairments result in personality conflicts with a particular manager or supervisor.[65] In one case decided in 1997, an individual's inability to work under several supervisors was determined not to be a substantial limitation on the major life activity of working because it did not prevent the individual from working in a class of other jobs.[66]

The next chapter examines how the determination of a substantial limitation in working does not indicate necessarily that the individual is "qualified" to perform the job in question, and therefore may be discharged or not hired without an employer violating the ADA. The test to determine if a disability is covered by the law focuses on whether the individual's access to the relevant labor market or job is limited due to the substantial nature of his impairment. A subsequent determination is required of whether he is qualified for the job and whether the employer discriminated against him because of his disability.[67]

2.9 A Case Example Involving the Definition of "Disability" for an Individual with Mild Mental Retardation: *Anderson v. General Motors*

In *Anderson v. General Motors*[68] the plaintiff was an individual with mild mental retardation working for General Motors (GM) on the sealer assembly line in the paint department. On the sealer line, plaintiff's single job was to apply paint sealer to the seams on an unpainted auto body. Some time after plaintiff had been working as a sealer, GM reorganized its plant around a team concept, in which groups of employees worked together on several related tasks, and no individual had a single job function. Under the team concept, the plaintiff was required to learn seven job tasks and to rotate through each position.

Plaintiff encountered difficulties in learning the job tasks of the new sealer position and was unable to fulfill her job responsibilities. Her frustration culminated in a breakdown and

---

[61] *See EEOC v. Joslyn Manufacturing Co.*, 1996 U.S. Dist. LEXIS 9882 (N.D. Ill. 1996) (finding that the impairment excluded individual from a wide variety of jobs at employer in question). An individual may show a substantial limitation on a major life activity other than working and thereby be a covered person with a disability. Burgdorf, **supra Ch. I § 1.4,** at 156–57.

[62] 29 C.F.R. § 1630.2(j)(3)(i–ii).

[63] *See Joslyn,* **supra Ch. II § 2.8,** at *16 (*citing* cases in support); *Sherrod v. American Airlines, Inc.*, 132 F.3d 112 (5th Cir. 1998) (same).

[64] *Id.* (*citing* in support *Cook v. Rhode Island,* 10 F.3d 17, 25–26 (1st Cir. 1993); *EEOC v. Chrysler Corp.*, 917 F. Supp. 1164, 1169 (E.D. Mich. 1996)). *Cf.* Burgdorf, **supra Ch. II § 2.7,** at 573 (arguing that the access to labor market test is overly broad and discrimination in one job should be enough to invoke ADA protections).

[65] *See* **infra Ch. III § 3.5** (reviewing cases involving mental characteristics); Fram, **supra Ch. II § 2.5,** at I-22–I-23 (same).

[66] *See Siemon v. AT&T,* 113 F.3d 1175 (10th Cir. 1997) (disability only precluded individual from working at one employer location).

[67] 42 U.S.C. § 12112(b).

[68] 1997 U.S. Dist. LEXIS 7829 (D. Kan. 1997).

hospitalization, and GM placed her on sick leave. After several months plaintiff's psychologist and psychiatrist released her to return to work under the job restriction of working only one job function.

GM claimed that plaintiff was not an individual with a "disability" covered by the ADA. In its analysis the court accepted that plaintiff's mental retardation qualified as a mental impairment but rejected the position that her mental retardation substantially limited her major life activity of working. Plaintiff had argued that her mental retardation substantially limited her major life activity of working through her inability to take care of her "business affairs," which were managed by her mother. The court rejected the view that taking care of one's business affairs was a major life activity for purposes of ADA analysis. Thus, plaintiff was not found to be "disabled" based on her inability to handle her business affairs.

In addition, plaintiff argued that her mental retardation prevented her from being able to learn and perform more than one job junction on the assembly line. Because of this inability, she argued that she was unable to perform a broad range or class of jobs at the GM plant. As discussed earlier, to be "substantially limited" in the major life activity of working, a plaintiff must be significantly restricted in the ability to perform a class of jobs. The court therefore concluded that the plaintiff did not demonstrate that she was disqualified from performing other jobs within the plant that would use similar skills or abilities. For these reasons the court found the plaintiff not disabled as defined under the ADA.

The *Anderson* case highlights several issues discussed in this and subsequent chapters in this book. Prominent among them is that an individual with mild mental retardation, who may be qualified for a single job but not for working in a class of jobs, will not necessarily be considered a person with a disability for purposes of analysis under the ADA. As discussed in Chapter V, such a plaintiff would fail to establish a required element of the "prima facie" case for employment discrimination under the ADA.[69]

Second, the *Anderson* court concluded summarily (for instance, as opposed to a fact-based inquiry at trial) that persons with mild mental retardation who require at least some assistance in their daily lives—such as in the management of their business affairs—may nonetheless not be disabled for purposes of the ADA. The difficult issue presented for persons with mental retardation, and others with disabilities, is what types of life activities, such as caring for oneself and performing everyday life tasks, are considered "major" for purposes of ADA analysis.

Third, as Chapter IV discusses, the *Anderson* court did not examine whether GM had explored the availability of effective workplace accommodations to enable the plaintiff to perform the essential functions of the jobs at the GM plant. Job coaching or coworker natural supports may have enabled the plaintiff in *Anderson* to learn to perform more than one task on the assembly line.[70] The chapters in the final part of the book examine how these and other workplace strategies cost far less than the pursuit of litigation in federal court, and enable qualified workers with mental retardation to remain on the job.

2.10 The Second and Third Prongs of the Definition of Disability

Unlike the first prong, the second and third prongs of the definition of disability (that is, an individual with a "record of" or "regarded as having" an impairment) are meant to prevent employment discrimination on the basis of biased and unjustified attitudes toward individuals with perceived, presently asymptomatic conditions, or not "substantially limiting" conditions.[71] Many times, an applicant's or employee's actual or perceived impairment is

---

[69] *See* **infra Ch. V § 5.2** (discussing elements of ADA case).

[70] *See* **infra Ch. IV § 4.7** (discussing these strategies as workplace accommodations).

[71] An example of a case involving all three prongs is *Joslyn*, **supra Ch. II § 2.8** (involving a plaintiff who contended that he: was qualified for the job; was regarded as a person with carpal tunnel syndrome; had a record of this impairment that substantially limited his major life activity of working; and was denied employment on that basis).

substantially limiting only as a result of the biased attitudes of others.

One example of a case implicating the second or third prong of the definition of disability might involve a qualified person with a record of mild mental retardation. In a situation where an employment action is taken because of that individual's perceived or misclassified record of mental retardation, and not on a worker's present capabilities, productivity or output—that is, not on actual work qualifications—an ADA employment discrimination claim may succeed. In this situation the economic value of the worker to the employer is distorted solely by the employer's discriminatory behavior.[72] A goal of Title I is to enable qualified workers with only perceived disabilities to receive the actual "value of their labor in a nondiscriminatory environment."[73]

An individual is perceived as or "regarded as" having a substantially limiting impairment if that individual:

- has an impairment that does not substantially limit major life activities but is treated by an employer as having such a limitation;
- has an impairment that substantially limits major life activities only as the result of the unjustified attitudes of others; or
- has no impairment but is treated by an employer as having a substantially limiting impairment.[74]

In "regarded as" cases, an individual's underlying impairment does not have to be "substantially limiting" to be covered by the ADA.[75] This is because the "regarded as" prong is meant to protect individuals from unjustified prejudice and stereotypes about disability, particularly in cases where the individual does not have an impairment or has an impairment that does not substantially limit a major life activity.[76] These issues, in relation to biased attitudes toward mental and genetic conditions, are revisited in Chapter XV.

Analysis of issues associated with employers' attitudes about "record of" and "regarded as" disabilities—for instance, conditions such as mental retardation that are not always immediately obvious—serves several purposes related to the analysis of the definition of disability and to the study of employment integration in this book.

First, studies suggest that increasing numbers of individuals with perceived disabilities are entering the workforce and are denied integrated employment opportunity solely on the basis of biased attitudes and prejudice about their impairments.[77] Some studies find that the most common health impairments associated with disability are "hidden" conditions.[78]

Second, the study of attitudes toward persons with mental disabilities is illustrative of underlying biases and discrimination unrelated to actual worker value or productivity in the labor

---

[72] Title I imposes liability for discrimination whenever the prohibited motivation based on disability affects the employer's decision, that is, "when it is a 'but-for' cause." *See McNely v. Ocala,* 99 F.3d 1068 (11th Cir. 1996), cert. denied 117 S. Ct. 1819 (1997) (concluding a literal reliance on the phrase "solely" by reason of disability leads to results inconsistent with Congressional intent).

[73] *See* John J. Donohue III, Employment Discrimination Law in Perspective: Three Concepts of Equality, 92 **Mich. L. Rev.** 2583, 2585 (1994) (defining this concept as "intrinsic equality").

[74] 29 C.F.R. § 1630.2(l), Appendix A (1997).

[75] EEOC Compliance Manual, § 902.8(e), at 49–50. *See also* Arlene B. Mayerson, Restoring Regard for the "Regarded As" Prong: Giving Effect to Congressional Intent, 42 **Vill. L. Rev.** 587–612 (1997) (arguing that the "regarded as" prong of the definition of disability should be analyzed differently than the first prong of the definition to give Congressional intent to the law).

[76] Nevertheless, some courts have concluded that a plaintiff cannot maintain a claim under the "regarded as" prong by alleging that the employer believes that some physical characteristic (e.g., obesity or height) automatically renders the plaintiff "disabled." *See Francis v. City of Meriden,* 129 F.3d 281 (2nd Cir. 1997). A successful plaintiff must show that the employer believed, even erroneously, that the plaintiff had an impairment that, if it existed, would be covered under the ADA's first prong of the definition of disability (e.g., substantially limiting a major life activity). *See Andrews v. State of Ohio,* 104 F.3d 803 (6th Cir. 1997).

[77] *See* **Disability Watch, supra Ch. II § 2.6,** at 3–4 (finding most common health impairments are "hidden" conditions, and persons with "hidden disabilities," such as those with mental impairments, encounter severe attitudinal bias in the workplace).

[78] *Id.* at 3.

market.[79] Diminished worker value, reflected in lower wages for comparable work, is not related to actual productivity or to customers' preferences but to unfounded attitudinal discrimination.

Unjustified discrimination may involve biased attitudes toward the work qualifications of many individuals with mental retardation. As reflected by the "black hole" findings from the present investigation (see Chapters XI and XII) regarding trends in employment integration of persons with mental retardation, discrimination may be reflected in unfounded expectations for continued sheltered workshop placement for many qualified persons with mental retardation. Unlike race or gender employment discrimination, the characteristics associated with many mental disabilities may not be immediately obvious to the employer, either at the time of hiring or during employment, thereby making the provision of effective workplace accommodation more difficult.[80]

2.11 A Taxonomy of Employment Discrimination Based on Disability

Theories of Title I discrimination based on attitudinal bias are emerging. Elsewhere, Mollie Marti and I have proposed a taxonomy for the analysis of the definition of disability under Title I.[81] Figure 2.1 highlights legal case outcomes that reflect judicial interpretations of the definition of disability.

A hypothetical case involving attitudinal bias and the "regarded as" prong of the definition of disability might involve a qualified individual with moderate mental retardation. This hypothetical case is analogous to an example that involves an individual with an asymptomatic impairment. In this type of case, the individual may be denied employment solely because of the employer's unfounded negative attitudes about the individual's present abilities or predisposition for future health-related problems. This case type is illustrated by the lower left cell in Figure 2.1. In this situation, an employer's discriminatory and biased attitudes determine employment decisions, rather than the individual's actual abilities or market value of that individual's labor.[82]

A second scenario involves alleged employment discrimination and perceived disability in circumstances where the appropriateness of an employee's workplace behavior is at issue. This case type is illustrated in the top left cell in Figure 2.1. In a case of this sort, the behavior at issue is not always related to an underlying impairment recognized by the law. In one such case, *Fenton v. Pritchard Corp.*,[83] an employee terminated for inappropriate and threatening behavior toward a fellow employee was deemed not qualified and thereby not entitled to Title I protections. The employee contended unsuccessfully that his behavior toward coworkers led his employer to perceive him as a covered person with a mental disability.

Cases of this type suggest that an employer's negative attitudes toward an employee resulting in an adverse employment decision nevertheless must be based on defined impairments that fall under the purview of the ADA. Employment decisions based on perceptions of an employee's personality or behavior problems, such as a short temper or poor judgment in the workplace, are not discriminatory if the underlying impairment is not regarded as a covered disability.

---

[79] *See* Harlan Hahn, Antidiscrimination Laws and Social Research on Disability: The Minority Group Perspective, 14 **Behav. Sci. & Law** 41 (1996) (discussing a minority group model of disability, which stresses attitudinal discrimination as the principal problem facing disabled persons); Linda Hamilton Krieger, The Content of Our Categories: A Cognitive Bias Approach to Discrimination and Equal Employment Opportunity, 47 **Stan. L. Rev.** 1161–248 (1995); Charles R. Lawrence, The Id, The Ego, and Equal Protection: Reckoning with Unconscious Racism, 39 **Stan. L. Rev.** 317 (1987).

[80] *See Hedberg v. Indiana Bell Telephone Co.*, 47 F.3d 928, 931–32 (7th Cir. 1995) (discussing similarity between nonobvious nature of religious discrimination and disability discrimination in cases involving hidden disabilities).

[81] *See* **Attitudes and the ADA, supra Ch. I § 1.1.**

[82] *See Runnebaum v. Nationsbank of Md.*, 123 F.3d 156 (4th Cir. 1996). According to EEOC regulatory guidance, the access to labor market test may not apply to analysis of the second and third prong definition of disability; that is, an individual could be covered under these parts of the definition regardless of whether the employer's attitudes "were shared by others in the field...," 29 C.F.R. 406 (app. to pt. 1630) (providing a commentary on § 1630.2(l)(1993)).

[83] 926 F. Supp. 1437 (D. Kan. 1996).

Figure 2.1

Analysis of ADA Title I: Definition of Disability*

	"KNOWN" IMPAIRMENT COVERED BY TITLE I — **NO** ("no substantial limitation on major life activity" or no impairment)	**"KNOWN" IMPAIRMENT COVERED BY TITLE I** — **YES** ("substantial limitation on major life activity")
NO PERCEIVED IMPAIRMENT	**Not Covered** (e.g., personality or behavior problem) ***Cases:*** Stewart v. County of Brown, 86 F.3d 107 (7th Cir. 1996) (excitability); Dutcher v. Ingalls Shipbuilding, 53 F.3d 723 (5th Cir. 1995) (arm injury); Fenton v. Pritchard Corp., 926 F. Supp. 1437 (D. Kan. 1996) (threatening behavior).	**Hidden, Asymptomatic Condition** (e.g., genetic or psychiatric illness) ***Cases:*** Hedberg v. Indiana Bell Tel. Co., 47 F.3d 928 (7th Cir. 1995) (primary amyloidosis); Johnson v. Boardman Petroleum, Inc., 923 F. Supp. 1563 (S.D. Ga. 1996) (depression); Stola v. Joint Indus. Bd., 889 F. Supp. 133 (S.D.N.Y. 1995) (anxiety disorder).
YES PERCEIVED IMPAIRMENT	**Misdiagnosis, Misconceptions and Biased Attitudes** (e.g., gay lifestyle equates with presence of HIV disease, obesity or heart disease equates with lack of present ability) ***Cases:*** Deane v. Pocono Med. Ctr., 7 A.D. Cases 555 (3d Cir. 1997) (sprained wrist); Katz v. City Metal Co., 87 F.3d 26 (1st Cir. 1996) (heart disease); La Paz v. Henry's Diner, 946 F. Supp. 484 (N.D. Tex. 1996) (homosexuality); EEOC v. Texas Bus Lines, 923 F. Supp. 965 (S.D. Tex. 1996) (obesity).	**Obvious, Readily Apparent Impairment** (e.g., cerebral palsy) ***Cases:*** Abbott v. Bragdon, 107 F.3d 934 (1st Cir. 1997) (HIV); Koblosh v. Adelsick, 1996 WL 675791 (N.D. Ill. 1996) (cerebral palsy). **or** **Impairment Substantially Limiting Only as Result of Attitudes of Employer** (e.g., toothlessness) ***Cases:*** Vande Zande v. Wisconsin Dep't of Admin., 44 F.3d 538 (7th Cir. 1995) (paralysis (dicta)); Hodgdon v. Mt. Mansfield Co., 624 A.2d 1122 (Vt. Sup. Ct. 1992) (toothlessness).

* Categorization of a case in one of the four quadrants or cells does not indicate whether a person is "qualified" for the job in question for purposes of Title I analysis. Although the cases cited are illustrative of a primary cell category, factual aspects of a particular case may enable categorization in multiple cells. For instance, in many Title I cases, plaintiffs allege multiple charges of discrimination under each of the three prongs of the statutory definition of disability.

A third scenario that implicates attitudes toward disability may involve decisions by employers to grant or refuse the provision of workplace accommodations, a topic discussed in Chapter IV. In cases of this kind, employment discrimination will not be found in circumstances where the employer does not perceive or treat an employee's hidden impairment (for instance, mild mental retardation) as a substantial limitation on the employee's present ability to work. This case type is illustrated in the top right cell in Figure 2.1.

A fourth scenario may involve alleged employment discrimination, where a qualified employee is perceived by an employer as having *and* has a covered impairment, and is discharged on that basis. This case type is illustrated in the lower right cell in Figure 2.1. In cases of this kind, an employee may allege not only that the employer regarded her as having the impairment, but also that the impairment substantially limited the employee's ability to work.

In some circumstances, an individual with a covered impairment, such as a person with more than mild mental retardation, may be "substantially limited" in a job only due to the unjustified attitudes of others. Thus, many severe and obvious impairments, which independently may be covered under Title I's definition of disability, are "disabling" in the workplace only as a result of employers' misperceptions about individual performance capabilities or about the efficacy of workplace accommodations or supports.

In each of the four generalized scenarios illustrated, the employee must show a connection between an employer's biased attitudes toward the employee's actual or perceived disability and that employer's subsequent adverse behavior.[84] This places a heavy evidentiary burden on plaintiffs in Title I employment discrimination cases. Although the test is meant to ensure that Title I's definition of disability does not distort the economic value of labor to employers, it also is not meant to alter their rational labor market behavior. Thus, an employer's negative attitudes about people with actual or perceived disabilities do not by themselves constitute unjustified discrimination under Title I, unless they form the basis for subsequent discriminatory behavior toward "qualified" individuals.[85]

Proof of the link between discriminatory attitudes and behavior, or "discriminatory animus," toward a qualified individual with a covered disability is one essential element of a successful Title I case.[86] Employment discrimination under Title I will not be found where the employer does not "know" of, perceive, or treat an employee's impairment as a substantial limitation on a "qualified" employee's present ability to work.[87]

An employer's economic or humanitarian decision to grant a leave, educational or vocational training, job coaching, workplace accommodations, or flexible supports to a worker are not by themselves indicative of that employer's perceptions of a defined disability.[88] Likewise, an employer's decision not to hire an individual with an impairment for a position does not demonstrate that it perceives the employee as disabled for purposes of Title I

---

[84] Donohue, **supra ch. II § 2.9,** at 2584.

[85] *See Gordon v. Hamm,* 100 F.3d 907 (11th Cir. 1996) (finding that as with actual impairments, a perceived impairment must be substantially limiting and significant, presumably perceived to substantially limit an individual to work in a class of jobs).

[86] *See Johnson v. Boardman Petroleum, Inc.*, 923 F. Supp. 1563 (S.D. Ga. 1996); *Bultemeyer v. Fort Wayne Community Schools,* 100 F.3d 1281 (7th Cir. 1996). *See also* **Ch. V § 5.2** (discussing elements of ADA employment discrimination case).

[87] *See Stewart v. County of Brown,* 86 F.3d 107 (7th Cir. 1996) (finding that employee did not make valid perceived disability claim even though employer thought he was excitable, ordered psychological evaluations for him, and stated that he considered employee to be psychologically imbalanced, because the employer was advised the employee was mentally fit for his job); *Holihan v. Lucky Stores,* 87 F.3d 362 (9th Cir. 1996) (finding issue of material fact as to perceived disability claim where employer called employee into meetings to discuss his "aberrational behavior," asked him if he had problems and encouraged him to seek counseling); *EEOC v. Joslyn Manufacturing Co.,* 1996 U.S. Dist. LEXIS 9882 (N.D. Ill. 1996) (finding genuine issue of fact where employer contended it did not treat plaintiff's carpal tunnel syndrome as an impairment that substantially limited his ability to work at one job and plaintiff was not disqualified from a class of jobs).

[88] *See Johnson,* 923 F. Supp. at 1569 (discussing that Title I lawsuits on the basis of perceived disability may "chill" employers' attempts to humanize their relationships with their employees).

analysis, regardless of whether an accommodation is required.[89]

2.12 Summary

ADA Title I prohibits discrimination against qualified persons with covered disabilities. This is accomplished by enabling persons covered by the law to have an equal opportunity to participate in employment. Title I requires employers to accommodate the needs of qualified persons with disabilities only so that they have equal, but not advantageous, opportunity for employment.

As described in the final part of the book, the findings of the present investigation support the view that many qualified employees with mental retardation are engaged successfully in competitive work. The next chapter examines issues related to employment integration and economic opportunity that may be clarified through study of whether a person with mental retardation is a "qualified individual" for purposes of ADA analysis.

---

[89] *Joslyn,* 1996 U.S. Dist. LEXIS 9882 (finding that the "test for whether a perceived impairment substantially limits a major life activity is not whether the employer's rejection of the applicant was due to a good faith, narrowly-based decision that the applicant's characteristics did not match specific job requirements. Rather, the proper test is whether the impairment, as perceived, would affect the individual's ability to find work across a class of jobs or a broad range of jobs in various classes."); *Barnes v. Cochran,* 944 F. Supp. 897 (S.D. Fla. 1996), affirmed *Barnes v. Broward County Sheriffs',* 130 F.3d 443 (11th Cir. 1997) (the fact that an employer finds an applicant unqualified does not mean that it did not perceive applicant as disabled).

CHAPTER III

Central Provisions of ADA Title I: Qualified Individuals with Disabilities

When I grow up, I want to be a firefighter. If there is a house on fire, I will help to squirt out the fire. I want to live in my own apartment. I will need a job to pay for the apartment. I will need food and clothes. Rules about working should be easy. Rules should help me get a job.

Tiffany Zimenoff [1]

3.1 Introduction

The previous chapter discussed a number of impairments and conditions that result in a "disability" recognized by the ADA, including mental retardation.[2] The definition of mental retardation set forth by the American Association on Mental Retardation (AAMR) in 1992 covers individuals who have substantial limitations in present functioning characterized by subaverage intellectual functioning, with limitations in adaptive skill areas such as work,[3] communication, social skills, community use, and health and safety skills.[4]

As discussed in Chapter II, a person with mental retardation will not be automatically considered an individual with a disability covered by Title I. The investigation described in this book uses a framework to address questions regarding the nature and severity of an individual's impairment—for instance, the extent to which it may be substantially limiting in a major life activity—and the relation of an impairment to subsequent employment integration and economic opportunity.

This chapter examines the definition of a "qualified" individual with mental retardation under the ADA. The definition of a qualified

---

[1] National Council on Disability, **Removing Barriers to Work: Action Proposals for the 105th Congress and Beyond** (Sept. 24, 1997) (statement before NCD by a 14-year-old with Down syndrome).

[2] 29 C.F.R. § 1630.2(h) (1991); Chai R. Feldblum, The Americans with Disabilities Act Definition of Disability, 7 **Lab. Law.** 11 (Winter 1991) (overview of Act).

[3] *Cf.* Richard J. Hernstein & Charles Murray, **The Bell Curve: Intelligence and Class Structure in American Life** (1994) ("In focusing on those who did drop out of the labor force and those who were unemployed, we do not want to forget that most white males at every level of cognitive ability were in the labor force and working, even at the lowest cognitive levels. Among physically able white males [at] the bottom 5 percent of the IQ distribution, comprising men who are intellectually borderline or clinically retarded, seven out of ten were in the labor force for all fifty-two weeks of 1989.").

[4] *See* American Association on Mental Retardation, **Mental Retardation: Definition, Classification, and Systems of Support** 1 (1992) **[hereinafter AAMR]** (mental retardation manifests before age 18); Burgdorf, **supra Ch. I § 1.4**, at 31–46; James W. Ellis, Decisions by and for People with Mental Retardation: Balancing Considerations of Autonomy and Protection, 37 **Vill. L. Rev.** 1779, 1781–82 (1992) (describing definition).

individual is central to the interpretation of the ADA and tied to the long-term research purposes of the present project.

The following questions related to the definition of a "qualified" individual under the ADA are addressed by the present research model:

1. What constitutes a substantial limitation on the major life activity of work (for instance, quality of health status alone) for persons with differing degrees of mental retardation and with different job capabilities and qualifications?[5]
2. How may substantial limitations on major life activities change over time for individuals with different degrees of mental retardation (for instance, as reflected in changes in individual capabilities and job qualifications with age or with job support and training)?
3. How do the living environments of individuals with mental retardation support or limit the ability to attain and retain work (for instance, the importance of independent living, job supports and accommodations, and family and governmental supports)?
4. How may the work qualifications of job applicants and employees with mental retardation be assessed?
5. How may essential and marginal workplace tasks be assessed for workers with mental retardation?

In addressing these and other questions, the present research framework is consistent with the recent shift in the definition of mental retardation and of disability generally. Rather than viewing impairments and conditions as static absolute traits, the research model enables examination of impairment as a function of the individual capabilities and qualifications of the person *and* supports and barriers in the social and physical environment. Professor Harlan Hahn and others have described the importance of social, attitudinal, and political forces in shaping conceptions of impairment and disability in our society.[6]

The importance of personal, familial, attitudinal, and social factors to employment integration and economic growth is highlighted in the model presented in Figure 1.1 by factors such as individual "capabilities and qualifications," "inclusion," and "empowerment" factors.[7] The information collected assesses reported limitations for persons with differing degrees of mental retardation in employment and daily life activities. This information may help clarify the applicability in practice of the substantially limiting language of Title I.[8]

As Chapter II highlighted, study is required to determine if a degree of mental retardation, or for that matter any impairment or condition, is substantially limiting, and thereby "disabling," for purposes of analysis under Title I's definition of disability.[9] This analysis is warranted for those persons with mental retardation who function well in society and yet are excluded from employment on the basis of myths and misconceptions about their condition (for instance, they are "regarded as" disabled).

---

[5] In *Mowatt v. Transportation Unlimited, Inc.*, 984 F.2d 230, 231–32 (8th Cir. 1992), the Eighth Circuit Court of Appeals held, under the Rehabilitation Act, that a truck driver who was unable to perform his job for the defendant employer was not substantially limited in a major life activity because he could not show he was unable to drive truck for another company.

[6] *See* Harlan Hahn, Antidiscrimination Laws and Social Research on Disability: The Minority Group Perspective, 14 **Behav. Sci. & L.** 41–59 (1996).

[7] *See* Ellis, **supra Ch. III § 3.1**, at 1781–82 (reviewing new definition); Donald L. MacMillan, et al., Conceptual and Psychometric Concerns About the 1992 AAMR Definition of Mental Retardation, 98 **Am. J. Mental Retardation** 325 (1993) (arguing that the new definition represents a "radical departure from previous definitions").

[8] *Cf.* **Comments on the EEOC's Proposed Regulations for Title I of the ADA**, Thresholds National Research and Training Center on Rehabilitation and Mental Illness, at 1 (Apr. 25, 1991) (noting that the EEOC's description of "major life activities" include activities relevant to persons with mental disabilities, such as reasoning, concentrating, and interacting with others).

[9] The substantial limitation determination is made on the job-related capabilities and qualifications of the individual. It is difficult to determine the exact extent of a disabling condition, especially for those persons with impairments who function well in work and society. Peter David Blanck & Robert Folberg, The Americans with Disabilities Act: Emerging Issues for Ophthalmologists, 101 **Ophthalmology** 1635 (1994). In the case of an individual with mild mental retardation, the individual must demonstrate that he or she can perform the essential job functions. *See also* Perritt, **supra Ch. I § 1.4,** at 35 (noting a "Catch 22" because if persons with disabilities are "too disabled," or they cannot perform essential job functions, they may not be covered by the law).

Research is needed of individuals with mental retardation who are excluded solely on the basis of attitudinal bias addressed by the second and third prong of the definition of disability.[10] Chapter XV of this book concludes that the bases for many individualized judgments of employee "qualifications" without the benefit of systematic data often result in unnecessary litigation on the subject.

3.2 "Qualified" Individuals with Disabilities

An understanding of the ADA's definition of a "qualified individual with a disability" is central to assessing the employment opportunity for persons with mental retardation covered under the law. This assessment must be individualized and will be affected by the degree of mental retardation, related developmental and physical disabilities, and their relation to required job skills.[11]

ADA Title I does not require an employer to hire or retain individuals with covered disabilities who are not qualified, nor to hire or retain individuals with covered disabilities over equally or more qualified individuals without disabilities.[12] Under the ADA employers are not discouraged from searching for the most qualified individuals with or without disabilities.[13] Nor are employers required to incur inefficiencies, productivity losses, or opportunity costs, whether defined in terms of economic value in the relevant labor market or in retaining nonqualified workers with or without covered disabilities.[14]

As mentioned in Chapter II, Title I's "qualified individual" requirement is meant to ensure that the value of a worker's labor or productivity should equal or exceed the worker's wage in a given labor market.[15] Workers with covered disabilities are not deemed "equal" by their Title I status to workers without disabilities, nor are they provided preferential treatment in any aspect of employment.

The goal of the qualified individual provision is to ensure that a worker with a disability who can perform essential job functions, with or without a reasonable accommodation, receives wages or other compensation that are comparable to his or her labor market value. In other words, qualified individuals with disabilities may not be treated differently than similar others without disabilities.

3.3 Determination of a Qualified Individual with a Disability

The determination of whether an individual with a disability is qualified for a job is made in two steps. The first step is to determine if the person *currently* satisfies the prerequisites for the job, such as educational background or employment experience.[16] The first case brought by the EEOC under ADA Title I involved a business executive with brain cancer who was fired, not because the company feared that he was currently unqualified for his job, but because the company feared that he may become disabled in the future.[17]

Title I requires that decisions about the qualifications of a potential employee be made at the time of hiring. The first step enables employers to consider jobs appropriate to the

---

[10] *See* 42 U.S.C. § 12102(2); 29 C.F.R. § 1630.2(j) (1991).

[11] *See Southeastern Community College v. Davis*, 442 U.S. 397 (1979) (construing section 504 so that college could consider legitimate physical requirements in making admission decisions as long as they are not discriminatory in nature). *See also* C. Geoffrey Weirich, Reasonable Accommodation Under the Americans with Disabilities Act, 7 **Lab. Law.** 27 (Winter 1991).

[12] 42 U.S.C. §12111(8).

[13] *Cf.* Walter Oi, Employment and Benefits for People with Diverse Disablities, in **Disability, Work and Cash Benefits** 112 (Jerry L. Mashaw, et al., eds., 1996).

[14] *See* Blanck, The Economics of the Employment Provisions of the ADA, **supra Ch. I § 1.1**, at 888–91 (reviewing cases finding that employers may regulate production standards if it is essential that job be performed with speed and quality, and that this does not necessarily discriminate against employees with disabilities).

[15] *See* Donohue, **supra Ch. II § 2.10**, at 2584.

[16] 29 C.F.R. § 1630.2(m). This is analogous to the determination of whether an individual is "otherwise qualified" for the job under the Rehabilitation Act (*citing* S.Rep. at 33; H.Rep. at 64–65).

[17] *See EEOC v. AIC Security*, 55 F.3d 1276 (7th Cir. 1995).

applicant's experience and skill level. It prevents employment decisions based on fears or myths that employees with mental retardation may not be able to perform their jobs or become unable to perform their jobs in the future.[18]

The second step in assessing whether an applicant or employee is qualified to perform the job is to determine if the individual can perform the "essential functions" of that job with or without reasonable accommodation. Essential functions are those that the employee must perform unaided or with the assistance of an accommodation.[19]

The second step ensures that persons with disabilities are not denied employment because they cannot perform nonessential or marginal job functions. As illustrated by the *Anderson v. General Motors* case discussed in Chapter II, in the absence of systematic analysis, essential and marginal functions of a job are difficult to assess, particularly for persons with varying degrees of mental retardation. This investigation explores the assessment of employment-related skills for a group of persons with mental retardation.

Title I provides that consideration is to be given to the employer's judgment as to what functions are essential.[20] However, persons with disabilities may challenge an employer's contention that a function is essential to a job. The factors relevant for the assessment of essential job functions vary among persons with different disabilities and within the group of persons with mental retardation.

Essential and marginal job functions may be different for the same job performed by persons with varying degrees of developmental disabilities, or even in companies of different sizes and in different business sectors. In a mail room job, a person with mild mental retardation may sort and box letters while a person with severe retardation may be able only to sort the letters. Both employees perform central job elements, but not all of the work tasks. At least in a large firm with many employees, eliminating one function may not alter the essential job requirements in the mail room or force the hiring of a "shadow" employee who, in effect, performs the essential functions for an employee with a disability.[21]

3.4 "Essential" Job Functions

Three factors are used in determining whether a job function is essential for purposes of ADA analysis.[22] These factors include:

1. the reason the job exists is primarily to perform that function;
2. the number of employees available to perform that job function, suggesting that essential functions are defined with regard to the total number of employees and to particular business demands; and
3. the degree of skill required to perform the job function.

Courts have considered these factors on a case-by-case basis in determining whether a job function is essential. The inquiry into essential job functions is not meant to second-guess an employer's business judgment. But given that the determination of employee qualifications is made by employers at the time of the hiring decision, many employers have little information about how to assess essential and marginal job functions and how assessment varies with type of impairment.[23]

Concerns by employers about the qualifications of their workers are not without merit. Yet, in the absence of empirical information, it is often difficult to determine who is a qualified individual with a disability and what exactly constitutes a reasonable accommodation for that individual. ADA analyst David Fram has suggested that the most important factor in determining if a job function is essential is whether the employee is required to and actually performs the particular function.[24] A written job

---

[18] *See* Disability Rights Education Defense Fund, **Comments on the EEOC's Proposed Regulations for Title I**, at 4 (Apr. 1991) (employment decisions should not be based on anticipated health coverage, insurance) (*citing* ADA Judiciary Report, at 34; House Education & Labor Rep., at 136).

[19] 29 C.F.R. § 1630.2(n) (1991) (providing the example that typing may be an essential function of a job if, in fact, the employer requires any employee in that particular position to type).

[20] *See id.*

[21] *Id.* (some functions may become essential if there are a limited number of employees to perform the task).

[22] Relevant evidence is considered, such as an established job description, work experience of past employees in the job or similar jobs, or time spent performing the particular job function. *See Hall v. U.S. Postal Service*, 857 F.2d 1073 (8th Cir. 1988).

[23] 29 C.F.R. § 1630.2(m) (1991).

[24] *See* Fram, **supra Ch. II § 2.5**, at II-5.

description that is prepared and validated before the employee begins a particular job is important evidence that certain functions are essential to the work task.[25]

A job description prepared after an employee's discharge that contains nonessential or marginal work functions likely would be determined by a court to be invalid and not related to actual business needs.[26] Although the employer bears the legal burden of proving that a particular job function is essential, the employee bears the legal burden of proving that he can perform the essential job tasks.[27]

The outcome of many ADA cases has turned on whether a particular job function is essential or marginal. Many common job functions at issue in ADA cases have been viewed by employers—sometimes justifiably and sometimes not justifiably—as relevant to assessing the qualifications of persons with mental retardation.

3.5 Mental Characteristics and Essential Job Functions[28]

Courts have held that characteristics such as "mental stability," "ability to handle stress," "mental ability to follow supervisor's instructions," and "ability to interact with coworkers and customers" may be essential job functions.[29] As discussed in Chapter IV, the development of job abilities related to interpersonal skills in the workplace for employees with mental retardation often is obtained through supported employment programs and job coaching.

In cases in which courts have concluded that "mental stability" is an essential job function, employees who have been disruptive at meetings or abusive toward others have been determined to be "not qualified" for purposes of the law.[30] The ability to work independently and to rotate through multiple job duty positions, as illustrated by the *Anderson* decision discussed in Chapter II, has been considered an essential job task.[31]

In another case involving an employee with severe depression, the court concluded that the employee was not "qualified" for the job because he was unable to work independently. Working independently was found to be an essential job task.[32] The court concluded that the requested workplace accommodation of increased supervision was not required under the ADA.

Overall, mental characteristics, such as the ability to get along with coworkers and supervisors or the ability to work independently, are skills valued as essential job functions by many employers. However, the assessment of mental characteristics, in comparison to work-related physical conditions, often depends upon the subjective judgment of a supervisor in the work setting.[33] For this reason, some courts have concluded that the lack of required work-related mental characteristics do not constitute a disability under the ADA because they do not

---

[25] *See* 29 C.F.R. § 1630.2(n), Appendix.

[26] *See Muller v. The Hotsy Corp.*, 917 F. Supp. 1389 (N.D. Iowa 1996) (job description prepared after employee's accident not valid).

[27] *See Bensen v. Northwest Airlines*, 62 F.3d 1108 (8th Cir. 1995) (employer bears burden of proving essential job functions); *Bombard v. Fort Wayne Newspapers, Inc.*, 92 F.3d 560 (7th Cir. 1996) (employee bears burden of proving ability to perform essential job tasks).

[28] *See* Fram, **supra Ch. II § 2.5**, at II-6–II-29 (discussing categories of cases involving "mental stability" as an essential job function); **Attitudes and the ADA, supra Ch. I § 1.1**, at 365–69 (discussing mental characteristics and ADA coverage).

[29] *Id.*, at II-6–II-7 (discussing cases); *Soileau v. Guilford of Maine, Inc.*, 105 F.3d 12 (1st Cir. 1997) ("ability to get along with others" does not constitute a major life activity); *Weiler v. Household Finance Corp.*, 101 F.3d 519 (7th Cir. 1996) (employee with depression not "qualified" where she is only able to work for one boss); *Pesterfield v. Tennessee Valley Authority*, 941 F.2d 437, 441–42 (6th Cir. 1991) (ability to get along with supervisors and coworkers held to be essential job function).

[30] *See Palmer v. Circuit Court of Cook County*, 117 F.3d 351 (7th Cir. 1997) (individual not a qualified worker under the ADA when engaging in disruptive behavior in the workplace).

[31] *See Miller v. Ill. Dept. of Corrections*, 107 F.3d 483 (7th Cir. 1997) (employer may have legitimate job-related reason for requiring employees to rotate essential job functions).

[32] *Bolstein v. Reich*, 1995 WL 46387 (D.D.C. 1995), affirmed, 1995 WL 686236 (D.C. Cir. 1995).

[33] *See Soileau v. Guilford of Maine, Inc.*, 105 F.3d 12, 15 (1st Cir. 1997) (describing mental characteristics such as the ability to get along with others as "remarkably elastic").

substantially limit an individual in the major life activity of working.[34]

Increasingly, courts also will be called upon to distinguish between claims brought under the ADA involving personal conflicts with supervisors or coworkers as a result of a worker's mental characteristics such as temperament and irritability, which are not defined disabilities, and medically diagnosed mental conditions and impairments, which are recognized disabilities under the ADA.[35]

Courts have examined other skills related to mental characteristics in determining essential job tasks and employee qualifications, many of which are relevant to analysis in the present investigation and to employment providers, families, and workers with mental retardation.[36] These include:

- *regular and predictable work attendance as an essential job function*: courts have concluded that the ability to maintain a regular work schedule is an essential function, in particular where the company has a policy addressing unscheduled absences;[37]
- *ability to work a regular shift or a rotating assignment as an essential job function*: courts have concluded that the ability to work particular assignments or as part of a work team may be an essential job function;[38] and
- *ability to stand, lift, and perform tasks involving manual dexterity as an essential job function*: courts have concluded that particular abilities, if legitimately required by an employer and not amenable to reasonable accommodation, may be essential job functions.

With increasing frequency, ADA cases arise in which courts also must examine the nature of employment discrimination based on a disability alone (e.g., assessment of ability to perform essential job functions) versus discrimination based on misconduct by the disabled person.[39] For instance, the ADA expressly permits employers to disregard the fact that a disability may have "caused" an employee to engage in abusive behavior toward coworkers or the illegal use of drugs or be an alcoholic.[40] In these circumstances an employer may discharge the disabled employee under the same workplace standards that would apply to all employees, regardless of the employee's job qualifications.[41]

As Chapter V discusses, the availability to employers of affirmative legal defenses—such as the "direct threat" defense—to a plaintiff's charge of ADA employment discrimination provide that certain levels of disability-caused conduct need not be tolerated or accommodated by employers.[42] Nevertheless, the ADA contemplates that certain disability-caused

---

[34] *See Breiland v. Advance Circuits, Inc.*, 976 F. Supp. 858 (D. Minn. 4th Div. 1997) (finding that inability to get along with others not a major life activity under the ADA). *Cf.* EEOC Compliance Manual § 902.3 (concluding that interacting with others is a major life activity under the ADA).

[35] *See Duda v. Board of Education of Franklin Park Public School District No. 84*, 133 F.3d 1054 (7th Cir. 1998) (finding psychiatric illness a disability covered by the ADA in circumstances where plaintiff was unable to work and communicate with coworkers).

[36] For a review, *see* Fram, **supra Ch. II § 2.5**, at II-6–II-29 (discussing categories of cases); Blanck, **supra Ch. I § 1.2** (reviewing essential job functions and their relation to mental and physical characteristics).

[37] *See* Fram, **supra Ch. II § 2.5**, at II-9 (discussing finding, in *Carlson v. InaCom Corp.*, 885 F. Supp. 1314 (D. Neb. 1995), that employer cannot claim attendance is an essential job task when it has no formal policy on unscheduled absences).

[38] *See* **supra Ch. II § 2.9** (discussing *Anderson v. General Motors* court finding that ability to work on several job tasks as part of a work team may be an essential job function).

[39] *See Den Hartog v. Wasatch Academy*, 129 F.3d 1076 (10th Cir. 1997) (discussing disability-caused misconduct under the ADA).

[40] 42 U.S.C. § 12114(a) & (c)(4) (1994) (providing term "qualified individual with a disability" does not include illegal drug users). *See also Den Hartog*, 129 F.3d 1076 (concluding that the disability versus disability-caused conduct dichotomy is unique to alcoholism and drugs).

[41] *See, e.g., Adamczyk v. Chief of Police of Baltimore County; Baltimore County Maryland*, 134 F.3d 362 (4th Cir. 1998) (finding officer demoted because of his misconduct not because of possible disability of alcoholism).

[42] *See* **infra Ch. V § 5.4** (discussing direct threat defense). *See also Harris v. Polk County, Iowa*, 103 F.3d 696 (8th Cir. 1996) (finding that ADA does not obligate an employer to ignore an employee's misconduct, regardless of a disability); *Breiland v. Advance Circuits, Inc.*, 976 F. Supp. 858 (same).

conduct by qualified workers may be accommodated effectively and tolerated by employers. In *Den Hartog v. Wasatch Academy*, the Tenth Circuit Court of Appeals comments that "[t]o permit employers carte blanche to terminate employees with mental disabilities on the basis of any abnormal behavior would largely nullify the ADA's protection of the mentally disabled."[43] The next two sections describe cases illustrating many of these issues.

3.6 A Case Example Involving the Definition of a "Qualified" Individual with a Developmental Disability: *Taylor v. Food World, Inc.*

Taylor v. Food World[44] involved a grocery store bagger, Gary Taylor, with Asperger's disorder—a form of autism involving pervasive developmental disorders. As a result of his disorder, Taylor is impaired in communication and social interaction.[45] At work, Taylor tended to make inappropriate remarks or ask personal questions of Food World customers. After a number of incidents, Food World discharged Taylor on the basis of his behavior.

Food World did not contest that Taylor was "disabled" for purposes of ADA analysis. Rather, it argued that Taylor was not a "qualified" employee because he could not "interact appropriately with customers"—a purported essential job function of a bagger. The question before the court was whether Taylor could, with or without reasonable accommodation, perform the essential duties of a bagger clerk without offending the store's customers.

In fact, some Food World customers had complained about Taylor's loud and inappropriate behavior and asking of personal questions. Other customers, however, praised Taylor for his attempt to work despite his impairment. At trial, expert testimony by mental health professionals ranged from suggestions that Taylor was "only capable of working in a sheltered environment, away from contact with the general public" to suggestions that he was capable of working in supported employment with the assistance of a job coach.

The bagger position at Food World was the store's lowest paying position available. Job reassignment, as an accommodation, would have resulted in a promotion under the terms of the collective bargaining agreement. After the ADA lawsuit was commenced, Taylor's mother filed for Supplemental Security Income (SSI) benefits on his behalf. Taylor was deemed "disabled" under the Social Security regulations and granted SSI benefits.

The two main issues for judicial resolution centered on the ADA's definition of a qualified individual with a disability. First, Food World claimed that Taylor was precluded as a matter of law—that is, "judicially estopped"—from claiming that he was a qualified employee because he had applied for and received SSI benefits. Second, Food World argued that, because Taylor was unable to function in a work environment in which he, by necessity, had contact with the store's customers, he was not qualified for the position of grocery bagger.

In reversing the lower court's ruling, the U.S. Court of Appeals for the Eleventh Circuit concluded that Taylor was not judicially estopped from bringing an action under the ADA. The appellate court also ruled that Taylor was entitled to a trial to determine whether he was qualified as a bagger under the purview of the ADA.

With regard to the application of the doctrine of judicial estoppel, the Eleventh Circuit concluded that, although Taylor declared himself to be disabled for purposes of receiving SSI benefits, he was not per se judicially estopped from bringing a claim that he was a "qualified" individual under the ADA.[46] The court reasoned that the Social Security Administration's definition of disability does not take into account the effect of a workplace accommodation on an individual's ability to work in determining whether an individual is entitled to SSI benefits.

Thus, the application of the judicial estoppel doctrine to the definition of disability under the

---

[43] *Den Hartog*, 129 F.3d 1076.

[44] 133 F.3d 1419 (11th Cir. 1997).

[45] *Id.* (Taylor often speaks loudly and engages in "echolalai," which is constant repetitive speech).

[46] *See also Blanton v. Inco Alloys, Inc.*, 108 F.3d 104 (6th Cir. 1997) (no judicial estoppel in state disability case where plaintiff applied for SSI benefits).

ADA in Taylor's case ultimately will depend on other evidence presented at trial related to the provision of workplace accommodations.[47] Experts testifying at the trial recommended that Taylor seek supported employment with the assistance of a job coach and with appropriate supports he could perform his job at Food World.

Other courts have supported the conclusion of the *Taylor* court, finding that an SSI application is not necessarily a per se admission of total disability and the inability to perform a particular job, particularly when an employee's discharge is due to the employer not providing a workplace accommodation.[48] In a 1997 case before the District of Columbia Circuit, *Swanks v. Washington Metropolitan Area Transit Authority*,[49] the court found that receipt of Social Security Disability Insurance (SSDI) benefits did not estop an individual with spina bifida from pursuing his ADA employment discrimination claims. The court nevertheless concluded that Mr. Swanks' receipt of SSDI benefits meant that he could not perform the essential functions required of his job with or without workplace accommodations. In fact, Swanks had requested and had been denied workplace accommodations prior to his discharge from employment.

In its 1997 Enforcement Guidance on the issue, the EEOC has taken the position that an individual's statements in applying for any disability benefit is never an absolute bar to a finding that an individual is qualified for purposes of the ADA.[50] As discussed in Chapter IV, in some cases job reassignment or workplace accommodations may enable an individual with a serious impairment to perform essential job functions and be "qualified" for a particular job. Once the employee is discharged, perhaps in violation of the ADA's requirement to provide reasonable accommodations, he or she may only then become disabled for purposes of ADA analysis—for instance, if the employee's impairment worsens as a result of an unjustified discharge.[51]

The second issue addressed by the Eleventh Circuit was whether Taylor was a qualified individual with a disability for purposes of the ADA. The district court ruled that Taylor's behavior at work rendered him unqualified for the job of bagger clerk. Food World argued that

---

[47] In *Taylor*, the district court concluded that reassigning Taylor to another job would have been a promotion in violation of the store's collective bargaining agreement (CBA). The district court found that as a matter of law an accommodation that forces an employer to violate its CBA is not "reasonable" under the purview of the ADA. The Eleventh Circuit ruled that on remand Taylor bears the burden of proof at trial to show the existence and reasonableness of any proposed accommodation. *See* **infra Ch. IV § 4.10** (discussing accommodations under the ADA in the context of a CBA).

Thus, Food World could have investigated the possibility of other accommodations, through the "interactive process" (**infra Ch. IV § 4.5**), that may have been shown to be reasonable and cost-effective. Such accommodations might have included the provision of a part-time job coach provided at no cost to the store by a state-sponsored rehabilitation program or the provision of natural supports from coworkers in the work environment. The case *EEOC v. Hertz*—**infra Ch. V § 5.8**—turned on the reasonableness of the request for a job coach as a workplace accommodation for an employee with mental retardation in circumstances in which that coach was to be provided by an outside agency at no cost to Hertz.

[48] *See Overton v. Reilly*, 977 F.2d 1190 (7th Cir. 1992) (determination of disability by the SSA does not necessarily preclude individual from performing a particular job); *Robinson v. Neodata Services*, 94 F.3d 499, 502 n.2 (8th Cir. 1996) (same); *Griffith v. WAL-MART Stores*, 135 F.3d 376 (6th Cir. 1998) (same); *Mitchell v. Washingtonville Central School*, 1998 U.S. Dist. LEXIS 831 (S.D.N.Y. 1998) (same, but on the facts of the particular case applying judicial estoppel doctrine).

[49] 116 F.3d 582 (D.C. Cir. 1997).

[50] *See* **Enforcement Guidance on the Effect of Representations Made in Applications for Benefits on the Determination of Whether a Person Is a 'Qualified Individual with a Disability' Under the ADA**, EEOC Notice No. 915.002, at 12 (Feb. 12, 1997) (concluding that context and timing issues are relevant to the determination of a qualified individual). *See also* Federal Agency Compliance Act, Bill H.R. 1544 (May 7, 1997) (proposed legislation to require federal agencies, such as the Social Security Administration, to follow legal precedents in the federal courts, such as in the provision of disability benefits for qualified workers with disabilities).

[51] Nevertheless, some courts have concluded that an individual's representation in applying for SSI or other related benefits—that he or she is unable to work or perform essential job functions—establishes that the person is not "qualified" for a job for purposes of ADA analysis. For decisions reaching this conclusion, see *Cleveland v. Policy Management Sys. Corp.*, 120 F.3d 513 (5th Cir. 1997); *Budd v. ADT Security Systems, Inc.*, 103 F.3d 699 (8th Cir. 1996); *McNemar v. Disney Stores*, 91 F.3d 610 (3d Cir. 1996).

interacting appropriately with customers was an essential job function of a bagger.

As discussed earlier in this chapter, courts have concluded that certain mental characteristics, such as the ability to get along with coworkers or customers, are skills that may be viewed as essential job functions under the ADA. The issue before the court was whether Taylor, with or without an accommodation, could perform the essential functions of a bagger clerk without offending customers.

In reversing the lower court, the Eleventh Circuit held that, as a matter of law, the trial record did not show that Taylor could not carry out the essential job tasks of a bagger. Some customers complained about Taylor's behavior. Other customers and store employees testified that they received no complaints about Taylor's behavior. Thus, the appellate court held that there was a genuine issue of fact to be determined at trial as to whether Taylor was qualified for purposes of ADA analysis.

3.7 A Case Example Involving the Definition of a "Qualified" Individual with Mental Retardation: *Wilson v. State Insurance Fund*

A 1997 case before the United States Court of Appeals for the Tenth Circuit, *Wilson v. State Insurance Fund*,[52] illustrates the complexities involved in assessing essential job functions and qualifications for a worker with mental retardation. Mr. Wilson, the plaintiff, a person with mild mental retardation, was hired by State Insurance Fund as a light vehicle driver. During Wilson's employment tenure, he had a history of absenteeism and noncompliance with attendance procedures, particularly after he sustained an on-the-job injury. Eventually Wilson was asked to resign. He alleged that he was constructively discharged, or coerced to resign, by the company in violation of ADA Title I.

The Tenth Circuit Court of Appeals upheld the decision of the lower trial court and dismissed Wilson's Title I claims. The court concluded that although Wilson may be a person with a disability covered by Title I, his work absences demonstrated that he was unable to perform the essential job functions of a vehicle driver. Therefore, Wilson was not a "qualified" individual for purposes of Title I analysis.

The *Wilson* court did not address the important underlying inquiry that is relevant to the study of Title I implementation for persons with mental retardation—the reasons for Wilson's work absences. The court determined that the company was justified in denying Wilson's request even to take a leave to consult with his vocational rehabilitation counselor about his work absences.

The court did not review Wilson's claim that the company did not accommodate his disability, thereby violating Title I. Although Wilson's absences may have been due to a lack of workplace supports and not to his lacking of qualifications for the job, the court did not address such reasons or whether expert professional testimony would be helpful to explain the reasons for the absences. The issues raised by the *Wilson* case suggest analysis is needed of the interaction among job skill and performance (such as Wilson's absences), workplace accommodations and supports, and the prevalence of workplace injury.[53]

In a series of studies, Professor Craig Zwerling and his colleagues find that persons with certain disabilities, primarily visual and hearing impairments, are more susceptible to subsequent occupational injury.[54] Zwerling's

---

[52] 106 F.3d 414 (10th Cir. 1997).

[53] *See* Weirich, **supra, Ch. III § 3.2**, at 27 (discussing the need for employers to understand the ADA requirements for compliance with the reasonable accommodation provision of the Act); *Henchey v. Town of North Greenbush*, 831 F. Supp. 960, 966–68 (N.D.N.Y. 1993) (holding that under the Rehabilitation Act an evidentiary finding at trial is necessary to determine qualifications, essential job functions, and appropriateness of reasonable accommodations).

[54] Craig Zwerling, Paul S. Whitten, Charles S. Davis, & Nancy L. Sprince, Occupational Injuries Among Workers with Disabilities: The National Health Interview Survey, 1985–1994, 278 **JAMA** 2163–66 (1997) (study not accounting for severity of disability and provision of workplace accommodation by employers, finding that 8.5 percent of occupational injuries in the workplace explained by prior disability); Craig Zwerling, Nancy L. Sprince, Robert B. Wallace, Charles S. Davis, Paul S. Whitten, & Steven G. Heeringa, Risk Factors for Occupational Injuries Among Older Workers: An Analysis of the Health and Retirement Study, 86 **Am. J. Pub. Health** 1306–09 (1996) (same).

findings show increased risk for persons with disabilities for occupational injuries, suggesting the need for study of workplace accommodations and injury prevention programs. The study of the relation of job capabilities and qualifications, workplace accommodations, and job attainment and retention for persons with mental retardation are discussed in Chapter XIII.

3.8 Summary

Prior study shows that the reform potential of Title VII of the Civil Rights Act of 1964 was limited because many employers and qualified persons tended not to understand their basic obligations under the law.[55] Information on the relation between the type and degree of actual or perceived impairments and the qualifications required to perform certain jobs or work functions is emerging.[56] Yet more study is needed of job qualifications and standards, particularly as they apply to persons with mental retardation.

The present investigation explores the usefulness of job-related skill measures (such as "capabilities and qualifications"), as well as other background factors (such as age and gender), for understanding the term "qualified individual with a disability" in the employment context. Such information may be useful to employers, employees, and employment providers, in tailoring jobs and workplace accommodations for qualified employees with mental retardation that support their entry and retention in the workforce.

---

[55] *See* Kristin Bumiller, **The Civil Rights Society** 98–117 (1988) (showing that the reform potential of employment and affirmative action law is limited).

[56] Peter David Blanck, The Americans with Disabilities Act: Issues for Back and Spine-Related Disability, 19 **Spine** 103 (1994) (discussing back-related disability under the ADA, job calibration, and assessment of employee qualifications).

CHAPTER IV

Central Provisions of ADA Title I: Reasonable and Effective Workplace Accommodations

At bottom line, when Sears hires, works with, and accommodates qualified employees with disabilities, Sears enhances its customer base, employee morale, and its overall business strategy goals.

Edward Brennan, former CEO and president, Sears[1]

4.1 Introduction

An individual with a disability covered by the ADA is considered qualified if he or she can perform essential job functions with or without "reasonable accommodation."[2] Under the ADA this element obliges employers to make individualized adjustments to jobs, thereby allowing qualified persons with "known"[3] disabilities equal employment opportunities.[4]

4.2 Categories of Workplace Accommodations

There are three types of accommodations,[5] including those that:

1. ensure equal opportunity to the application process;
2. enable qualified employees with disabilities to perform essential job functions; and,
3. enable qualified employees with disabilities to enjoy the benefits and privileges of employment.

---

[1] *See* **Sears I, supra Ch. II § 2.3**; Peter David Blanck, **Communicating the Americans with Disabilities Act: Transcending Compliance, 1996 Follow-up Report on Sears, Roebuck and Co.,** at 8 (1996) [**hereinafter Sears II**].

[2] 42 U.S.C. § 12111(9); 29 C.F.R. § 1630.2(o) (1991). *Cf. Coley v. Secretary of Army*, 689 F. Supp. 519, 521–22 (D.C. Md. 1987) (holding under Rehabilitation Act that person who can perform essential functions of job with or without reasonable accommodation is a "qualified" individual with a disability).

[3] *See Hunt-Golliday v. Metropolitan Water District*, 104 F.3d 1004 (7th Cir. 1997) (finding no duty to accommodate where employer does not know of employee's mental disability).

[4] **BNA Report, supra Ch. I § 1.5,** at 114–16 (*citing* House Judiciary Committee Report stating requirement "central to the non-discrimination mandate of the ADA," H. Rep. 101–485 Part 3, 39).

[5] *See* Fram, **supra Ch. II § 2.5,** at III-1 (reviewing these categories); 29 C.F.R. § 1630.2(o) (1991) (defining categories of reasonable accommodation).

Accommodations may include permitting the use of accrued paid leave, flexible scheduling of work hours, restructuring of nonessential job functions, making employer-provided transportation accessible, or providing job coaching or workplace assistants. The Sears studies, discussed throughout this and other chapters, examine more than 500 of that company's workplace accommodations and their related costs and benefits to workers with mental and physical disabilities. An example of an accommodation posing no direct cost to Sears for a qualified employee with mental retardation included flexible scheduling of work hours to allow the employee to coordinate his schedule with that of public transportation.[6]

The determination of the appropriateness of an accommodation involves a dialogue, referred to by the EEOC as an "interactive process," between employer and employee (or the employee's representative, who sometimes is a job coach or family member). The interactive dialogue is ongoing, because the needs and interests of employees and employers change over time. This dialogue aids in the determination of whether the accommodation poses an "undue hardship" or economic burden to the business, a concept discussed in Chapter V.[7]

4.3 Concepts of Workplace Accommodations

Several aspects of the concept of workplace accommodation are relevant to coverage under Title I for persons with mental retardation. The obligation for employers to make accommodations applies to all aspects of the employment relationship.[8] This obligation may extend to the provision of assistants or job coaches in supported employment arrangements to help the employees with essential job duties.[9]

Employers are not required to provide accommodations that are primarily personally based (for instance, hearing aids, eye glasses, or communication devices), unless such accommodations are required to meet job-related needs. As the *Wilson* case illustrated in Chapter III, the evidentiary burden is on the qualified employee or job applicant with a disability to show a connection between the disability and the need for an accommodation.

Employers may require individuals with disabilities to provide documentation supporting the need for an accommodation when it is not obvious. This requirement underscores the importance of developing information useful to employers, employees, and employment providers that helps to identify the magnitude and scope of costs and benefits associated with particular accommodations.

For the population with mental retardation, as for persons with other disabilities, it is sometimes difficult to separate job supports or accommodations that are important to job-related interests from supports or accommodations for off-the-job interests. In many cases an employer may not be obligated under the law to provide an employee with mental retardation the services of a job coach at times during or after the workday, unless it can be shown that such accommodations meet job-related needs.[10]

In other cases, personal and job-related supports, training, and accommodation needs are intimately linked. In comparison to the court's analysis in the *Wilson* case described in Chapter III, employment training often is part of a more integrated plan for daily living. The goals of such plans are not separated easily, because daily living skill development is necessary for employment skill development and vice versa. Coordinated study is needed on the relation of vocational rehabilitation pro-

---

[6] **Sears II, supra Ch. IV § 4.1**, at 60.

[7] *See* **infra Ch. V § 5.3** (discussing concept of undue hardship).

[8] 29 C.F.R. § 1630.9 (1991).

[9] 29 C.F.R. § 1630.2(o) (1991). *Cf.* **infra Appendix E** (in *EEOC v. Hertz* decision provision of job coach held not to be required as a reasonable accommodation for employees with mental retardation).

[10] *Id.* (*citing* S. Rep., at 31; H. Rep., at 62). The appendix to the EEOC regulations lists examples of accommodations that are not necessarily job-related such as wheelchairs or eyeglasses. For many persons with severe disabilities, accommodations are required to assist in daily and job-related activities (e.g., a person serving as a page turner for an employee with a disability of the hands). *See* Z. M. Lutfiyya, P. Rogan, & B. Shoultz, Supported Employment: A Conceptual Overview, **Center on Human Policy Monographs** 2–3 (1991) (discussing relations of self-care and job-related accommodations for persons with severe disabilities).

grams, workplace supports, and accommodations for persons with mental retardation.

The aspect of workplace supports that has received the most attention involves ADA Title I's affect on employers' ability to provide "reasonable" workplace accommodations for qualified job applicants and employees with disabilities. As discussed in Chapter III, an employer may legitimately determine an employee's work tasks or production requirements as long as they are job-related and not a pretext for discrimination against persons with disabilities covered by the law. The employer's right to structure jobs, however, may not violate Title I's requirement that the employer provide "reasonable accommodations" for a qualified employee with a covered disability.[11]

As mentioned, an accommodation is a modification or adjustment to a workplace process or environment that makes it possible for a qualified person with a disability to perform essential job functions, such as physical modifications to a work space, flexible scheduling of duties, or provision of assistive technologies to aid in job performance.[12] To be eligible for an accommodation, an employee must disclose his or her disability to the employer and request an accommodation. Chapters II and III discussed that exactly how a disclosed or "known" disability is defined for purposes of the ADA has been the subject of some debate.[13]

The requirement to disclose a disability places a particular burden on an individual with hidden, nonobvious mental disabilities to identify the claimed disability and request that the employer provide an accommodation.[14] Once the request is made, the employer retains the right to choose the accommodation, as long as it is effective and the employee has a "good faith" (that is, a meaningful) opportunity to participate in the process.[15] Chapter III described how an employee is not "qualified" for purposes of the law if he or she cannot perform essential job functions with or without an accommodation.

Critics of Title I have characterized an employer's obligation to provide accommodations to qualified persons as a form of market

---

[11] *See* 29 C.F.R. § 1630.2(o) (1991); Barbara Lee, Reasonable Accommodation Under the Americans with Disabilities Act: The Limitations of Rehabilitation Act Precedent, 14 **Berkeley J. Emp. & Lab. Law,** at 212–35 (1993).

[12] 42 U.S.C. § 12111(9)(B) (qualified employee may request reasonable accommodation of being transferred to a vacant and similar position with the employer). *See Kent v. Derwinski*, 790 F. Supp. 1032 (E.D.Wash. 1991) (requiring accommodation for employee with mental retardation of sensitivity training of coworkers and use of care by supervisor in disciplining to avoid criticism or undue stress); *Overton v. Reilly*, 977 F.2d 1190 (7th Cir. 1992) (approving accommodation for chemist with depression of restricting job to decrease contact with public where contact with public occupied small percentage of employee's time); *Arneson v. Sullivan*, 946 F.2d 90 (8th Cir. 1991) (when employee with apraxia, a neurological disorder characterized by disruptions in concentration, performs satisfactorily when placed in a semiprivate work space, employer must take reasonable efforts to provide a "distraction-free environment"). *Cf. Hudson v. MCI Telecommunications Corp.*, 87 F.3d 1167 (10th Cir. 1996) (request by employee with carpal tunnel syndrome for unpaid leave for an indefinite amount of time not reasonable); *Pesterfield v. Tennessee Valley Auth.*, 941 F.2d 437 (6th Cir. 1991) (plaintiff's inability to handle criticism made it impossible to perform essential job functions and it was not reasonable to require employer to provide a stress-free environment to accommodate disability); *Kuehl v. Wal-Mart Stores, Inc.*, 909 F. Supp. 794 (D. Colo. 1995) (individual who rejected accommodation was not a qualified individual with a disability).

[13] *See Hutchinson v. United Parcel Service,* Inc., 883 F. Supp. 379, 394 (N.D. Iowa 1995) (finding that the "ADA does not require clairvoyance") (*quoting Hedberg v. Indiana Bell Telephone Co., Inc.*, 47 F.3d 928, 932 (7th Cir. 1995)) (employer cannot be liable without knowledge of disability); *Morisky v. Broward County*, 80 F.3d 445, 448 (11th Cir. 1996) (same). *See* Burgdorf, **supra Ch. I § 1.4,** at 129–54.

[14] *See Fussell v. Georgia Ports Authority*, 906 F. Supp. 1561, 1569 (S.D. Ga. 1995), affirmed, 106 F.3d 417 (11th Cir. 1997). *See also* 29 C.F.R. Pt. 1630, App. § 1630.9 at 414 (1995) (responsibility of employee to inform employer of need for accommodation).

[15] *See Bultemeyer v. Fort Wayne Community Schools*, 100 F.3d 1281 (7th Cir. 1996) (accommodation process requires good faith communication between employer and employee, and in case involving employee with mental illness, communication process is even more critical); *Beck v. University of Wisconsin Board of Regents*, 75 F.3d 1130 (7th Cir. 1996) (university not liable under ADA where plaintiff responsible for breakdown in accommodation process); *Peterson v. Univ. Wisconsin*, 818 F. Supp. 1276 (W.D. Wis. 1993) (employee may not refuse all good faith and reasonable attempts by employer at accommodation); *Taylor v. Principal Financial Group*, 93 F.3d 155, 164 (5th Cir. 1996) (responsibility for fashioning accommodation shared between employer and employee). *See also* 29 C.F.R. § 1630.2(o)(3) (1995) (accommodation process regulations).

distortion by the government leading to economic inefficiencies.[16] They claim that the duty of accommodation creates for persons with disabilities an employment privilege or subsidy, in that it provides covered workers the wages they would not have received in a nondiscriminatory free market.[17] The duty of accommodation is cast as compromising the ideal of free market efficiency by imposing upon employers an affirmative duty to retain less economically efficient workers.[18]

Chief Judge Richard Posner of the U.S. Seventh Circuit Court of Appeals, in the case *Vande Zande v. State of Wisconsin Department of Administration*, writes: "[W]e do not think an employer has a duty to expend even a modest amount of money to bring about absolute identity in working conditions between disabled and nondisabled workers."[19] He continues: "The duty of reasonable accommodation is satisfied when the employer does what is necessary to enable the disabled worker to work in reasonable comfort."

In contrast to Judge Posner's view, Professor Chai Feldblum has contended that the " 'reasonable' part of 'reasonable accommodation' refers only to whether a requested accommodation is *effective* in ensuring the person with a disability can perform the job up to the standards required by the employer" and not to the costs or benefits of the request.[20] Feldblum has suggested that although the "failure to provide a reasonable accommodation is a form of *discrimination*; it is not a remedy for discrimination in the way that various forms of affirmative action might serve as remedies." The next section in this chapter examines the concept of a "reasonable" accommodation, in light of cost-benefit analysis by courts to determine whether a particular accommodation is mandated by the ADA.[21]

4.4 Assessing Whether Workplace Accommodations Are "Reasonable"

There are at least three simplified hypothetical situations that illustrate the distribution of possible economic implications of the required provision of accommodations for qualified job applicants or employees covered by the ADA.[22] A first example involves two equally qualified workers, that is, workers who are equally productive and of equal economic value to the employer. Stanford Law Professor John Donohue has set forth such a hypothetical: "[G]iven the choice between two equally productive workers, one requiring the expenditure of significant sums in order to accommodate him, one requiring no such expenditures, the profit-maximizing firm would prefer the worker who is less costly to hire."[23]

Donohue's hypothetical is not problematic for Title I economic impact analysis. Title I does not require an employer to hire or retain a qualified individual with a covered disability, regardless of the need for accommodation, over an equally or more qualified individual without a disability. There is no resultant distortion of labor market or economic efficiencies by Title I's antidiscrimination provisions, nor is there a

---

[16] *See* Donohue, **supra Ch. II § 2.10,** at 2608. *Cf.* Burgdorf, **supra Ch. II § 2.7,** at 529–36 (discussing whether ADA accommodation requirement is preferential treatment for disabled workers).

[17] *Id.* at 2609. *Cf. Gile v. United Airlines*, 95 F.3d 492, 499 (7th Cir. 1996) (accommodation process does not require employer to "bump" other employees to reassign disabled employee, nor does it require employer to create new position for disabled employee); *Weiler v. Household Finance Corp.*, 101 F.3d 519 (7th Cir. 1996) (same).

[18] *See* Karlan & Rutherglen, **supra Ch. II § 2.2,** at 14 ("Reasonable accommodation is affirmative action, in the sense that it requires an employer to take account of an individual's disabilities and to provide special treatment to him for that reason.").

[19] 44 F.3d 545.

[20] Chai R. Feldblum, The (R)evolution of Physical Disability Anti-discrimination Law: 1976–1996, 20 **Men. & Phys. Dis. L. Rep.** 613, 618–19 (1996).

[21] *See Vande Zande*, 44 F.3d 542 (finding that the cost of an accommodation should not be disproportionate to its benefit); *Borkowski v. Valley Central School District*, 63 F.3d 131, 138 (2d Cir. 1995) (finding plaintiff bears burden of showing that an accommodation is reasonable).

[22] For related discussion, *see* Carolyn L. Weaver, Incentives Versus Controls in Federal Disability Policy, *in* **Disability and Work** 14 (Carolyn L. Weaver, ed., 1991) (discussing economic impact of accommodation provision).

[23] Donohue, **supra Ch. II § 2.10,** at 2608.

requirement "to make the disabled equal."[24] Employer prerogative and economic need is not disturbed and the employer is not discouraged from searching for the most qualified worker.[25] Moreover, to the extent that many accommodation costs for workers with disabilities are fixed or sunk, the economic incentive would be to retain the qualified disabled worker over an equally or less qualified nondisabled worker.[26]

A similarly simple hypothetical involves two workers whose productivity varies. In this case one individual with a covered disability is more "qualified" than an individual without a disability, say by three units of value to the employer. It requires a certain amount of unit value to accommodate this qualified worker with a disability, say three units of value.

Thus, the net cost to the employer of employing the individual with a disability is comparable to employing the individual without the disability and their "value" is identical. Title I would require the employer to hire the more qualified worker, regardless of disability and require the provision of accommodation. A decision by the employer in this scenario to refuse the provision of accommodation to this qualified individual with a covered disability would constitute discrimination under Title I, assuming no undue hardship is associated with the provision of the accommodation.

The more controversial third hypothetical involves two workers whose productivity varies. In this case one individual with a covered disability is more "qualified" than an individual without a disability by three units of value to the employer. However, it requires 30 units of employer value to accommodate the qualified worker with a disability, or 10 times the direct cost of the accommodation. Here, the net cost to the employer of employing the qualified individual with a disability is considerably more than the cost of employing the less qualified individual without the disability.

In this third scenario, a decision by the employer to refuse to provide an accommodation to the qualified individual with a covered disability may or may not constitute discrimination under Title I. This may be true, even though provision of the accommodation may be economically inefficient to the employer, assuming actual direct and indirect costs and benefits of the decision could be calculated. Discrimination may be found if no undue hardship is associated with the provision of an effective accommodation.

Alternatively, employment discrimination may not be found if the element of cost or efficiency is interpreted to be implicit in the concept of a "reasonable" accommodation.[27] Under this latter view, an employer has no duty to incur even a modest loss in value, because it would not be "reasonable" (i.e., economically rational) to accommodate the disabled employee.[28]

It is this third scenario that critics of Title I use to suggest that the accommodation provision, absent the high evidentiary burden on employers of showing financial undue hardship, in effect, is an affirmative subsidy to employees with disabilities.[29] Critics argue that the accommodation provision reflects a cost to employers incurred for employees with disabilities that is not spent on other employees without disabilities who arguably are more economically efficient but possibly less qualified or productive to perform the job in question.[30] Others argue that the ADA reflects a judgment by society that qualified persons with disabilities should be able to work, even when "the value of their output does not equal the cost neces-

---

[24] *See id.* at 2611. *See also* William G. Johnson, The Future of Disability Policy: Benefit Payments or Civil Rights?, 549 **Annals, AAPSS [hereinafter Annals]** 160, 164 (Jan. 1997) (arguing that Title I "goes beyond the concept of equal opportunities for equally productive workers by requiring employers to modify job requirements or work environments to compensate for impairment-related limits on productivity.").

[25] *Cf.* Oi, **supra Ch. III § 3.2,** at 112 (arguing that Title I forces employers to hire less productive workers). *But see Martin v. General Mills, Inc.*, 1996 WL 648721 (N.D. Ill., E. Div. 1996) (Title I does not require employers to retain less productive employees).

[26] Donohue, **supra Ch. II § 2.10**, n.72. *See also* **infra Ch. XIV § 14.3** (discussing the economics of workplace accommodations).

[27] *See Vande Zande*, 44 F3d. 542–45.

[28] *See* Feldblum, **supra Ch. IV § 4.3,** at 619–20 (discussing Judge Posner's reasoning in *Vande Zande* decision).

[29] *See* Sherwin Rosen, Disability Accommodation and the Labor Market, *in* **Disability and Work** 27 (Carolyn L. Weaver, ed., 1991).

[30] *See* Oi, **supra Ch. III § 3.2,** at 112.

sary to accommodate them in the workforce."[31]

Chapters XIII and XIV of this book examine findings from studies addressing the economic effect on employers of the provision of accommodations. Additional study is required of the costs and benefits associated with accommodations in different businesses, jobs, labor markets, and involving persons with varying disabilities. Many qualified individuals with perceived disabilities or with a record of impairment covered under the second and third prong of the definition of disability may not need an accommodation, even though they are denied employment opportunity on the basis that their employer believes an accommodation may be required in the future. In such cases Title I's antidiscrimination provisions are implicated and should impose no economic inefficiencies on employers.[32]

Study is needed of the actual occurrence of the hypothetical cases discussed above. This analysis may show that, in practice, accommodating qualified workers with and without disabilities leads to efficient and cost-effective workplace operation. In the absence of accurate and reliable measures of worker "value," however, economic efficiency arguments of accommodation implementation may need to be reevaluated.

4.5 The "Interactive Process" and Workplace Accommodations

A major issue in the *Hertz v. EEOC* case, discussed in Chapter V, was whether Hertz had failed to engage in a meaningful discussion regarding possible accommodations for their employees with mental retardation who were discharged. The EEOC claimed that Hertz failed in its obligation to engage in the interactive process mandated by the ADA's implementing regulations and case law interpreting the meaning of that process.

The EEOC implementing regulations address the role of the interactive process:

> Once a qualified individual with a disability has requested provision of a reasonable accommodation, the employer must make a reasonable effort to determine the appropriate accommodation. The appropriate reasonable accommodation is best determined through a *flexible, interactive process that involves both the employer and the qualified individual with a disability*.[33]

The EEOC regulations set out a framework within which this interactive process is to take place. When a qualified individual with a disability has requested a reasonable accommodation to assist in the performance of essential job functions, the employer should use a problem solving approach to:

1. Analyze the particular job involved and determine its purpose and essential functions;
2. Consult with the individual with a disability to ascertain the precise job-related limitations imposed by the individual's disability and how those limitations could be overcome with a reasonable accommodation;
3. In consultation with the individual to be accommodated, identify potential accommodations and assess the effectiveness each would have in enabling the individual to perform the essential functions of the position; and,
4. Consider the preference of the individual to be accommodated and select and implement the accommodation that is most appropriate for both the employee and the employer.[34]

Courts have found that when an employer knows of an employee's disability and what would enable that employee to perform the essential functions of his job, that employer has a duty to engage in the interactive process.[35] As the Seventh Circuit has explained,

> [C]ourts should look for signs of failure to participate in good faith or failure by one of the parties to help the other party determine

---

[31] Richard V. Burkhauser, Post-ADA: Are People with Disabilities Expected to Work?, 549 **Annals, supra Ch. IV § 4.4,** 71, 80–81 (Jan. 1997) (arguing that Title I provisions force taxpayers to bear part of the cost of accommodations, either through higher costs or tax credits).

[32] *See* Weaver, **supra Ch. IV § 4.4,** at 14.

[33] 29 C.F.R. pt. 1630, app. § 1630.9 (emphasis added).

[34] *Id. See also* **infra Appendix C** (reviewing regulations in context of *EEOC v. Hertz*).

[35] *See Bombard v. Fort Wayne Newspapers, Inc.*, 92 F.3d 560, 563 (7th Cir. 1996); *Bultemeyer*, 100 F.3d at 1285.

what specific accommodations are necessary. A party that obstructs or delays the interactive process is not acting in good faith. *A party that fails to communicate, by way of initiation or response, may also be acting in bad faith. In essence, courts should attempt to isolate the cause of the breakdown and then assign responsibility.*[36]

In situations where an employer knows of an applicant's or employee's disability and the need for a workplace accommodation, but the employee is unable to articulate the specific accommodation—for instance, because of a mental disability—courts have determined the employer still has an obligation to provide an accommodation.[37] In one case involving a request by a janitor with mental illness for a workplace accommodation, the court in ruling for the employee commented:

> [A]n employer cannot expect an employee to read its mind and know that he or she must specifically say 'I want a reasonable accommodation,' particularly when the employee has a mental illness. The employer has to meet the employee half-way, and if it appears that the employee may need an accommodation but doesn't know how to ask for it, the employer should do what it can to help.[38]

This view is similar to the position taken by the plaintiff in the *Taylor v. Food World* case that was described in Chapter III. Finally, the interactive process itself may be an effective accommodation for many qualified workers with mental disabilities. Courts recognize that meaningful discussions alone between employer and employee with a mental disability often lead to improved work performance.[39]

4.6 Emerging Issues Related to Workplace Accommodations Under the ADA

In a potentially far-reaching decision by the Third Circuit in *Deane v. Pocono Medical Center*,[40] the court concluded that an individual who is "regarded as" disabled by an employer is not entitled to workplace accommodation if that individual is not in fact disabled under the first prong of the definition of disability. The *Deane* court commented that "if an individual is perceived to be but is not actually disabled, he or she cannot be considered a 'qualified individual with a disability' unless he or she can, without accommodation, perform all the essential as well as the marginal functions of the position held or sought."

In a dissenting opinion, Judge Becker strongly disagreed with the *Deane* majority view that a "regarded as" plaintiff must be able to perform all the functions of the job without reasonable accommodations to be considered qualified under Title I.[41] In mid-1997, the Third Circuit vacated the decision of its three-judge panel, so that the case will be reargued before the entire Circuit Court *en banc*. If upheld, the *Deane* decision would have the effect of preventing an entire class of plaintiffs with "regarded as" impairments, but ones that do not rise to the level of an ADA disability, from bringing suit.[42]

In a case of first impression that also has important implications for interpretation of the ADA's reach for persons with family members with disabilities, the Tenth Circuit Court of Appeals, in *Den Hartog v. Wasatch Academy*,[43]

---

[36] *See Beck v. University of Wisconsin Bd. of Regents*, 75 F.3d 1130, 1135 (7th Cir. 1996) (emphasis added) (involving employee with severe depression).

[37] *Cf. Schmidt v. Safeway, Inc.*, 864 F. Supp. 991 (D. Ore. 1994) (finding that an employer's failure to engage in the interactive accommodation dialogue is not necessarily a violation of the ADA); *with Willis v. Conopco*, 108 F.3d 282 (11th Cir. 1997) (finding that an employee's failure to engage in the interactive process—for instance, by not attending meetings or not providing medical documentation of disability—may result in denial of ADA claim).

[38] *Bultemeyer v. Fort Wayne Community Schools*, 100 F.3d 1281 (7th Cir. 1996); *Miller v. Illinois Department of Corrections*, 107 F.3d 483 (7th Cir. 1997) (finding if employee has difficulty communicating to employer because of a mental disability then employer is on notice that it may have to provide accommodation).

[39] *See Erickson v. Board of Governors of State Colleges and Universities for Northeastern Illinois University*, 1997 U.S. Dist. LEXIS 13313 (N.D. Ill., E.D. 1997).

[40] 7 A.D. Case 555 (3d Cir. 1997).

[41] *See id.* (Becker, J., dissenting).

[42] On October 3, 1997, the Third Circuit vacated its three-judge panel decision and decided to rehear the Deane appeal *en banc*. *Deane*, 1997 WL 500144 (3d Cir. 1997).

[43] *See Den Hartog v. Wasatch Academy*, 129 F.3d 1076 (10th Cir. 1997) (discussing disability-caused misconduct under the ADA).

has concluded that the protections afforded to nondisabled workers who have an association with a person with a disability differs from the protections afforded qualified workers with disabilities. The difference is that the ADA does not require an employer to make *any* workplace accommodations to the disabilities of relatives or associates of an employee who is not disabled.

The *Den Hartog* decision suggests that only job applicants or employees, but not their relatives or associates, are entitled to be accommodated under the ADA. Nevertheless, as discussed in Chapter XIV, independent of ADA requirements many companies expend large sums of money "accommodating" the needs of workers without disabilities so that they may care for their relatives or associates with disabilities. Employee wellness programs, flexible hours for workers with young children, employer-sponsored child care enters, job sharing strategies for workers with limited time availability and employee assistance programs (EAPs) enable qualified workers without disabilities, who have economic value to their employers, to retain employment.

In summary, most courts continue to find that employers are free to choose a workplace accommodation as long as it is effective and does not result in an undue burden or a direct threat.[44] If a qualified employee is able or chooses to provide his or her own accommodation, at no expense and hardship to the employer, the employer is obligated to allow the accommodation. The concepts of undue hardship in the provision of workplace accommodations and direct threat are discussed in the next chapter. The following sections examine types of workplace accommodations that may be effective for qualified persons with mental retardation.

4.7 Supported Employment and Job Coaching as Workplace Accommodations

Supported employment programs, such as those examined in this investigation, assist persons with mental retardation in securing and retaining competitive employment. The use of supported employment programs are not required by employers as an accommodation under the ADA. Chapter V examines the issues in dispute in the *Hertz* case involving interpretation of the EEOC regulations regarding the use of job coaches and supported employment. In that case the plaintiffs argued unsuccessfully that Hertz misinterpreted EEOC views concerning the provision of a job coach and the provision of reasonable accommodations in the workplace.

In 1997 the EEOC issued Enforcement Guidance on the implementation of ADA Title I for persons with mental disabilities.[45] The guidance reiterates that in certain circumstances an employer may be required to provide a job coach as an accommodation, unless it is shown to be an undue hardship to the employer. In some circumstances a reasonable accommodation may include an employer allowing a job coach paid for by an outside agency (private or state sponsored agency) to accompany the employee at work.[46]

In many cases the provision of a temporary, part-time or full-time job coach therefore may constitute an effective and reasonable accommodation. The 1997 EEOC guidelines for the application of ADA to individuals with mental disabilities addresses the issue of whether it is a "reasonable" accommodation to provide a job coach:

> An employer may be required to provide a temporary job coach to assist in the training of a qualified individual with a disability as a reasonable accommodation, barring undue hardship. An employer also may be required to allow a job coach paid by a public or private

---

[44] *See Stewart v. Happy Herman's Cheshire Bridge, Inc.*, 117 F.3d 1278 (11th Cir. 1997) (finding employee entitled to accommodation, but employer may choose type of accommodation); *Hankins v. The Gap, Inc.*, 84 F.3d 797 (6th Cir. 1996) (same).

[45] *See* **infra Appendix F**, **Enforcement Guidance on the ADA and Psychiatric Disabilities,** March 25, 1997, EEOC Office of Legal Counsel (guidance refers broadly to persons with mental disabilities, including those with mental retardation).

[46] *Cf.* **infra Appendices C and D** (briefs filed in *EEOC v. Hertz*), *with* **infra Appendix E** (opinion in case).

social service agency to accompany the employee at the job site as a reasonable accommodation.[47]

Studies suggest that almost two thirds of those receiving supported employment services are persons with mental retardation.[48] These supports and accommodations are considered on a case-by-case basis without regard to whether that assistance is referred to as supported employment.[49] The present investigation provides information concerning the potential need for accommodations for persons with mental retardation, including supported employment programs, modified training materials, restructuring of essential job functions, and job coaching to assist in job training.

Study is needed of the extent to which employers may cost effectively restructure job functions as part of an accommodation plan for qualified workers with mental retardation. Although job restructuring is not required under Title I, an employer is not prohibited from providing any personal modifications or to engage in supported employment programs.

In sum, in most situations supported employment and the provision of a job coach may constitute a reasonable accommodation. In adopting this view, the EEOC has recognized that supported employment may be economically beneficial to the employee and the employer. As discussed in Chapter XI of this book, studies show that employees using supported employment generally have lower absenteeism rates, lower turnover rates, fill positions that many people consider "undesirable," and in many cases have lower salary requirements than those not using supported employment.

4.8 Personal Attendant Services (PAS) and Workplace Accommodations

For many persons with mental retardation, particularly those who also have physical disabilities, personal attendant services (PAS), accessible transportation to work, and adequate health care and insurance benefits are linked to the ability to attain and retain employment.[50] Chapter XVI examines in greater detail how analysis of the measures in the present investigation illuminate the relation of PAS needs to employment opportunity and job retention.[51]

The President's Committee on Employment of Persons with Disabilities has argued that PAS should be viewed as a particularly important workplace accommodation for persons with severe disabilities.[52] While a "reasonable" accommodation of PAS in the workplace under the purview of the ADA may not require employers to provide, for instance, skilled medical attendants, it may include aides who assist qualified employees with certain job functions. Like job coaching supports, PAS in the workplace may include helping a qualified employee with mental retardation to perform job tasks—for instance, assisting an individual to read technical business instructions if that employee has difficulty reading.[53]

In recognition of the need to empower and support qualified persons with disabilities in the workplace, Speaker of the House Newt Gingrich has introduced the Medicaid Community Attendant Services Act of 1997 (MiCASA—"my

---

[47] **EEOC Enforcement Guidance, supra Ch IV § 4.7,** at 27 (citations omitted) (emphasis added).

[48] *See* Frank Rusch, Laird W. Heal, & Robert E. Cimera, Predicting Earnings of Supported Employees with Mental Retardation: A Longitudinal Study, 101 **Am. J. Mental Retardation** 630–44 (1997), *citing* W.G. Revell, Paul Wehman, J. Kregel, M. West, & R. Rayfield, Supported Employment for Persons with Severe Disabilities: Positive Trends in Wages, Models, and Funding, *in* **New Directions in Supported Employment: Volume 1** (Paul Wehman & J. Kregel, eds., 1996) at 40–51.

[49] 29 C.F.R. § 1630.9 (1991) (not making reasonable accommodation).

[50] Disability Rights Education Defense Fund, **Comments on the EEOC's Proposed Regulations for Title I of the ADA,** at 4 (noting that daily attendant care may be a reasonable accommodation and for persons with severe disabilities it is of the highest priority) (*citing* ADA Senate Report, at 33; H. Ed. & Lab. Rep., at 64).

[51] *See* Judith E. Heumann, Building Our Own Boats: A Personal Perspective on Disability Policy, *in* **Rights and Responsibilities, supra Ch. I § 1.1,** at 251, 253–54 (discussing personal assistance services).

[52] **Ability: The Bridge to the Future,** President's Committee on Employment of People with Disabilities, Educational Kit (July 1997).

[53] The President's Committee on Employment of Persons with Disabilities has developed a database on instances in which PAS has served as an effective workplace accommodation. *See id.*

house" in Spanish).[54] MiCASA would amend Title XIX of the Social Security Act to provide for coverage of community attendant services (i.e., PAS) under the Medicaid program. The bill is projected to reach 2.3 million Americans with disabilities.

MiCASA would give individuals with mental retardation, and others with disabilities, who are eligible for Intermediate Care Facility Services for the Mentally Retarded (ICF-MR programs) or nursing facility services the option to use their program dollars for Qualified Community-Based Attendant Services in a workplace or school setting. States participating in the Medicaid program would be required to allow individuals to receive Community-Based Attendant Services in the most integrated setting appropriate to the needs of the individual. If enacted into law, MiCASA would enhance funding opportunities for work accommodations for qualified persons with serious disabilities.[55]

4. 9 Workplace Accommodations Through Dialogue Among Employer, Employee, and Service Providers and Families

Although an accommodation must meet the job-related needs of the individual and be effective, it does not have to be the best accommodation available.[56] Employers have discretion in the type of accommodation they select for an individual. However, often employers lack information to make such determinations. Persons with mental retardation, their families, or their service providers typically have most of the information to determine an appropriate accommodation.[57]

For persons with mental retardation, as well as for others with disabilities, a family member, representative, guardian, or friend may request an accommodation on behalf of the individual with a disability. ADA Title I requires that employers be receptive to such accommodation requests through the interactive process.[58] Nevertheless, employers may require a job applicant to describe or demonstrate how, with or without accommodation, the applicant may perform job-related functions.[59] In cases where the qualified individual provides or pays the cost associated with accommodation—for instance, the provision of PAS or job coaching in the workplace—the employer is obligated to allow the individual to use that accommodation.[60]

Professor Mank and his colleagues have demonstrated that effective dialogue among employers, employees with mental retardation, and their families and coworkers leads to enhanced integration in employment and higher wages for these individuals with mental retardation.[61] In a series of studies, Mank finds that natural support strategies, emphasizing dialogue among employees with mental retardation, their families, and advocates and coworkers, result in higher monthly earnings for workers with mental retardation, even when statistically controlling for level of retardation. Workers with mental retardation earn higher wages—presumably because they are more qualified and valuable to their employers—in employment settings where coworkers receive training from supported employment personnel and job coaches in effective workplace accommodation strategies.

---

[54] H.R. 2020, introduced on June 24, 1997, currently is referred to House Commerce Committee.

[55] *See* **infra Ch. XVI § 16.5** (discussing H.R. 2020 and other related proposed legislation affecting persons with disabilities such as S. 879 and S. 1544).

[56] 29 C.F.R. § 1630.2(o) (1991) (*citing* S. Rep., at 35; H. Rep., at 68).

[57] *See* Lavelle, **supra Ch. I § 1.1,** at 1172 (sharing of consumer information with employers during the phase-in period of Title I should reduce transaction costs in hiring persons with disabilities) *(citing* Report from the Committee on Labor and Human Resources, S. Rep. No. 116, 101st Cong., 1st sess., 34–35 (1989)).

[58] **Enforcement Guidance on the ADA and Psychiatric Disabilities,** Mar. 25, 1997, EEOC Office of Legal Counsel; 29 C.F.R pt. 1630 app. § 1630.9 (1996) (**infra Appendix F**).

[59] 29 C.F.R. 1630.14(a) (1991).

[60] 29 C.F.R. § 1630.2(p).

[61] David Mank, Andrea Cioffi, & Paul Yovanoff, Patterns of Support for Employees with Severe Disabilities, 35 **Mental Retardation** 433–47 (1997) (studying employment outcomes for 462 individuals with severe disabilities, of whom 84 percent had mental retardation).

4.10 Work Leave, Job Restructuring, and Reassignment as Workplace Accommodations

Chapter V examines the ADA's "undue hardship" provision, particularly in light of requests by employees for work leave, restructuring job functions, and job reassignment as accommodations. Hardship may take the form of economic or logistical inefficiencies due to a fundamental alteration of the required job. These inefficiencies depend upon relative costs and benefits associated with the specialization of the task, the size and nature of the business, the availability of worker substitutes in the relevant labor market, or cyclical changes in the market or economy that affect labor and production requirements.[62] The determination of the reasonableness of such accommodations, or conversely their inefficiencies, is made on a case-by-case basis.

Most courts have interpreted unpaid leave as a form of accommodation that may be effective and reasonable, depending upon the circumstances.[63] The amount of leave that is reasonable depends upon the context and business demands. A request for an indefinite leave likely would not be a reasonable or effective accommodation because it does not enable the employee to work.[64]

Job reassignment may be a form of reasonable accommodation.[65] The effective reallocation of marginal as compared to essential job functions through job restructuring has been held to be a reasonable accommodation.[66] As mentioned, an employer need not alter essential job functions as a workplace accommodation under the ADA.

David Fram has noted the scope of the employer's obligation to provide accommodations related to job restructuring and reassignment:[67]

- reassignment is available only to employees, and not to job applicants;
- an employer does not have to promote or raise the salary of an employee with a disability as a reassignment;
- an individual must only be reassigned to a position for which he or she is qualified; and
- an employer does not have to reassign another employee to create a vacancy to accommodate an employee with a disability.

In this last regard, courts have found that the ADA does not require employers to alter a collective bargaining agreement (CBA) to accommodate a worker with a disability. In the leading case on the issue, *Eckles v. Consolidated Rail Corp.*,[68] the Seventh Circuit Court of Appeals concluded that the ADA's accommodation provision does not require a disabled worker be given special job protection from "bumping" in violation of a seniority agreement of a CBA.

In *Eckles*, the Seventh Circuit Court reasoned that reassignment to a "vacant" position is not required by the ADA if it violates collectively bargained seniority rights of all workers.[69] Thus, workers with mental retardation and other disabilities in a union setting are not necessarily entitled to specific workplace accommodations that affect the collectively bargained rights of coworkers. However, to the extent that the work rights at issue, in a union or nonunion setting, are independent nonnegotiable rights found under the ADA (for instance, relating to an employer's general duty of reasonable accommodation), then such rights may not be preempted automatically by a CBA.[70]

---

[62] Burgdorf, **supra Ch. I § 1.4,** at 210 (1995 book); 29 C.F.R. §1630.2(n)(2) (1993) (commentary on §1630.2(n)(ii)).

[63] *See* C.F.R. § 1630.2(o) (Appendix with **EEOC Guidance**); *Williams v. Widnall*, 79 F.3d 1003 (10th Cir. 1996) (leave appropriate for medical treatment or rehabilitation therapy).

[64] *See Rogers v. International Marine Terminals, Inc.*, 87 F.3d 755 (5th Cir. 1996); *Johnson v. Foulds,* Inc., 1997 U.S. App. LEXIS 3386 (7th Cir. 1997).

[65] *See Gile v. United Airlines, Inc.*, 95 F.3d 492 (7th Cir. 1996).

[66] *See also Bensen v. Northwest Airlines*, 62 F.3d 1108 (8th Cir. 1995).

[67] *See* Fram, **supra Ch. II § 2.5,** at III-30 (setting forth these categories and reviewing related cases).

[68] 94 F.3d 1041 (7th Cir. 1996), *cert denied*, 117 S. Ct. 1318 (U.S. Mar. 21, 1997).

[69] For a review and analysis of this issue, *see* Condon A. McGlothlen & Gary N. Savine, *Eckles v. Consolidated Rail Corp.*: Reconciling the ADA with Collective Bargaining Agreements: Is This the Correct Approach?, 46 **DePaul L. Rev.** 1043–55 (1997).

[70] *See Ralph v. Lucent Technologies, Inc.*, 135 F.3d 166 (1st Cir. 1998) (finding independent nonnegotiable work rights not preempted by CBA, and duty to provide workplace accommodation is an ongoing responsibility of employer).

4.11 Summary

ADA Title I requires employers to accommodate the needs of qualified persons with disabilities. Workplace accommodations ensure equal opportunity to the application process (e.g., by providing job application forms in alternative formats such as braille and large print), enable qualified employees with disabilities to perform essential job functions (e.g., by providing adaptive equipment or flexible work schedules), and enable employees with disabilities to enjoy the same benefits as employees without disabilities (e.g., by providing equitable health and life insurance and benefit plans).

There is a developing body of information on the costs and benefits of accommodations in the workplace. Findings for persons with mental retardation suggest that workplace accommodations often are inexpensive and not burdensome to employers.[71]

The research model in this book focuses on a type of accommodation, the adaptive-equipment needs for these participants.[72] The appropriateness of an accommodation for a qualified person with mental retardation will be difficult to assess without the guidance from empirical information.[73] Employee skills, level of workplace involvement and self-advocacy, available assistive technology, and job requirements change with time. This is true for those accommodations involving job coaching or PAS.

Study may help to assess the long-term usefulness of different accommodations, which in turn may lead to enhanced and cost-effective services and technology for employees with different disabilities and their employers.[74] Chapter V next describes how, with or without the provision of a workplace accommodation, the evidentiary burden remains with the employee to demonstrate that he or she is a qualified individual with a covered disability.[75]

---

[71] *See* Thomas Baffuto & Elizabeth M. Boggs, What ADA Has Meant and What It Can Mean for People with Mental Retardation, **Am. Rehabilitation,** at 10–14 (Winter 1990–91) (reviewing cost-effective approaches by companies that obviate the need for accommodations each time an employee with a disability is hired).

[72] *See* **infra Chapter VIII § 8.4** (discussing the adaptive equipment factor).

[73] Assistive technology is the use of commercial or custom-designed devices and technical services that enhance the capabilities of individuals with disabilities. *See* The Technology Related Assistance for Individuals with Disabilities Act of 1988 (reauthorized in 1994 and codified as amended at 29 U.S.C. § 2201 et seq.) (defining assistive technology, and distinguishing assistive technology devices and assistive technology services).

[74] *See* **infra Ch. XIV § 14.5** for discussion of how advances in accommodations translate into new and universally accessible consumer products in the home that have direct and indirect economic benefits to ADA stakeholders.

[75] *See Chandler v. City of Dallas*, 2 F.3d 1385, 1394 & n.43 (5th Cir. 1993) (outlining the burden of proof).

CHAPTER V

Central Provisions of ADA Title I: Affirmative Defenses and Enforcement

[A]s long as there is lingering prejudice against the disabled, we cannot rely on free labor markets alone to provide appropriate employment opportunities for the handicapped, any more than we can rely on free markets alone to provide equal opportunity for racial minorities while substantial racial prejudice exists.

Gregory Kavka [1]

5.1 Introduction

Chapter II described several forms of employment discrimination that may be claimed under ADA Title I. Employment discrimination may be alleged because of the "disparate treatment" toward qualified workers with mental retardation as compared to other similarly situated nondisabled employees who are treated more favorably.[2] Discrimination may be based on an employer not making reasonable accommodations for a qualified job applicant or employee with a covered disability.[3] This chapter explores the legal defenses employers may raise in response to a charge of discrimination under ADA Title I. It also examines trends in ADA enforcement and compliance.

5.2 Affirmative Defenses to Charges of ADA Title I Discrimination: "Prima Facie Case" and Burdens of Proof

There are a number of "affirmative defenses" available to employers or other entities covered by the law to rebut a charge of Title I discrimination. One such defense is that a proposed accommodation presents an undue hardship on the operation of the entity. A second is that the employee poses a significant risk or "direct threat" to him- or herself or others in the workplace.

An employee or job applicant alleging a claim of discrimination under the ADA must

---

[1] Gregory S. Kavka, Disability and the Right to Work, 9(1) **Soc. Phil. & Pol'y,** 262–90, at 268 (1992).

[2] *See* 42 U.S.C. § 12112(b). *See Bultemeyer*, **supra Ch. IV § 4.3** (discussing burden-shifting test in Title I context using direct or indirect evidence of discrimination). Discrimination may be alleged also on the basis of the "disparate impact" of an employment practice on a group of qualified employees with disabilities. Disparate impact cases often involve a challenge to a business practice that unfairly impacts a group of qualified individuals with disabilities, such as benefit or medical testing policies discussed **infra Ch. XV § 15.4**.

[3] *See* 42 U.S.C. § 12112(b)(5)(A)–(B) (delineating qualified individual with a disability provision).

present to the court a "prima facie" legal case.[4] To be successful, a plaintiff must prove each of these statutorily required legal elements. In a case where a plaintiff alleges employment discrimination under ADA Title I on the basis of an employer's refusal to provide workplace accommodations, as part of his prima facie case the employee bears the evidentiary burden of proving that he or she:

- is "disabled" under the purview of the ADA [*see Chapter II*];
- can perform "essential job functions" with or without reasonable accommodations, and therefore is "a qualified individual" [*see Chapter III*];
- requested workplace accommodations that would have been effective and reasonable [*see Chapter IV*]; and
- received an adverse employment decision from the employer on the basis of the employee's disability and not on the employee's present qualifications.[5]

If an employee plaintiff satisfies the elements of proof required by the prima facie case, the evidentiary burden shifts to the employer defendant to rebut the claim of employment discrimination.[6] An employer may attempt to prove that the plaintiff is not a person with a "disability," is not "qualified" for the job in question, did not request a "reasonable" workplace accommodation, or that any accommodation would not be possible because it would present an undue hardship to the employer or a "direct threat" to the employee or others.

The successful prima facie ADA Title I case establishes that a qualified individual with a disability covered by the law suffered an adverse employment decision because of his or her disability on the basis of the employer's discriminatory fears, myths, or misconceptions.[7] At its core, ADA Title I is meant to prevent unjustified employment discrimination on the basis of "discriminatory animus," unfounded prejudice and fear.

5.3 Undue Hardship

Through the concept of "undue hardship," Title I limits an employer's obligation to provide workplace accommodations.[8] Undue hardship occurs when the employer would undergo significant difficulty or expense in providing an accommodation.[9] This provision focuses on the economic impact of an accommodation on covered firms; that is, businesses with 15 or more employees.[10]

As mentioned later in this chapter in regard to the *EEOC v. Hertz* case, even if an employer shows that the cost of an accommodation would impose an undue hardship, the employer

---

[4] *See Monette v. Electronic Data Systems*, 90 F.3d 1173 (6th Cir., 1996) (discussing elements of disparate treatment cases).

[5] *See Miners v. Cargill Communications, Inc.*, 113 F.3d 820 (8th Cir. 1997) (discussing that final element of prima facie case is that an adverse employment determination was made "under circumstances giving rise to an inference of unlawful discrimination.").

[6] *See Katz v. City Metal Co., Inc.*, 87 F.3d 26, 30 (1st Cir. 1996) (discussing essential elements of prima facie ADA Title I case); *Sherback v. Wright Automotive Group,* 987 F. Supp. 433 (W.D. Pa. 1997) (discussing that the U.S. Supreme Court may have modified the traditional formulation of a plaintiff's prima facie case in employment discrimination cases to a case-by-case determination—*citing O'Connor v. Consolidated Coin Caterers Corp.*, 517 U.S. 308 (1996). *Cf. McDonnell Douglas Corp. v. Green*, 411 U.S. 792 (1973) (U.S. Supreme Court discussion of disparate treatment cases under Title VII of the Civil Rights Act of 1964), *with Bultemeyer*, **supra Ch. IV § 4.3** (McDonnell-Douglas test does not apply in ADA cases based on discrimination in the provision of workplace accommodations).

[7] *EEOC v. Amego*, 110 F.3d 135, 141 (1st Cir. 1997) (discussed **infra Ch. V § 5.5**).

[8] 29 C.F.R. § 1630.2(p) (1991). *See* Jeffrey O. Cooper, Overcoming Barriers to Employment: The Meaning of Reasonable Accommodation and Undue Hardship in the Americans with Disabilities Act, 139 **U. Pa. L. Rev.** 1423, 1430 (1991).

[9] *See* 42 U.S.C. § 12111(10); 29 C.F.R. § 1630.2(p) (1991) (referring to accommodation that would be unduly costly, extensive, disruptive, or fundamentally alter the nature of the business); R.H. Gardner & C.J. Campanella, The Undue Hardship Defense to the Reasonable Accommodation Requirement of the Americans with Disabilities Act of 1990, 7 **Lab. Law.** 37 (Winter 1991).

[10] **BNA Report, supra Ch. I § 1.5,** at 119 (listing economic factors including nature and cost of accommodation, financial resources and workforce of facility and of the parent entity; composition of the workforce, and relation between facility and parent entity); Lavelle, **supra Ch. I § 1.7,** at 1186 (arguing this is significant protection afforded small businesses by Title I and that undue hardship likely means something less than threatened existence of the business).

may be required to provide the accommodation if it may be effective and its funding is available from another source. One external source of funding for an accommodation for an employee with mental retardation might be provided from a state department of vocational rehabilitation for job coaching services in a supported employment program. Where the individual or state agency provides the accommodation or pays for that portion of the costs that constitute the undue hardship on the business, the employer is obligated to provide the accommodation.[11]

Many workers with mental retardation receive job training and work supports from state and private programs.[12] Chapter XVI describes how under the ADA, federal, state or local tax credits are available to offset the cost of the accommodation. To the extent that partial monies are used by an individual with a disability to offset the cost of the accommodation, only the remaining net cost to the employer is considered in determining undue hardship.

One goal of this book is to provide information to national, state, and local agencies that helps support efforts toward equal opportunity for qualified persons with mental retardation. The findings summarized in Chapter XII suggest that some employers have expressed concerns about of the costs associated with the hiring and retention of persons with mental retardation through supported employment programs. The present findings suggest, however, that most employers in this investigation did not view the costs associated with supported employment programs as a significant disincentive to the hiring of qualified workers with mental retardation.[13]

Accommodations that have adverse effects on coworkers may result in an undue hardship to an employer, and in some cases would not be required under the ADA.[14] In *Turco v. Hoechst Celanese Corp.*,[15] the Fifth Circuit Court of Appeals concluded that an employee with diabetes was not "qualified" because he could not perform essential job functions and because of the safety risk in the workplace he posed to himself and others. The employee's position required him to work with complicated machinery and dangerous chemicals.

The *Turco* court found that a diabetic episode or loss of concentration occurring while operating machinery or working with chemicals had the potential to create additional work burdens for other employees and the risk of harm not only to the employee himself but to coworkers. The court concluded that the impact of the employee's disability on the work requirements of other workers created an undue hardship and direct threat in the workplace, terms which are discussed in following sections.[16]

---

[11] 29 C.F.R. § 1630.2(p) (1991).

[12] *See also* Disability Rights Education Defense Fund, **Comments on the EEOC's Proposed Regulations for Title I of the ADA,** at 5 (arguing for clarification in the regulations that even if a job coach—permanent or temporary—is an undue hardship for the employer, the employer may not refuse to allow an employee to use a job coach who has been paid for in another manner) (*citing* EEOC proposed regulations).

[13] *See* **infra Ch. XI § 11.6** (discussing the present findings for a sample of employers surveyed regarding the participants in this study). *Cf.* **infra Ch. V § 5.8** (discussing *EEOC v. Hertz* case in which the federal court found that the provision of a job coach was not a reasonable workplace accommodation).

[14] *See* Lisa E. Key, Co-Worker Morale, Confidentiality, and the Americans with Disabilities Act, 42 **Vill. L. Rev.** 1003–42 (1997) (arguing that coworker morale should be a factor in assessing whether a workplace accommodation poses an undue hardship on an employer); Fram, **supra Ch. II § 2.5,** at III-48 (reviewing cases).

[15] 101 F.3d 1090 (5th Cir. 1996) (*per curium*).

[16] Research indicates that for many employers the provision of accommodations has not proven to be costly, controversial, or an "undue hardship." *See* **infra Chs. XIII & XIV;** Stanley S. Herr, The ADA in International and Development Disabilities Perspectives, *in* **Rights and Responsibilities, supra Ch. I § 1.1,** at 229, 238 (noting implications of ADA for persons with mental retardation and the potential costs of accommodating these individuals); U.S. Gen. Accounting Office, **Persons with Disabilities: Reports on Costs of Accommodations** (Pub. No. GAO/HRD-90-44BR, 1990) (providing summaries of various studies of accommodation costs); Lawrence P. Postol & David D. Kadue, An Employer's Guide to the ADA—From Job Qualifications to Reasonable Accommodations, 24 **John Marshall L. Rev.** 693, 713 (1991) (listing examples of accommodations including a telephone headset with a $49.95 price tag, a $45 lighting system, and a $26.95 timer with an indicator light).

5.4 Direct Threat

A second affirmative defense asserted by employers to ADA charges of employment discrimination often involves persons with disabilities who are alleged to be "unqualified" for a job in circumstances in which they are believed to pose a direct safety or health threat to themselves or others in the workplace.[17] Under the ADA, "direct threat" means "a significant risk to the health or safety of others that cannot be eliminated by reasonable accommodation."[18]

Factors considered by courts in determining whether a threat exists include the duration of the risk, nature of potential harm, and likelihood that the harm will occur.[19] Chapter XV discusses that cases in which a direct threat defense is used by an employer have implicated underlying attitudinal biases about hidden or perceived impairments such as genetic, mental, addictive, and contagious conditions as derived from medical testing.[20]

The ADA does not require that a medical examination or test be conducted to assess a direct threat when objective evidence is available.[21] In cases involving persons with mental disabilities, there may be objective evidence from a worker's behavior that the person has made threats that caused harm to other workers directly or indirectly.[22] However, the ADA is meant to prevent the exclusion of qualified employees from employment solely on the basis of unjustified fears about the possibility of threat to self or others in the workplace.

The determination by employers of direct threat is to be made, therefore, on the basis of tests of current medical judgment.[23] Chapter XV examines the uses and abuses of employment-related medical tests to assess disability under the ADA in cases involving persons with mental retardation.[24] A central issue to be addressed by the United States Supreme Court in *Bragdon v. Abbott*[25]—the case discussed in Chapter II involving a plaintiff with asymptomatic HIV disease—will be the extent to which courts should defer to the reasonable judgment of public health officials in assessing whether an

---

[17] 42 U.S.C. § 12113(a); 29 C.F.R. § 1630.2(r) (1991) (defining direct threat as a "significant risk of substantial harm to the health or safety of the individual or others that cannot be eliminated or reduced by reasonable accommodation"); 28 C.F.R § 36.208 (Title I may require accommodations that eliminate or sufficiently reduce a direct threat); 29 C.F.R. § 1630.2 (r) (1991) (where a mental or emotional disability is involved, employer must identify the behavior on the part of the individual that would pose a direct threat). For a review, *see* Laura F. Rothstein, The Employer's Duty to Accommodate Performance and Conduct Deficiencies of Individuals with Mental Impairments Under Disability Discrimination Laws, 47 **Syracuse L. Rev.** 931–86 (1997).

[18] 42 U.S.C. § 12111(3). *See also* 29 C.F.R. § 1630.2(r) (1996) (EEOC supplementing statutory definition by adding the following words in its ADA regulations: "a significant harm to the health or safety of the individual or others that cannot be eliminated or reduced by reasonable accommodation.").

[19] 29 C.F.R. § 1630.2(r) (1996).

[20] *See Judice v. Hospital Serv. Dist. No. 1*, 919 F. Supp. 978 (E.D. La. 1996) (finding hospital did not violate ADA by requesting recovering alcoholic surgeon to undergo second medical evaluation before reinstatement of staff privileges); *Doe v. University of Maryland Medical System Corp.*, 50 F.3d 1261 (4th Cir. 1995) (finding hospital did not violate ADA when it suspended HIV-positive surgical resident because of threat to patients); *Scoles v. Mercy Health Corp.*, 887 F. Supp. 765 (E.D. Pa. 1994) (ruling for defendant hospital and against surgeon with HIV disease in suit involving nonstaff hospital privileges because of safety threat to patients). *See* Phillip L. McIntosh, When the Surgeon Has HIV: What to Tell Patients About the Risk of Exposure and the Risk of Transmission, 44 **U. Kansas L. Rev.** 315–64 (1996); Pope L. Moseley, Peter David Blanck, & Randy Merrit, Hospital Privileges and the Americans with Disabilities Act, 21 **Spine** 2288–93 (1996); McDonald, et al., Mental Disabilities Under the ADA: A Management Rights Approach, 20 **Empl. Rel. L.J.** 541–69, 557–58 (Spring 1995); Mary E. Sharp, The Hidden Disability That Finds Protection Under the Americans with Disabilities Act: Employing the Mentally Impaired, 12 **Ga. St. U.L. Rev.** 889, 921–26 (1996).

[21] *See* 29 C.F.R. § 1630.2(r) (1996). *See also Den Hartog v. Wasatch Academy*, 129 F.3d 1076 (10th Cir. 1997) (finding that direct threat defense not require medical test as basis for determination).

[22] *Id.* (discussing similar example of worker with mental illness).

[23] 29 C.F.R. § 1630.2(r).

[24] *See* **infra Ch. XV § 15.4** (discussing medical testing in employment).

[25] 118 S. Ct. 554 (1997).

activity poses a direct threat to the health or safety of others.[26]

Employers are required to make an *individualized* and objective determination of a purported direct threat, based on the employee's current ability to safely perform essential job functions. Blanket exclusions by employers of applicants or employees on the basis of a perceived direct threat from a particular disability is prohibited under the ADA.[27]

In some cases such as in *EEOC v. Amego* described in the next section, the issue of direct threat is not related clearly to the employee's performance of essential job functions. In those cases the question is whether the employer has the legal burden of proving that the employee is a threat to others in the workplace.

The direct threat defense has been raised also in circumstances where the threat came from relatives of the quailfied worker. In such a case, the Tenth Circuit in *Den Hartog v. Wasatch Academy* concluded that the ADA permits an employer to discharge a nondisabled employee whose son with a mental disability posed a direct threat in the workplace.[28]

Examination is needed of attitudes and behavior linked to job qualifications and the reality of the perceived risk associated with "direct threats" involving persons with different disabilities, such as those with mental retardation. Under the ADA's direct threat analysis, a court must balance protecting individuals and society from exposure to unacceptable health and safety risks with protecting qualified individuals with disabilities covered by the law from discrimination "that is rooted in prejudice or baseless fear."[29]

5.5 An Illustration of an ADA Case Involving Direct Threat: *EEOC v. Amego*

As mentioned, an employer bears the burden of proving that the employee in question poses a direct threat in the workplace setting.[30] In situations where the ability to perform essential job functions impacts the safety of coworkers or others, the employee, to be considered a qualified individual for purposes of Title I analysis, has the burden of showing that he can perform those functions safely.

In a 1997 case *EEOC v. Amego*,[31] the First Circuit Court of Appeals concluded that an employee has the burden of showing that he or she is not a direct threat when the inability or failure to perform essential job functions would create a risk to others.[32] The *Amego* case involved Ms. Guglielmi, a team leader at Amego, Inc., a small not-for-profit provider of care for persons with mental retardation and other mental disabilities. One of Guglielmi's essential job functions was to administer medications to the clients Amego served.

Guglielmi suffered from depression and had twice tried to commit suicide by overdosing on medications. After internal analysis, Amego concluded that Guglielmi could not safely dispense medication, an essential function of her job, and that there was no other job available to her as an accommodation.

Amego terminated Guglielmi and she brought an ADA employment discrimination claim on the grounds that she was discharged solely on the basis of her disability. The major question before the court involved the legal burden of proof in an ADA case. The issue was whether Amego bore the burden of proving that Guglielmi posed a significant risk to other individuals in the workplace—the affirmative

---

[26] *See also EEOC v. Prevo's Family Market, Inc.*, 135 F.3d 1089 (6th Cir. 1998) (finding that the medical examination of an alleged HIV positive employee was job-related, consistent with business-necessity and did not violate the ADA because purpose was to protect health of employee and coworkers).

[27] *See Mendez v. Gearan*, 956 F. Supp. 1520 (N.D. Cal. 1997) (employer must perform individualized medical screening to assess nature of direct threat possibility).

[28] *Den Hartog*, 129 F.3d 1076.

[29] *Abbott v. Bragdon*, 107 F.3d at 943.

[30] *See EEOC v. Chrysler Corp.*, 917 F. Supp. 1164 (E.D. Mich. 1996) (employer bears burden of proving employee is a direct threat).

[31] 110 F.3d 135, 143–45 (1st Cir. 1997).

[32] *Cf. Moses v. American Nonwovens, Inc.*, 97 F.3d 446 (11th Cir. 1996), *cert denied*, 117 S. Ct. 964 (1997) (employee retains burden of persuading jury that he was not a direct threat or that reasonable accommodations were not available).

defense of direct threat to the charge of discrimination—or whether the burden of proof remained with Guglielmi to show that she was qualified for the job.

The *Amego* court concluded that it was Guglielmi's legal burden, as part of her prima facie ADA case, to show that she could safely perform essential job functions, and therefore be considered a "qualified" individual within the meaning of the ADA. The ruling suggests that in instances where essential job functions implicate the safety of others, a plaintiff bears the legal burden of proving that she can perform those functions without endangering the safety of others. Most courts will defer to the employer's judgment—if set forth in good faith and well founded—about the potential risks of an employee's workplace behavior.

In the *Amego* case, the court concluded that there was no workplace accommodation that Amego could make that would not cause it an undue hardship. Neither the hiring of additional staff nor the job reassignment of Guglielmi would be a "reasonable" accommodation, given that a small employer like Amego would incur excessive costs from such accommodations in relation to their benefits.

5.6 ADA Title I Compliance and Enforcement

The EEOC is charged with enforcing ADA Title I. In 1996, 23 percent of the employment discrimination charges received by the EEOC alleged an ADA violation.[33] In contrast, 47 percent of the charges involved race discrimination and 41 percent gender discrimination.

The procedures for filing an ADA Title I charge with the EEOC are set forth in Title VII of the Civil Rights Act of 1964.[34] An individual first must file a charge with the EEOC within 180 days of the alleged discriminatory conduct. The agency then informs the employer or other covered entity (i.e., the respondent) of the charge and conducts an investigation. If the EEOC concludes that there is reasonable cause to believe the charge, it may attempt to conciliate the dispute informally, initiate a civil action itself on behalf of the charging party in federal district court, or issue to the charging party a "right-to-sue" letter.

After exhausting its administrative remedies, a charging party may pursue the matter through a private right of action in federal district court. To be timely, a private civil action must be filed within 90 days of EEOC issuance of a right-to-sue letter. The ADA provides that a prevailing plaintiff in an ADA Title I lawsuit may recover attorney's fees and experts' costs.[35]

The legal remedies available under ADA Title I are set forth in the Civil Rights Act of 1991.[36] The 1991 Civil Rights Act strengthens the ban on discrimination in employment against people with disabilities. The law limits compensatory and punitive damages in cases of intentional discrimination in small firms (15 to 100 employees) to $50,000, and in larger firms (more than 500 employees) to $300,000. The law provides for the right to a jury trial in ADA cases.

The Civil Rights Act of 1991 is intended also to provide effective deterrence and compensation for the victims of discrimination. The 1991 Act established a Glass Ceiling Commission to study issues facing those covered by the law, such as promotion practices, training programs to enhance employment advancement, and barriers to advancement in employment. The compliance and enforcement remedies set forth in the 1991 Civil Rights Act have yet to be examined empirically. Increasingly, empirical information will be required to assess areas such as employment integration, job advancement patterns, and "glass ceiling" barriers facing qualified persons with disabilities.

Study of the kind illustrated by the present investigation may help to address improvements in the lives of qualified persons with disabilities, changes in public attitudes and behavior, and structural changes in the economy resulting from the implementation and enforcement of the ADA. The research model in this book explores the independent and combined effects of personal background, job skill, inclusion,

---

[33] For a review, *see* Miller, **supra Ch. I § 1.1,** at 788–96 (discussing EEOC enforcement statistics for the ADA).

[34] *See* 42 U.S.C. §§ 2000e-4, et seq.

[35] *See* 42 U.S.C. § 12205 (**infra Appendix A**).

[36] 42 U.S.C. § 1981a(b)(3)(Supp. IV 1992), & § 1981a(c) (**infra Appendix B**). *See also* The Congressional Accountability Act of 1995, **Pub. L. No.** 104-1 (making the ADA applicable to Congress and its staff and offices).

empowerment, and workplace accessibility factors on employment integration and economic opportunity for participants with mental retardation.

5.7 Trends and Emerging Issues in ADA Title I Compliance and Enforcement

The present research addresses compliance and enforcement issues such as:

1. How far will ADA enforcement strategies affect employers' attitudes, ability, and willingness to maintain a workforce of persons with disabilities?
2. In what ways will ADA enforcement enhance employment opportunity and economic growth for qualified women and men, younger and older workers, workers from different ethnic groups, and workers with varying disabilities?
3. How will the EEOC and the courts assess and foster compliance with and enforcement of the law?

Chapter XV describes in detail the types of employment discrimination charges filed since Title I's effective date on July 26, 1992. Of the approximately 85,000 Title I charges filed to date, roughly 0.4 percent have involved persons with mental retardation. Of the cases involving mental retardation, approximately two thirds involved discharge of the worker.

Approximately 20 percent of the charges brought by persons with mental retardation involved workplace harassment issues, and another 20 percent involved the request for or provision of workplace accommodations. Chapter XIV examines issues related to workplace accommodations for persons with mental retardation and the need for related strategies to reduce disputes in the workplace, implement cost-effective workplace design, and lessen unjustified attitudinal bias toward workers and applicants with mental retardation.

Recently courts have addressed whether an employee's agreement with an employer not to sue an employer under the ADA may be enforceable.[37] To be valid, the "release" of ADA claims must be "knowing and voluntary"—a particularly important standard for persons with mental disabilities.

The EEOC has taken the position that most employee rights under the ADA may not be waived as a matter of public policy, because they hinder the agency's ability to eliminate unlawful employment discrimination.[38] According to the EEOC, agreements that unfairly extract promises from employees not to pursue their ADA claims may amount to a separate violation of the antiretaliation provisions under the law. This is because such agreements themselves may have a "chilling" effect on the willingness and ability of individuals with information to help eliminate unlawful employment discrimination.

5.8 An Illustration of Compliance and Enforcement Issues: *EEOC v. Hertz*

As mentioned in prior chapters, in 1996 the EEOC filed the agency's first Title I lawsuit on behalf of two individuals with mental retardation in *EEOC v. Hertz Corporation*.[39] The EEOC charged that Hertz had discharged the two employees, not because of their capabilities and qualifications, but because of the alleged inappropriate behavior of their job coaches.

The two Hertz employees, Messrs. Klem and Miller, worked with supported employment job coaches, provided by the state vocational rehabilitation program at no cost to Hertz. Klem and Miller received positive job evaluations over the course of their employment. At some point during the tenure of Klem and Miller, a Hertz manager reported seeing their two job coaches (a male and female) hugging. The supervisor proceeded to fire Klem and Miller and told the

---

[37] *See Riveria-Flores v. Bristol-Myers Squibb Carribean*, 112 F.3d 9 (1st Cir. 1997) (discussing that release may be upheld where employee participation was voluntary, received additional benefits from release, and had legal counsel review the agreement).

[38] **EEOC: Guidance on Waivers Under the ADA and Other Civil Rights Laws** (Apr. 10, 1997).

[39] 1998 U.S. Dist. LEXIS 58 (E.D. Mich. S.D. 1998). *See also* Tamar Lewin, Hertz Sued for Firing Retarded Men, **N.Y. Times** New Service (Nov. 28, 1997); *EEOC v. Hertz Corp*., U.S. Dist. Ct. Detroit, June 6, 1996 (summarized in 8(2) **Disability Compliance Bull.** (June 6, 1997).

job coaches to leave the premises immediately.

Based on these facts, EEOC Commissioner Paul Miller has stated that the *Hertz* case "may be a particularly egregious case of blaming the victim."[40] According to the EEOC, Hertz did not attempt to accommodate Klem and Miller—for instance, by exploring ways to retain new job coaches or attempting to have coaches provided by the outside supported employment agency at no cost to the company. Instead, Hertz chose to terminate Klem and Miller.

The allegations made in the *Hertz* case illustrate to the community of persons with mental retardation the importance of the EEOC to Title I compliance and enforcement.[41] At a minimum, the *Hertz* case highlights the need for study of unfounded corporate attitudes toward their qualified workers with mental retardation.

Unfortunately, the federal district court opinion in the *Hertz* case furthers conceptions about workers with mental retardation as "recipients of 'charity' and corporate 'generosity' " that is all too common.[42] In ruling for Hertz, Judge Feikens writes: "How does the EEOC expect to *further the goal of assisting handicapped persons that employers will seek to hire if it seeks to punish them for their generosity?*" He continues: "[i]t is not the duty, obligation or responsibility of Hertz to provide job coaches, either on a temporary basis or on a permanent basis, to train and supervise these handicapped individuals."[43]

Judge Feikens' legal conclusions and underlying assumptions in *EEOC v. Hertz* have important implications for workers with mental retardation and other disabilities.[44] The court concludes:

> *If a temporary job coach providing job training to a qualified individual may be a reasonable accommodation, the clear implication is that a full-time job coach providing more than training to unqualified individuals is not....* EEOC, in the face of this precedent and in spite of its inability to point to any case mandating that a full-time job coach is a reasonable accommodation, advances the incredible argument that, because Hertz could have obtained a job coach for Messrs. Klem and Miller at no cost to itself, the provision of a job coach is a per se reasonable accommodation, and must be provided.
>
> Plaintiff seeks to establish an expanded liability for putative employers who consider hiring handicapped persons, i.e., that *once an employer evidences an intent to and does provide employment for a handicapped person with support for that person of a job coach, it is obligated to continue that relationship in perpetuity and without regard to any event(s) that make that employment relationship untenable. The ADA does not require this.*[45]

On its face, Judge Feikens' decision is inconsistent with prior interpretations of the ADA and its case law described in earlier chapters. The ADA does not mandate job coaching as a reasonable accommodation in all cases. As discussed in Chapter IV, in certain circumstances an employer may be required to provide a job coach as an accommodation, but only after an individualized inquiry has been made through the "interactive process" and it is shown that the accommodation is not an undue hardship to the employer.[46]

Despite the court's analysis in *EEOC v. Hertz*, workers with mental retardation or any other disability are not automatically considered "qualified individuals with a disability" under the purview of the ADA. Chapter III described that the ADA does not require an employer to hire or retain individuals with covered disabilities who are not qualified, or to hire or retain individuals with covered disabilities over equally or more qualified individuals without disabilities.[47]

---

[40] *Id.*

[41] *See* Miller, **supra Foreword.**

[42] *See* Miller, **supra Foreword.**

[43] *See EEOC v. Hertz* Opinion, **infra Appendix E** (emphasis added).

[44] *Cf.* **supra Ch. IV § 4.7** (discussing role of personal attendant services in the workplace for workers with severe disabilities).

[45] *See EEOC v. Hertz* Opinion, **infra Appendix E** (emphasis added).

[46] *See* **supra Ch. IV § 4.7** (discussing job coaching as workplace accommodation required by the ADA). *See also Drawski v. Department of General Administration, State of Washington*, 1998 Wash. App. LEXIS 84 (Wash. Ct. App. 1998) (finding that the employer had attempted to reasonably accommodate an employee with mental retardation by changing his job duties, and by providing a worksite job coach and job training; and finding that the employer is not required under the ADA to provide a worksite job coach with extraordinary experience and credentials because this would not be a reasonable accommodation).

[47] *See* **supra Ch. III § 3.2** (discussing these issues and citing in support 42 U.S.C. § 12111(8)).

Employers are not discouraged from searching for the most qualified individuals with or without disabilities under the ADA, and they are not required to incur productivity losses or economic costs in retaining nonqualified workers with disabilities. Klem and Miller need not have been provided preferential treatment in any aspect of their employment with Hertz.

On a deeper and more disturbing level, the language of the *Hertz* decision is, at best, paternalistic and, at worst, condescending toward these Hertz employees with mental retardation. In contrast to the research findings described in later chapters in the book, the opinion perpetuates myths and stereotypes about the capabilities of workers with mental retardation that the ADA was designed to remove.[48]

Chapter IX describes the findings from the present investigation suggesting that the growing grass-roots community of self-advocating persons with mental retardation and their families increasingly may take a stand against outdated and stereotyped thinking about workers with mental retardation. The implications of such "sanist" attitudes toward workers with mental retardation are discussed next.

5.9 "Sanism" and ADA Title I Enforcement and Compliance

Many cases involving the direct threat defense have involved persons with mental disabilities. Persons with hidden and perceived disabilities (e.g., a history of psychiatric illness or mild mental retardation) are alleged to be "unqualified" for a job in circumstances in which they are believed to pose a direct safety or health threat to themselves or others in the workplace.

As discussed in Chapter XV of this book, while the decision to disclose a hidden disability is a complex one, disclosure by a qualified employee is necessary to assist the employee in obtaining workplace accommodations. But it is difficult to predict how employers and coworkers will respond to individuals with mental disabilities who self-disclose or whose condition is divulged from medical tests.[49]

Fear of negative attitudes and discriminatory behavior often prevents qualified workers from disclosing their mental disabilities.[50] Studies suggest that employers' attach greater stigma to employees with mental disabilities than to those with physical disabilities.[51] Fueled by common prejudice, employers and coworkers interpret work and personal difficulties or symptoms experienced by an individual with a mental disability as related directly to that individual's ability to perform a job. This tendency may be especially true if the employee previously requested an accommodation for a known mental disability.[52] This situation was illustrated in the *Wilson* case described in Chapter III.

Professor Michael Perlin has argued that for the ADA to lessen employment discrimination against persons with mental disabilities, society

---

[48] *See generally* **infra Ch. XII.**

[49] *See* B.G. Link, et al., The Consequences of Stigma for Persons with Mental Illness: Evidence from the Social Sciences, **Stigma and Mental Illness** (P.J. Fink & A. Tasman, eds.) (1992); O.F. Wahl & C.R. Harman, Family Views of Stigma, 15 **Schizophrenia Bull.** 131–39 (1989).

[50] *See* **infra Ch. XV § 15.6** (discussing this issue).

[51] Ira H. Combs & Clayton P. Omvig, Accommodation of Disabled People Into Employment: Perceptions of Employers, 52 **J. Rehabilitation** 42–45 (1986) (mental illness ranked 13 out of 16 severe disabilities surveyed for relative employability and ease of accommodations); John B. Allen, Jr., Don't Judge a Book by Its Cover: Qualified Employees Under the ADA, 6 **J. Cal. Alliance Ment. Ill,** at 29–30 (1995) (ADA makes it possible for persons with disabilities to become employed, but philosophical beliefs are a barrier to employment); Louis Harris & Associates, Inc. National Organization on Disability, **Public Attitude Toward People with Disabilities** (1991) (finding that 19 percent of respondents reported being "very comfortable" when meeting someone known to have a mental illness, compared to 22 percent for someone who has mental retardation, 47 percent for someone who is blind, and 59 percent for someone who uses a wheelchair).

[52] George Howard, The Ex-Mental Patient as an Employee, 45 **Amer. J. Orthopsychiat.** 479–83 (1975) (employees with history of psychiatric prob lems indistinguishable from randomly selected employees in job performance, human relations, and overall ratings); J. Mintz, et al., Treatments of Depression and Functional Capacity to Work, 49 **Arch. Gen. Psychiatry** 761–68 (1992) ("behavioral impairments, including missed time, decreased performance, and significant interpersonal problems are common features of depression that appear to be highly responsive to symptomatically effective treatment given adequate time").

must address "sanist attitudes."[53] Sanism, like racism and sexism, is an irrational prejudice based upon biased attitudes.[54] The disproportionate prominence attached to Title I's "direct threat" language in the media reflects one example of sanist bias.[55]

Despite the low base-rate occurrence of alleged workplace violence by workers with mental disabilities,[56] disability policy and views of employment screening have been influenced in profound ways by negative attitudes toward these individuals.[57] The research model herein is meant to stimulate a body of research that helps employers, policy makers, researchers, the disability community, and others debunk prejudicial attitudes about qualified people with disabilities. It is meant to further the examination of myths and stereotypes about persons with mental retardation, as exemplified in the *Wilson* case, and their relation to emerging issues in Title I compliance and enforcement.

It is possible that nonviolent yet dysfunctional work performance associated with a known mental disability may be accommodated reasonably.[58] Title I cases have recognized as a covered mental disability an employee's inability to function under a diagnosed stress disorder, and the employer's requirement to provide accommodations to enable the qualified employee to function properly on the job.[59] The goal of accommodation is not to further inappropriate and non-job-related workplace behavior, but to provide equal employment opportunity to the qualified employee in ways that ensure a productive work environment.[60]

5.10 Disability Harassment and Retaliation

A growing number of plaintiffs are alleging hostile work environment or disability harassment.[61] As mentioned earlier, approximately 20 percent of ADA employment discrimination charges brought by workers with mental retardation allege disability harassment. Courts addressing the issue have found that hostile

---

[53] Michael L. Perlin, Sanism and the ADA: Thinking About Attitudes, 6 **J. Cal. Alliance Mentally Ill,** at 10–11 (1995); Michael Perlin, The ADA and Persons with Mental Disabilities: Can Sanist Attitudes be Undone?, 8 **J. L. & Health** 15, 20 (1993) (arguing that sanist attitudes dominate discourse about persons with mental illness); Michael L. Perlin, On "Sanism," 46 **S.M.U. L. Rev.** 373 (1992) (same).

[54] *Cf.* George F. Will, Protection for the Personality-Impaired, **Wash. Post,** at A31 (Apr. 4, 1996) (providing an example of "sanism" and arguing that ADA Title I encourages inappropriate behavior in the workplace).

[55] *Cf.* Catherince C. Cobb, Challenging a State Bar's Mental Health Inquiries Under the ADA, 32 **Hous. L. Rev.** 1384 (1996) (examining ADA implications of mental health inquiries routinely included in applications for bar admissions).

[56] *See* Jeffrey W. Swanson, et al., Violence and Psychiatric Disorder in the Community: Evidence from the Epidemiologic Catchment Area Surveys, 41 **Hosp. & Community Psychiatry** 761, 769 (1990) (finding that those with anxiety disorder or affective disorder had similar rates of violence as those with no disorder).

[57] *See* H.R. Rep. No. 485, 101st Cong., 2d Sess., pt 4, at 81, 84 (1990), reprinted in 1990 U.S.C.C.A.N. 267, 564 (members of Congress expressing concern that ADA would provide a shield for mentally unstable people); *Stradley v. LaFourche Communications, Inc.*, 869 F. Supp. 442, 443–44 (E.D. La. 1994) (finding that employer may have regarded employee as having a disability because understood that employee was suffering from acute anxiety and depression and believed that employee's condition made him potentially violent and hostile in the workplace).

[58] *See* **supra Ch. III § 3.5** (discussing mental characteristics and workplace accommodations).

[59] *See Bryant v. Compass Bank*, 1996 U.S. Dist. LEXIS 10137, at 16 (N.D. Ala. S.D. 1996) (employer does not violate Title I when criticizing an employee's work performance as long as the criticism is job-related and not a subterfuge for discrimination, even though employer is aware that criticism may cause additional stress to hypersensitive employee).

[60] Bruce G. Flynn, Violence, Mental Illness and Reasonable Accommodation in the Workplace, 6 **J. Cal. Alliance Ment. Ill** 13–16 (1995).

[61] *See* Jerome L. Holzbauer & Norman L. Berven, Disability Harassment: A New Term for a Long-standing Problem, 74(5) **J. Couns. & Dev.** 478–83 (May 1996) (reviewing behavioral definitions of disability harassment and rise in Title I harassment charges before EEOC); Brian T. McMahon, et al., An Empirical Analysis: Employment and Disability from an ADA Litigation Perspective, 10 **NARPPS J.** 3–14 (1995) (reviewing EEOC charges involving harassment); Frank S. Ravitch, Beyond Reasonable Accommodation: The Availability and Structure of a Cause of Action for Workplace Harassment Under the Americans with Disabilities Act, 15 **Cardozo L. Rev.** 1475 (1994) (analysis of cause of action for disability harassment and hostile environment).

work environment theory and disability harassment claims are actionable under Title I.[62]

In finding that an employer creates a hostile work environment, courts have considered behavioral factors worthy of study, such as the severity, humiliating, and threatening nature of the alleged conduct and whether the conduct interfered with the work performance of a qualified employee.[63] Under a hostile environment or disability harassment theory, Title I would be violated if the employer's behavior discriminated against the qualified employee because of the disability.[64] The relation of prejudicial attitudes about workers with disabilities to subsequent harassment in the workplace is an area worthy of future study and of great practical consequence.

Under the ADA, an employer or other covered entity also may not discriminate against an individual because that individual has brought a charge of employment discrimination.[65] The retaliation provision of the ADA employs the same framework for retaliation claims as does Title VII of the Civil Rights Act.[66] A plaintiff must prove that retaliatory attitudes (i.e., "animus") played a role in the employer's adverse employment decision toward that individual.

In contrast to the prima facie elements that must be proven in an ADA employment discrimination case, a plaintiff in a retaliation case need not establish that he is a "qualified individual with a disability."[67] This is because the ADA expressly protects any individual who has opposed any act or practice of an employer made unlawful by the ADA.

Thus, a person's status as a "qualified individual with a disability" is not relevant in assessing a claim for retaliation under the ADA. In addition, in contrast to the cases discussed in Chapter III, a plaintiff is not disqualified or "judicially estopped" from bringing an ADA retaliation claim because of that individual's prior representations or claims to receive disability insurance benefits (for instance, Social Security Disability Insurance), disability pension benefits, or workers' compensation benefits.[68]

5.11 Summary

ADA Title I prohibits discrimination by employers against qualified individuals with covered disabilities. But Title I is not intended to limit employers in choosing and maintaining a qualified and economically efficient workforce. The ADA does not require that employers create jobs or award job preferences for employees with disabilities. However, the ADA prohibits employers from restricting employment opportunities solely on the basis of stereotypes and myths about persons with disabilities. The following chapters examine many of these myths.

---

[62] *See Bryant,* **supra Ch. V § 5.9,** at 12 (reviewing cases of hostile environment theory under Title I).

[63] *See Harris v. Forklift Sys., Inc.*, 510 U.S. 17 (1993) (conduct must be severe enough that a reasonable person would find it hostile). *See also Miranda v. Wisconsin Power & Light Co.*, 91 F.3d. 1011 (7th Cir. 1996) (claim of constructive discharge from hostile work environment cognizable under Title I); *Gray v. Ameritech*, 937 F. Supp. 762 (N.D. Ill. 1996) (same).

[64] *See* 42 U.S.C. § 12112(a).

[65] 42 U.S.C. § 12203(a).

[66] The analysis depends on whether the suit is characterized as a "pretext suit" or a "mixed motives" suit. For a review of the "pretext analysis," *see Krouse v. American Sterilizer Co.*, 126 F.3d 494 (3d Cir. 1997) (discussing prima facie case and burdens of proof).

[67] *Id.*; *see* **supra Ch. V § 5.2** (discussing required elements of ADA case).

[68] *Cf.* **supra Ch. III § 3.6** (discussing concept of judicial estoppel in ADA cases).

CHAPTER VI

Prior Empirical Study of Employment Integration and ADA Title I

It would be irresponsible if, twenty years [from the enactment of the ADA], we still were not sure whether the social reform sought by the ADA had a positive impact. Indeed, if the legislation is not having the impact intended, we need to know as soon as realistically feasible so that the legislation or its implementation can be corrected or improved.

Frederick Collignon[1]

6.1 Introduction

Prior chapters have provided an overview of the central terms of ADA Title I and their potential impact on persons with mental retardation. The passage of the ADA, like other major civil rights legislation, involved many aspects of the political process. The Act's format reflects the Congressional intent that it be modeled on the Rehabilitation Act of 1973.[2] Yet systematic baseline data were never gathered on the degree of employment integration occurring during the implementation of the Rehabilitation Act. Detailed longitudinal study of the Rehabilitation Act of the kind described in the present investigation therefore is not possible.

At the time of the ADA's passage in 1990, limited study had been conducted on the employment of persons with disabilities.[3] The majority of information available was generated by telephone polling, survey research, and by analysis of U.S. Census Bureau data. Research was required to establish a baseline data set for tracking over time key indicators of Title I implementation. Research in this regard was needed from the perspective of individuals covered by the law and from those required to comply.[4]

---

[1] Frederick C. Collignon, Is the ADA Successful?: Indicators for Tracking Gains, 549 **Annals, supra Ch. IV § 4.4,** 129, 130 (Jan. 1997).

[2] 29 C.F.R. § 1630.1(a) (1991).

[3] *See* Burgdorf, **supra Ch. I § 1.4,** at 415–26 (overview of empirical study).

[4] *See* Collignon, *in* **Annals**, **supra Ch. IV § 4.4,** at 129 (emphasizing the need for collecting baseline data); Corinne Kirchner, Disability Statistics: The Politics and Science of Counting, 4 **J. Disability Pol'y Stud.** 1–7 (1993) (discussing role of disability research and statistics in policy development); Irving K. Zola, Disability Statistics: What We Count and What It Tells Us, 4 **J. Disability Pol'y Stud.** 9–39 (1993) (suggesting multidimensional approach to measuring disability); Harlan Hahn, The Political Implications of Disability Definitions and Data, 4 **J. Disability Pol'y Stud.** 41–52 (1993) (arguing that there is a need for new measures of definition of disability that take into account the interaction of the individual and society).

This chapter highlights the role that empirical information played in the passage of Title I and the continuing need for such information to guide effective implementation. In a 1997 report entitled *Equality of Opportunity: The Making of the Americans wth Disabilities Act*, the National Council on Disability (NCD) presented a history of the enactment of the law.[5] This chapter builds on that effort in discussing empirical study of ADA implementation.

6.2 Empirical Study in Support of the Passage of the ADA

The effort to enact a federal antidiscrimination law to assure the rights of persons with disabilities began formally in 1986 with the publication of a policy and empirically based report by the National Council on the Handicapped (later called the NCD) entitled *Toward Independence*.[6] As part of the report, a nationwide survey was conducted by Harris & Associates involving 1,000 telephone interviews.[7] The stated purpose of the survey "was to obtain data on disabled people's experiences and attitudes that would provide a clear information framework of the NCD's recommendations on public policy for disabled people."[8] This was the first nationwide survey in which people with disabilities were asked about their perceptions of their quality of life.

According to the NCD's interpretation of the 1986 survey findings, "unemployment more than anything else seemed to define disability, and the correlation between employment and life satisfaction cried out for attention."[9] In many ways this statement expresses the rationale for the present longitudinal study of employment integration and economic opportunity under the ADA for persons with mental retardation.

Lex Frieden, staff member at the NCD at the time of the survey, noted: "I doubt that the recommendations in *Toward Independence*, particularly [those regarding] civil rights, would have been taken seriously by the policy makers had we not had the data."[10] The same may be said to be true with regard to the future of effective ADA implementation.

Based in part on the findings from the Harris survey, the NCD's report *Toward Independence* analyzed current federal programs and presented legislative recommendations for enhancing the quality of life of persons with disabilities. The NCD set forth three major policy conclusions from its analysis:[11]

1 approximately two thirds of working-age persons with disabilities did not receive Social Security or other public assistance income;
2 federal disability programs overemphasized income support and underemphasized initiatives for equal opportunity, independence, and prevention; and
3 a need existed for federal programs to assist the private sector in promoting opportunities and independence for individuals with disabilities.

The report included a proposal for a comprehensive antidiscrimination law for people with disabilities.

6.3 The NCD's Findings and the Present Investigation

The NCD's recommendations provide several avenues of analysis relevant to the present investigation. First, the investigation described in this book explores employment integration and economic opportunity over time for a large sample of persons with mental retardation

---

[5] Prepared July 26, 1997, by the National Council on Disability [**hereinafter Equality of Opportunity**]. This document is an excellent historical archive, written for a broad audience, including members of the disability community, policy makers, academics, and others. Little discussion is made, however, on the empirical support underlying the goals of the ADA. For a critical review of the history of the ADA, *see* Thomas F. Burke, On the Rights Track: The Americans with Disabilities Act, *in* **Comparative Disadvantages? Social Regulations and the Global Economy** (Pietro S. Nivola, ed., 1997) (in the absence of data in support, claiming that the ADA has not brought people with disabilities into the labor force).

[6] National Council on the Handicapped, **Toward Independence**, at 18 (1986) [**hereinafter Toward Independence**]; **Toward Independence—Appendix:** Topic Papers (Feb. 1986).

[7] **Equality of Opportunity, supra Ch. VI § 6.1,** at 59.

[8] *Id.* at 59 (*quoting* ICD Executive Director John Wingate).

[9] *Id.* at 60.

[10] *Id.* at 60–61 (*quoting* Frieden).

[11] **Toward Independence**, **supra Ch. VI § 6.2**, at vi–xiii & A-3 (appendix).

before and after ADA Title I implementation. This baseline and follow-up information may help to identify broader policy strategies for reducing dependence on maintenance support programs and enhancing initiatives for equal employment opportunity, independence, and self-sufficiency.

A second goal of the present investigation is to examine ways in which empirical study of the issues may help to support fair, effective, and economically sound employment strategies for qualified individuals with disabilities, consistent with the spirit of the ADA. The framework for assessing the capabilities, qualifications, health status, and other individual measures presented in the research model in Chapter I may help in the development of strategies designed to enhance equal employment opportunities for qualified disabled people and for those who may become disabled in the future.

A third goal of this investigation is to provide information useful in the development of programs important to increasing employment among qualified people with disabilities by enhancing individual and social support related to employment environments (for instance, development of a knowledge base on workplace accommodations), family support strategies, private sector initiatives, and job placement, training, and development programs. As mentioned, only recently has the implementation of the Rehabilitation Act of 1973 been assessed with regard to its indirect impact on the job training and placement of qualified persons with disabilities.

In such studies Professor Frederick Collignon and his associates have examined the earnings of persons with disabilities—primarily those of persons with severe disabilities—who have received job training and vocational rehabilitation services and supports before and after implementation of the Rehabilitation Act.[12] These researchers found positive gains in earnings over time for those receiving job training, adjusting for inflation. Among other reasons, Collignon attributes the income gains of qualified workers with disabilities to the ability to work longer hours.

In his studies Collignon finds also substantial gains in integrated employment opportunities for persons with severe disabilities since 1973. Over time, for instance, individuals with severe disabilities are less likely to be employed in nonintegrated sheltered workshops. Nevertheless, Collignon and others find that over time the real earnings of the individuals—earnings accounting for inflation—were declining due to minimum wage levels in the 1980s that were not adjusted for inflation.

6.4 Aggregating Empirical Information on Employment Integration and ADA Title I

Although the policy recommendations set forth in *Toward Independence* were driven by empirical information, the report concludes that, at least at the time, it was almost impossible to aggregate the available data on persons with disabilities because of differing definitions of disabilities, divergent sources of data, and inconsistent survey methods.[13]

At the time the report was written, existing studies of persons with disabilities primarily involved one of two methodological approaches: a "health conditions" approach that assessed the conditions that impair the health or functioning of an individual,[14] and a "work disability" approach that focused on individual reports and employer interviews about disability.[15] Each approach has strengths and weaknesses. It was difficult, however, to compare the findings of studies using various methodologies.

One of the recommendations in *Toward Independence* was that the U.S. Bureau of Census incorporate questions that assess the numbers and types of persons with disabilities and provide a uniform database for federal

---

[12] *See* Collignon, *in* **Annals**, **Ch. IV § 4.4,** at 146–47 (discussing employment of persons with disabilities).

[13] **Toward Independence**, **supra Ch. VI § 6.2,** at 3.

[14] *Id.* at 3 (health survey of types of problems, but because of medical orientation of such studies, data is limited about such conditions as learning disabilities and mental conditions).

[15] *Id.* at 4 (noting problems with this empirical approach because such studies tend to underestimate the total numbers of people with disabilities, and overestimate the unemployment of people with disabilities).

policy planning and service delivery.[16] *Toward Independence* suggested the need for information on individuals with varying disabilities as compared to individuals without disabilities.[17]

One goal of the present investigation, albeit on a smaller scale than anticipated by the NCD, is to develop a framework for gathering systematically a range of information about persons with mental retardation in employment. A longer-term goal is to compare the resultant database with other analogous data sources that would enable the assessment of persons with and without disabilities in comparable employment on a number of dimensions related to legal, social, and policy questions.

6.5 Empirical Information and the Legislative History of the ADA

The legislative history of the ADA refers to a few studies on the experiences of employers in hiring and accommodating workers with disabilities. In one study the DuPont Corporation conducted a survey of its employees with disabilities and explored managers' perceptions of employees with disabilities on such dimensions as job performance, attendance, and safety.[18]

DuPont found that the job performance, safety records, and attendance of employees with disabilities were comparable to employees without disabilities.[19] Yet in the absence of explicit discussion of research methods and process, it has been difficult for researchers to replicate the DuPont findings and aggregate the findings with those of other studies.

Collignon has suggested a number of methodological issues useful for future aggregation and comparison of findings regarding employment integration and economic growth under Title I.[20] Several such strategies are employed in the present investigation and reflected in the research model illustrated in Chapter I, including the use of:

1. multiple indicators of employment integration and economic growth;
2. multiple indicators of the definition of disability;
3. multiple indicators of background characteristics, individual capabilities and qualifications, and measures of inclusion and empowerment in work and daily life;
4. multiple indicators of attitudes about disability and satisfaction in work and daily life, from self-reported perspectives of the consumers of the law;
5. multiple indicators of health care and medical needs;
6. multiple measures of education and training activities related to the attainment and retention of work;
7. composite measures of independence in living, reflecting an essential component of inclusion and empowerment in work and daily life;[21]
8. composite measures of individual involvement in self-advocacy, legal, and citizenship activities;

---

[16] **Toward Independence** is accompanied by an appendix containing papers on the laws and programs affecting persons with disabilities. One paper is devoted to increasing employment opportunities for persons with disabilities (topic paper B) and relies on census and survey data as the basis of its recommendations (1980 census showed 15.1 million Americans have physical or mental disabilities that prevent them from working; *citing* Vachon (1985) analysis of data from the Social Security Administration's 1978 **Survey of Disability and Work** forecasting a 30 percent increase in the number of work disabled individuals by the year 2000). *See* Mitchell P. LaPlante, Data on Disability from the National Health Interview Survey, 1983–1985, **National Institute on Disability and Rehabilitation Research,** at 2 (1988) (providing data from national estimates from National Health Interview Survey for prevalence of work limitations as a result of disability).

[17] **Toward Independence, supra Ch. VI § 6.2,** at 4. The remainder of the report summarizes statistical information from existing empirical studies of individuals with disabilities. These empirical studies provide a rough profile of the population of individuals with disabilities.

[18] DuPont de Nemours and Company, **Equal to the Task: 1981 DuPont Survey of the Handicapped** (1982).

[19] *See* **Toward Independence**, **supra Ch. VI § 6.2,** at 13.

[20] Collignon, *in* **Annals, supra Ch. IV § 4.4,** at 132–34.

[21] For a review of this area, *see* Robert Bruininks & Charles K. Lakin, eds., **Living and Learning in the Least Restrictive Environment** (1994).

9. changes in measures related to the central goals of Title I implementation, such as self-reported integration in employment and living setting, and tracking of gross and earned income levels; and
10. self-reported perceptions by persons with disabilities of access to employment (Title I issues), to governmental and transportation services (Title II issues), and to public accommodations (Title III issues).

In a comprehensive effort, Professors Robert Schalock and William Kiernan have summarized the central findings of the major studies to date on employment integration before and during ADA implementation.[22] Several conclusions from their work may be drawn with regard to the state of studies on employment integration. Consistent with the core findings drawn from the present investigation summarized in Chapter I and described in detail in the following chapters, there are increasing numbers of qualified persons with disabilities working in integrated employment settings.

6.6 Information from the Harris Polls

As mentioned above, coinciding with the publication of *Toward Independence* in 1986, a nationwide telephone poll of individuals with disabilities was conducted by Harris and Associates.[23] The survey gathered information about how people cope with physical or mental disabilities and the barriers they face in everyday life.[24] No nationwide survey had measured the self-reported impact of disability, what persons with disabilities thought about being disabled, and what actions they believed necessary to enable equal participation in society.[25]

The first Harris survey was based on 1,000 telephone interviews of noninstitutionalized persons with disabilities aged 16 and over. The findings showed that, of those persons interviewed:

1. two thirds were not working;
2. two thirds of those not working would like to have a job;
3. one quarter reported they had encountered job discrimination because of their disabilities;
4. almost half who were not employed or not employed full time said an important reason for this status was that employers would not recognize that they were capable of holding a full-time job because of their disability;
5. one quarter of those not working or working part-time said they do not need adaptive equipment devices or accommodations to help them work or communicate with other workers; and
6. one third of those employed said that their employer made some accommodation for their disability.

In 1988 the NCD summarized the implications for federal policy of the Harris poll findings.[26] Three major suggestions for study were identified, again each consistent with the broader goals of the present project.

First, the NCD recognized the need for studies to document and employ multiple methodologies to develop the criteria for a working definition of "disability" so that findings may be aggregated in the future. In this regard the definition of an individual with a disability covered under Title I was different than that employed by the Harris poll. The Harris poll defined a person as "disabled" if that person (1) had a disability or health problem that prevented participation in major life activities, (2) had a physical, mental, learning or emotional disability, or (3) considered him- or herself to be a disabled person or other people considered him or her disabled. Chapter II discussed the definition of disability under the purview of the ADA.

---

[22] Kiernan & Schalock, **supra Ch. 1 § 1.1,** at 11–12.

[23] **The ICD Survey of Disabled Americans: Bringing Disabled Americans into the Mainstream** (Mar. 1986) (a nationwide telephone survey of 1,000 persons with disabilities) [**hereinafter 1996 Harris Poll**].

[24] *Id.* at i (questions about the impact of disability on quality of life, work, and education).

[25] *Id.* at i–ii (the survey provided measures of persons with disabilities' perceptions of how their life has changed in the past decade, the impact of federal laws designed to enhance opportunities for the disabled, and comparisons between persons with and without disabilities in terms of quality of life, work opportunities, and attitudes about disabilities).

[26] National Council on Disability, **Implications for Federal Policy of the 1986 Harris Survey of Americans with Disabilities** (Nov. 1988).

Second, as mentioned, the NCD stressed the need for the U.S. Bureau of Census and other federal agencies to conduct large-scale demographic studies of persons with disabilities.[27] This investigation contributes to that goal by providing a research framework for sampling demographic and other relevant information for a large sample of persons with mental retardation.

Third, the NCD highlighted the limits of the Harris telephone polling method and urged that future research allow persons with disabilities to speak for themselves on the issues.[28] In building on the approaches of the Harris organization and others who have conducted studies of persons with disabilities, the present investigation explores information derived directly from a group of persons with mental retardation. The present investigation attempts to replicate and extend over time aspects of the Harris surveys with a different sample of persons with disabilities who were interviewed not on the telephone but in person, including a comparison group of institutionalized persons with disabilities.[29]

6.7 Information from the EEOC and Related Data Collection Efforts

Consistent with the emphasis described above, the EEOC has relied on empirical information in reaching its conclusions regarding ADA Title I compliance and enforcement. In one cost-benefit study presented during the Congressional hearings on the passage of the ADA, the EEOC estimated that positive economic effects were likely to result from Title I implementation.[30] The benefits were derived from estimates of the minimal cost to employers of workplace accommodations,[31] and increased productivity gains and tax revenues with corresponding decreased support and social welfare payments from qualified workers with disabilities.[32] Analysis of these issues with regard to recent health care and welfare reform policies are discussed in Chapter XVI of this book.

In its economic analysis, the EEOC estimated the costs to employers for the provision of workplace accommodation to be $16 million. The EEOC estimated productivity gains resulting from the provision of effective workplace accommodations to be at more than $164 million, with decreased support payments and increased tax revenue at an additional $222 million. The EEOC concluded that the estimated lost benefits could exceed $400 million.

In other studies the EEOC estimated the magnitude of the potential wages of qualified employees with disabilities. In relying on its own studies and those of others, the EEOC predicted that the real wages of employees with disabilities (that is, those adjusted for inflation) were only 71 percent of nondisabled employees with a comparable education.[33] These wage disparities grew substantially when comparisons

---

[27] *Id.* at 11–12 (suggesting limited census data on persons with disabilities and call for Census Bureau and other federal agencies to develop information on persons with disabilities by including questions to identify numbers and geographic distribution).

[28] *Id.* at 53–58 (recognizing the methodological limitations, including nonrepresentativeness of sample and small sample size, failure to use Telecommunication Devices for the Deaf (TDDs), high rate of responses by proxies (17 percent of the interviews not conducted with the person with a disability but with member of the household), and lack of observations of actual behavior).

[29] *Id.* at 60 (calling for research on persons with disabilities living in institutional and community settings).

[30] The EEOC acknowledges the scarcity of relevant data for the development of an "ideal" application of a cost-benefit analysis. *See* 29 C.F.R. § 1630.2 (preliminary regulatory impact analysis).

[31] 56 Fed. Reg. 8583 (concluding the cost of most accommodations will be minimal, *citing* **Equal to the Task: 1981 DuPont Survey of Employment of the Handicapped** 17–18 (1982), concluding that more than 80 percent of all accommodations may cost less than $500; **A Study of Accommodations Provided to Handicapped Employees by Federal Contractors, Vol. 1: Study Findings,** Berkeley Planning Associates for the U.S. Dept. Labor, Employment Standards Administration, at 29 (June 17, 1982); and that only 35 percent of workers require accommodation); 56 Fed. Reg. 8584 (*citing* Finnegan, Reuter, & Taff, **The Costs and Benefits Associated with the Americans with Disabilities Act,** at 38 (Sept. 11, 1989) (estimated average cost of accommodations $200, and 50 percent of accommodations require no cost)).

[32] 56 Fed. Reg. 8579.

[33] 56 Fed. Reg. 8581 (*citing* Haveman & Wolfe, The Economic Well-being of the Disabled, 1962–1984, 25 **J. Hum. Resources** 32–54 (1990); Johnson & Lambrinos, Employment Discrimination, **Society** 47–50 (Mar.–Apr. 1983)).

were made of individuals with lower educational levels.[34] One study cited during the Congressional hearings on the ADA estimated that 35 percent of the difference between the real wages of persons with and without disabilities was due to discrimination.[35]

In recent studies Professor Marjorie Baldwin and her colleagues have examined the potential economic benefits of ADA Title I on the real wages and employment opportunities for more than 25,000 persons with disabilities.[36] Baldwin finds that men and women with disabilities experience discrimination in access to employment and with regard to their earnings capacity.

Baldwin finds that the annual economic losses estimated to be attributed to discrimination against workers with disabilities is a staggering $37 billion. Of this amount Baldwin estimates that $27 billion in annual economic losses are related to employment discrimination and $10 billion to discriminatory wages. Baldwin's analysis provides an important framework in which to assess the true economic impact of effective ADA implementation, a topic that is revisited in the final chapters of this book.

6.8 A Renewed Call for Research

In 1988 the NCD issued *On the Threshold of Independence*, its report on the progress that had been made in implementing the Council's recommendations in *Toward Independence*.[37] The 1988 report described progress in relation to the previous legislative recommendations, relying on data from the U.S. Census Bureau, various national data banks, and the prior Harris surveys as support for the need for a comprehensive federal antidiscrimination disability law.[38]

The bulk of the information relied on in *On the Threshold of Independence* was data compilations on the incidence and prevalence of disability.[39] Though these sources were important, the NCD appeared most influenced in its policy recommendations by the Harris surveys.[40] The idea for the Harris surveys evolved from the NCD's expressed frustration with the lack of data regarding the status and opinions of persons with disabilities.[41]

In 1996 the NCD issued a report, *Achieving Independence: The Challenge for the 21st Century*, on the progress that had been made in the prior decade in implementing the NCD's recommendations in the area of disability policy.[42] Once again, a primary recommendation was the need for interdisciplinary, multimethod, and longitudinal study of people with disabilities. The NCD concluded that disability policy and the implementation of disability-related laws to date have been limited by a lack of study of people with disabilities. The NCD wrote:

> Regular reporting of statistics, such as employment rates, will promote policy development, implementation and public understanding. Without such data, people with disabilities and policy makers are unable to accurately assess the nation's progress in meeting the goals of the ADA and achieving independence for people with disabilities.[43]

---

[34] *Id.* (employees with disabilities with less than 12 years of education earned less than one third earned by employees without disabilities).

[35] *Id.* (*citing* Johnson & Lambrinos, Employment Discrimination, **Society** 47–50 (Mar.–Apr. 1983)).

[36] Marjorie L. Baldwin, Estimating the Potential Benefits of the ADA on the Wages and Employment of Persons with Disabilities, **Obermann ADA Seminar Paper** (1997).

[37] National Council on the Handicapped, **On the Threshold of Independence** (A. Farbman, ed., 1988) (progress on legislative recommendations from **Toward Independence**).

[38] *Id.* at 9–18, 23 (*citing* Census Bureau Study, Disability, Functional Limitation and Health Insurance Coverage: 1984/85 (Dec. 1986)). In 1988, the Social Security Administration concluded in a study that SSA and other social programs supporting the estimated 43 million Americans with disabilities cost the taxpayers $46.3 billion annually.

[39] **On the Threshold of Independence**, **supra Ch. VI § 6.8,** at 10 (*citing* Digest of Data on Persons with Disabilities, The Compilation of Statistical Sources on Adult Disability, and The Summary of Data on Handicapped Children and Youth).

[40] *Id.* at 11. *See also* Arlene Mayerson The Americans with Disabilities Act—An Historic Overview, 7 **Lab. Law.** 1, 4–5 (Winter 1991).

[41] **On the Threshold of Independence**, **supra Ch. VI § 6.8,** at 11.

[42] National Council on Disability, **Achieving Independence: The Challenge for the 21st Century—A Decade of Progress in Disability Policy, Setting an Agenda for the Future** (July 26, 1996) [**hereinafter Achieving Independence**].

[43] *Id.* at 6.

In 1997 the NCD issued *National Disability Policy: A Progress Report*, which provides an update on the progress made in advancing the recommendations set forth in *Achieving Independence*.[44] The report identifies several data collection and statistical activities that occurred during and since the preparation of *Achieving Independence*, which are central to empirical assessment of the labor force participation of people with disabilities and ADA implementation.

First, a multiagency working group was established—with participation from federal agencies with expertise in disability policy such as the National Institute on Disability and Rehabilitation Research at the U.S. Department of Education—to collaborate with the U.S. Census Bureau and the Bureau of Labor Statistics to develop new questions to measure disability status for Census 2000 and the Current Population Survey. The questions ask about a broader range of functional limitations—for instance, about many of the major life activities defined by the ADA[45]—and deemphasize the link between disability and the presumption toward an individual's inability to work.

Second, the Bureau of Labor Statistics, in collaboration with other federal agencies with disability expertise, has begun to reexamine and articulate the assumptions underlying its disability data collection efforts. Consistent with the approach discussed in Chapter VIII of this book, Bureau of Labor Statistics data collection activities are being refocused toward a post-ADA multidisciplinary view of disability.[46] This approach focuses on individual, societal, and environmental barriers to equal participation in employment and society. It focuses also on the development of measures to assess the nation's goals for the inclusion and empowerment of people with disabilities as articulated in the ADA.

6.9 Summary

This chapter and those that follow explore ways to examine systematically emerging trends in equal employment for a large sample of persons with mental retardation. This chapter has highlighted the role of empirical study in the development and interpretation of disability law and policy. Additional study is warranted, given the ADA is in its initial implementation period. For analysis by policy makers and others, baseline information must be collected on employees with various disabilities and comparable employees without disabilities.

This line of study is required to assess the economic implications associated with effective implementation of the ADA and of related antidiscrimination laws and policy. Professor Dana Gilmore and her colleagues have argued that "[t]he lack of a comprehensive, nationally based employment data system has hampered efforts to document fully the movement of persons with disabilities into integrated employment."[47] The chapters following in Part 3 describe the present investigation's process for studying employment integration and economic opportunity during early ADA implementation for the participants with mental retardation.

---

[44] National Council on Disability, **National Disability Policy: A Progress Report, July 26, 1996–October 31, 1997** (Oct. 31, 1997) [**hereinafter National Disability Policy**].

[45] *See* **supra Ch. II § 2.6** (discussing ADA definition of major life activities).

[46] *See* **supra Ch. VIII § 8.5** (discussing data collection assumptions in the present research model and empirical investigation); *see also* **supra Ch. VII §§ 7.4 & 7.5** (discussing collaborative approach to data collection and empirical investigation of employment of persons with disabilities).

[47] Dana S. Gilmore, Robert L. Schalock, William E. Kiernan, & John Butterworth, National Comparisons and Critical Findings in Integrated Employment 49, *in* **Integrated Employment, supra Ch. I § 1.1.**

PART III:

The Investigation's Methods and Research Model

CHAPTER VII

The Present Investigation's "Process of Study"

I think there is a big difference between the gathering of data and the implementation and use of that data...[W]e had better start looking at the effects of the Americans with Disabilities Act, and we had better start evaluating the ADA in light of the numbers and costs and so on.

Paul Hearne[1]

7.1 Introduction

Prior chapters have examined the central provisions of the ADA and empirical information on which the passage of the law was based. The chapters in this part discuss the process by which the present investigation explores employment integration during initial ADA implementation.

The discussion in this chapter and the next is detailed, for several reasons. First, as the NCD has concluded in its reports, it is becoming increasingly important for social, behavioral, legal, and medical researchers to articulate their philosophy and methods of study of persons with disabilities.[2] Although questions have been raised about the social and economic impact of ADA implementation, at this point few answers to such questions are based on facts from actual consumers of the law.

Second, as the NCD and other bodies have recognized, there is an absence of description of the methods on which the empirical bases underlying disability-related research rest. The bulk of the information to date about the employment-related issues have been generated from telephone surveys or aggregate census data and not from face-to-face contact with research participants. The Harris and National Organization on Disability surveys described in Chapter VI remain some of the most comprehensive national polls of persons with disabilities and their employers. Insufficient study has been conducted on the longitudinal assessment of the lives of persons with disabilities.

Third, attention must be directed toward the processes that social scientists and policy makers will employ in the coming years in studying the behavior and economic and social status of persons with disabilities. Professor Donald Campbell, in his classic article "Reforms as Experiments," writes:

> Many of the difficulties [in the analysis of the effectiveness of social programs such as the

---

[1] Paul Hearne, President Dole Foundation, Remarks on the Uses of Disability Statistics, Disability Forum Report, **The Future of Disability Statistics: Proceedings of the First Policy Forum** 17 (Mar. 1996).

[2] Peter David Blanck, The "Process" of Field Research in the Courtroom, 11 **Law & Hum. Behav.** 337 (1987) (in other contexts, the Supreme Court has highlighted this need by emphasizing the value and legal relevance of studying real-world behavior).

> ADA] lies in the intransigences of the research setting and in the presence of recurrent seductive pitfalls of interpretation....What is essential [sic] is that the social scientist research advisor understand the political realities of the situation, and that he aid by helping create a public demand for hard-headed evaluation, by contributing to those political inventions that reduce the liability of honest evaluation, and by educating future administrators to the problems and possibilities.[3]

This chapter makes explicit the methods used in the present investigation.[4] It is not intended as a handbook or manual about how to conduct research on disability. More study is needed in the communities, homes, and workplaces of persons with disabilities. This chapter reflects on the experience of managing that undertaking.

Nevertheless, description of the present research process is not hard-and-fast about how to conduct study. Nor is it meant to substitute for practical learning gained from first-hand evaluation research experience. The process of study does not lend itself to such a check-list of such principles. Rather, the complexities of study often are best understood upon description of reflection of such undertakings.[5]

7.2 The Research "Process"

The emphasis on making explicit research methods is as old as social science study itself. With regard to the impact of social science research on policy making, however, these ideas were expressed with increasing frequency at the turn of the last century by legal and social science scholars.[6] As these early scholars have written, research method sometimes is difficult to divorce from policy goals, particularly when study of new social and legal reform issues are involved.[7] Understanding these relationships furthers appreciation of the implications of research on social reform policies, such as the ADA.

The present investigation documents how the policies and legal requirements set forth in the ADA may help to eliminate discrimination against qualified persons with disabilities in aspects of their employment and daily lives. This approach may be contrasted with that of those who suggest, without reliance on any data, that the ADA has resulted in economic burdens for employers trying to comply with the law.[8]

Social scientists and policy makers have recognized that description of the process of research study aids in program evaluation of social reform legislation.[9] To date, little has been said by legal scholars and policy makers concerning the process of studying the legal and social reforms embodied in the ADA.

Derek Bok, the former president of Harvard University and former dean of its law school, has commented that "[e]ven the most rudimen-

---

[3] Campbell, **supra Ch. I § 1.1,** at 409.

[4] The investigation examines process of study through interviews with research team members. Interviews cited are with Dennis Bean, project director for the State of Oklahoma Developmental Disabilities Services Division, Apr. 3, 1991; Professor Lynn Atkinson, project manager, Apr. 8, 1991; Yolanda Dow, project manager, interviewer and quality assurance coordinator, Apr. 11, 1991; Dan Broughton, developmental disabilities project administrator, June 29, 1991 [**hereinafter Bean, Atkinson, Dow, or Broughton Interview**]. For discussion of this method, *see* D.C. Hagner & S.T. Murphy, Closing the Shop on Sheltered Work: Case Studies of Organizational Change, 55(3) **J. Rehabilitation** 68, 69 (1989) (noting that interview method focuses on understanding experiences and perspectives of people).

[5] *See* William F. Whyte, **Street Corner Society** (3d ed. 1981) (classic description of field study).

[6] Professor Llewellyn, in his famous passage, has described the importance of this approach as the "temporary divorce of Is and Ought for purposes of study." Karl Llewellyn, Some Realism About Realism—Responding to Dean Pound, 44 **Harv. L. Rev.** 1222 (1931).

[7] *See* Peter David Blanck, ed., **Interpersonal Expectations: Theory, Research, and Applications** (1992) (importance of expectancy effects in determining social and research outcomes); David L. Faigman, To Have and Have Not: Assessing the Value of Social Science to the Law as Science and Policy, 38 **Emory L. J.** 1005, 1026–27 (1989) (understanding potential bias of social science research is crucial).

[8] *See* Thomas Barnard, The Americans with Disabilities Act: Nightmare for Employers and Dream for Lawyers?, 64 **St. Johns L. Rev.** 229 (1990) (*citing* Harris polls). *See generally* **infra Chs. XIII & XIV** (discussing myths about ADA implementation).

[9] *See* **infra Ch. XIV § 14.5** (discussing study of unintended economic benefits of the ADA).

tary facts about the legal system are unknown or misunderstood."[10] Professor Michael Saks, a leading proponent of empirical study of law and policy, writes: "A major part of the problem is that the legal system has no systematic methodology for producing knowledge about its task or about how well it is accomplishing that task."[11]

This chapter is meant to help advance discussion of research process with regard to the analysis of the ADA. It points out the strengths and limitations of the present project, which may help to foster the replication of the research before confident generalizations may be applied to other populations of persons with disabilities covered by the law.[12]

One benefit of describing the research process is to gain an understanding of the complex social situation that is impacted by the policy and legal processes associated with ADA implementation.[13] Description may prove helpful in clarifying the use of empirical information in defining disability or the scope of the reasonable accommodation provision under the ADA. It also may aid in the development of nonlitigious solutions that are helpful to dispel myths about the capabilities of qualified employees with mental retardation.

7.3 Pilot-Testing the Research

The purpose of this investigation is to develop an in-depth view of the employment issues facing the participants with mental retardation against the backdrop of initial ADA implementation. Of particular interest is how description and interpretation vary with the setting and circumstances under study, and with the role of the research team.

After defining the research questions and framework and choosing an array of measuring instruments, the interviewers (primarily trained in social work) ventured into the field to test and refine the process of study. The experience gained from this initial exposure helped in the selection of methods and in gaining the trust and consent required to conduct subsequent phases of the project.

In pilot-testing the questionnaires, surveys, and observational methods for the assessment of the lives of individuals with mental retardation, the research team sought the feedback from the participants, their families, and employers. The team attempted to understand whether the questions asked were understood by the participants.

7.4 Researcher and Participant Collaboration

Many support and direct care staff—those responsible for aiding in the daily needs of many of the participants with mental retardation—did not understand the ways in which their clients may be discriminated against because of their disabilities.[14] Aides responded that "this is the way society treats these individuals, and this has always been the case." Or, "it is easier to take clients with mental retardation residing in the institutions to the community in large groups by bus." Many support staff did not understand the meaning of integrated employment opportunity for the participants.

These and other attitudes suggested that the participants and staff may hold different views about discrimination, integration, employability, community accessibility, and other issues related to ADA implementation. One study conducted by Professor Janis Chadsey-Rusch and her colleagues examined beliefs about employment and social integration from the perspectives of persons with mental retardation, their job coaches, and their employers—referred to as ADA "stakeholders."[15] Their findings showed disagreement by the stakeholders on

---

[10] Derek Bok, Report to the Harvard Board of Overseers 1981–82, *reprinted in* Bok, A Flawed System of Law Practice and Training, 33 **J. Legal Educ.** 570, 581 (1983).

[11] Saks, **supra Ch. II § 2.1,** at 808.

[12] Laird W. Heal & Carol K. Sigelman, Methodological Issues in Quality of Life Measurement, *in* **Quality of Life: Vol. I: Conceptualization and Measurement** 91–101 (Robert L. Schalock, ed., 1996) (overview of research process involving persons with mental retardation).

[13] *See* Peter David Blanck & Arthur N. Turner, Gestalt Research: Clinical-Field-Research Approaches to Studying Organizations *in* **Handbook of Organizational Behavior** (J.W. Lorsch, ed., 1987).

[14] **Dow Interview, supra Ch. VII § 7.1.**

[15] Janis Chadsey-Rusch, Dan Linneman, & Billie Jo Rylance, Beliefs About Social Integration from the Perspectives of Persons with Mental Retardation, Job Coaches, and Employers, 102 **J. Mental Retardation** 1–12 (1997).

issues related to employment integration and coworker interaction in the employment setting. These differences in beliefs among the stakeholders require further examination, particularly if they are shown to affect employment integration strategies.

The pilot-testing phase of the present project trained the research interviewers to take the time necessary at each interview to ensure that the participants understood the process. To aid in this learning process, videotapes of initial interview sessions and mock interviews were conducted and reviewed by the research team to standardize the interview process.[16] Throughout the project, retraining of interviewers was conducted and measures were adapted as new experiences or issues were faced by the team.[17]

As part of the initial research phase, the team contacted the participants and families and guardians who would participate in the project. The team explained the project, and emphasized that knowledge was needed about employment-related issues under the ADA for persons with mental retardation. The team stressed that the development of knowledge may be useful to the future implementation of the ADA.

7.5 Developing a Collaborative Research Process

Throughout the initial phase, the researchers approached the project as a collaborative effort. Researchers in the area of mental retardation have explored collaborative research methods.[18] Building on the work of William Kiernan and his associates, Professor Whitney-Thomas has formulated a model for collaboration in the research process involving persons with mental retardation.[19]

Similarly, Professor Tamar Heller and her colleagues have developed guidelines to foster meaningful involvement in research activities for individuals with mental retardation.[20] Consistent with this approach, the present investigation emphasized a collaborative process with special focus on consumer involvement in the refinement of the research protocol, understandable informed consent documents, and a removal of physical and communicative barriers to participation, among other areas.[21]

As part of the collaborative approach, the participants, sometimes through their guardians or others, helped define issues and ensure that the study had personal relevance and meaning. This did not mean that the study was developed in a completely joint manner or that we did not proceed from preformulated hypotheses. Rather, on the basis of pilot-testing and the empirical framework, the investigation's research measures and goals reflected issues affecting the participants. Too often researchers of mental retardation have adopted methodologically "cleaner" investigations that result in the use of ineffectual methods that reduce the usefulness of the findings.[22]

Over time, the research measures were reevaluated to meet the demands of the project and of the participants. Flexibility in research process is crucial in longitudinal projects because the relevant legal, social, and economic issues facing persons with disabilities change over the implementation period of the ADA.

Gaining the ongoing trust and cooperation of

---

[16] *Id.* (actual and videotaped interviews are regularly critiqued by the interview team; this is important for interview and observational methods that required impressionistic ratings by the interviewers).

[17] **Atkinson Interview**, **supra Ch. VII § 7.1** (interviewers kept field notes to share with the research team their experiences; field notes were also kept to document any potentially serious behaviors, such as abusive behaviors, so that they might be transmitted to the proper authorities).

[18] *See* Jean Whitney-Thomas, Participatory Action Research as an Approach to Enhancing Quality of Life for Individuals with Disabilities, in **Quality of Life: Vol. II: Application to Persons with Disabilities** (Robert L. Schalock, ed., 1996), 181–97.

[19] *Id.* at 181–97.

[20] Tamar Heller, Esther Lee Pederson, & Alison B. Miller, Guidelines from the Consumer: Improving Consumer Involvement in Research and Training for Persons with Mental Retardation, 34 **Ment. Retardation** 141–48 (1996).

[21] *Id.* at 141–48 (1996).

[22] **Dow Interview, supra Ch. VII § 7.1** (commenting that it was important for the researchers to learn to roll with the environment and needs of the clients, interview is a dynamic process, important to develop rapport and define terms—e.g., the meaning of employment itself).

the research participants and their families were some of the most challenging aspects of the research.[23] Discussions were conducted with each research participant and employer. The researchers emphasized to the participants that the participants might receive value from the project experience. The researchers explained to the participants that they might receive benefits from the involvement. For many of the participants with mental retardation, this was the first time that they had been asked their opinions about their employment, their living setting, and the quality of the support services received.[24]

Developing a meaningful exchange of information between the participants and research team members reinforced the cooperation required to conduct an investigation of this sort. From a practical point of view, cooperation was crucial, given the necessity to track longitudinally large numbers of participants as they changed residences and jobs. In some cases the research team telephoned family and case workers to find participants, and this raised ethical issues of the degree to which the team should respect the privacy rights of the participants.[25]

One methodological problem, a so-called threat to the "internal validity," was that not all individuals with mental retardation and employers chose to participate. Self-selection problems are part of any large study. Attempts were made to contact and recruit all individuals with mental retardation served by the state, either directly or through their families or guardians. This effort served to reduce potential selection bias within the sample of persons with mental retardation, as a subset of the participants had been class members in a deinstitutionalization lawsuit in the state during the initial period of ADA implementation.[26]

7.6 The "Research Contract"

Before beginning large-scale data collection, the research team explained, in writing, the purpose of the present project in language that would make sense to the participants. This "research contract" documented the researchers' responsibilities to the participants and the participants' responsibilities to the project. The writing was a formal sign of the importance of the project, serving motivational and instructional purposes.

Letters to the participants and their families sent before the study began described the investigation and emphasized that the data would remain confidential and anonymous.[27] The interviewers were made sensitive to the possible stigma within community if information about the participants was leaked to neighbors, potential employers, or others living in the community.

As part of the research contract, the participants completed a consent agreement.[28] The consent agreement stated that participation would involve interviews and data collection about the participants' employment and living situation. It was made clear that research participation was completely voluntary. This statement was important, given that many of the participants with mental retardation relied on the state for services and an appearance of coercion to participate was to be avoided.[29]

---

[23] For classic description of this issues, R.L. Kahn & F. Mann, Developing Research Partnerships, 8(3) **J. Soc. Issues** 4–10 (1952). *See also* **Dow Interview, supra Ch. VII § 7.1** (noting need to get your foot in the door, important not to threaten the clients, or the staff, for instance, in terms of threat to their job).

[24] *Id.* (Noting that some of the participants were completely nonverbal and nobody had ever taken the time to ask their opinion of their surroundings).

[25] **Atkinson Interview, supra Ch. VII § 7.1** (describing the need to track telephone numbers of participants, relatives, and case workers).

[26] *See* James W. Conroy, Letter to Dennis Bean, director of Oklahoma Quality Assurance for the Human Services Division of Developmental Disabilities (May 1, 1997) (describing how the data collection effort was directed toward all individuals with mental retardation in the state).

[27] **Dow Interview, supra Ch. VII § 7.1** (noting that the interviewers were expected and did not show up and surprise the participants); **Atkinson Interview, supra Ch. VII § 7.1** (noting that the letter stated that the research team would be contacting the participants, and what information would be asked of them).

[28] **Bean Interview, supra Ch. VII § 7.1** (describing that the consent agreement was primarily for consent for the research team to publish, in aggregate form, the results of the project; and that in subsequent years of the project consent for a service audit became a part of provider contract with the state DDSD and a condition of their state funding, raising ethical concerns for the research team).

[29] The agreement stated expressly that "there is no penalty for refusal to participate." *See* Conroy & Bradley, **supra Ch. I § 1.1,** at 120–21 (ethical issues associated with this type of research).

Individuals were assured that refusal to participate would involve no penalty or loss of benefits to which the individuals were entitled. Research participation could be discontinued at any time and the consent form listed contact addresses and phone numbers so that participants could discuss problems that might arise. The project representative verified in writing to each participant that the elements of the consent form had been explained to each participant.

Where appropriate, the consent agreement was witnessed or signed by an advocate or guardian for the participant. Each participant or a guardian received a copy of the consent agreement. During the 1990 baseline year, approximately 10 out of 1,900 individuals with mental retardation did not agree to participate in the project, indicating the reason for not participating related to their privacy rights.[30]

The research contract became an expression of the researcher's respect for the integrity of the participants in their living setting and of the participants' commitment to the project. For the researchers, this meant the relative freedom to collect information and communicate findings; for the participants, it meant freedom to pursue their lives unencumbered.[31]

7.7 Ethical Considerations

Ethical decisions confronted the research team at every stage of the project. Ethical and legal considerations were made explicit via the research contract. Emphasis was placed on the ethical principle of respect for participants, requiring actions by the team that fostered the autonomy, integrity, privacy, and dignity of individuals.[32] The research contract and informed consent agreements reinforced the view that participants were entitled to make their own decisions on matters affecting their lives.

Because of the sensitive nature of the issues under study, the goal was to avoid harm or embarrassment to any participant, under conditions of complete informed consent. Interviews with persons with mental retardation were conducted in a private room or setting, under quiet conditions.

The research process involved taking steps to safeguard the welfare, rights, and privacy of the participants.[33] In the past the rights of individuals with mental retardation as research participants have received little attention in the research context.[34] Despite the precautionary measures, ethical issues remained throughout the study. Issues included such factors as what constituted valid and informed consent for persons with mental retardation without advocates or guardians or with severe disabilities.[35]

The present investigation followed the

---

[30] **Bean Interview, supra Ch. VII § 7.1** (noting high level of individual support and participation); **Atkinson Interview, supra Ch. VII § 7.1** (noting less emphasis on consent issues over time and more emphasis on quality of services and monitoring of services).

[31] *See* Leonard Schatzman & Anselm L. Strauss, **Field Research: Strategies for a Natural Sociology,** at 29 (1973).

[32] American Psychological Association (APA), Ethical Principles of Psychologists, 36 **Amer. Psychologist** 633–38 (1981) (Principle 9); Thomas Grisso, Elizabeth Baldwin, Peter David Blanck, & Mary Jane Borus-Rotheram, Standards in Research, 46 **Amer. Psychologist** 758–66 (1991); Herbert C. Kelman, Privacy and Research with Human Beings, 33(3) **J. Soc. Issues** 169– 95 (1977).

[33] *Cf.* Conroy & Bradley, **supra Ch. I § 1.1,** at 121 (noting in the past that people living in institutional settings have been part of studies that never would have been approved if the participants had not been labeled mentally retarded).

[34] *See* Federal Guidelines for the Protection of Human Subjects, 45 C.F.R. § 46 (1983) (Health and Human Services guidelines). The guidelines cover three categories of research activities, depending upon the level of risk involved, including data collection (1) from existing data, documents that are not publicly available, where individual participants are not used directly in the gathering of information; (2) which involved minimal risk to the participants, such as through interviews, observation or surveys (minimal risk means potential harms from the research are not greater than those ordinarily encountered in daily life or during the performance of routine physical or psychological examinations or tests); and (3) which involves risks to the participants that are greater than those encountered from customary everyday activities, such as any from medical procedures or physical body intrusion.

[35] **Dow Interview, supra Ch. VII § 7.1** (noting that the interviewers described confidential information as that which will be kept "secret" and not told to others). *See also* Conroy & Bradley, **supra Ch. I § 1.1,** at 120.

approach for addressing ethical issues in research involving persons with mental retardation set forth by the work of James Conroy and Valerie Bradley in the *Pennhurst Longitudinal Study.* Individuals were included in the present project if:

1. the individual or his or her representative stated explicitly that he was willing to be interviewed or observed;
2. the individual appeared to be capable of responding (either him or herself or through an aide);
3. the individual was judged not to be at risk of any harm by the study; and
4. the individual or a representative signed the consent agreement.

7.8 Data Gathering, Reporting Findings, and Dissemination

The next chapter describes in detail the data collection and data organization processes. The methods employed in the investigation included the use of surveys, questionnaires and interviews, and general observation techniques.

Surveys, questionnaires, and interviews conducted in person and by mail were employed to gather data. Graduate and undergraduate students were hired to interview the participants. The interviews lasted approximately 40 to 50 minutes and employed structured questions, with such questions requiring a set of responses (such as reported satisfaction with services provided), and open-ended questions, in which the participants are able to expand on the directive questions.

Many participants supplemented the structured question format, providing important views. Questions that did not seem to allow participants to answer in their own words generated little interest or motivation to reply thoughtfully.

Where appropriate, communication assistance devices were employed so that participants with verbal disabilities could interact directly with the interviewer. Interviewers or staff employed sign language to communicate with nonverbal participants. In one instance, a participant with moderate mental retardation had developed a language of her own that only her roommate of 18 years understood; in that case, the roommate acted as interpreter for the research interviewer. Because many of the participants are nonverbal, in some instances interview responses may more accurately reflect the views of the interviewers than that of the participants.[36]

Observational methods were used to assess the physical quality of the participants' environment.[37] The researchers were trained to collect observational data on the physical quality and accessibility of the living settings. An ethical justification for proceeding with caution when observing participants relates to their privacy rights. Some observations provided information that was considered personal by the participants or their families. For this reason, physical quality and accessibility observational ratings were not regularly recorded in family home settings, where unsupervised observation into the family home was thought to be intrusive.

Many observations were made of the participants' living areas at the invitation of the participants. The research team followed the ethical principles of the right to privacy and complete informed consent in these situations. The observational data gathering techniques were made flexible to meet the needs of the participants and of the project.[38] The research process involved assessment of a particular data collection method in terms of informational accessibility, accuracy and relevance, economy of resources, and ethical considerations.

After data was gathered, data confidentiality, usefulness and clearance considerations remained. Among the related issues, researchers considered the proper subsequent use of the

---

[36] *See* Conroy & Bradley, **supra Ch. I § 1.1,** at 119 (citing studies that individuals with mental retardation often have difficulty in expressing themselves in a consistent fashion).

[37] *See* Steven J. Taylor & Robert Bogdan, **Observing Community Residences,** Center on Human Policy Monographs, Syracuse Univer. (1991) (guide to observe and monitor residences).

[38] *See, e.g.,* Eugene J. Webb, Donald T. Campbell, Richard D. Schwartz, & Lee Seachrest, **Unobtrusive Measures: Nonreactive Research in the Social Sciences** (1966) (discussing field research methods).

database in decisions involving service delivery or employment opportunity for persons with mental retardation.[39] Protecting the confidentiality of the participants required excising certain identifying information from the questionnaire and observational and interview data.[40] The research contract helped to clarify who would have access to the information.

The research findings were made available, prior to their publication, to the participants and to the relevant state agency. This was done as a check on validity of the findings, to obtain final clearance for publication, to check for errors of fact, and to disguise information that could be harmful if published in an undisguised form. The research team provides a yearly summary report on the findings of the investigation to the participants.

7.9 Summary

This chapter described the research process in this investigation. It highlighted the importance of making explicit the research methods on which the investigation rests so that others studying these issues may better assess the foundation on which the findings are based.

---

[39] *See* Peter David Blanck & Mollie Weighner Marti, Genetic Discrimination and the Employment Provisions of the Americans with Disabilities Act: Emerging Legal, Empirical, and Policy Implications, 14 **Behav. Sci. & L.** 411–32 (1996); **Bean Interview, supra Ch. VII § 7.1** (noting meetings with providers to share information, provide feedback and retain interest in the project).

[40] **Dow Interview, supra Ch. VII § 7.1** (noting how names and identifying information were stricken from the data and identification numbers left).

CHAPTER VIII

Participants, Data Sources, and the Research Model

Future generations will look back on the passage of the ADA as a watershed public policy. Now is the time to preserve a record about the creation and passage of this historic, landmark legislation.

Marca Bristo & Gerben DeJong[1]

There is a relationship between data needs and statistical policy at both the theoretical and applied levels.... We also need integrated data sets that combine health, economic, and social measurements and the individual and environmental levels.... What I am urging is that it would be more profitable for disability research and policy to have a survey that could simultaneously cover many of these areas.

Mitchell LaPlante [2]

8.1 Introduction

This chapter presents information on the investigation's participants, data sources, and development of the research model set forth in Figure 1.1. The model identifies measures to be studied to achieve a systematic understanding of employment integration and economic opportunity during ADA implementation.

The research process focuses on the participants' views and attitudes concerning their living arrangements, employment, and other aspects central to their lives. As discussed in the prior chapter, an important goal of the present investigation is to highlight the collaborative research process between the researchers and the participants with mental retardation. As Professor Tamar Heller and her colleagues have written: "Individuals with mental retardation often have profound insights related to their lives that add valuable contributions to research and training activities."[3]

8.2 The Research Participants

Prior chapters have stated the central purpose of this investigation: to explore the lives and experiences of citizens with mental

[1] Marca Bristo & Gerben DeJong, **Equality of Opportunity: The Making of the Americans with Disabilities Act,** at xv (July 26, 1997).

[2] **Disability Report Forum, The Future of Disability Statistics: Proceedings of the First Policy Forum**. Remarks by Mitchell P. LaPlante, at 3 & 7 (Mar. 1997).

[3] *See* Tamar Heller, Esther Lee Pederson, & Alison B. Miller, Guidelines from the Consumer: Improving Consumer Involvement in Research and Training for Persons with Mental Retardation, 34 **Mental Retardation** 141–48 (1996).

retardation during the early implementation period of the ADA. The research activities include the collection of information that may enhance integrated employment opportunities for "qualified" persons with mental retardation.[4]

The study involves more than 5,000 adults and children with mental retardation residing in various living arrangements in Oklahoma.[5] Many of these individuals have physical disabilities. In 1990 of the roughly 1,400 adult participants, approximately two thirds (67 percent) lived in institutions and one third (33 percent) lived in community settings around the state. Analysis of these participants who were residing in the community shows that 19 percent lived in family or foster homes, 75 percent in group homes, and 6 percent in independent living.

In 1996, of the roughly 3,000 adult participants who were assessed, approximately half (52 percent) lived in institutional settings and half (48 percent) in the community. Of those living in the community in 1996, 7 percent resided in family or foster homes, 46 percent in group homes, and 46 percent in independent living (representing an almost eightfold increase in this category from 1990).[6]

Prior to the development of the present investigation, in 1985 one of the three large state-run institutions in Oklahoma for persons with mental retardation (The Hissom Center) was the subject of a deinstitutionalization lawsuit mandating the placement of residents into community settings.[7] The case, *Homeward Bound v. Hissom,*[8] was brought by a group of parents whose relatives resided at the institution.

The *Hissom* litigation eventually led to a settlement between the plaintiffs and the state to close the institution in May 1994 and to place its approximately 350 to 400 residents in community settings.[9] The present investigation is based on information collected from all persons with mental retardation served in the State of Oklahoma.

8.3 Data Organization for the Present Investigation

The data in this investigation are arrayed by the participants' type and degree of integration in employment and in living arrangement. For purposes of analysis, the data are organized into four types of employment involvement, ranging from less to more integrated types of employment involvement:[10]

1. *No employment*—no actual employment and minimal employment training.
2. *Sheltered employment*—program of work or work-related training. Jobs are primarily in nonintegrated group settings, including trash pick-up, greenhouse work, and pamphlet folding. Wages are paid but they are usually half of the minimum wage.[11]
3. *Supported employment*—individual job placement supported by a job coach, at least minimum wages are paid. Job coaches' responsibilities include job placement, job training, skills assessment, and assistance in

---

[4] *Cf.* Conroy & Bradley, **supra Ch. I § 1.1** (Pennhurst Longitudinal Study involving persons with mental retardation during the process of court-ordered deinstitutionalization).

[5] For purposes of the analyses, an adult was defined as an individual 18 years of age or over.

[6] These trends in living arrangement as assessed between the years 1990 and 1996 involve cross-sectional analyses. *Cf.* Figure 9.8 **infra Ch. IX** (displaying findings for the longitudinal analysis of living arrangement for the same 952 participants assessed in 1990 and again in 1996).

[7] For an overview, *see* David L. Braddock, et al., **The State of the States in Developmental Disabilities** (1998) (discussing statistics about developmental disabilities).

[8] *Homeward Bound v. Hissom*, 963 F.2d 1352 (10th Cir. 1987).

[9] For review of the Hissom litigation and its results, *see* Conroy, **The Hissom Outcomes Study, supra Ch. I § 1.6,** at 1–3.

[10] *Cf.* 34 C.F.R. § 252, 254 Ch. III (7-1-88 Edition), Part 363—The State Supported Employment Services Program. (HBC Waiver Program—§ 1915(c) of the Social Security Act as part of the Omnibus Budget Reconciliation Act of 1981 (§ 2176, Pub. L. No. 97-35).

[11] **Dow Interview, supra Ch. VII 7.1.** *See also* **Toward Independence, supra Ch. VI § 6.2,** at B-75–B-76 (appendix). (sheltered employment as non-competitive and nonintegrated work setting). Most sheltered workshops provide vocational and rehabilitation services such as evaluation, training, and placement services. *Id.* at B-81. Sheltered workshops are allowed under the Fair Labor Standards Act to pay persons with disabilities at a lower rate than the statutory minimum wage (but not less than 50 percent of minimum wage unless specifically exempted).

job retention.[12] Support services involve coaching and training provided at the worksite and accommodations provided at or away from work, such as transportation, PAS, and family counseling.[13] Many employment-related services in Oklahoma are supported by the Medicaid home and community-based waiver program (HBC Waiver Program). These services include prevocational services, assistive and adaptive equipment, transportation, case management, and therapy services. According to studies by Kregel and Wehman, in 1993 approximately 70 percent of supported employment participants are persons with mental retardation, up from 63 percent in 1991.[14]

4. *Competitive employment*—job placement is made primarily without the services of a job coach, at least minimum wages are paid for full- or part-time work in settings where most coworkers are not disabled and individuals with disabilities are not part of a work group of individuals with disabilities. Competitive employment is found in private industry where a worker with a disability is independent of any support services.[15]

The present investigation also gathers information about the participants' living arrangements that are arranged from less to more integrated as follows:[16]

1. *Institutional residences*—residence in the three state-run facilities. Professor Braddock and his colleagues have found that by the year 1992, 52 percent of the 347,000 persons with developmental disabilities in residential settings lived with 15 or fewer residents;[17]
2. *Family homes*—residence in birth home, a relative's home, or in an adult companion home, such as in a foster care arrangement;
3. *Group homes*—residence with 4 to 12 other adults with mental retardation (average number, 6 residents) living in a structured setting, receiving varying levels of program support from state and private agencies; and
4. *Semi-independent/supported living homes*—residence in own home individually or with one roommate, and receiving varying levels of program support from state and private agencies.

8.4 Data Instruments

The data instruments are designed to explore the needs, behavior, and attitudes of the participants with mental retardation (see Figure 1.1, for model display) and include measures of:

1. adaptive equipment needs;
2. adaptive behavior and job skill scores;
3. general medical needs;
4. financial information, citizenship, and advocacy;
5. service planning and delivery;
6. consumer satisfaction with employment and daily living services; and
7. accessibility in living and community settings and physical quality of settings.

Adaptive Equipment Needs[18]

This measure explores physical equipment aids that are needed or used by the participants in their employment settings. The physical equipment needs assessed included wheelchairs, walkers, braces or canes, and communication

---

[12] **Dow Interview, supra Ch. VII § 7.1** (job coaches start one-on-one with the client—e.g., teaching food preparation—and fade out allowing the client to develop independent work skills). *See* **Toward Independence, supra Ch. VI § 6.2,** at B-30 (appendix) (discussion of supported work program approach).

[13] *See* The Federal Office of Special Education and Rehabilitative Services (OSERS, 5/12/88 Final Regulations); *see also* The Developmental Disabilities Assistance and Bill of Rights Act, **Pub. L.** 101-496, § 102(14).

[14] John Kregel & Paul Wehman, Supported Employment: A Decade of Employment Outcomes for Individuals with Disabilities, *in* **Integrated Employment, supra Ch. I § 1.3,** at 37.

[15] *See* Robert L. Schalock & William E. Kiernan, How We Got to Where We Are, *in* **Integrated Employment, supra Ch. I § 1.3**, at 5.

[16] Although the conceptual ordering of the living arrangements were determined through interviews with the research participants, living arrangements within a category may vary in its degree of integration.

[17] The present sample included individuals residing in private ICF-MRs. For a review of national demographics, *see* Braddock, et al., **supra Ch VIII § 8.2**.

[18] This term is related to the concept of assistive technology services, set forth in The Developmental Disabilities Assistance and Bill of Rights Act, **Pub. L.** 101-496, § 102(29).

devices. Based on descriptive analysis of these individual measures, a composite measure of equipment needs for the participants was developed.

Adaptive Behavior Scores

The adaptive behavior scale contains 54 interview items that measure individual functioning and developmental growth.[19] A general adaptive behavior score for each participant was developed as a measure of the person's capabilities and job skills, reflecting abilities in employment-related and self-care activities, personal and environmental mobility, communication and interpersonal skills, and opportunities for interaction with family, friends, and the general population.

The adaptive behavior scale measures related to employment abilities including: body balance, sense of direction, money handling, purchasing, writing, verbal and preverbal communication, reading, comprehension of instructions, time and numbers, job complexity, table clearing, food preparation, attention, initiative, interaction with others, and participation in groups. Because researchers measuring adaptive behavior find that a single measure best reflects individual scores on this measure, a summed score or index of adaptive behavior on the above-listed measures was used for analytical purposes.[20]

Medical Needs

Study has shown that a family's medical needs and contacts with physicians increase when a family member has a disability.[21] The measures in the investigation explore the general medical needs of the participants. The needs assessed included general need for medical care, prior contact with medical personnel, and prior difficulty in receiving medical services.[22] A composite measure of medical need was developed for analytical purposes.

Financial Information, Citizenship, and Advocacy

This information covers several areas related to employment. The participants' average monthly gross and earned income from employment or other sources is assessed. Issues related to guardianship, advocacy, and legal assistance are

---

[19] The adaptive behavior questions were a modified version of the Behavior Development Survey used by Conroy and Bradley in the Pennhurst Longitudinal Study. The adaptive behavior total (or sum) score in this study ranged from 1–100, with 1 being a low score and 100 a high score. Conroy and Bradley have reported the adaptive behavior to be highly reliable, with test-retest reliability of .96, and interrater reliability of .94. *See* S. Devlin, Reliability Assessment of the Instruments Used to Monitor the Pennhurst Plaintiff Class Members, paper submitted in partial fulfillment for degree of Doctor of Philosophy, Philadelphia: Temple University Developmental Disabilities Center/UAP, March 1989.

In a 1996 report, an assessment was conducted of the reliability of the adaptive behavior measures and other measures used in the research model during the years 1990 to 1996. The items making up the adaptive behavior scale showed high test-retest reliability, ranging on individual items from .66 to 1.00. Patricia A. Bell, Richard Dodder, & Barbara Murray, Developmental Disabilities Quality Assurance Research Project, 1996 Yearly Report: A Longitudinal Assessment of Consumer Outcomes 1990–1996, and an Examination of the Reliability of the Measurements (1996).

[20] *See* Arndt, A General Measure of Adaptive Behavior, 85(5) **Am. J. Mental Deficiency** 554 (1981) (adaptive behavior is better and more reliably measured using a single general score). *Cf.* Aanes & Moen, Adaptive Behavior Changes of Group Homes Residents, 14 **Mental Retardation** 36, 40 (1976) (discussing implications of adaptive behavior scores in individual programming and evaluation of community services).

[21] *See* Mitchell P. LaPlante, Dawn Carlson, H. Stephen Kaye, & Julia E. Bradsher, Families with Disabilities in the United States, 8 **Disability Stat. Rep.** 2, 12–13 (Sept. 1996).

[22] Data were collected on the participants' history and frequency of seizure activity, and medication schedule and management. For a review of this aspect of the Oklahoma study, *see* Scott Spreat, James W. Conroy, & Jennifer C. Jones, Use of Psychotropic Medication in Oklahoma: A Statewide Survey, 102 **J. Mental Retardation** 80–85 (1997) (finding 23 percent of individuals with mental retardation served by the state receiving psychotropic medication, with higher levels in less integrated living settings). *See also* E.S. Uehara, B.J. Silverstein, R. Davis, & S. Geron, Assessment of Needs of Adults with Developmental Disabilities in Skilled Nursing and Intermediate Care Facilities in Illinois, 29 **Mental Retardation** 223, 229 (1991) (finding high frequency of chronic health problems).

explored. These measures include the participants' civic involvement and citizenship-oriented activities, and whether the participant has a guardian appointed by a court, is involved with organizations promoting self-advocacy for persons with mental retardation or civic organizations, or has sought legal advice to assist with civil rights, entitlements, or other service delivery matters.

Service Planning and Delivery

These measures explore the scope of supported services the participants receive to enhance employment or community living opportunities. The measures identify service planning goals to support employment and community living goals.

Behavioral goals are measured for employment skills areas such as food service, machine operation, maintenance, construction and delivery. Other employment goals are measured, including those related to employee attendance, punctuality, productivity, task accuracy, and independence. Information is collected on the average number of hours during the month prior to the data collection period that the participants received training in occupational therapy, prevocational skills, employment activities, and social, physical, and employment-related skills.

Consumer Satisfaction and Choice

This measure reports the participants' own views of their employment and daily living needs, concerns, and opportunities.[23] Satisfaction is assessed through a standardized consumer interview.[24] The measure assesses the participants' impressions of their living situation, social interaction, use of public facilities, and employment.

The questions include whether the participant likes the activities during the day, makes money and chooses how his or her money is spent, and uses transportation that other people without disabilities use. The questions are combined to form two indices of satisfaction and choice, one for employment-related satisfaction and choice and one for self-care and daily living satisfaction and choice.[25]

Accessibility in Living Settings and Physical Quality of Settings

These measures explore whether the participants are denied or limited access to community or employment opportunities because of their disability. The questions explore the participants' accessibility to buildings, employment services, educational and human services, transportation, interactions with nondisabled friends, civic events, and recreation and leisure activities.

Accessibility in the home may relate to the participants' ability to adapt to or their need for accommodations in the work setting. Accessibility may be related to reported satisfaction in daily life and in employment opportunities. Composite variables are developed to assess

---

[23] Researchers have found that persons with mild mental retardation are reliable reporters about their social supports. *See* Yona Lunsky & Betsey A. Benson, Reliability of Ratings of Consumers with Mental Retardation and Their Staff on Multiple Measures of Social Support, 102 **Am. J. Mental Retardation** 280–84 (1997).

[24] The Consumer Interview was developed as part of the Pennhurst Longitudinal Study, *see* Conroy & Bradley, **supra Ch. I § 1.1,** at 119–26. *See* Lynn Atkinson, **Project for Quality of Life Improvement of Oklahomans with Developmental Disabilities,** Grant Proposal, at 11 (May 1, 1990); David A. Goode, Quality of Life Research: A Change Agent for Persons with Disabilities, **Presentation at AAMR National Meeting** (May 20–23, 1991) (citing studies).

[25] *See* Steven J. Taylor & Robert Bogdan, Quality of Life and the Individual's Perspective, *in* **Quality of Life: Vol. I, supra Ch. VII § 7.2,** at 19 (pointing out methodological issues such as interpretation and reliability of data). The issue of participant acquiescence with the researcher has been examined in studies of persons with mental retardation, with some researchers finding that persons with mental retardation in interview setting are likely to say "yes" to a question that is not clear. *See* Conroy & Bradley, **supra Ch. I § 1.1,** at 119, 126. Some studies show no relationship between aquiescence and level of mental retardation. *See, e.g.,* Leena M. Matikka & Hannu T. Vesala, Acquiescence in Quality-of-Life Interviews with Adults Who Have Mental Retardation, 35 **Mental Retardation** 75–82 (1997) (no relation for quality-of-life interviews, but women acquiesced more than men).

reported accessibility in daily life and employment.[26]

8.5 The Research Model: Overview

Several assumptions, in part derived from principles set forth by the AAMR, guided the development of the research model. The assumptions are consistent with the recent multidimensional approach adopted to broaden the conceptualization of mental retardation, avoid reliance on standardized tests, define disability with greater precision, and match individual needs in the workplace more closely to appropriate levels of support from society.[27]

The assumptions include that:

1. valid descriptions of the concept of disability require interdisciplinary analysis;
2. disability is a function of limitations in skills or capabilities but must be defined within the context of the individual's work and living environment and level of support from the environment;
3. for all people, disabilities coexist with individual strengths and capabilities;[28] and
4. with appropriate supports, the functioning of persons with disabilities improves.

These assumptions focus on individual strengths and capabilities, on the importance of living and working in integrated settings, and on the importance of appropriate access to supports and services.[29] Professor Chai Feldblum has commented that discrimination under the ADA "must be viewed in the context of the *interaction* between social realities and choices and the individual's disability, rather than in the context of the individual's disability per se."[30]

The research model allows for the comprehensive analysis of employment integration and economic opportunity in five ways:

1. *over time*—from 1990 to 1996, reflecting a period before and after Title I implementation (cross-sectional analysis during the period 1990 to 1996);
2. *on a "matched" set of participants*—based on information collected annually from the participating adults (longitudinal analysis during the period 1990 to 1996);
3. employing a *state as a unit of analysis*—based on information from an entire state system examining its citizens with mental retardation;
4. *from an interdisciplinary perspective*—information derived from multiple research methods and disciplines; and
5. *in ways consistent with the major goals of the ADA*—exploration of the ADA's goals of equality and opportunity, full participation, independent living, and economic self-sufficiency.[31]

The research model explores the relationship of employment integration and economic opportunity with combinations of the independent measures in Figure 1.1. Examination of the findings is not focused on the assessment of statistically significant results, but rather on the general magnitude and direction of trends in the data.[32]

Where appropriate, statistical testing techniques are used to provide an estimate of the

---

[26] The ratings made by the observers on the physical quality and accessibility measures include: the attractiveness of neighborhood and residence, physical accessibility to the site/residence (overall and on a room-by-room basis). Many of the environmental measures are sensitive to the characteristics of the participants living in the residence being rated. *See* Conroy & Bradley, **supra Ch. I § 1.1,** at 159.

[27] *See* **AAMR, supra Ch. III § 3.1,** at 1, 23.

[28] *See* Alison B. Miller & Christopher B. Keys, Awareness, Action, and Collaboration: How the Self-Advocacy Movement Is Empowering for Persons with Developmental Disabilities, 34 **Mental Retardation** 312–19 (1996) ("An empowerment perspective emphasizes awareness of individual strengths and potential over deficits and limitations.").

[29] **AAMR, supra Ch. III § 3.1,** at 135; Louis Rowitz, Prologue to: **Mental Retardation in the Year 2000,** at 5 (Louis Rowitz, ed., 1992) (discussing the changing paradigms of disability).

[30] *See* Feldblum, Antidiscrimination Requirements of the ADA, *in* **Rights and Responsibilities, supra Ch. I § 1.1,** at 35, 36.

[31] **ADA Watch, supra Ch. I § 1.2,** at 7.

[32] The information within the tables is presented either by absolute numbers of responses or by weighted percentages of the responses. The absolute raw number is simply the tally for that variable. Absolute raw numbers and percentages are presented for a particular cell. The marginal numbers (i.e., those on the perimeter of the table) are weighted by the number of responses for a particular cell. Weighted percentages present the impact of a particular set of responses based on the number of responses for that cell.

relationship (not the "causes and the effects") among the measures of interest. Statistical analyses are performed on the various dependent measures. Simple (bivariate) correlational analysis[33] and principle components factor analysis are used to reduce the individual measures scores to a single measure.[34] Chi square tests, multiple regression, and partial correlation analysis assess the impact of the measures on the participants' level of integrated employment and income levels.[35]

8.6 The Research Model Components

One major challenge in the study of employment integration and economic opportunity for persons with mental retardation is the establishment of appropriate and useful outcome variables. Professors Schalock and Kiernan have summarized many of the key indicators of employment integration that have been used in prior research involving persons with mental retardation.[36] Several of the measures identified by Schalock and Kiernan are examined in this investigation, including measures of employment movement, earned income, and consumer satisfaction.

The present investigation focuses on two major types of dependent or outcome measures. The first is a measure of "employment integration," as assessed by employment category in 1996 and by changes in employment category from 1990 to 1996 (referred to as "employment movement").[37] The second outcome measure, "economic opportunity," is defined by measures of earned income in 1996 and by changes in gross monthly income from 1990 to 1996 (i.e., reflected in economic growth).

Employment Integration

The four categories of employment type described above are arranged from less to more integrated as follows:[38] no employment; sheltered employment;[39] supported employment;[40] and competitive employment.[41] For purposes of analysis, hypothetical weights are assigned to the various cells to calibrate employment movement and integration. These weights range from –3 to +3, reflecting the

---

[33] Statistical significance is indexed by a probability value that an observation would have been found if, in the population from which we sampled, the true correlation were zero. The correlation coefficient (r) can take on values between –1.00 and +1.00. A value of –1.00 means that there is a perfect negative relationship; a value of +1.00 means there is a perfect positive relationship, and a value of .00 means there is no linear relationship between the two variables.

[34] Using principle-components analysis with varimax rotation, composite measures for capabilities and qualifications, empowerment, and ADA legal variables were developed. The analyses reduce the number of variables required to describe behavior. The conceptual grouping or composite is used as an index in the model.

[35] One challenge in conducting large-scale study is collecting information for all the participants. Data were missing for a variety of reasons, including lost information, oversight in collection, and participant unwillingness to share information. There was no systematic pattern in the missing data and missing data appeared to be randomly distributed. Another issue relates to the statistical reliability and validity of the measures. Reliability is the degree to which the interviewers and observers agree in their ratings of the same behaviors. To assess reliability, a sample of data from different raters for the interviews and observations was compared and the result of this rater-reliability test was high, $r = .85$, for the adaptive behavior score. Absolute differences among raters ranged from 1 to 22, with a median absolute difference of 8 points. The largest differences were found for the higher functioning individuals, indicating that care must be taken in assessing scores when targeting higher functioning individuals. Some measures showed a higher degree of reliability than others. Validity is the degree to which the measures assess what they are intended to assess. External validity relates to the generalizability of the results to other samples of persons with mental retardation or populations of persons with disabilities.

[36] Kiernan & Schalock, **supra Ch. 1 § 1.1,** at 9–10.

[37] Questions concerning the quality of the movement and its relation to long-term independence in work and daily living warrant study. *See* Barbara Altman & Peter J. Cunningham, Dynamic Process of Movement in Residential Settings, 98 **Am. J. Mental Retardation** 304 (1993) (finding great mobility among living settings for persons with mental retardation and citing studies emphasizing the quality of the movement and long-term outcomes); Paul Wehman & John Kregel, Supported Employment: Growth and Impact, *in* **Supported Employment: Strategies for Integration of Workers with Disabilities** 3–6 (Paul Wehman, et al., eds., 1992) [**hereinafter Supported Employment**] (reviewing supported employment programs and integrated work programs for persons with disabilities).

magnitude of potential movement over time from one employment category to another category as follows: 0 for no employment; 1 for sheltered employment; 2 for supported employment; and 3 for competitive employment.

If a participant was not employed in 1990 and not employed in 1996, the score for employment movement or degree of integration over time is 0 (i.e., no change). If a participant was not employed in 1990 but attained competitive employment in 1996, the score for employment movement would be +3.

Likewise, if a participant was in supported employment in 1990 (+2) and in sheltered employment in 1996 (+1), employment movement would be considered to have regressed and be coded at -1. The cell weights allow the model to illustrate the magnitude of employment integration over time for these participants.

Economic Opportunity and Changes in Income

National census data from 1991 to 1992, collected prior to the effective date of Title I of the ADA, show that persons with disabilities are more likely to have low incomes.[42] The NCD finds that the earnings of women with disabilities working full time are only two thirds of men with disabilities employed full time.[43] The analysis of economic indicators, such as gross and earned income rates, as reflective of progress toward social inclusion and empowerment for persons with mental retardation, has received limited attention.

In a longitudinal study of 197 persons with mental retardation in supported employment, Professor Frank Rusch and his colleagues found that measures of intelligence (similar to the capabilities and qualifications measures in Figure 1.1) predicted individual future earnings.[44] Another study by Professor David Mank and his associates of 462 persons with mental retardation found that higher levels of natural supports in the workplace and of interactions with coworkers without disabilities in the workplace corresponded to higher hourly and monthly wages for these individuals.[45] Few studies have examined the independent and combined effects over time of various predictor variables, such as the effect of individual capabilities or empowerment measures on the income levels and economic growth for qualified persons with mental retardation.

---

[38] *See* State Supported Employment Services Program, 34 C.F.R. § 252, 254 (1991) (explaining that integrated settings involve job sites where coworkers are not disabled and individuals with disabilities are not part of a group of other individuals with disabilities).

[39] *See* **Toward Independence, supra Ch. VI § 6.2,** at app. at B-75–B-76 (1986) (portraying sheltered employment as noncompetitive and nonintegrated work). Under the Fair Labor Standards Act, sheltered workshops may pay persons with disabilities a lower rate than the statutory minimum wage, but not less than 50 percent of minimum wage unless exempted by the Act. *Id.* at B-85; Shapiro, **supra Ch. I § 1.1,** at 143 (the absence of nondisabled coworkers in a sheltered workshop is confirmation of a prejudiced opinion that people with disabilities cannot work); John Kregel, The Subtle and Silent Points of Program Evaluation: An Illustration from Supported Employment, 2 **J. Voc. Rehab.** 53–54 (1992) (the ADA and consumer empowerment movement focused scrutiny on appropriateness of sheltered workshop programs).

[40] Analysis of national trends suggest that roughly 63 percent of persons in supported employment are individuals with mental retardation. *See* W.G. Revell, Paul Wehman, J. Kregel, M. West, & R. Rayfield, Supported Employment for Persons with Severe Disabilities: Positive Trends in Wages, Models, and Funding, *in* **New Directions in Supported Employment: Vol. I** (Paul Wehman & J. Kregel, ed., 1996), at 40–51.

[41] *See* Frank R. Rusch & Carolyn Hughes, Overview of Supported Employment, 122 **J. Applied Behav. Analysis** 351 (1989); Michael S. Shafer, et al., Competitive Employment and Workers with Mental Retardation: Analysis of Employers' Perceptions and Experiences, 92 **Am. J. Mental Retardation** 304–11 (1987) (examining competitive and supported employment for workers with mental retardation).

[42] McNeil, **supra Ch. I § 1.1,** at 11.

[43] **Achieving Independence, supra Ch. VI § 6.8,** at 59 (*citing* Frank Bowe, **Adults with Disabilities: A Portrait** (1992)).

[44] Frank R. Rusch, Laird W. Heal, & Robert E. Cimera, Predicting the Earnings of Supported Employees with Mental Retardation: A Longitudinal Study, 101(6) **J. Mental Retardation** 630 (1997) (finding that prior earnings and federal job subsidy also predicted future earnings).

[45] David Mank, Andrea Cioffi, & Paul Yovanoff, Analysis of the Typicalness of Supported Employment Jobs, Natural Supports, and Wage and Integration Outcomes, 35 **Mental Retardation** 185–97, at 193 (1997).

Examination of Gross and Earned Income

The research model examines the participants' earned income in 1996 and changes in their average gross monthly income from 1990 to 1996 (for instance, from employment and other sources such as Supplemental Security Income (SSI), controlling for inflation) and relates them to other independent variables. This design facilitates analysis of economic growth and opportunity during the early implementation phase of Title I. Nevertheless, a limitation of the 1990 baseline analysis of income was that, without controlling for the severity of disability, it was not clear whether income disparity is due to disincentives in the disability benefit system, to the functional limitations of the participants, or to both.

Beginning with the 1993 data collection efforts, the measures were modified to examine earned income from employment and income from governmental support programs or private sources. The findings for earned income may be influenced by differences in income support or educational levels among persons with different levels of disability.[46] The relationships are analyzed between income levels and other factors in the model, such as background measures and capabilities and qualifications.[47]

Personal Background Measures

Personal background variables refer to the participants' age, gender, and minority status. The cross-sectional demographics in 1996, based on the participating sample size of 3,057 adults, show that the majority of participants are white (86 percent) with 14 percent minority. In that same cross-section, the demographics within minority status are as follows: 8 percent African-American; 5 percent American Indian; 0.5 percent Hispanic; and 0.2 percent Asian/Oriental-American. The research model examines the relationship between background variables and employment integration and economic opportunity.[48]

Studies have examined the relationship of gender, race, and disability to workforce participation, economic opportunity, and career advancement. Professor William Hanna and his colleagues have analyzed the 1984 Census Bureau survey on health and disability, conducted interviews with women with physical disabilities, and gathered information from a 1988 questionnaire on attitudes toward people with disabilities. These researchers find that only 25 percent of black women with disabilities were employed full time, as compared to 77 percent of white men, 44 percent of white women, and 57 percent of black men with disabilities.[49] Other studies of persons with mental retardation in supported employment show no relation to background variables such as ethnicity and income levels.[50]

Capabilities and Qualifications Composite Measure

Individual job capabilities and qualifications are defined as the interaction between intellectual, physical, and social functioning and the demands of the environment.[51] The ADA stands

---

[46] *See* **infra Ch. X § 10.4** (discussing findings of partial correlations controlling for job skill level).

[47] The 1990 findings for income are based on results with varying cell sample sizes. The group with the highest monthly gross and earned incomes comprises participants who reside in integrated settings and who are competitively employed.

[48] *Cf.* **ADA Watch**, **supra Ch. I § 1.2,** at 5 ("Minorities with disabilities, overrepresented in the disability community, are significantly under-reached by current ADA information and technical assistance efforts.").

[49] *See* William J. Hanna & Elizabeth Rogovsky, On the Situation of African-American Women with Physical Disabilities, 23 **J. Applied Rehab. Counseling** 39–45 (1992); McNeil, **supra Ch. I § 1.1,** at 10 (supplying data from 1991–1992 showing differences among races and ethnicity groups in severe disability prevalence rate); Daniel J. Reschly & Susan M. Ward, Use of Adaptive Behavior Measures and Overrepresentation of Black Students in Programs for Students with Mild Mental Retardation, 96 **Am. J. Mental Retardation** 257–68 (1991) (summarizing studies showing overrepresentation of minority students in special education classes versus mainstreamed classrooms; arguing that the debate over educational placement has been about biased intelligence testing; and asserting that the use of adaptive behavior measures is necessary to ensure valid classification and placement for students with mild mental retardation).

[50] Rusch, et al., **supra Ch. VIII § 8.6,** at 641 (1997) (finding that earnings are not predicted by ethnicity and reviewing related studies).

[51] **AAMR, supra Ch. III § 3.1,** at 11.

for the proposition that "[a] person's disabilities have little to do with his or her inabilities. Often it is society's reactions to the person with disabilities or society's structural barriers that disable the person."[52]

In the model, two measures comprise the capabilities and qualifications composite factor: adaptive skill scores and general health status. These two measures reflect one working definition of the term "qualified" within the meaning of the ADA.[53] Although the term is central to legal disputes involving the ADA,[54] Chapter III discussed that to date little research has been devoted to defining "qualified."[55] The common approach has been to define "qualifications" retroactively, on a case-by-case basis.[56]

The adaptive skill measure contains items that assess an individual's functioning and developmental growth.[57] For each participant an adaptive skill score is generated, reflecting abilities in employment, self-care, personal mobility, communication skills, and the participant's opportunities for interaction with family, friends, and the public.

The health-status measure assesses the health status and medical needs of the participants. Chaper XVI discusses how, for persons with mental retardation, health status alone often relates to the need for supports and services and the opportunity for integrated work. Yet many persons with mental retardation and good health status face limitations in employment integration and advancement as a result of employment discrimination and the lack of access to private health insurance.[58]

The model explores the relationships among health status, employment integration, and economic opportunity.[59] Initial analysis of the model showed that as the participants' community living arrangements became more integrated, their general health status improved. This finding is consistent with the historic trend to place persons with severe and complex medical needs in less integrated living arrangements. The question remains whether persons with less pressing medical needs have greater opportunity for integrated employment and living. Other studies suggest that as employment type becomes more integrated, medical needs decrease.[60]

---

[52] Justin W. Dart, Jr., Preface, *in* **Rights and Responsibilities**, **supra Ch. I § 1.1,** at xiii ("The mandate of civil rights law is to destroy those negative reactions and dismantle those barriers in order to restore equal opportunity and full participation in daily life activities with dignity, not charity.").

[53] *Cf.* Rusch, et al., **supra Ch. VIII § 8.6,** at 631–32 (1997) (employing measures of IQ as predictors of earnings).

[54] *See Daubert v. U.S. Postal Serv.*, 733 F.2d 1367 (10th Cir. 1984) (ruling that an employee with a back injury was not "otherwise qualified" because of inability to do heavy lifting); *Diaz v. U.S. Postal Serv.*, 658 F. Supp. 484 (E.D. Cal. 1987) (ruling that an employee with a back injury was "otherwise qualified" because he could perform the job's essential functions); *Rosiak v. U.S. Dep't of the Army*, 670 F. Supp. 444 (M.D. Pa. 1987) (holding that a carpenter unable to work around cement fumes was not "otherwise qualified"), *aff'd*, 845 F.2d 1014 (3d Cir. 1988).

[55] *See* Thomas H. Barnard, The Americans with Disabilities Act: Nightmare for Employers and Dream for Lawyers?, 64 **St. John's L. Rev.** 229, 242–45 (1990) (concluding that the ADA will result in considerable litigation to determine who is "qualified"); Kim F. Ebert & Joseph M. Perkins, New Era in Employment Litigation: Overview of Americans with Disabilities Act, 34 **Res Gestae** 318, 319–20 (1991) (arguing that the ADA invites litigation over definition of the term "qualified").

[56] 29 C.F.R. § 1630.5 (1991).

[57] *See* **AAMR**, **supra Ch. III § 3.1,** at 38 (comparisons of measures of intellectual functioning (e.g., IQ measures) and indices of adaptive behavior must proceed with caution and consider factors related to degree of mental retardation).

[58] *See* **Achieving Independence, supra Ch. VI § 6.8,** at 96–106 (call for research on the interaction among employment opportunity, access to health insurance, and individual capabilities and qualifications, such as those identified in Figure 1.1); Paula M. Minihan & Deborah H. Dean, Meeting the Needs for Health Services of Persons with Mental Retardation Living in the Community, 80 **Am. J. Pub. Health** 1043, 1046–48 (1990) (ADA-related barriers to health care include negative attitudes by health care providers toward people with mental retardation).

[59] *See* **AAMR, supra Ch. III § 3.1,** at 68 (noting acute need for research on the health status of persons with mental retardation living in the community).

[60] Based on the 1996 cross-section of the sample, the components of the composite measure illustrate: (1) the majority of participants did not show an urgent (life-threatening) need for medical care (94 percent overall, 93 percent for those residing in institutions, and 95 percent for those residing in the community); (2) for all participants, more integrated levels of employment are related to relatively less urgent need for medical care (91 percent for those not employed, 96 percent for those in sheltered workshops, 98 percent for those in supported employment, and

Equipment/Accommodation-Needs Measure

The equipment/accommodation-needs[61] measure is a preliminary index of potential accommodations required for these participants. Although more sophisticated measures are warranted, little attention has been devoted to assessing the relation of equipment needs to employment integration or economic opportunity.[62] As a result, employers have little information about the employment-related equipment needs of employees with disabilities. The adaptive equipment studied is an approximation of other equipment types that the participants may need for employment purposes.

Inclusion Factors

Full inclusion into society for persons with disabilities is a major goal of the ADA. Inclusion in employment brings opportunity and participation.[63] The model measures inclusion in two ways: degree of integration and independence in living arrangement (the integration aspect), and satisfaction and choice with employment and daily living (the consumer interview measure).

Integrated and independent living is central to civil rights for people with disabilities.[64] Judy Heumann, assistant secretary in the U.S. Department of Education, has written: "The key force behind a rethinking of policy toward persons with disabilities has been the independent living movement."[65]

Research shows that people with mental retardation who live in integrated settings show significant advancements in capabilities and participation in society.[66] People with mental retardation often face a loss of access to adequate health care services when they move from institutional to community-based settings.[67] Professor Braddock finds that, for a variety of reasons, roughly 80 percent of persons with mental retardation in community-based settings return to institutional settings.

The research model allows for the analysis of the relation of independence in living to employment and economic integration for this sample of persons with mental retardation. Prior

---

98 percent for those in competitive employment); (3) for all three types of community settings, there was not a general urgency for medical care (89 percent in foster/family settings, 97 percent in group homes, and 94 percent in supported/semi-independent living). A related issue was whether the participants had difficulty in receiving medical services. Restricted access to medical care was less for those participants residing in the institutions (1.2 percent) than for those residing in the community (4 percent). Access to medical care is reported generally good, with 81 out of 2972 (3 percent) participants expressing difficulty receiving medical care. *See* **infra Ch. XVI § 16.4** (discussing managed care and persons with mental retardation).

[61] *See* Developmental Disabilities Assistance and Bill of Rights Act, **Pub. L.** 101–496, § 102(29), 104 Stat. 1191, 1194 (1991).

[62] The baseline findings in this study suggested that participants' adaptive equipment needs were met in the majority of cases. The baseline finding may be contrasted with the 1986 Harris Poll result showing that almost one quarter of those surveyed not working or working part time did not need adaptive-equipment accommodations to help them work. Louis Harris & Assocs., **The ICD Survey of Disabled Americans: Bringing Disabled Americans into the Mainstream** 73–74 (1986).

[63] The ARC, **The Employment of People with Mental Retardation and the ADA: Issues and Barriers** (Working paper, May 1993) (citing studies).

[64] *See* West, **supra Ch. I § 1.1,** at 9 (commenting that: "[T]his consciousness of independent living that has evolved over the last 2 decades has been a significant contributor to the development of a sense of disability community and a call for civil rights reforms....The independent living consciousness has shepherded in a gradual shift in policy focus from custody to cure to care to rights."). ADA Title II (state and governmental services) and Title III (public accommodations) cover discrimination in housing against persons with disabilities. For a discussion of ADA Titles II and III, *see* **infra Ch. XVI §§ 16.2–16.3.**

[65] Heumann, **supra Ch. I § 1.1.**

[66] *See* **AAMR, supra Ch. III § 3.1,** at 114 (summarizing research); Carol A. Howland, et al., Independent Living Centers and Private Sector Rehabilitationists: A Dynamic Partnership for Implementing the ADA, 8 **NARPPS J.** 75 (1993) (discussing how independent living improves empowerment, inclusion, and self-sufficiency); *Lelsz v. Kavanagh*, 673 F. Supp. 828, 842 (N.D. Tex. 1987) (reflecting the ADA view that "[n]o longer are mentally retarded persons shackled by notions that they cannot learn and grow, that they are eternal children, that they have no ability to care for themselves, or that they cannot live dignified and productive lives").

[67] *See* David Braddock, Community Mental Health and Mental Retardation Services in the United States: A Comparative Study of Resource Allocation, 149 **Am. J. Psychiatry** 175 (1992).

studies have shown that inclusion into society, as reflected in independence in living, is an important predictor of integration in employment for persons with mental retardation.[68]

The second inclusion component, the consumer interview measure, is based on participants' views of their employment and daily living opportunities and is obtained from a subset of participants responding directly to the research interviewers. The investigation examines the relationship of satisfaction and choice in work and daily life to employment integration and economic opportunity.

Future studies may examine individual and social perceptions related to ADA implementation and address questions such as: to what extent are the self-images of persons with mental retardation enhanced or diminished as a result of experiences with ADA implementation? In what ways have antidiscrimination laws such as the ADA produced a victim status that negatively affects self-image of those covered in the shadow of the law?

Empowerment Factors

The ADA follows a policy of equal opportunity, full participation, and choice in life, rejecting the traditional role of "patient" for persons with disabilities. The Act reflects a consumer-driven approach to civil rights.

Senator Tom Harkin, a Congressional sponsor of the ADA, has said: "[T]he clearly implied promise of ADA is that all Americans with disabilities will be empowered to fulfill their potential as equal, as prosperous and as welcome members of the mainstream."[69]

Research shows that inclusion into society results in enhanced personal satisfaction and perceptions of choice and control in life.[70] Persons with mental retardation report that enhanced choice in life stimulates their growth and development. Professor Wendy Parent finds that "[t]he opportunity for an individual to make choices and participate in life decisions improves his or her quality of life and the outcomes achieved, while also positively influencing his or her dignity, self-worth, and independence."[71]

Few studies have examined the process of persons with mental retardation in empowerment efforts.[72] In their studies, Professor Fabricio Balcazar and his colleagues find that empowerment involves an ongoing process of gaining access and control over societal resources through group participation centered at local community levels.[73] Three measures explore the process of empowerment in the present investigation: self-advocacy involvement measures, family and governmental supports measures, and education and job training measures.

The self-advocacy measure reflects the participants' contact and participation with self-advocacy programs from 1990 to 1996. David Braddock has described self-advocacy as

> teaching people with a disability how to advocate for themselves and to learn how to speak out for what they believe in. It teaches the individuals how to make decisions and choices that affect their lives so that they can become more independent along with learning about their rights [and]...responsibilities.[74]

---

[68] *See* Laird W. Heal & Frank R. Rusch, Predicting Employment for Students Who Leave Special Education High School Programs, 61 **Exceptional Children** 472–87 (1995) (integrated living among white males strong predictor of employment integration).

[69] *See* 137 **Cong. Rec.** S11,107 (daily ed. July 26, 1991) (statement of Sen. Harkin); *see also* Justin W. Dart, Jr., The ADA: A Promise to Be Kept, *in* **Rights and Responsibilities, supra Ch. I § 1.1** (discussing "empowerment policy").

[70] *See* Wendy Parent, Quality of Life and Consumer Choice, *in* **The ADA Mandate for Social Change** (Paul Wehman, ed., 1993) 19, 20 [**hereinafter ADA Mandate**].

[71] *Id.*; **AAMR, supra Ch. III § 3.1,** at 27 (*citing* studies by Moseley (1988) and by Conte, Murphy, and Nisbet (1989) on persons with mental retardation).

[72] Fabricio E. Balcazar, Christopher B. Keys, Joyce F. Bertram, & Thomas Rizzo, Advocate Development in the Field of Developmental Disabilities: A Data-Based Conceptual Model, 34 **Mental Retardation** 341–51 (1996).

[73] *Id.* (*citing* Cornell Empowerment Group, **Empowerment Through Family Support.** Networking Bulletin: Empowerment & Family Support, 1, 2–12 (1989)).

[74] *See* David Braddock, Responding to the Self-Advocacy Movement, **AAMR News & Notes,** at 2 (July–Aug. 1993) (self-advocacy movement is now organized in almost every state); American Ass'n on Mental Retardation, **Policy Positions on Legislative & Social Issues** 8–10 (1994) (discussing need for individuals with disabilities to speak for themselves in making lifestyle choices); Thomas J. Zirpoli, et al., Partners in Policymaking: Empowering People, 14 **J. Assoc. for Persons with Severe Handicaps** 163

Self-advocacy is a means for ensuring equal participation in society by persons with mental retardation. The analyses examine the amount of meaningful contact by participants with self-advocacy organizations (e.g., involvement with People First). Participants are asked about their contact with state advocacy programs, their sponsorship of meetings, their work with local self-advocacy groups, their participation in civic organizations, and voting behavior.[75]

The participants' family and governmental supports also are assessed.[76] Studies show that the use of cost-effective and natural supports[77] in homes, employment, and communities empower persons with disabilities.[78] Supports substantially improve the capabilities and functioning of persons with mental retardation.[79] Family and governmental supports are important to employment integration and economic opportunity because they provide "a more natural, efficient, and on-going basis for enhancing a person's independence, productivity, community integration, and satisfaction."[80]

Family support programs may be private (e.g, employer Employee Assistance Programs), informal and natural (e.g., from neighbors, extended family, and community members), or public (e.g., state or federal family support program, general welfare program, or disability-related program).[81] Analysis of the research model for the years 1990 and 1996 showed a positive relationship between formal and informal supports and participation in self-advocacy.

Finally, education and training, which are critical to employment integration and economic opportunity, are becoming increasingly individualized and coordinated across many disciplines for persons with mental retardation. To assess job or skill educational goals, the model uses a measure consisting of work, self-care, recreation, independent living, communication, social skills, and citizenship factors. The investigation also examines levels of service planning goals for employment-related skills and educational training actually received. The relation among education and job training measures and job attainment and retention measures in the model will be important to study over time to assess Title I implementation.

Legal Factors and Measures of ADA Implementation

The ADA composite measure examines the participants' perceptions of their degree of access to employment (ADA Title I issues) and daily life opportunities. As discussed in prior

---

(1989) (explaining program designed to provide information and training for self-advocates); Patricia H. Crist & Virginia C. Stoffel, The Americans with Disabilities Act of 1990 and Employees with Mental Impairments: Personal Efficacy and the Environment, 46 **Am. J. Occupational Therapy** 434–42 (1992) (identifying psychological components that predict whether persons with mental disabilities engage in self-advocacy and seek competitive employment).

[75] *See* Shapiro, **supra Ch. I § 1.1,** at 195–207 (discussing the self-advocacy movement for persons with mental retardation); Dart, *in* **Rights and Responsibilities, supra Ch. I § 1.1,** at xxvi ("United advocacy is the fundamental basis of power for any group in any form of society. Real-life empowerment occurs only through the consistent advocacy, action, and vigilance of those who seek it.").

[76] The investigation assesses the degree of contact with and support from family and case managers. This measure is not equivalent to the definition of mental retardation based on intensities of supports (e.g., intermittent, limited, extensive, or pervasive support). *See* **AAMR, supra Ch. III § 3.1,** at 26; Kerri Melda & John Agosta, Human Servs. Research Inst., Pol'y Brief on Family Support: Results of a National Study, **Families Do Make a Difference** (1992) (reporting survey of role of family support programs).

[77] *See* **CARF Standards, supra Ch. I § 1.7,** at 162 ("[Natural supports]...assist the person served to attain the goals of independence and productivity and...facilitate...integration into the community. Natural supports are provided by persons who are not paid staff of a service provider, but may be planned, facilitated, or coordinated in partnership with such a provider.").

[78] Shapiro, **supra Ch. I § 1.1,** at 232–36 (discussing the importance of family involvement); **AAMR, supra Ch. III § 3.1,** at 101 (same).

[79] *Id.* at 101–03 (noting that this belief is exemplified by the current emphasis on supported employment programs).

[80] *Id.* at 101 (noting that the rehabilitation profession emphasizes personal satisfaction, individual choices, decisions, and empowerment, and recognizes the need for fiscal and programmatic accountability).

[81] *See* Robin Cunconan-Lahr & Mary Jane Brotherson, Advocacy in Disability Policy: Parents and Consumers as Advocates, 34 **Mental Retardation** 352–58 (1996) (finding importance of family supports to self-advocacy activities).

chapters, ADA Title I requires employers to ensure that employees with disabilities have physical access to equal educational and employment services and other elements that make it possible to find and retain a job. Studies show that accessibility in the home relates to the ability to adapt to accommodations in the work setting.

Participants are asked about their access to educational and governmental training services, as well as to public transportation (ADA Title II issues). Chapter XVI describes how ADA Title II covers state and local agency services, as well as public transportation services. In addition, lack of access to education and transportation forecloses the possibility of employment for many people with mental retardation.

Participants also are asked about access to public accommodations (ADA Title III issues). Chapter XVI discusses the ways in which Title III requires public accommodations to make modifications to their facilities so that they may be accessible to persons with disabilities.

8.7 Summary

This chapter presented information on the research participants, the data sources, and the development of the measures in the research model. The outcome measures to be studied help achieve a more systematic understanding of employment integration and economic opportunity during ADA implementation. The next part of this book describes the findings of the research investigation.

PART IV:

Findings from the Research Model

CHAPTER IX

Empirical Findings over Time

Depending on who is speaking, the estimate of people with a disability may range from 25 to 60 million.... What may have looked initially like a methodological debate—what is the "real" number of people with disabilities—has become one that goes to the heart of our current policy formulation.... The empirical reality is that everyone... will in fact acquire one or more disabilities with all their consequences. This is the reality on which future conceptualization, measurement, and policy must be based.

Irving Zola [1]

9.1 Introduction

This chapter sets forth the findings of the research model, presenting analysis of the participants' backgrounds, attitudes, and behaviors relevant to employment integration and economic opportunity under the ADA. The findings document relationships among measures in the research model prior to and after ADA Title I implementation.

The findings illustrate the relationships among variables, provide insight into previously unexamined relationships, and help to develop future hypotheses. Nevertheless, at this point causal inferences and generalizations about the findings to other persons with different disabilities must be made with caution.[2]

9.2 Employment Integration: Movement from 1990 to 1996

Figure 9.1 shows employment movement over time for a matched set of participants across the four categories of employment type from 1990 to 1996. The figure reports cell percentages and the corresponding sample sizes for this longitudinal analysis.

Examination of the findings in the diagonal cells in Figure 9.1 (that is, the four cells in which no employment movement occurred) is a useful starting point for analysis. The top left cell shows that 83 of 973 participants (9 percent) were not employed in 1990 and remained unemployed in 1996. A little more than one third (36 percent) of the participants remained in nonintegrated sheltered workshops during this time.[3] Over the 1990 to 1996 time period,

---

[1] Irving Kenneth Zola, The Sleeping Giant in Our Midst: Redefining "Persons with Disabilities," *in* **Rights and Responsibilities, supra Ch. I § 1.1,** at xvii & xix.

[2] Conroy, **Hissom Outcomes Study**, **supra Ch. I § 1.6,** at 4 (discussing 1995 Hissom Outcomes Study and assessing the statistical reliability of measures in the present model).

[3] *See* **infra Ch. XII § 12.5** (discussing nonintegrated employment as a "black hole" for people with disabilities).

Figure 9.1

Employment Movement: Sample Sizes

		EMPLOYMENT STATUS IN 1996				
		None	**Sheltered**	**Supported**	**Competitive**	**Row Total**
Employment Status in 1990	**None**	9% (83)	24% (233)	3% (32)	2% (17)	38% (365)
	Sheltered	5% (45)	36% (352)	9% (88)	5% (50)	55% (535)
	Supported	0% (1)	2% (22)	1% (7)	1% (9)	4% (39)
	Competitive	0% (1)	2% (15)	0% (3)	2% (15)	3% (34)
	Column Total	13% (130)	64% (622)	13% (130)	9% (91)	100% (973)

Note: Reported above are percentages of participants in a particular cell with sample sizes in parentheses. 47% no change; 44% improve; 9% regress.

only 3 percent of the participants in supported or competitive employment remained in these programs.

Thus, from 1990 to 1996 almost half of the participants (47 percent) show no change in their employment category, 44 percent transition into more integrated employment settings, and 9 percent regress into less integrated work settings. Almost three quarters of the participants (73 percent) *remain* in nonintegrated employment settings (i.e., comprising those not employed or in sheltered workshops), while only 3 percent of the participants are *retained* in integrated settings (i.e., in supported and competitive employment).[4]

The column and row totals in Figure 9.1 show that in 1990, 3 percent of the participants were in competitive employment and that by 1996 this group tripled in size to 9 percent. The same pattern is evidenced for supported employment programs, with participation increasing from 4 percent in 1990 to 13 percent in 1996.[5] Figure 9.1 illustrates that employment movement from the category of unemployed in 1990 to the category of sheltered workshop employment in 1996 was most common (233 participants, or 24 percent of the total).[6]

9.3 Employment Integration: Comparison with Trends Prior to and After ADA Passage

Professor William Kiernan and his colleagues have conducted a state-by-state examination of the employment services provided by state agencies to individuals with mental retardation from the years 1988 to 1990.[7] These researchers separate state programs into two categories: (1) segregated employment services—defined as in the present investigation as no employment or employment in sheltered workshop settings, and (2) integrated employment programs—defined in Chapters VII and VIII as employment in supported and competitive work settings.

Kiernan's findings with regard to integration in employment services in Oklahoma and nationally during 1988 to 1990 may be compared to the present findings illustrated in Figure 9.2.

---

[4] *See* Conroy, **Hissom Outcomes Study, supra Ch. I § 1.6,** at 38–41 (analysis of subset of 427 individuals from the present sample finding substantial increases in opportunities for integrated employment and prevocational training).

[5] *Cf.* Paul Wehman & John Kregel, Supported Employment: Growth and Impact, *in* **Supported Employment: Strategies for Integration of Workers with Disabilities** (Paul Wehman, et al., eds., 1997) at 15 (showing growth in numbers of supported employment participants for all persons with disabilities in Oklahoma during fiscal years 1986–1988—FY 86, 0 participants; FY 87, 20 participants; FY 88, 78 participants).

[6] For findings of relative percentage change in employment status, *see* **Ch. XI § 11.4.**

[7] *See* Kiernan, Gilmore, & Butterworth, *in* **Integrated Employment, supra Ch. I § 1.1,** at 18–19.

Figure 9.2

Percentage of Persons in Integrated Employment

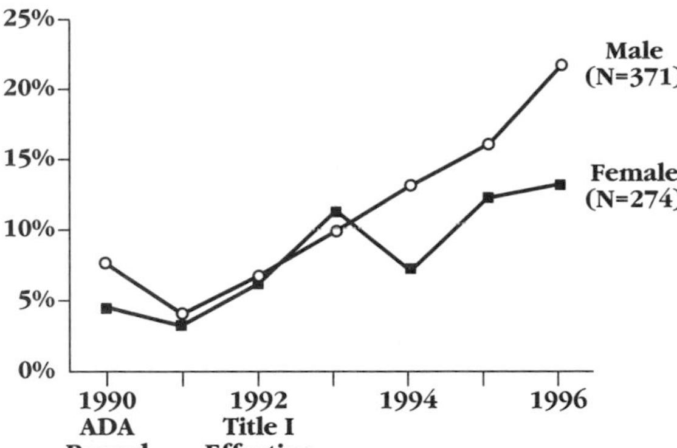

Analysis of Variance

	F	P
Gender	3.66	.06
Time	26.29	.0001
Gender * Time	3.25	.004
DF Error =	637	& 3822

Figure 9.2 displays, separately for men and women, the proportion of the participants attaining integrated employment from 1990 when the ADA was passed into law, until the year 1996. The trend toward movement into integrated employment is substantial, with male participants showing particularly strong movement into integrated employment.[8]

Figure 9.2 illustrates the increasing disparity in integrated employment levels for men and women participants.[9] During the initial years of ADA implementation, from 1990 to 1993, employment gains for men and women are comparable.[10] However, from 1994 to 1996 the gap in employment levels for men and women widens.[11] Chapter XIII discusses the findings in relation to labor force trends for persons with disabilities and their relation to both ADA implementation and future policy making in the area.

The present findings support Kiernan's analysis of Oklahoma and national data showing that during the two-year period studied prior to ADA passage, there had been a substantial trend toward the provision of services for integrated employment activities and a relative decline in services supporting segregated work settings. Kiernan's findings suggest that in Oklahoma there was a strong trend toward the attainment of integrated employment services, with the number of individuals served during the two-year period prior to ADA passage increasing more than twofold and increasing at a rate greater than the national average.

As discussed in depth in Chapter XII, the present findings reflect "black hole" trends of continued segregation in nonintegrated work settings facing many qualified persons with mental retardation. During pre-ADA and early implementation period there is a strong and continued reliance on nonintegrated and segregated work for individuals with mental retardation.

Kiernan has conducted a post-ADA implementation period study of state employment activities during the years 1990 to 1993. These findings again are consistent with the trends found in the present investigation, showing an increasing trend for qualified people with mental retardation to integrated work.[12]

---

[8] Findings are: for trend toward employment integration over time, $F = 26.29$, $p < .0001$; for time by gender interaction effect, $F = 3.25$, $p < .004$. These findings are based on a matched-set of 645 participants on whom data were available each year from 1990 to 1996.

[9] The difference in the trends for men and women is significant, $F(1, 3892) = 3.66$, $p = .06$.

[10] The increase in integrated employment over time for all participants is $F(1, 3892) = 26.29$, $p = .0001$.

[11] The increase in integrated employment over time for men versus women participants is statistically significant, $F(6, 3822) = 3.25$, $p = .004$ (interaction effect of gender and time).

[12] William E. Kiernan, **Integrated Employment: Status, Approaches, and Challenges** (1996).

Kiernan found a 95 percent increase in service utilization from 1990 to 1993 in the provision of integrated employment services and supports provided by the states, and a 353 percent increase in these services from 1988 to 1993. Conversely, Kiernan finds that during the same time periods the use of segregated employment services did not grow substantially.

9.4 Trends in Unemployment Levels During Initial ADA Implementation

From 1990 to 1996, relative unemployment levels for the participants in the present investigation decreased substantially, with an overall absolute drop of 25 percentage points, from approximately 38 percent in 1990 to 13 percent in 1996.[13] Figure 9.3 displays the decreasing trends in unemployment for these participants, separately for men and women.

As Figure 9.3 illustrates, by the year 1996 male participants, relative to female participants, had higher unemployment rates.[14] Other researchers have found that men with mental retardation without job training are more likely to be unemployed than similarly situated females.[15] Chapter XIV discusses the possible reasons for changes in the labor force participation by qualified persons with disabilities.

To summarize the findings to date, assessment of the changes in marginal unemployment rates for all the participants with mental retardation show the following:

1. for all participants (n = 973), unemployment rates decline significantly (Chi Square = 44.39, $p = .001$, reduction from 38 percent to 13 percent);
2. for all men (n = 568), unemployment rates decline significantly (Chi Square = 24.38, $p = .001$, reduction from 38 percent to 10 percent);
3. for all women (n = 405), unemployment rates decline significantly (Chi Square = 20.77, $p = .001$, reduction from 38 percent to 18 percent); but these declines are relatively less than declines by men ($F(1, 969) = 6.77$, $p = .01$, interaction of gender and time period);
4. For all minorities (n = 166), unemployment rates decline significantly (Chi Square = 15.49, $p = .001$, reduction from 40 percent to 11 percent); and
5. for all nonminorities (n = 807), unemployment rates decline significantly (Chi Square = 31.60, $p = .001$, reduction from 37 percent to 14 percent), at rates comparable to minority participants.

By way of comparison to the present findings, the 1994 Harris *Survey of Americans with Disabilities*, commissioned by the National Organization on Disability, showed an *increase* in the unemployment rate of working-age adults with disabilities between 1986 and 1994. In 1986 the unemployment rate was 66 percent, and by 1994 the unemployment rate increased to 68 percent.[16]

---

[13] *Cf.* Richard Butler & James J. Heckman, The Government's Impact on the Labor Market Status of Black Americans: A Critical Review, *in* **Equal Rights and Industrial Relations** 235, 244–46 (Leonard J. Hausman, et al., eds., 1977) (discussing differences in the unemployment rate of blacks and whites and noting changes made as labor force composition changes).

[14] The finding for test of the gender by time interaction effect is, $F = 3.71$, $p < .002$. Analysis is based on the subset of participants for whom data were available each year.

[15] *See* Mark L. Hill, et al., Benefit-Cost Analysis of Supported Competitive Employment for Persons with Mental Retardation, 8 **Res. Developmental Disabilities** 71 (1987) (summarizing literature on unemployment rates among adults with mental retardation and showing benefit-cost analysis of supported- or competitive-employment programs); Stephen A. Richardson, et al., Job Histories in Open Employment of a Population of Young Adults with Mental Retardation, 92 **Am. J. Mental Retardation** 483–91 (1988) (mentally disabled males without job training are more likely to be unemployed than similarly situated females); McNeil, **supra Ch. I § 1.1,** at 8–9 (citing data from 1991–1992 showing that disability rates were higher among women than men, but mental disability rates were higher among men than women).

[16] Louis Harris & Associates, **Survey of Americans with Disabilities** 37 (1994). *See also* Oklahoma Employment Sec. Comm'n, Economic Research and Analysis Div. (1994); McNeil, **supra Ch. I § 1.1,** at 4 (providing data from 1991–92 showing that the employment rate for persons without disabilities was 81 percent while the rate for persons with severe disabilities was 23 percent).

Figure 9.3

Unemployment Levels from 1990 to 1996

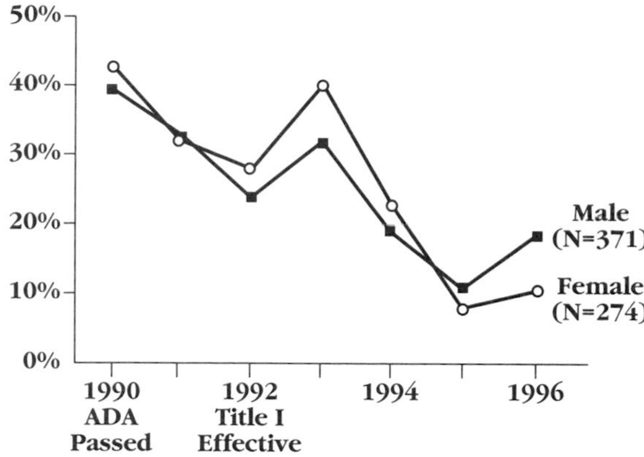

Analysis of Variance

	F	P
Gender	0.30	.59
Time	71.30	.0001
Gender * Time	3.71	.002
DF Error =	643	& 3858

Similarly, McNeil's studies, discussed in Chapter I, analyzing the Census Bureau's Survey of Income Participation (SIPP) data between October 1994 and January 1995 show that 74 percent of adults with severe disabilities (ages 21 to 64 years) were not employed.[17] McNeil found that the unemployment rate for all people with disabilities was 48 percent, as compared to 18 percent for the total U.S. working-age population.

9.5 Trends in Individual Growth Prior to and After ADA Implementation

The design of the investigation allows for the study of change during the initial years of ADA implementation (i.e., from 1990 to 1996) for these participants.[18] Figure 9.4 summarizes the dramatic changes that are occurring in the lives of these participants with mental retardation.

From 1990 to 1996 participants work in more integrated employment settings.[19] Their monthly incomes grow.[20] By way of comparison, a 1994 Harris survey showed that 40 percent of adults with disabilities live in households with annual incomes of less than $15,000. In 1986, 50 percent of adults with disabilities lived similarly. More adults with disabilities live in households with annual incomes in excess of $35,000 in 1994 (20 percent) as compared to 1986 (12 percent).

The growth over time in income levels found in the Harris findings may be skewed, however, because that survey failed to account for changes in income due to inflation. Nevertheless, as discussed in Chapter XII, growth in income

---

[17] **Ability: The Bridge to the Future, supra Ch. II § 2.4.**

[18] Presented for each measure are the sample size ("n"), the score on that variable in 1990 and 1996, the statistical test of the difference in the scores for 1990 and 1996 (i.e., reflected by the t-test, and the associated effect-size correlation, *"r"*), and the statistical significance of the change (i.e., reflected by the "*p*-value"). For a discussion of the effect-size correlation, *see* Robert Rosenthal, **Essentials of Behavioral Research** 22 (2d ed. 1992).

[19] Employment category is coded from 0 = no employment to 3 = competitive employment. *See* John McDonnell, et al., An Analysis of the Procedural Components of Supported Employment Programs Associated With Employment Outcomes, 22 **J. Applied Behav. Analysis** 417 (1989) (suggesting a growing need for competitive-employment positions for persons with mental retardation).

[20] Median monthly gross income, in terms of actual dollars, increased from $63 in 1990 to $536 in 1996. This increase is attributable to the corresponding decrease in overall unemployment rates. In analyses involving income (gross or earned), actual dollar amounts are transformed into "log dollars." Researchers find that a distribution of earnings often is skewed, with median earnings lower than the mean of the earnings. *See* Ernest R. Berndt, **The Practice of Econometrics: Classic and Contemporary** 161 (1991) (discussing practice of using log dollars). Compared to other distributions, the log-normal distribution better "fits" the data on earnings and reduces the influence of extreme values that make the use of standard statistical techniques unreliable. The log transformation reduces errors associated with large

Figure 9.4

Changes on Measures in the Model from 1990 to 1996

Variable	n[a]	Score[b] 1990	Score[b] 1996	*t*-value	*r*[c]	*p*-value
Employment Integration						
Employment Category	973	.73	1.19	16.00	.46	<.001
Monthly Income log dollars[d]	722	4.60	5.80	22.64	.64	<.001
Dollars		$99.00	$330.00			
Capabilities & Qualifications						
Adaptive Skills	973	51.10	55.00	11.15	.34	<.001
Health Status	973	7.50	8.40	10.89	.33	<.001
Equipment/Accommodation	973	.93	.95	1.95	.06	.06
Inclusion Factors						
Living Arrangement	952	.50	1.46	21.41	.57	<.001
Job/Life Satisfaction & Choice	199	34.20	38.70	13.81	.70	<.001
Empowerment Factors						
Self-Advocacy	911	.17	.36	10.31	.32	<.001
Family & Government Support	967	14.90	18.90	12.27	.37	<.001
Job/Skill Educational Goals	901	9.50	3.80	19.75	.55	<.001
Legal Factors						
ADA Composite[e]	973	.03	.32	7.37	.23	<.001
Title I	973	.85	.96	8.39	.26	<.001
Title II	973	.87	.95	6.07	.19	<.001
Title III	973	.76	.84	4.05	.13	<.001

[a] n = sample size

[b] Higher scores indicate more integrated employment and higher income, higher adaptive skills and health status, fewer equipment/accommodation needs, more integrated living arrangement and higher job/life satisfaction and choice, more self-advocacy, family & government support and job/skill educational goals, and more integrated opportunities as defined by the ADA.

[c] *r* = Effect size correlation on score between 1990 and 1996.

[d] 1996 gross monthly income information is derived from the addition of two sources: (1) weekly employment income (multiplied by 4), and (2) monthly entitlement income (e.g., SSI, Social Security, etc.).

[e] Composite score comprised of first principal component for Titles I–III.

---

income values and is employed in similar sociological or economic research. *See* Hubert M. Blalock, Jr., **Social Statistics** 427–29 (2d ed. 1986) (describing "diminishing returns effects" in models requiring transformation); Ronald J. Wonnacott & Thomas H. Wonnacott, **Econometrics** 123 (1979) (illustrating how nonlinear models require log transformation).

Standard linear regression analyses require that the data be "normal" as opposed to skewed. For the present data set, the log transformation produces a more "normal" distribution as tested by the Kolmogorov Statistic (D) for income differences. The Shapiro-Wilk statistic (w) for testing lack of fit for difference in income from 1990–1996 was .85 and for difference in log-income from 1990–1996 was .87. For consistency, the log transformation was used on the 1996 earned income from wages. The D statistic showed no improvement resulting from the log transformation of 1996 earned income alone: D = .10 for 1996 earned income, and D = .19 for log 1996 earned income.

The inflation rate from 1990–1996, based on the consumer price index, was approximately 21.3 percent. When 1996 earned income levels are corrected for inflation (i.e., multiplied by .824), participants still show a significant increase in their monthly gross incomes [$t(722) = 19.23$, $p < .001$].

21 *Cf.* Harris Poll-1994, **supra Ch. IX § 9.4,** at 93, 110 (satisfaction levels of persons with disabilities remained relatively constant between 1986 (69 percent satisfied, 24 percent dissatisfied) and in 1994 (67 percent satisfied, 24 percent dissatisfied); also 63 percent of persons with disabilities in 1994 perceive that the quality of life for people with disabilities has improved).

Figure 9.5

Percentage of Persons in Integrated Employment[1]

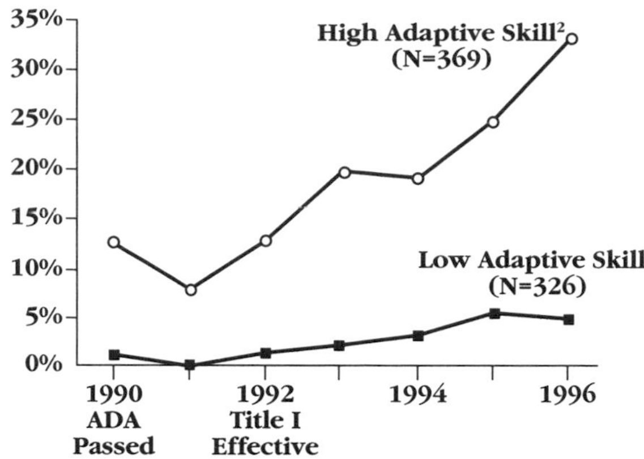

Analysis of Variance	F	P
Skill High	131.15	.0001
Time	29.53	.0001
Skill High * Time	12.56	.0001
DF Error =	637	& 3822

[1] Integrated employment is defined as either competitive or supported employment.

[2] High/Low adaptive skill defined by: High: > 50, Low: ≤ 50 as measured in 1996.

levels for qualified workers with mental retardation is an important outcome measure to assess the effectiveness of ADA implementation.

Along with improvements in adaptive skills and health status, the work capabilities and qualifications of the participants improve substantially over the time period measured.[21] Figure 9.5 shows that, from 1990 to 1996, those participants with higher adaptive job skills are much more likely to attain integrated employment, relative to those with lower skill scores. The trends underscore the importance of job skill development to help people attain and retain integrated employment.[22]

In an extensive analysis related to the closure of Oklahoma's Hissom Memorial Center care facility for individuals with mental retardation, James Conroy has analyzed gains in adaptive behavior scores for a subset of 382 individuals from the present larger sample. Conroy finds that for the subset of participants visited by the research team in 1990 and 1995, employment-related skills show the overall greatest gains among the skills assessed during the period. The percentage gains from the baseline 1990 year to 1995 in employment-related skills exceed 80 percent.[23]

Figure 9.4 shows that from 1990 to 1996 the participants' health status and their self-reported perceptions of satisfaction and choices in work and daily life improve substantially. Conroy's analysis of a subset of participants shows that the majority of individuals responding to the verbal interview report substantially more opportunities for choice in work and daily life in the year 1995 than they reported in 1990.[24]

Consistent with prior studies, the present participants who are working and living in integrated settings also report greater satisfaction with their daily lives. These findings are comparable to those of the 1994 National Consumer Survey showing that people with mental retardation working and living in nonintegrated settings perceive themselves as having fewer choices and control in their daily lives than do respondents without disabilities.[25]

---

[22] *See* Conroy, **Hissom Outcomes Study, supra Ch. I § 1.6,** at 18–20 (concluding that the adaptive skill scale is a central measure of growth and development in the field of developmental disabilities, and finding positive longitudinal findings in changes in adaptive behavior scores for 382 of the participants from the years 1990 to 1995).

[23] *Id.* at 21–25 (showing dramatic changes in other skill areas, such as reading, attention, and money use; and concluding that much of the individual growth is due to Oklahoma deinstitutionalization efforts).

[24] *Id.* at 27–29 (finding that the average scale score on this measure in 1990 was 77.2 and in 1995 was 84.9 and the difference is statistically significant, $t(87) = 2.98$, $p = .002$).

[25] *Cf.* Michael L. Wehmeyer & Christina A. Metzler, How Self-Determined Are People with Mental Retardation?: The National Consumer Survey, 99 **Am. J. Mental Retardation** (1994).

Figure 9.6

Gains in Monthly Earned Income: Mediated by Job Skill Level[1]

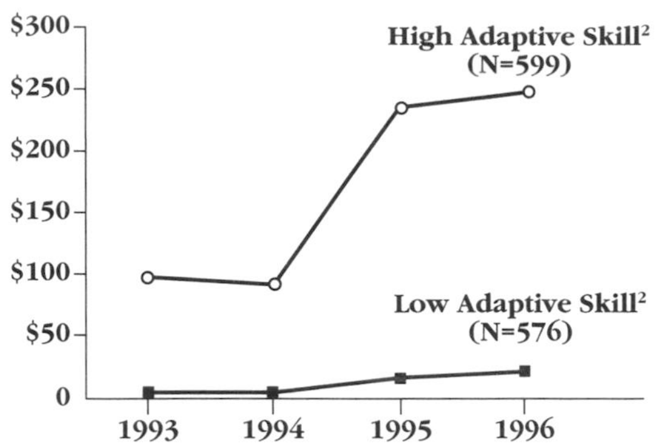

Analysis of Variance

	F	P
Skill High	405.99	.0001
Time	128.70	.0001
Skill High * Time	85.16	.0001
DF Error =	1173 & 3519	

1 Depicts average monthly earned income from employment. This amount does not include SSI or other governmental payments.

2 High/Low adaptive skill defined by: High: > 50, Low: ≤ 50 as measured in 1996.

9.6 Rise in Earned Income During Post-ADA Title I Implementation

Figure 9.6 displays the rise in monthly earned income for the participants with high and low job skills during the post-Title I effective years from 1993 to 1996. Participants with higher job skills, relative to those with lower skills, show dramatic increases in earned income during the time period.

Figure 9.7 shows that from 1993 to 1996, participants in integrated employment earned substantially higher levels of income, relative to those in nonintegrated work settings.[26]

Other studies show consistent findings for substantial increases over time in income as qualified workers with mental retardation move from segregated to integrated employment. Professors John Kregel and Paul Wehman find that individuals with mental retardation increase their annual earnings by 500 percent when they move from segregated to integrated work.[27]

Although all the participants in the present study displayed higher levels of earned income from 1993 to 1996, total yearly earned income for this sample is low relative to workers without disabilities. The participants' relatively low income levels suggest either that these individuals are not working full time or that they experience only periodic employment. Preliminary analysis of the work hours for 1996 participants indicate that these individuals worked on average 25 hours per week in each of the three types of employment settings (i.e., sheltered, supported, and competitive).

Chapter XIV of this book describes a recent investigation of Manpower Inc., the largest temporary staffing employer in the United States. The Manpower study is designed to explore the importance of the staffing industry as a bridge for enhancing part-time and full-time work opportunity for qualified persons with disabilities. More information is needed on the degree to which these participants with mental retardation and other persons with disabilities work part or full time and the quality of their work hours.

---

[26] For integrated versus nonintegrated employment, $F(1,2196) = 351.46$, $p < .0001$; for gender $F(1,2196) = 8.68$, $p = .004$; for time $F(3,2196) = 48.17$, $p < .0001$.

[27] Kregel & Wehman, *in* **Integrated Employment, supra Ch. I § 1.1,** at 38–39.

[28] **AAMR, supra Ch. III § 3.1,** at 114 (summarizing research); Carol A. Howland, et al., Independent Living Centers and Private Sector Rehabilitationists: A Dynamic Partnership for Implementing the ADA, 8 **ARPPS J.** 75 (1993) (discussing how independent living improves empowerment, inclusion, and self-sufficiency); *see also Lelsz v. Kavanagh*, 673 F. Supp. 828, 842 (N.D. Tex. 1987) (finding persons with mental retardation should not be shackled by myths that they cannot learn, that they have no ability to care for themselves, or that they cannot live productive lives).

Figure 9.7

Gains in Monthly Earned Income: Mediated by Degree of Integration in Employment[1]

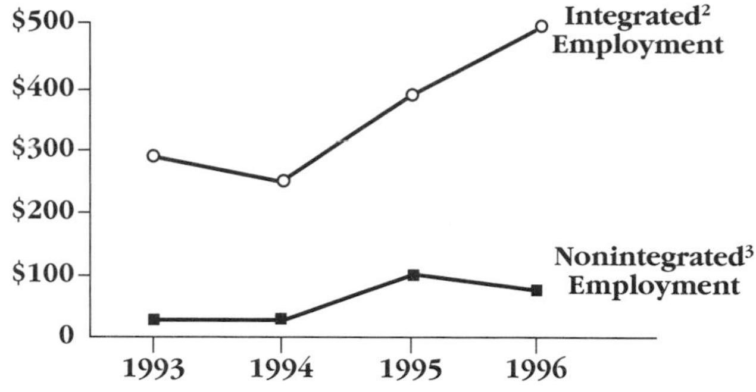

[1] Depicts average monthly earned income from employment. This amount does not include SSI or other governmental payments.
[2] Integrated employment includes competitive and supported employment.
[3] Nonintegrated employment includes sheltered workshops and unemployed.

9.7 Rise in Opportunities for Integrated Community Living

Chapter VIII described the central importance of independent living to the inclusion into society of people with disabilities. People with mental retardation who live in integrated settings show significant advancements in capabilities and participation in society.[28]

Figure 9.8 shows the trends in the four living arrangement types studied from 1990 to 1996. As in the assessment of integration in employment, hypothetical weights are assigned to the various cells in Figure 9.8 to calibrate degree of change in independence in living over time. The weights range from -3 to +3, reflecting the magnitude of movement toward inclusion and independence over time. Living arrangement category is coded as follows: 0 for institutional residences, 1 for family or foster care, 2 for group homes, and 3 for independent living.

The top left cell of Figure 9.8 shows that 41 percent of the participants remain in institutional residences between 1990 and 1996. Only 1 percent of the participants were in independent living settings in 1990 and in 1996. Examination of the diagonal cells in Figure 9.8 shows that from 1990 to 1996, 58 percent of the participants show no change in living category, 39 percent improve their degree of independence of living, and 3 percent regress.[29]

From 1990 to 1996, more than 10 times as many participants move into more integrated living settings as compared to those who regressed. The column and row totals show that the percentage of participants in institutional living drop substantially, from 74 percent in 1990 to 43 percent in 1996, while the percentage of participants in independent living increases substantially (from 2 percent to 33 percent).[30]

By way of summary, changes in marginal rates of institutional living from 1990 to 1996 show that:

1. for all participants (n = 952), rates decline significantly (Chi Square =186.82, p = .0001, reduction from 74 percent to 43 percent);
2. for all women (n = 393), rates decline significantly (Chi Square = 77.09, p = .0001, reduction from 69 percent to 38 percent);
3. for all men (n = 559), rates decline significantly (Chi Square = 107.13, p = .0001, reduction from 78 percent to 46 percent);

---

[29] *Cf.* Robert L. Schalock, et al., Placement into Nonsheltered Employment: Findings from National Employment Surveys, 94 **Am. J. Mental Retardation** 80, 83 (1989) (approximately 68 percent of 65,000 persons with mental retardation surveyed were placed in sheltered employment).

[30] *See* **supra Ch. VIII § 8.2** (discussing that the closure of the Hissom Memorial Center was accomplished entirely by the movement of its residents to community-based living settings).

Figure 9.8

Integration in Living Settings: 1990 and 1996

		LIVING ARRANGEMENT IN 1996				
		Institution	Family/Foster	Group	Independent	Row Total
Living Arrangement in 1990	Institution	41% (393)	0% (2)	6% (55)	27% (258)	74% (708)
	Family/Foster	0% (1)	1% (11)	1% (7)	1% (8)	3% (27)
	Group	1% (12)	0% (1)	15% (146)	4% (41)	21% (200)
	Independent	0% (0)	0% (0)	1% (12)	1% (5)	2% (17)
	Column Total	43% (406)	1% (14)	23% (220)	33% (312)	100% (952)

Note: Reported above are percentages of participants in a particular cell with sample sizes in parentheses. 58% no change; 39% improve; 3% regress.

4. for all minorities (n = 162), rates decline significantly (Chi Square = 28.46, p = .0001, reduction from 83 percent to 46 percent); and
5. for all nonminorities (n = 790), rates decline significantly (Chi Square = 158.19, p = .0001, reduction from 73 percent to 42 percent).

Figure 9.9 illustrates the substantial rise in the percentage of the participants living in the community, for the subsample of 645 individuals for which information is available for each year of analysis.[31]

Thus, during the years 1990 to 1996, living arrangements become more integrated. There is a substantial rise in the proportion of the participants in community-based living (e.g., in group homes, family living, or independent living). Many more participants move into integrated living settings as compared to those who regress into nonintegrated settings. The proportion of participants in institutional living drops and the proportion of participants in independent living increases substantially.[32]

The present findings showing movement trends toward integrated living arrangements do not necessarily reflect the quality or magnitude of basic and professional support services provided in various living arrangements. The quality of services varies across and within institutional and community-based settings.

Professor Charlie Lakin and his colleagues find that the type of support services received in community residences by persons with mental retardation is influenced by a number of factors that are independent of the residents' mental, physical, and health needs.[33] Lakin finds that the best predictors of the provision of specialized professional services for persons with mental retardation—for instance, medical, occupational, and psychological services—are the state and federal funding mechanisms (e.g., Medicaid reimbursement rates) available to support the particular community residence.[34] Careful evaluation of the type, quality, and funding of community living services is needed.

---

[31] Rise in community living (versus institutional living) is statistically significant, $F(1, 627) = 220.14$, $p < .0001$.

[32] Despite the encouraging present findings, tens of thousands of persons with mental retardation across the U.S. who could and want to live in integrated community settings continue to live in nonintegrated institutional settings. *See, e.g.*, Bob Mims, Mentally Retarded Left Languishing for State Support, 255(26) **Salt Lake Tribune** (Nov. 9, 1997) (citing recent study by the ARC finding that nationwide waiting lists for community-based living opportunities have risen in the past 10 years, with more than 220,000 requests currently pending as compared to 140,000 in 1987). *See also* **infra Ch. XVI** (discussing economic and attitudinal barriers to integrated work and living for persons with mental retardation).

[33] *See* K. Charlie Lakin, Angela N. Amado, Robert H. Bruininks, Mary F. Hayden, & Xiaoming Li, Programs and Services Received by Persons with Mental Retardation in Three Models of Small Community Residences, 3 **J. Disability Pol'y Stud.** 17–44 (1992).

[34] *See* **infra Ch. XVI §§ 16.6 & 16.7** (discussing economic and noneconomic barriers to integration in work and daily life).

Figure 9.9

Percentage of Persons Living in the Community

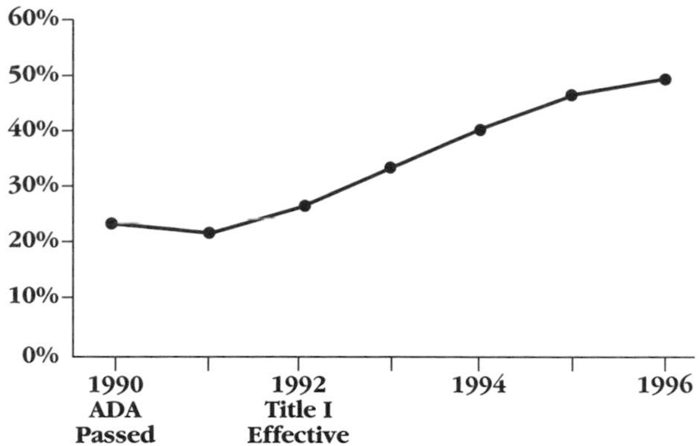

9.8 Rise in Self-Advocacy Activities

A core principle of the ADA is to empower people with disabilities to fulfill their potential as equal members of American society.[35] One measure of empowerment in society for persons with mental retardation has been involvement in self-advocacy activities. Figure 9.10 shows that the proportion of participants involved in self-advocacy activities more than doubles—from 16 percent in 1990 to 35 percent in 1996.[36] The rise in self-advocacy activities is more dramatic for men than women.

A 1994 Harris poll found that 27 percent of persons with disabilities participated in group or organized activity on behalf of people with disabilities. Of those individuals aged 25 to 60, 40 percent reported such involvement. The number of persons with disabilities who report a strong sense of common identity with other individuals with disabilities has increased from 40 percent in 1986 to 54 percent in 1994.

By way of summary, for the present participants, involvement in self-advocacy is greater for those who:

1. are younger ($r = -.26$, $p = .0001$);
2. are men ($r = .08$, $p = .0001$);
3. have higher capabilities and job qualifications composite scores ($r = .32$, $p = .0001$);
4. have better health status ($r = .10$, $p = .0001$);
5. live in more integrated settings ($r = .28$, $p = .0001$);
6. do not need adaptive equipment devices ($r = -.08$, $p = .0001$);
7. receive more family and governmental supports ($r = .06$, $p = .002$);
8. report more satisfaction in work and daily life ($r = .22$, $p = .0001$);
9. report perceived barriers to accessibility in work, education, and public transportation ($r = -.04$, $p = .02$, for ADA composite accessibility measure).

As work and daily life become more integrated and independent, the participants with mental retardation focus greater attention on involvement in self-advocacy activities. The trends in the present study are consistent with the growing national self-advocacy movement for persons with mental retardation[37] and with the spirit of individual empowerment fostered by the ADA.[38]

---

[35] *See* 137 **Cong. Rec.** S11,107 (daily ed. July 26, 1991) (statement of Sen. Harkin); Dart, *in* **Rights and Responsibilities, supra Ch. I § 1.1,** at xxi, xxiv–xxv (discussing "empowerment policy").

[36] For rise in self-advocacy over time, t(910) = 10.31, $p < .001$. *Cf.* **AAMR, supra Ch. III § 3.1,** at 2 (*citing* study showing that the number of participants in the self-advocacy movement has increased substantially in the last several years).

[37] *See* **AAMR, supra Ch. III § 3.1,** at 2 (*citing* the Pennhurst Study).

[38] *See* Shapiro, **supra Ch. I § 1.1,** at 181–207 (discussing need for integration and empowerment of persons with disabilities); Gary E. Holmes, The Historical Roots of the Empowerment Dilemma in Vocational Rehabilitation, 4 **J. Disability Pol'y Stud.** 1–20 (1993) (discussing concept of empowerment in employment training context).

Figure 9.10

Trends in Self-Advocacy from 1990 and 1996

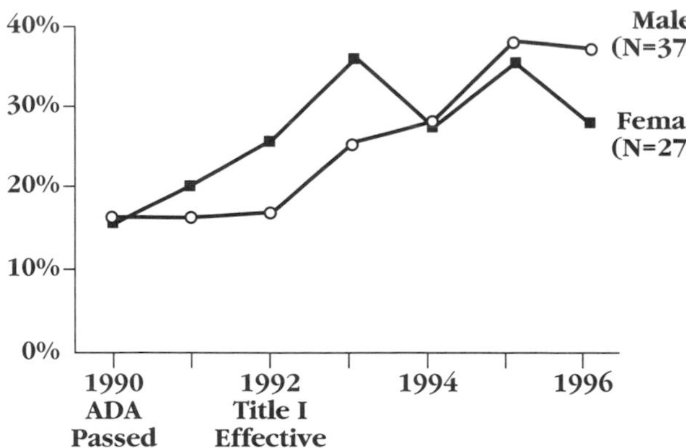

Analysis of Variance

	F	P
Gender	0.83	.37
Time	27.13	.0001
Gender * Time	3.82	.0008
DF Error =	554 &	3324

Further analysis of the trends in self-advocacy is warranted because the movement's major objectives are closely related to the long-term goals of the ADA: namely, support for independent living, fair wages, empowering changes in laws, and equitable modifications to entitlement programs.[39] Professor Balcazar and his colleagues have reported that there may be developmental stages in advocacy involvement for persons with mental retardation.[40] Over time, those individuals most active in self-advocacy show increased activity in school presentations, public hearings, and volunteer activities.

9.9 Rise in Family and Governmental Supports That Reduce Barriers to Work

The findings described in Chapter VIII illustrate that the use of natural supports and workplace accommodations in employment may empower qualified workers with disabilities.[41] Natural supports in the workplace have been shown to reduce the barriers to employment faced by qualified workers with mental retardation.[42]

Chapter XVII of this book examines the ways in which community and governmental supports are crucial to enhance employment integration and to lessen the barriers to work for many qualified people with mental retardation.[43] Related education and vocational training programs are critical to employment integration and economic opportunity under ADA implementation.

During the years 1990 to 1996, family and governmental supports available to the participants rise. In his analysis of a subset of the present participants, James Conroy finds both improvements and declines in the provison of several work-related supports, such as improvements in the areas of daily living training and in speech and communication skills, yet declines in the areas of occupational and physical therapy.[44] Further study is needed on the magnitude, quality, and individualized nature of

---

[39] *See* **AAMR, supra Ch. III § 3.1,** at 2.

[40] Fabricio E. Balcazar, Christopher B. Keys, Joyce F. Bertram, & Thomas Rizzo, Advocate Development in the Field of Developmental Disabilities: A Data-Based Conceptual Model, 34 **Mental Retardation** 341–51 (1996).

[41] Shapiro, **supra Ch. I § 1.1,** at 232–36 (discussing the importance of family involvement); **AAMR, supra Ch. III § 3.1,** at 101–03 (noting that this belief is exemplified by the current emphasis on supported employment programs).

[42] *See* **supra Ch. II § 2.9** (discussing natural workplace supports in the context of *Anderson v. General Motors*).

[43] *Id.* at 101 (noting that the rehabilitation profession emphasizes personal satisfaction, individual choices, decisions, and empowerment, while recognizing the need for fiscal and programmatic accountability).

[44] Conroy, **Hissom Outcomes Study, supra Ch. I § 1.6,** at 48–50 (reviewing growth support areas).

these supports, a topic discussed in Chapter XVI in the context of welfare reform policy and breaking down barriers to work.

Analysis of the relation of work-related supports to individual growth and empowerment is warranted. Balcazar finds that those individuals more involved in self-advocacy activities tend to receive greater family and governmental supports with regard to how to implement change.[45]

During the period under study in this investigation, many of the job- and life-skill educational goals for these participants decrease. Thus, as participants become more "qualified" for work, they require lower levels of subsequent training in traditional vocational training programs. This finding is consistent with Balcazar's suggestion that individuals with mental retardation proceed through developmental stages of involvement in self-advocacy, increasingly becoming more independent in their work activities.

9.10 Changes in Perceptions of ADA Implementation

Few studies have examined changes in the self-reported perceptions of consumers with disabilities after ADA implementation. The 1994 Harris poll found that more persons with disabilities believe that access to employment opportunity has improved since 1990 than believe it has regressed (44 percent versus 28 percent).

Likewise, substantially more people believe that access to public transportation, an area covered by ADA Title II, improved between the years 1990 and 1994 (60 percent reported improvements over the period). In the area of access to public accommodations, covered by ADA Title III issues, 75 percent of those surveyed reported improvements.

A 1994 federal General Accounting Office (GAO) report on the positive effects of ADA Title III on access to goods and services supported the Harris findings.[46] Yet barriers were reported to remain, including insufficient signs with raised print or braille, insufficient assistive devices in hotel rooms for persons with hearing impairments, inaccessible showers, tubs, toilets, and sinks in hotel rooms, and public telephones with no text telephone or amplification systems.

Half the businesses examined in the 1994 GAO report had failed to remove existing accessibility barriers and had no plans to remove them in the future. Contributing to this trend was the lack of information that many businesses reported in determining the extent to which they were in compliance with the ADA. The 1994 GAO report concluded that the demand for technical assistance and information on ADA implementation and compliance exceeded the current resources of the federal and local governments.

The present investigation explores the participants' self-reported views of accessibility to society during the years 1990 to 1996, the period of early ADA implementation. The findings for the ADA composite measure, and the analysis of the individual Title I, II, and III measures, suggest that these participants report improved access over time to work, education, transportation, and public accommodations.

Figure 9.4 showed that reported accessibility to employment (Title I issues) increased over the time period from 85 percent to 96 percent. Similarly, reported access to state and local governmental services (ADA Title II issues) increased from 87 percent to 95 percent. Reported access to public services (ADA Title III issues) increased from 76 percent to 84 percent. One reason for the high proportion of participants reporting accessibility may be the self-selecting nature of these respondents—that is, this analysis is conducted on those individuals who have experienced access to work and daily life.

Figure 9.11 summarizes the participants' reported attitudes concerning perceptions of access to work, daily life, and society during the years 1990 to 1996.

From 1990 to 1992, in the early years of implementation, perceptions of ADA effectiveness and of access to society increased. Starting in 1992, and through 1994, attitudes about rights and access dropped. From 1994 to 1996,

---

[45] Balcazar, et al., **supra Ch. IX § 9.8.**

[46] U.S. Gen. Accounting Office, **Americans with Disabilities Act: Effects of the Law on Access to Goods and Services** (Pub. No. GAO/PEMD-94-14, 1994).

Figure 9.11

Perceptions of ADA Rights over Time

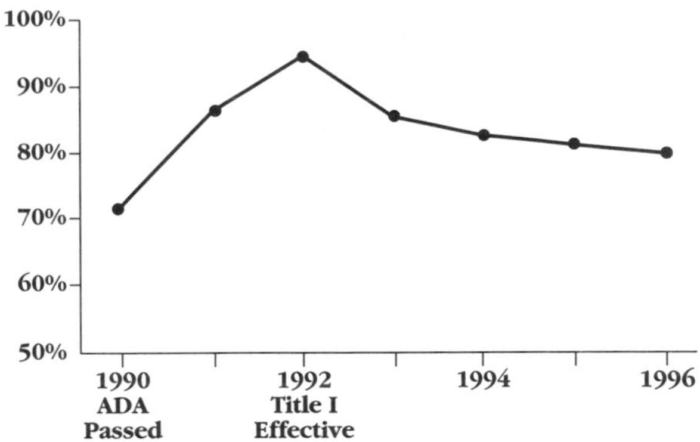

reported levels are almost comparable to those reported in 1990. Further analysis is needed to understand the dramatic changes in individual growth that are occurring during ADA implementation.

According to the 1994 Harris survey, more than one third (35 percent) of adults with disabilities mistakenly believed that no law granting protection to people with disabilities had been implemented since 1990. Not even half of those surveyed (42 percent) were aware that disability antidiscrimination laws had been passed. Less than half (40 percent) had neither read nor heard about the ADA. Although these figures show a relatively low level of awareness of the ADA, they show a marked improvement in awareness since 1991, when only 16 percent of adults with disabilities were aware of the law. Analysis of ADA stakeholders' perceptions and individual growth during implementation may contribute to greater awareness of the law.[47]

The present findings suggest that upon passage of the ADA, during the two-year period from 1990 to 1992, expectations were high for a new civil rights era for people with disabilities. In just seven years, however, ADA implementation may not have achieved the promise of full inclusion and empowerment in society. Although it is too early to make definitive conclusions about these trends, research must examine over time the relation of attitudes and behavior in society to equal employment opportunity for qualified persons.[48] This topic is revisited in Chapter XVII, in the context of barriers to work and to society.

9.11 Summary

The findings from the present investigation illustrate substantial changes in individual growth and empowerment during the early years of ADA implementation. According to James Conroy's analysis of a subset of participants from the present investigation, the magnitude of individual growth and empowerment evidenced from 1990 to 1995 is greater than he and Valerie Bradley found in their classic *Pennhurst Longitudinal Study* conducted over a 14-year period.[49]

---

[47] Melinda Henneberger, Technology Revolution Reaches the Retarded, **N.Y. Times,** at AI (Sept. 7, 1993) (discussing the increased role of assistive technology in independent living, education, and employment); Timothy L. O'Brien, A PC Revolution: Aided by Computers Many of the Disabled Form Own Businesses, **Wall St. J.,** at 1 (Oct. 8, 1993).

[48] *See* Paul Wehman, Employment Opportunities and Career Development, *in* **ADA Mandate, supra Ch. VIII. § 8.6,** at 255.

[49] Conroy & Bradley, **supra Ch. I § 1.1,** at 66–67.

CHAPTER X

Simple and Complex Relationships in the Research Model

Fundamentally, what is at issue in the current policy debate over expanding transfer rolls is how society should treat people with disabilities. Should people with disabilities be expected to work or not?

Richard Burkhauser[1]

The effort to understand behavior must itself be one of the oldest of human behaviors. But for all the centuries of effort, there is no compelling evidence to convince us that we do understand human behavior....The application of scientific method has not simplified human behavior. It has perhaps shown us more precisely just how complex it really is.

Robert Rosenthal[2]

10.1 Introduction

The prior chapter examined changes in the participants' characteristics on the measures identified by the research model set forth in Figure 1.1. The findings illustrate substantial individual growth and empowerment during the early years of ADA implementation.

Although the magnitude of growth and empowerment evidenced is encouraging, the descriptive findings cannot fully inform ADA stakeholders about many of the complex and ongoing issues related to employment integration and economic opportunity during early ADA implementation. This chapter examines the predictive value of the measures in the research model using correlational (simple bivariate) and regression (complex multivariate) analyses.

10.2 Predicting Employment Integration: Correlational Analysis

Only recently have questions been raised about trends in employment integration and economic opportunity for qualified persons with disabilities. Research is emerging on how particular job types may influence career advancement for men and women with disabilities. Professor David Braddock and his colleagues have described the "glass ceiling" that many qualified

[1] Burkhauser, *in* **Annals, supra Ch. IV § 4.4,** at 73.

[2] Robert Rosenthal, **Experimental Effects in Behavioral Research** (1976).

Figure 10.1

Employment and Earned Income in 1996: Simple Correlations

Variable	Employment Category	Earned Income
Personal Background		
Age	–.35****	–.34****
Female	–.12****	–.12****
Minority	.03*	.004
Capabilities & Qualifications[a]	.50****	.59****
Adaptive Skill	.54****	.66****
Health Status	.27****	.29****
Equipment/Accommodation	–.09****	–.09****
Inclusion Factors		
Living Arrangement	.48****	.46****
Job/Life Satisfaction & Choice	.38****	.46****
Empowerment[b]	.27****	.30****
Self-Advocacy	.33****	.44****
Family & Government Support	.12****	.09****
Job/Skill Educational Goals	–.02	.002
Legal Factors		
ADA Composite[c]	–.04**	–.05***
Title I	–.05***	–.08****
Title II	–.04**	–.07****
Title III	–.008	.01

Note: Presented above are Pearson correlations. All variables reflect scores in 1996, based on a sample size of 3,057. Earned income is based on log dollars. A positive correlation indicates that more integrated employment category and higher earned incomes are associated with higher or more integrated scores on the various factors. A negative correlation would indicate the converse.

[a] Composite score comprised of first principal component for adaptive skills and health status.

[b] Composite score comprised of first principal component for self-advocacy, family and government support, and job/skill educational goals.

[c] Composite score comprised of first principal component scores for Titles I–III.

* = statistical significance assessed at $p \leq .10$; ** = at $p \leq .05$; *** = at $p \leq .01$; **** = at $p \leq .001$. Significance levels are a function of the magnitude of the effect and sample size.

workers with disabilities face; it limits upward career advancement.[3] Careful study is warranted, given that some researchers argue that while a reduction in discrimination patterns against women and minorities with disabilities may occur as a result of the implementation of the ADA, the law's impact is not likely to be fully corrective.[4]

Figure 10.1 presents the simple correlations between the independent variables in the research model and the 1996 employment-category and earned-income measures. A

[3] David Braddock & L. Bachelder, **The Glass Ceiling and Persons with Disabilities,** Public Policy Monograph Series, No. 56 (1994).

[4] *See* William J. Hanna & Elizabeth Rogovsky, On the Situation of African-American Women with Disabilities, 23 **J. Applied Rehab. Counseling** 43–44 (1992) (arguing that "the changes in discrimination [against minorities and women with disabilities that] may occur as a result of the passage of the Americans with Disabilities Act are not likely to be fully corrective"); Stephen Labaton, Benefits Are Refused More Often to Disabled Blacks, Study Finds, **N.Y. Times,** at A1, A12 (May 11, 1992) (summarizing Congressional study that blacks are more likely than whites to be rejected for federal disability benefits).

positive correlation indicates that a more integrated employment category or higher earned-income level is associated with a higher or more integrated score on that independent measure.

The center column of Figure 10.1 shows that the majority of independent measures, assessed from 1990 to 1996, are useful for predicting the participants' degree of integration in 1996 employment. The emerging workforce of younger relative to older participants experience more integrated employment in 1996 (r = -.35). Men, compared to women, experience more integrated employment in 1996 (r = .12). Minority status tends to be related to a participant's degree of integration in employment category in 1996 (r = .03).

Understanding of background variables, such as age, gender, and race, and related trends in employment integration for persons with mental retardation require additional investigation, some of which is explored in the next chapter. As discussed in in Chapter XIV, study is required on the types of jobs attained by qualified persons with mental retardation.

Figure 10.1 shows that participants with better capabilities and job qualifications scores tend to be employed in more integrated work settings in 1996 (r = .50). In particular, those in more integrated work settings in 1996 have higher adaptive skills (r = .54), better health status (r = .27), and less adaptive equipment needs (r = .09).[5]

Examination of the "inclusion factors" in Figure 10.1 show that participants in integrated employment are more likely to reside in integrated living (r = .48) and are more satisfied with their job activities and daily life activities (r = .38). This finding is consistent with studies showing that integrated employment activities for employees with disabilities result in increased self-esteem.[6]

Participants in integrated work also tend to show higher scores on:

1. the empowerment composite measure (r = .27),
2. levels of involvement with self-advocacy (r = .33), and
3. family and governmental support for their employment activities (r = .12).

As discussed in Chapter VIII, analysis of trends in self-advocacy involvement suggest strategies for enhancing equal employment opportunity consistent with the goals of the ADA. Systematic study of the impact of People First self-advocacy groups is needed to assess the ways in which these groups aid people with developmental disabilities in making choices about work and daily living.[7] The sharing of information between employers and self-advocacy groups such as People First, now organized in almost every state, is an important link for enhancing employment opportunity for persons with disabilities.

Figure 10.1 shows that participants in integrated employment tend to report lower accessibility scores on the ADA composite measure (r = -.04). Participants in integrated work also perceive less accessibility to employment (r = -.05) and to governmental services (r = -.04), relative to those in less integrated work settings.

10.3 Predicting Economic Opportunity: Correlational Analysis

In an analysis of 1984 wages, Professor Robert Haverman and Barbara Wolfe have found the average earned income of men with physical and mental disabilities was roughly half that of nondisabled workers.[8] Using a similar sample from 1984, Professors Marjorie Baldwin and William Johnson reported this wage differential to be much smaller when analyzing only men with functional impairments.[9] Comparison is needed of the earned income of these partici-

---

[5] *See* McNeil, **supra Ch. I § 1.1,** at 13 (outlining census data from 1991–1992 that show a negative relation between earnings and disability severity).

[6] *See* Mary Sinnott-Oswald, et al., Supported and Sheltered Employment: Quality of Life Issues Among Workers with Disabilities, 26 **Educ. & Training in Mental Retardation** 388–97 (1991) (noting that self-esteem relates to competitive employment).

[7] New Directions: People First of Washington Provides Informed Choice and Advocacy, 21(6) **Pub. Nat'l Association of State Mental Retardation Program Directors** 1, 2 (June 1991).

[8] Robert Haverman & Barbara Wolfe, The Economic Well-Being of the Disabled, 1962–1984, 25 **J. Hum. Resources** 41 (1990).

[9] Marjorie L. Baldwin & William G. Johnson, Labor Market Discrimination Against Men with Disabilities, 29 **J. Hum. Resources** 6 (Winter 1994).

pants with mental retardation and of those without disabilities in comparable jobs. Before passage of the ADA, only a few studies had examined the relative wage levels of qualified workers with and without disabilities.[10]

In other studies Professor Baldwin and her colleagues have found that earned income patterns not only vary across different impairments, but with gender as well.[11] These researchers find that physical impairments generate relatively lower wage ratios for men than for women. The converse is found for mental impairments. Chapter XI profiles the types of jobs held by many of the participants and views of the participants by many of their employers. The regression analyses presented later in this chapter is undertaken to understand how job type, nature of impairment, and gender relate to the participants' earned incomes.

The right column of Figure 10.1 shows that 14 of the 17 independent measures examined by the research model are useful for predicting 1996 earned-income levels.[12] Younger, relative to older, participants earn more income in 1996 (r = -.34). Men, compared to women, earn more income in 1996 (r = .12). Earning higher incomes are participants who score better on the job capabilities and qualifications composite measure (r = .59). This finding is particularly apparent for those with higher adaptive skills (r = .66), better health status (r = .29), and fewer adaptive equipment needs (r = -.09).

Consistent with the findings for the employment category, participants with higher incomes live in more integrated settings (r = .46) and report greater choice and satisfaction with their jobs and their lives (r = .46). Participants with higher incomes also show greater levels of empowerment (composite r = .30), are more involved in self-advocacy (r = .44), and receive more family and governmental supports (r = .09).

Professor Beverly Lozano finds from a seven-year longitudinal study that individuals with mental retardation receiving greater independent living services and skills training were more likely to live independently.[13] Likewise, Professor Robert Schalock and his colleagues find that persons with learning disabilities and mental retardation are more successful in employment training programs when their families are involved with the development of the programs.[14] The present findings support these trends, illustrating that participants in more integrated employment settings and earning more income tend to receive more job and skill training and education.

Future analysis of growth in the participants' levels of earned income over time may reflect expanding workplace opportunities as well as the changing attitudes by employers about the work potential of qualified people with disabilities.[15] This suggestion is consistent with studies finding that "much of [a] law's [initial] effect occurs in its shadow," and that over time,

---

[10] *Cf.* Lynn A. Carol, The Trend in Inequality Among Families, Individuals, and Workers in the United States: A Twenty-Five Year Perspective, *in* **Uneven Tides** 54, 63 (Sheldon Danzoger & Peter Gottschalf, eds., 1993) (real median income for men in 1989 was 10 percent below the 1973 peak and, depending on methodology, real median income for women grew 10–30 percent in the same period; also women have experienced significant real wage gains over the past 25 years, with black men and women experiencing higher gains than white men and women from 1973–1989).

[11] Marjorie L. Baldwin, Lester A. Zeager, & Paul R. Flacco, Gender Differences in Wage Losses from Impairments, 29 **J. Hum. Resources** 881–83 (Summer 1994).

[12] Consistent with predictions, integration in 1996 employment category relates strongly to 1996 earned income levels (r = .75, p < .0001).

[13] *See* Beverly Lozano, Independent Living: Relation Among Training, Skills, and Success, 98 **Am. J. Mental Retardation** 249 (1993) (results of a seven-year study show that individuals receiving greater independent living services and skills training were more likely to live independently); Julie A. Racino & Judith E. Heumann, Independent Living and Community Life, Generations, **Aging & Disabilities** 45 (Winter 1992) (discussing the relationship of independent living to the development of a sense of personal empowerment for people with disabilities).

[14] Robert L. Schalock, et al., Post-secondary Community Placement of Handicapped Students: A Five-Year Follow-Up, 9 **Learning Disability Q.** 297–98 (1986).

[15] *Cf.* Edelman, **supra Ch. I § 1.3,** at 1535 n.6 (study of interplay between organizations and their legal environments based on nationwide data from 346 organizations and finding that organizations sensitive to their legal environments tend to conform, first symbolically, then institutionally, to legal norms to achieve legitimacy, noting that "by influencing organizations' environments, law has an important indirect effect on organizational behavior that goes significantly beyond the direct effect of law and legal sanctions.").

organizations may institutionalize the ADA's goals through good faith attempts at compliance.[16]

Study also is needed to understand the disparity in income for those residing in various degrees of integrated living and how this acts as a disincentive to work for those residing in the community.[17] The 1994 Harris poll results showed that two thirds (66 percent) of those persons with disabilities interviewed who were not working would like to have a job.

Consistent with the findings of *Toward Independence* described in Chapter VI, income levels and the related disability support programs may reflect an overemphasis on income supports and an underemphasis on initiatives for independence and self-sufficiency for those residing in the community.[18] The wage disparities for the present sample echo the findings of prior studies suggesting that wage differences result in higher unemployment rates for persons with disabilities. A limitation of the present analysis is that, without other measures of severity of disability, it is not clear whether income disparity and related unemployment is due to disincentives in the disability benefit system or to the functional limitations of the participants.[19]

10.4 Controlling for Job Skill: Partial Correlations

Professor Marjorie Baldwin has found that the strongest evidence of discrimination against qualified workers with disabilities may be derived from research models that control for the effects of functional limitations (that is, worker capabilities and qualifications in the research model) on worker productivity.[20] Studies by Professor Michael Shafer and his colleagues show that, when controlling for adaptive skill, many persons with severe disabilities are employed effectively over time in integrated work settings.[21] Of course the term "severely disabled" is open to interpretation. One definition refers to individuals in the lowest functioning 1 percent of the population.[22]

To explore the extent to which the present findings may be influenced by the participants' job capabilities and qualifications (that is, in economic terms, by worker productivity), partial correlation analysis was performed. Partial correlations describe the relationship of an independent variable with a dependent variable in the research model, statistically controlling for the effects of other variables in the model.[23] Partial correlations between employment integration and movement, income levels, and

---

[16] *Id.* at 1569; John J. Donohue III, Further Thoughts on Employment Discrimination Legislation: A Reply to Judge Posner, 136 **U. Pa. L. Rev.** 523, 539 n.62 (1987) (if Title VII stimulated favorable attitudinal changes, there would be additional benefits in reducing discrimination); John J. Donohue III & James Heckman, Continuous Versus Episodic Change: The Impact of Civil Rights Policy on the Economic Status of Blacks, in **Equal Employment Opportunity: Labor Market Discrimination and Public Policy** 1717 (Paul Burstein, ed., 1994) (Civil Rights Act of 1964 "at first, may not have changed the attitudes, but it appears to have altered the behavior, of discriminatory employers"); James J. Heckman & Brook S. Poyner, Determining the Impact of Federal Antidiscrimination Policy on the Economic Status of Blacks: A Study of South Carolina, 79 **Am. Econ. Rev.** 138, 173–74 (1989) (federal government, through Title VII of the Civil Rights Act of 1964 and Executive Order 11246, was agent of change in integrating the textile workforce).

[17] *See* G.T. Sav, Benefit-Cost Analysis of Transitional Employment Programs, 55 (2) **J. Rehab.** 44 (1989) (placement of persons with disabilities into competitive employment generates direct and indirect benefits for participants and society); D.L. Poole, Competitive Employment of Persons With Severe Physical Disabilities: A Multivariate Analysis, 53 **J. Rehab.** 20 (1987) (noting SSI SSDI reduce or eliminate motivation of a beneficiary to work).

[18] *See* J. tenBroek & F.W. Matson, The Disabled and the Law of Welfare, 54 **Cal. L. Rev.** 809, 830 (1966) (casting welfare support as a system of governmental paternalism over persons with disabilities).

[19] *See* Poole, **supra Ch. X § 10.3,** at 20.

[20] Marjorie L. Baldwin, Estimating Wage Discrimination Against Workers with Disabilities, 3 **Cornell J. L. & Pub. Pol'y** 277 (Spring 1994).

[21] Michael S. Shafer, et al., Employment Retention and Career Movement Among Individuals with Mental Retardation Working in Supported Employment, 29 **Mental Retardation** 103, 108–09 (1991).

[22] *See* Pat Rogan & Stephen Murphy, Supported Employment & Vocational Rehabilitation: Merger or Misadventure?, **J. Rehab.**, at 39–40 (Apr.–June 1991) (citing other studies).

[23] *See* Jacob Cohen & Patricia Cohen, **Applied Multiple Regression/Correlation Analysis for Behavioral Sciences** 83, 181–82 (2d ed. 1983) (explaining that partial correlation is the relationship between two variables, with all other independent variables held constant).

the variables in the model were calculated, controlling for the capabilities and qualifications composite.

Examination of the partial correlations controlling for the capabilities and qualifications composite reveals a pattern of findings similar to those produced by the simple correlations presented in Figure 10.1. The analyses suggest that, for this sample of individuals, employment integration and economic growth does not depend solely on the participants' capabilities and qualifications. In other words, integration in work is attained by qualified persons with varying degrees of mental retardation, not only those with the highest job skill levels.

As discussed in Chapter XVI, many factors independent of job skill levels—such as the availability of accessible public transportation to the workplace, the provision of coworker supports or training in the workplace, and the availability of adequate health insurance benefits—affect employment opportunity for qualified persons with mental retardation. In the absence of information on these barriers to work, employers may underestimate the potential contribution of qualified workers with mental retardation to their economic bottomlines.[24]

In a promising line of study, Professor David Mank and his colleagues have found that certain characteristics of work settings are more predictive of the degree of integration in employment and resultant wage levels for workers than are these individuals' level of mental retardation.[25] Mank finds that employees with mental retardation experiencing employment similar to people without disabilities—that is, with a "typical" employment status and better interactions with workers without disabilities—in the same workplace tend to be more integrated into the work setting and receive higher wages, relative to those individuals with less typical employment status. The link between "typicalness" in employment and higher wages is found even when controlling for individual levels of retardation.

Consistent with Mank's findings, the present analyses highlight the need for study of the relation among employment opportunity, wages, and incentives and barriers to work for qualified persons with disabilities, issues that are examined in greater detail in Chapter XVI. As Mank concludes, if level of disability and mental retardation do not explain adequately an individual's degree of integration in employment and wage levels, then other factors may need to be explored, such as corporate culture, degree of typicalness in employment, workplace accommodations and natural supports, and coworker training.[26]

In the absence of such study, many employers will continue to rely on degree of "disability" as a primary proxy for determining whether to employ persons with mental retardation.[27] Yet, as tenBroek and Matson suggested more than 25 years ago, to the extent that employers may be provided useful information about workers with disabilities related to "the goals of integration—that is, of economic opportunity, social equality, and personal dignity"—they will be empowered to further the effectiveness of ADA implementation.[28]

10.5 Predicting Employment Integration and Economic Opportunity: Regression Analysis

The prior sections in this chapter examine simple correlational relationships in the research model. This section describes findings from the regression analysis that explores the overall predictive power of the research model.[29] Multiple regression analysis describes relationships that characterize a complex set of variables in which a single dependent (outcome) variable is predicted from scores on two or more independent predictor variables.[30]

---

[24] Marjorie Baldwin, Can the ADA Achieve Its Employment Goals?, 549 **Annals, supra Ch. IV § 4.4,** 37, 46–47 (Jan. 1997).

[25] Mank, et al., **supra Ch. IV § 4.9,** at 444–45.

[26] *Id. See also* **infra Ch. XIV § 14.2** (discussing role of corporate culture in the provision of workplace accommodations).

[27] Baldwin, **supra Ch. IV § 4.4,** at 37, 46–47.

[28] tenBroek & Matson, **supra Ch. X § 10.3,** at 840.

[29] Standard regression diagnostics were employed from the SAS Computer Program (for instance, analysis revealed no multicollinearity among the independent variables, and which data outliers could be adjusted).

[30] Cohen & Cohen, **supra Ch. X § 10.4,** at 7.

Two illustrative regression analyses are used to assess the relationship between the set of predictor measures and the outcome variables of employment category in 1996 and earned income level in 1996.[31] The regression analyses use 11 predictor variables: age, gender, race, adaptive skill level, health status, adaptive equipment needs, living arrangement, perceptions of satisfaction and choices in work and daily life, self-advocacy involvement, family and governmental support, job or skill educational goals, and the ADA composite. Many combinations of these measures could be employed as variables in regression equations. The purpose of presenting the regression analysis is to illustrate how the composite measures are useful for modeling aspects of the employment integration and opportunity.

The two outcome measures are defined as the degree of integration in employment category and earned income levels in 1996. A positive relationship between the dependent variable and a particular independent measure suggests that a higher level of integrated employment or earned income is associated with the independent variable.

In the presentation of the findings, the Multiple *R* (or R^2) represents the relationship between the degree of integration in employment or earned income and the set of predictor demographic and composite measures. The explained variance for each independent variable represents the contribution of the variable in the model, controlling for the effects of the other variables.

The Multiple *R* takes on values between 0 and 1, with the former indicating no relationship and the latter indicating a perfect relationship between the variables. The *F* and *t* tests describe the level of confidence for the assertion that the linear relationship between the set of predictor and criterion variables is not zero in the sample population.[32]

Predicting Employment Integration

Figure 10.2 shows the findings for the test of the research model predicting degree of integration in 1996 employment category.

The Multiple *R* for this regression equation suggests that the equation consisting of these independent variables explains approximately 44 percent of the variation in 1996 employment category for these participants.[33] The individual findings of the regression show that participants in more integrated employment in 1996 tend to be younger, male, have higher adaptive skills, and better health status. These participants live in more integrated settings, are more involved in self-advocacy programs, receive less family and governmental supports, and tend to have fewer equipment needs.

The findings illustrate that when performing multivariate analysis, as opposed to simple correlational analysis alone, an enriched view

---

[31] John McDonnell, et al., An Analysis of the Procedural Components of Supported Employment Programs Associated with Employment Outcomes, 22 **J. Applied Beh. Analysis** 417, 422–23 (1989) (describing the use of regression analysis similar to this project); J.S. Trach & Frank R. Rusch, Supported Employment Program Evaluations: Evaluating Degree of Implementation and Selected Outcomes, 94 **Am. J. Mental Retardation** 134, 138 (1989) (calling for multiple-regression analyses similar to that conducted herein); M.W. Brown & S.H.C. Du Toit, Models for Learning Data, *in* **Best Methods for the Analysis of Change** 47, 50 (Linda M. Collins & John L. Horn, eds., 1991) (reviewing statistical aspects of longitudinal field investigations).

The independent variables in the linear regression models used to examine the findings are entered simultaneously into the regression equation. This approach is conservative statistically as opposed to using a step-wise or hierarchical regression model, because it places emphasis on the conceptual development of the model than on the magnitude of the statistical effects. This strategy avoids bias as to the conceptual ordering or placement of independent variables in the regression model. In many instances a sample size of participants as large as the present one will yield statistical significance for even the most conservative of approaches. The focus is on trends, directions, and magnitudes of the effects that appear. The independent measures chosen in the regressions represent the participants' 1996 status. An alternative approach for study is to examine relationships among the changes over time in independent and dependent measures.

[32] *See* Cohen & Cohen, **supra Ch. X § 10.4,** at 49–50, 104 (indicating that *df* refers to the "degrees of freedom" required for statistical significance testing). All tests of significance are two-tailed. "NS" refers to the result being statistically not significant at the $p < .10$ level, for a two-tailed test.

[33] *Id.* at 3 (regression yields measures of the magnitude of the relationship among the independent variables and their relationship to the dependent variable—integration in employment).

Figure 10.2

Integration in Employment in 1996: Regression Results

Variable	Regression Coefficient	t-value	p-value	Explained Variance[b]
Personal Background				
Age	–.011	–12.82	.0001	5.6%
Female	–.112	–4.20	.0001	0.6%
Minority	.000	0.00	.99	0.0%
Capabilities & Qualifications				
Adaptive Skill	.011	21.60	.0001	14.5%
Health Status	.036	5.23	.0001	1.0%
Equipment Needs	–.094	–1.64	.11	0.1%
Inclusion Factor[a]				
Living Arrangement	.173	13.09	.0001	5.9%
Empowerment Factor				
Self-Advocacy	.182	5.65	.0001	1.1%
Family & Government Support	–.005	–3.66	.0003	0.5%
Job/Skill Educational Goals	.001	0.12	.91	0.0%
ADA Composite	–.027	–1.02	.31	0.0%

For this model, $R^2 = .44$, $F(11,2747) = 196.34$, $p < .0001$

[a] Job/life satisfaction & choice composite was tested separately because of reduced sample size (N = 970) and found to have a t-value of 1.67 with an associated p-value of .10.

[b] Explained variance is the squared partial correlation, which is the unique variance accounted for by each variable after adjusting for the effects of all other variables in the model.

emerges. The regression reveals that different combinations of the individual variables predict 1996 employment.[34] As the right column of Figure 10.2 shows, participant age, skill level, and degree of independence in living predict degree of integration in 1996 employment (combined explained variance is roughly 26 percent), when statistically controlling for the other variables in the model.[35]

This finding suggests that these three variables, particularly skill levels, enhance the predictability of degree of integration in em-

---

[34] Regressions with the smaller sample sizes (n = 970) were performed with the job/life satisfaction and choice variable and the other 11 independent measures for both the employment category and earned income. For the employment category, with the addition of the consumer satisfaction variable, the $R^2 = .408$, $F(12, 957) = 55.00$, $p < .0001$ showed satisfaction to be a significant contributor ($p = .10$, .3 percent independent explained variance).

[35] *See* Cohen & Cohen, **supra Ch. X § 10.4,** at 39–43. For the individual variables in the model, a conservative estimate of explained variance is computed by dividing the sum of squares (Type II in SAS computer program) by the corrected total sum of squares. Type II sum of squares reflects the variance accounted for, assuming the variable in question is entered last in the regression equation. The combined individual explained variance will be less than the total explained variance. Caution must be used in relying on standardized skill measures alone to predict the individual explained variance in employment integration.

Regressions were conducted testing employment movement from 1990 to 1996. The same 11 predictor variables were used: age, gender, race, adaptive skill, health status, adaptive equipment needs, living arrangement, self-advocacy, family and government support, job or skill educational goals, and the ADA composite. The dependent measure is the degree of employment movement from 1990 to 1996. The R^2 for the regression equation is statistically significant: $R^2 = .03$, $F(11, 872) = 2.48$, $p < .005$. The finding suggests that this combination of variables predicts employment movement for these participants. The R^2 explains roughly 3 percent of the variance. The individual findings of this regression show that integrated employment movement from 1990 to 1996 is greater for participants who are younger and in better health.

ployment category. The externally driven empowerment variables, on the other hand, do not strongly predict degree of integration in employment category.[36] At this stage of ADA implementation, forces beyond that of the law itself may better predict employment integration.

Closer examination of the findings for the ADA composite, analyzed separately for those participants not employed versus those in some form of employment (e.g., sheltered, supported, or competitive), show almost all (92 percent) of those unemployed report no ADA-related accessibility problems, as compared to most of those (88 percent) in some form of employment reporting no problems.[37]

This finding suggests that for many people with disabilities the experience of employment itself heightens awareness of ADA-related accessibility barriers in work and daily life. Professors John Donohue and Peter Siegelman comment that "employment integration has not come about through direct changes in the law itself or the ways the courts have interpreted it [but rather] the nature of the protection provided by anti-discrimination legislation has been shaped by the behavior of plaintiffs, defendants, and the economy at large."[38]

Predicting Economic Growth

The second set of regressions assess the relationship between the same 11 predictor measures and the dependent variable of participants' earned income in 1996. In actual dollars, earned monthly income in 1996 for the participants ranged from $0 to $1,936. The actual mean monthly earned income for those not employed, $8 (with 97 percent earning no income), for those in sheltered workshops, $163 (with 26 percent earning no income), for those in supported employment, $430 (4 percent earning no income), and for those in competitive employment, $521 (with 1 percent earning no income).

Figure 10.3 illustrates the results of the regression. The explanatory power of the R^2 is again substantial and predicts 58 percent of the variance in the model.[39] Several independent measures predict 1996 earned income when controlling for the other measures in the model. Those individuals with higher earned incomes are younger, are men, and have higher skill scores and better health status. They tend to be in more independent living, involved with self-advocacy, and receive less family and governmental support.

The pattern of findings is consistent with those found for predicting changes in monthly gross income; that is, participants experiencing economic advancement are younger, have higher skill levels, and perceive accessibility limitations in employment and life activities.

The right column of Figure 10.3 shows that adaptive skill strongly predicts 1996 earned income (explained variance is 31 percent) when taking into account the other variables in the model. Skill level is a stronger predictor of earned income than it is of the degree of integration in employment. This finding suggests that once the qualified participants attain integrated employment, like persons without disabilities, their increased job skills are related directly to their wage levels.[40]

---

[36] *Cf.* Shapiro, **supra Ch. 1 § 1.1,** at 180 (stating that changes will occur not by the law alone).

[37] Chi Square test = 10.16, $p < .001$.

[38] John Donahue III & Peter Siegelman, The Changing Nature of Employment Discrimination, 43 **Stan. L. Rev.** 983, 1033 (1991).

[39] This test reflects findings for those individuals reporting 1996 wages and income. Because of the small sample size for the job or life satisfaction and choice variable, a separate regression was performed. For the regression with the smaller sample sizes with the job or life satisfaction, choice variable and the other 11 independent measures for 1996 earned income, $R^2 = .519$, $F(12, 838) = 100.78$, $p < .0001$, when controlling for the other variables, the satisfaction and choice variable predicts 1996 earned income, $t = 3.37$, $p = .0008$, 1.3 percent independent explained variance.

[40] A regression test of changes in monthly gross income from 1990 to 1996 also was conducted. In actual dollars, gross monthly income in 1996 (income from employment and entitlements) for these participants ranged from $0 to $2023. The actual mean monthly gross income for those not employed was $437 (90 percent earning no income), for those in sheltered workshops was $457 (31 percent earning no income), for those in supported employment was $757 (4 percent earning no income), and for those in competitive employment was $926 (1 percent earning no income).

This regression test uses the same 11 independent predictor variables. The R^2 for the test is statistically significant: $R^2 = .0908$, $F(11, 658) = 5.98$, $p = .0001$, suggesting that the combination of variables predicts income differences for these participants. The test reflects findings only for those individuals reporting wages and income. The results show that the

Figure 10.3

Earned Income in 1996: Regression Results[2]

Variable	Regression Coefficient Antilog[b]	t-value	p-value	Explained Variance[d]
Personal Background				
Age	.968	-13.54	.0001	7.0%
Female	.718	-4.51	.0001	0.8%
Minority	.857	-1.49	.14	0.1%
Capabilities & Qualifications				
Adaptive Skill	1.049	33.09	.0001	30.9%
Health Status	1.112	5.65	.0001	1.3%
Adaptive Equipment Needs	1.120	0.71	.48	0.0%
Inclusion Factor[c]				
Living Arrangement	1.433	9.84	.0001	3.8%
Empowerment Factor				
Self-Advocacy	2.672	10.98	.0001	4.7%
Family & Government Support	.979	-5.29	.0001	1.1%
Job/Skill Educational Goals	.995	-0.34	.74	0.0%
ADA Composite	.941	-0.88	.39	0.0%

For this model, $R^2 = .58$, $F(11,2453) = 306.27$, $p < .0001$

[a] Monthly earned income (actual) from employment ranged from $0 to $1936, with a mean of $155. The regression analysis uses log dollars.

[b] For each unit change in the independent variables, the corresponding 1996 income should be multiplied by the "regression coefficient antilog." A regression coefficient antilog of 1.0 signifies no effect. Antilogs above 1.0 indicate a positive increase in income associated with an increase in the independent variable. Antilogs below 1.0 indicate a corresponding decrease in income.

[c] Job/life satisfaction & choice measure was tested separately because of reduced sample size and was found to have a t-value of 3.37 with an associated p-value of .0008.

[d] Explained variance is the squared partial correlation, which is the unique variance accounted for by each variable after adjusting for the effects of all other variables in the model.

10.6 Predicting Other Measures in the Research Model

Other exploratory regression analyses may be employed to assess the relationship between a set of predictor measures and a dependent variable in the research model. For instance, regression analysis may be employed to predict the participants' degree of integration in their living arrangement (i.e., the dependent measure). As in the above analyses, it is possible to explore degree of independence in living as based on combinations of other measures in the model. Prior studies have shown that inclusion into society, as reflected in independence in living, is an important predictor of many other individual life factors, such as integration in employment for persons with mental retardation.[41]

The Multiple *R* for this regression equation suggests that the equation consisting of these independent variables explains approximately

monthly gross incomes of younger participants increase over time. Those with increasing incomes live in more integrated settings, higher family and governmental supports, and score lower on the ADA composite measure. Income advances are evidenced by young and "qualified" participants who perceive accessibility barriers in employment and everyday life. The findings suggest that younger qualified individuals may experience less economic discrimination than do older individuals.

[41] *See* Lakin, et al., **supra Ch. IX § 9.7.**

40 percent of the variation in the 1996 integration in living measure. The individual findings of this regression show that participants in more integrated living in 1996 tend to be younger, have higher adaptive skills, and better health status. These participants also are more involved in self-advocacy programs, receive greater family and governmental supports, and have more equipment/accommodation needs.

Chapter VIII described the ways in which self-advocacy in the field of mental retardation is a means for ensuring full participation in society. The research model may be useful for examining the predictors of self-advocacy involvement by the participants. In such a test of the model, the regression equation consisting of the independent variables set forth in the research model predict 1996 involvement in self-advocacy. The individual findings of the test show that participants more involved in self-advocacy in 1996 are younger, male, have higher skill scores, are less likely to need adaptive equipment, live in more integrated settings, and have more job or skill educational goals.

As mentioned in Chapter VIII, the consumer interview measure is based on participants' views of their employment and daily living opportunities. Prior study has suggested that persons with mental retardation who report enhanced choice in work and life are more likely to attain and retain employment.[42] The Multiple *R* for this regression equation suggests that the equation consisting of these independent variables explains approximately 30 percent of the variation in reported consumer satisfaction and choice in 1996. Again, the individual findings of the regression show that participants reporting more satisfaction and choice in 1996 tend to be younger, have higher adaptive skill and health status, live in more integrated settings, and report difficulties with accessibility to work, education, and daily life opportunities. These participants also are more involved in self-advocacy and receive greater family and governmental supports.

Finally, Chapter VIII describes how the present investigation's ADA composite measure examines participants' perceptions of their access to employment and daily life opportunities. ADA Title I requires employers to ensure that employees with disabilities have physical access to equal educational and employment services and other elements that make it possible to find and retain a job. Yet studies show that accessibility in the home relates to the ability to adapt to accommodations in the work setting. Likewise, the lack of access to education and transportation forecloses the possibility of employment for many people with mental retardation.

With regard to the prediction of perceptions of ADA implementation and the other measures in the research model, the Multiple *R* for this regression equation suggests that the equation consisting of these independent variables explains approximately 4 percent of the variation in perceptions of ADA implementation. The individual findings of the regression show that those experiencing less difficulty in access tend to be older, female, and residing in integrated settings.

10.7 Summary

The analyses presented in this chapter illustrate predictive relationships on measures in the research model that are useful to a comprehensive understanding of employment integration and economic opportunity for these participants. The analyses identify combinations of factors that help predict individual growth and change during ADA implementation.

The findings are not meant to suggest a hard-and-fast method for establishing the employment potential of persons with disabilities. Instead, they illustrate the usefulness of the research framework to the description of the capabilities and lives of persons with mental retardation in varying employment settings. The findings highlight the complexity of the study of behavior of persons with disabilities. Although the variables tested in combination and separately explain a good deal of the complexity in predicting employment integration and economic opportunity, more study is warranted before any definitive conclusions may be drawn.

---

[42] *See* **AAMR, supra Ch. III § 3.1.**

CHAPTER XI

Profiles of Employment: Improvers, Regressors, and Stayers

The particular labels often chosen in American culture can carry social and moral consequences while burying their choices and responsibility for those consequences. The labels point to conclusions about where an item, or an individual, belongs without opening for debate the purposes for which the label will be used.

Martha Minow[1]

11.1 Introduction

Prior chapters in this book have highlighted "profiles" of participants in the four employment categories—not employed, sheltered workshop, supported employment, and competitive employment—in terms of the measures identified by the research model set forth in Figure 1.1. This chapter describes the profiles of those participants showing improvement, regression, or no change in employment integration during the years 1990 to 1996.

The employment profiles do not represent a prescriptive list of the measures necessary to predict employment movement. In part, this is due to the exploratory nature of the present analyses, which are sometimes based on relatively small cell sample sizes. Any interpretation or generalization of these profiles to other samples, or to other persons with disabilities covered by the ADA, therefore must be made with caution.

An illustration of this last point may be found in Professor Walter Oi's recent criticism of the ADA. Oi, a distinguished economist, has provided an interpretation of the "employment profiles" of workers with developmental disabilities, based on his interviews with various employers.[2] In a discussion with a manager at a large company employing 200 persons with developmental disabilities, Oi reports that he was surprised at the large number of workers with developmental disabilities willing and qualified to work. Oi comments that the manager said, "We pay them at union scales, and with that kind of money, there are lots of developmentally disabled folks who want to work."

---

[1] Martha Minow, **Making All the Difference,** at 4 (1990).

[2] Walter Oi, Comment on Burke, **supra Ch. VI § 6.1,** at 295 (suggesting an elastic supply of disabled workers based on interviews with several large employers).

11.2 Research on Employment Profiles

Predicting a person's employability is controversial, especially for persons with mental retardation who historically have been subjected to unjustified myths and misconceptions about their employment potential. As discussed in Chapter III, without careful study, profiles of worker qualifications often reflect the unfounded expectations or biased attitudes of employers—a point illustrated in Oi's comments above—more than they predict individual employment potential or productivity.[3] The profiles provide a description of the characteristics of the present sample with regard to their employment integration and economic opportunity during early ADA implementation.

A number of studies have tracked changes over time in the work profiles of persons with mental retardation. A three-year longitudinal study followed 53 individuals with mental retardation who stayed in sheltered workshops ("stayers") and 53 individuals who moved from workshops to supported employment ("movers") during the early years of ADA implementation, from 1990 to 1993.[4] Movers were substantially more satisfied with their employment activities than were the stayers.

Professors Roger Stancliffe and Brian Abery tracked 127 current and former residents of institutional living settings who had severe and profound mental retardation.[5] Of the 127 participants, 56 were classified as "movers" from the institution to the community and 71 as "stayers," residing in the institution after a one-year baseline assessment. The findings of this study showed that movers displayed greater choice in daily life activities than did stayers. The finding is consistent with the results in the present investigation showing that the participants reported substantially higher degrees of choice and satisfaction in work and daily life activities when working and living in more integrated settings.

James Conroy has tracked a subset of approximately 400 of the participants in the present investigation to assess their employment profiles as they move from segregated to integrated community living settings as a result of a deinstitutionalization order carried out during the years 1990 to 1995. Conroy concludes that the employment profiles of these individuals suggest that "they are better off" in 1995 than they were in 1990.[6] He writes: "The positive outcomes in employment, particularly in supported employment, far outstrip the results of any other deinstitutionalization that I have seen."[7] Conroy finds that the only indicator that showed potential decline was in the area of access to health care, a topic examined in Chapter XVI as a major barrier to work.

11.3 Employment Profiles: The Present Investigation's Findings

Figure 11.1 summarizes the profiles for three categories of participants: improvers, stayers, and regressors.

Several trends emerge. First, almost half (47 percent) of the participants remain in the same employment category over the period, 44 percent improve, while 9 percent regress in degree of integration in employment category. Consistent with the simple correlational findings described in Chapter X, employment improvers tend to be younger than stayers or regressors. Substantially fewer women (37 percent) than men (63 percent) improve in their employment category. This finding highlights the earlier suggestion that men relative to women made substantial advances in employment integration over the 1990 to 1996 period.

Over time, regressors, relative to improvers and stayers, show higher average skill scores. Closer analysis reveals that almost half of the regressors (43 percent) moved out of integrated employment settings back to sheltered workshops

---

[3] *See* Rogan & Murphy, **supra Ch. X § 10.4,** at 39–42. The profiles are not meant to suggest the bases for job selection criteria as set forth in 29 C.F.R. § 1630.10.

[4] *See* Corporate Alternatives, Inc., Overview of the Second Year Longitudinal Study of Supported Employment in Illinois, Springfield, Ill. (1990), *cited in* **ADA Mandate, supra Ch. VIII § 8.6,** at 33.

[5] Roger J. Stancliffe & Brian H. Abery, Longitudinal Study of Deinstitutionalization and the Exercise of Choice, 35 **Mental Retardation** 159–69 (1997).

[6] *See* Conroy, **Hissom Outcomes Study, supra Ch. I § 1.6,** at 63–65.

[7] *Id.* at 67 (conclusions based on analysis of subsample of approximately 400 individuals).

Figure 11.1

Profiles of Employees in 1996

Variable[a] Total (%)	Improvers 429 (44%)	Stayers 457 (47%)	Regressors 87 (9%)	p-value from Chi-Square test[c]
Personal Background				
Age (average)	34.4	36.3	36.5	.0008[d]
Female	37%	46%	44%	.04
Minority	19%	16%	13%	.30
Capabilities & Qualifications				
Adaptive Skill High	44%	54%	60%	.001
Health Status High	57%	54%	52%	.63
Equipment/Accommodation Satisfied	90%	90%	85%	.36
Inclusion Factors				
Living Arrangement Integrated[b]	51%	62%	80%	.001
Job/Life Satisfaction & Choice High	54%	50%	52%	.86
Empowerment Factors				
Self-Advocacy Involvement	44%	42%	45%	.81
Family & Government Support High	49%	49%	67%	.007
Job/Skill Educational Goals High	52%	56%	42%	.05
Legal Factors Satisfied				
Title I	85%	79%	76%	.04
Title II	85%	82%	76%	.09
Title III	69%	61%	62%	.06
Employment Category Integrated[e]	38%	5%	47%	.001
Monthly Income High	42%	56%	64%	.001

[a] A median-split defined low and high score categories for the measures in the model.

[b] Defined by institutional living = low integration; family, group, & independent living = high integration.

[c] Chi square test with two degrees of freedom.

[d] p-value for age is from ANOVA.

[e] Defined by not employed & sheltered employment = low integration; supported and competitive employment = high integration.

during the period 1990 to 1996. The majority of the other regressors (54 percent) became unemployed. Virtually all stayers (95 percent) remain in nonintegrated employment settings.

Regressors, particularly those with higher job skill scores, tend to live more independently and receive more supports but have fewer educational and training goals relative to improvers and to stayers.[8] The majority of those not experiencing any employment movement during the period stayed in the "black hole" of nonintegrated work settings, leading to a possible cycle of failure, segregation, and personal frustration.[9]

[8] *Cf.* Mank, et al., **supra Ch. IV § 4.9,** at 445 (finding that individuals with mental retardation who experience employment similar to people without disabilities in the same workplaces are more likely to earn higher wages over time).

[9] Shapiro, **supra Ch. I § 1.1,** at 183; Parent, *in* **ADA Mandate, supra Ch. VIII § 8.6,** at 27 (*citing* Moseley's 1988 study for the proposition that individuals with severe mental retardation who were previously in sheltered employment and moved to supported employment are more satisfied).

Figure 11.2

Black Hole Trends in Employment: 1990 and 1996

		1996 EMPLOYMENT STATUS		
		Non-integrated[a]	**Integrated[b]**	**Row Total**
1990 Employment Status	**Non-Integrated**	79% (713)	21% (187)	100% (900)
	Integrated	53% (39)	47% (34)	100% (73)

X^2 (1) = 96.92, $p < .001$ (test of symmetry)
[a] None and sheltered workshop status
[b] Supported and competitive status

11.4 The "Black Hole" Profile of Employment Segregation

Joseph Shapiro described the societal consequences of the "black hole" of employment segregation when he wrote: "When disabled people are herded into sheltered workshops to earn below-minimum-wage salaries for piecework, employers lose the impetus to hire good workers, and taxpayers foot the bill."[10]

Figure 11.2 highlights the "black hole" of nonintegrated settings in which many qualified persons with disabilities stagnate.

Figure 11.2 displays the relative percentage change in participants' employment status from 1990 to 1996. Employment is categorized as nonintegrated (none or sheltered) or integrated (supported or competitive).

Seventy-nine percent of those participants in nonintegrated settings in 1990 remained in those settings in 1996 (the "black hole effect").[11] The lower "survival rates" for those in integrated employment amplify this finding—47 percent of those in integrated settings in 1990 remained in this category in 1996.[12]

Fifty-three percent of the participants in integrated employment in 1990 regressed to nonintegrated settings by 1996.[13] In comparison, 21 percent of those in nonintegrated employment in 1990 moved to integrated employment by 1996. The findings are consistent with studies suggesting that persons with disabilities experience high levels of movement in and out of the competitive labor market.[14]

Study is crucial to assess the relation among ADA implementation, "black hole" unemployment trends for persons with disabilities and complaints of employment discrimination under the ADA. Donohue and Siegelman have analyzed the changing nature of employment discrimination litigation from 1970 to 1989. They conclude that prior to ADA implementation, worsening employment conditions, reflected by higher unemployment rates, led to the filing of

---

[10] Shapiro, **supra Ch. I § 1.1,** at 183.

[11] *Cf.* Kathryn Haring & David Lovett, A Study of the Social and Vocational Adjustment of Young Adults with Mental Retardation, 25 **Educ. & Training in Mental Retardation** 52 (1990) (57 percent of 58 participants with mental retardation were placed in sheltered workshops and paid below minimum wage).

[12] *See* Michael D. West, Job Retention: Toward Vocational Competence, Self-Management, and Natural Supports, *in* **Supported Employment, supra Ch. VIII § 8.6,** at 176, 194–95 (discussing strategies related to job retention for persons with disabilities).

[13] The investigation conducted separate analyses to explore the relative percentage changes from 1990 to 1996 in living status for these participants. The following trends emerged: (1) 56 percent of those in institutional living in 1990 still remained in 1996; (2) 41 percent of those in family or foster living in 1990 still remained in 1996; (3) 73 percent of those in group homes in 1990 still remained in 1996; and (4) 29 percent of those in independent living in 1990 still remained in 1996.

[14] This is true when appropriate supports and services are not provided. *See* Shafer, et al., **supra Ch. X § 10.4,** at 106–09 (tracking 302 individuals with mental retardation and finding that 30 percent of these individuals were employed in their original employment category 24 months following initial placement, and that there was no significant relation between level of retardation and employment status 24 months after placement).

more employment discrimination lawsuits.[15]

The high unemployment levels and low rates of integrated employment revealed in Donohue and Siegelman's investigation suggest the need for study in the present context. As discussed in Chapter XV, this analysis may foster dialogue about the ADA so that disputes may be avoided or resolved without resort to costly litigation.[16] This dialogue will become increasingly important, given the rising numbers of young, qualified, and independent persons with disabilities in the emerging workforce highlighted in this investigation.[17]

11.5 Profiles of the Emerging Workforce

Separate exploratory analyses conducted on the subgroup of 261 young adults with mental retardation ages 21 to 24 in 1996 reveals several trends of interest and of concern. First, only 16 percent of this young adult cohort were in integrated employment in 1996, reflecting a proportion lower than the entire sample average in this category (i.e., overall proportion of 22 percent).[18]

Those young adults in integrated (when compared to nonintegrated) employment tend to have better job skills and live more independently. The group of young adults in integrated employment are more involved in self-advocacy activities, receive more family support and educational goals, and have substantially higher monthly gross and earned incomes. The average earned income of young adults in integrated employment is three times that of adults of the same age in nonintegrated settings ($354 versus $112).

Of concern is that the majority of the group of young adults (84 percent) are either unemployed or in sheltered workshop settings. How many of these young persons will be relegated to the black hole of segregated employment is a question requiring careful study. The challenge for policy makers, members of the disability community and their families, and other ADA stakeholders is how to enhance the opportunities for these young adults before they attempt to enter the labor force. Many of the issues related to education, job training, and creating economic incentives to work for qualified young people with mental retardation are discussed in Chapter XVI.

Exploratory regression analyses were performed on the young adult subgroup, employing the same model and dependent and independent variables set forth in Chapter X. For this cohort, degree of integration in 1996 employment category is predicted strongly by the independent measures in the research model.[19] The individual findings of this regression model show that those young adults in integrated employment have better job skills. Earned income in 1996 also is predicted by the independent measures in the model, with those young adults earning more income having better job skills.[20]

Additional study over time is required of the profiles of the participants and other members of the emerging workforce. Study is needed of job retention patterns, employer satisfaction and consumer satisfaction with work, and wage growth. Professors Kregel and Wehman report that more than two thirds of persons in supported employment retain their job for at least a year, and roughly half retain their job for three years.[21] They find that employers have favorable ratings of their workers participating in supported employment programs—for instance on dimensions such as attendance reliability and job skill.

In their projected analysis of the growth and development of services and funding for

---

[15] Donohue & Siegelman, **supra Ch. X § 10.5,** at 987–88 (suggesting that the availability of employment serves as an alternative to litigation, but not analyzing ADA claims).

[16] *See* Mark K. O'Melveny, The Americans with Disabilities Act and Collective Bargaining Agreements: Reasonable Accommodation or Irreconcilable Conflicts, 82 **Ky. L. J.** 219, 225–26 (1994) (arguing that the best way to resolve ADA disputes is through full communication among all parties).

[17] *Cf.* Donohue & Siegelman, **supra Ch. X § 10.5,** at 992–93 (citing studies showing that younger, well-educated women are more likely to report employment discrimination); Peter Kuhn, Sex Discrimination in Labor Markets: The Role of Statistical Evidence, 77 **Am. Econ. Rev.** 567, 568 (1987) (study of same).

[18] Rogan & Murphy, **supra Ch. X § 10.4,** at 39–42.

[19] $R^2 = .377$, $F(11, 150) = 8.25$, $p < .0001$.

[20] $R^2 = .633$, $F(11, 138) = 21.68$, $p < .0001$.

[21] Kregel & Wehman, *in* **Integrated Employment, supra Ch. 1 § 1.3,** at 40–42.

persons with mental retardation in the state of Oklahoma, Professor David Braddock and his associates find that in 1997 the state ranked 14th in per capita spending for supported employment programs.[22] Oklahoma had the seventh highest percentage of state service participants receiving supported employment services.

As a result of substantial advances in state spending on community-based services, deinstitutionalization trends, the development of self-advocacy and family support activities, and the policy momentum created by ADA implementation, citizens with mental retardation in Oklahoma appear to be improving in their empowerment and inclusion in society.[23]

11.6 Profiles of the Participants' Employers

As part of the initial phase of this investigation, during the years 1990 to 1991 the research team collected baseline information about the practices of employers of the participants. This study explored employers' attitudes and expectations for the employment relationship, satisfaction with employees, needs for information and support services necessary to enhance the employment relationship, and knowledge of the ADA and its impact on the employment relationship.[24]

Forty-seven employers participated, ranging in size from small family businesses to large corporate firms. The interviews were completed in late 1990 and early 1991, before the effective date of ADA Title I. The information gathered included:

1. the number of individuals employed with and without disabilities;
2. the average length of tenure for employees with and without disabilities;
3. the jobs in which individuals with mental retardation were employed;
4. the level of satisfaction of workers with mental retardation, in job attendance, productivity, customer and coworker interaction, initiative and dedication to work;
5. the average number of hours worked and hourly wages of employees with and without disabilities;
6. the job coaching supports available to employees with mental retardation, including assessment of the employers' general level of satisfaction with job support services;
7. the factors relevant to employers for increasing the number of employees with mental retardation, including improved local economy, referrals, assistance in work place and transportation accessibility, job coaching and support services, and financial incentives to accommodate employees with disabilities;
8. knowledge of the ADA and perceptions of how the Act affects the employment relationship; and
9. views on the myths of employing persons with disabilities, including attitudes toward employees with disabilities regarding turnover, absenteeism, job performance, safety risks, accommodation needs, acceptance by customers, funding sources available to help pay for accommodations, and insurance needs.[25]

11.7 Employers' Attitudes of Employee "Qualifications"

The businesses surveyed included restaurants, major hotels, large discount store chains, research laboratories, churches, hospitals, and public schools. The firms ranged in size from small family businesses with only 1 employee to large corporations with more than 400 employees. General managers and supervisors of the firms completed the questionnaire instrument. Nineteen firms had fewer than 25 employees, 15

---

[22] *See* Braddock, **supra Ch. VIII § 8.2,** at 393 (discussion of 1997 state rankings).

[23] *Id.* at 393 (estimating that in Oklahoma, from the years 1989 to 1996—a period reflecting pre-and post-ADA implementation—spending on community services grew 288 percent in inflation-adjusted terms).

[24] *Cf.* Daksha A. Thakker, Employers and the Americans with Disabilities Act: Factors Influencing Manager Adherence with the ADA, with Special Reference to Individuals with Psychiatric Disabilities, Univ. Minnesota, Dissertation Abstracts International, 58/03-A (1997) (study of 195 managers examining factors that contribute to adherence to the ADA, finding that managers more likely to recruit, interview and hire people with physical as compared to mental disabilities).

[25] Several of the questions are based on a summary of myths presented in the **BNA Report, supra Ch. I § 1.5,** at 171–72.

firms had 25 to 99 employees, and 13 firms had 100 or more employees and were categorized as relatively larger firms.

Predictably, larger firms, compared to smaller firms hired more persons with mental retardation. Participants were employed in customer service, maintenance, food preparation, kitchen or restaurant clean-up, clerical positions, product assembly, machine operations, laundry services, and as cardboard bundlers, stockroom clerks, and receptionists. In Robert Schalock's 1989 national employment survey, almost one quarter (23 percent) of employees with mental retardation were employed in food service jobs and 18 percent in building service jobs.[26]

In the smallest firms, employees with mental retardation worked approximately 23 hours per week, with a range of 12 to 40 hours per week. In firms with more than 25 workers, employees with mental retardation worked roughly 28 hours per week. Schalock has found that employees with mental retardation in more integrated employment settings generally work longer hours than those in sheltered workshops, and this trend is more pronounced for those employed by larger firms.[27]

The mean tenure of employees with mental retardation for employers of all sizes was approximately 12 months. Tenure at a particular job across employers ranges from 2 to 36 months. The findings are consistent with other studies showing that a majority of employees with mental retardation placed in competitive settings remain in their job.[28]

The mean hourly wage during the years 1990 and 1991 for employees with mental retardation for all employers is approximately $4.16 per hour, with a range of pay from $3.80 to $5.00 per hour. The mean hourly wage for nondisabled employees in similar jobs was somewhat higher at approximately $4.30 per hour, with a greater range in pay, from $3.80 to $8.00 per hour.

Several measures assessed the employers' level of satisfaction with their employees with mental retardation on work attendance, productivity, interactions with customers, interactions with coworkers, initiative, and dedication to work. The importance of each of these dimensions to the definition of a qualified individual with a disability covered by the ADA is described in Chapters II and III. On these dimensions there were no substantial differences in the responses of the firms of varying sizes.

Approximately three quarters of the employers (74 percent) are very satisfied with employees' work attendance. Feelings about employee productivity are strong, as 41 percent of the employers are very satisfied with their employees on this dimension. Similarly, slightly more than half (52 percent) of the employers are very satisfied with their employees' dedication to their work and 31 percent are very satisfied with their initiative.[29]

Satisfaction with employee interactions with coworkers is high (see Chapter III for related discussion of essential job tasks under ADA), with almost half of the employers (41 percent) very satisfied with their employees with disabilities on this dimension. Prior study shows the opportunity to interact and train with employees without disabilities is greater in more integrated work settings, particularly in firms in which the physical environment is modified to achieve greater integration for persons with severe disabilities.[30] Similarly, several studies have

---

[26] *See* Schalock, et al., **supra Ch. 1 § 1.1,** at 83.

[27] *Id.* at 83–84 (reporting that individuals in sheltered employment work 20 percent fewer hours than those in competitive employment).

[28] *Id.* at 83 (finding approximately 78 percent of individuals with mental retardation retained their jobs for 60 days or longer); Kregel & Wehman, *in* **Integrated Employment, supra Ch. 1 § 1.3,** at 40–41.

[29] *Cf.* Peter J. Krebs, The Americans with Disabilities Act: Employment at the Compliance Threshhold, Walden Univ., Dissertation Abstracts International, 58/03-A (1997) (study of 369 small employers finding that nearly 70 percent reported that persons with mental disabilities could not perform their jobs as well as others without disabilities).

[30] Kregel & Wehman, **Integrated Employment, supra Ch. I § 1.3,** at 40–41; Joel M. Levy, et al., Attitudes of Fortune 500 Corporate Executives Toward the Employability of Persons with Severe Disabilities: A National Study 30 **Mental Retardation** 67, 71–74 (1992) (reporting that executives who had contact with persons with disabilities had more positive attitudes than executives who did not have such contact); Frank R. Rusch, Carolyn Hughes, John R. Johnson, & Kathleen E. Minch, Descriptive Analysis of Interactions Between Co-Workers and Supported Employees, 29 **Mental Retardation** 207 (1991) (finding high level of advocacy among coworkers and persons with severe and profound mental retardation).

shown the effectiveness of coworker mentoring job training.[31] Satisfaction with employee interactions with customers, for those individuals employed in service jobs, was rated high, with 19 percent of the employers very satisfied and another 78 percent generally satisfied with their employees who work in customer-service positions.

11.8 Factors Important to Hiring of Workers with Mental Retardation

Employers were asked to describe the factors that would increase the number of individuals with mental retardation that they would hire, including:

1. improved local economy;
2. increased number of referrals;
3. more assistance in workplace accessibility;
4. more assistance in transportation to the workplace;
5. improved job coaches;
6. increased job coach service; and
7. expanded fiscal incentives.

Many of the myths ascribed to the negative economic impact of ADA implementation on smaller, relative to larger, firms have not been borne out. In the present survey, the seven factors listed above were not predicted by firm size. Chapter XVI suggests that the greater managerial flexibility of certain smaller firms may give them an advantage in complying with the ADA.[32]

Most employers recognize the importance of an improved local economy or expanded financial incentives to enabling them to hire more individuals with mental retardation. Of the employers surveyed, nearly two thirds (60 percent) rate the local economy as somewhat important, and over two thirds (68 percent) rate financial incentives, such as tax breaks to accommodate workers with disabilities, as somewhat important.

Employers are not certain that an increase in referrals from state services would enable them to hire more individuals with mental retardation.[33] Roughly half (51 percent) of the employers report that more assistance from the state in improving workplace accessibility is somewhat important for them to hire more individuals with mental retardation.

A little more than half of the employers (53 percent) report that more assistance from the state in the transportation of employees to the workplace is not particularly important to their decision to hire more individuals with mental retardation. Finally, a majority of employers (53 percent) do not see lack of improved and increased job coach services as an important barrier to hiring more individuals with mental retardation.[34]

The responses suggest that, during early ADA implementation, employers had mixed views about the factors that may be important to them for increasing the number of qualified employees with mental retardation.[35] The development of empirical information may aid employers to better understand the capabilities and qualifications of workers with disabilities. As discussed in Chapter XII, educational and training initiatives may help to enhance effective ADA implementation.

---

[31] Marilyn Likins, Charles L. Salzberg, Joseph J. Stowitschek, Ben Lignugaris, & Rita Curl, Co-Worker Implemented Job Training, 22 **J. Applied Beh. Analysis** 381 (1989); Michael S. Shafer, Kelly Trait, Randy Keen, & Carole Jesinlowski, Supported Competitive Employment: Using Co-Workers to Assist Follow-Along Efforts, **J. Rehab.,** at 68, 73 (Apr.-May-June 1989) (an essential element of supported employment is the opportunity for persons with severe disabilities to work alongside workers without disabilities).

[32] Regardless of size, many businesses may be classified as places of public accommodation under Title III. *See* **infra Ch. XVI § 16.3** (discussing ADA Title III). As with larger firms, small firms with fewer than 15 employees must accommodate their patrons with disabilities as they would have to accommodate their employees with disabilities.

[33] *Cf.* **supra Ch. V § 5.8** (discussing *EEOC v. Hertz* case and the nature of the workplace accommodation of job coaching services provided at no cost to employers by employment providers).

[34] *Cf.* **supra Ch. V § 5.8** (decision of federal court in *EEOC v. Hertz*).

[35] Kevin Pritchett, Provisions of Disabilities Act Puzzle Many Firms, **Wall St. J.,** at B1 (Nov. 29, 1991) (noting that the vagueness of the EEOC regulations is creating apprehension among employers); Randall Samborn, Disabilities Act Regs Draw Mixed Reactions, **Nat'l L. J.,** at 10 (Aug. 12, 1991) (describing a survey that indicated that many employers are not preparing to comply with the ADA).

11.9 Employers' Myths About Their Workers with Mental Retardation

Employers were asked to agree or disagree with a series of questions relating to common myths about the hiring of persons with mental retardation. The categories of myths assessed include: performance issues, costs of accommodations, impact on insurance rates, and general perceptions of employees with disabilities.

The majority of employers (95 percent) do not believe that employees with mental retardation have higher turnover rates than nondisabled employees. All of the employers report that their disabled employees do not exhibit higher absenteeism rates than their comparable nondisabled employees.

More than two thirds of the employers (69 percent) do not believe that the job performance and productivity of disabled employees is necessarily lower than that of nondisabled employees. In addition, a high percentage of the employers (93 percent) do not believe that disabled employees create a safety risk at the workplace. Chapter XV of the book discusses the nature of employers' perceptions of safety risks in the workplace and the use of employment-based medical testing.

Most employers surveyed (91 percent) do not believe that making accommodations at the workplace for employees with disabilities is too expensive. Moreover, almost two thirds of employers (65 percent) believe that adequate funding sources are available to help pay for accommodations at the workplace for employing people with mental retardation or other disabilities.

Although most employers report that they do not believe that providing accommodations at the workplace is expensive, it is possible that the sample of responding employers represents only those employers having positive experience with accommodating workers with disabilities. Chapter XV examines in greater detail the economic implications of ADA accommodations.

Nearly all employers (95 percent) believe that insurance rates will not skyrocket if they hire more individuals with mental retardation. This is an important finding in light of the discussion in Chapter XVI suggesting that the loss of governmental health insurance coverage (e.g., Medicaid insurance) is a major disincentive to work for qualified persons with disabilities. Exclusion from employer-sponsored or private health insurance is a major disincentive to employment for many persons with severe disabilities.

Most employers surveyed (82 percent) do not believe that employees with mental retardation are overly demanding. Almost all employers (98 percent) believe that employees with mental retardation are not an embarrassment at the workplace. Notably, a majority of employers (84 percent) have communicated their positive experiences in employing persons with mental retardation to their colleagues in other businesses. This finding underscores the importance of enhancing communication, as well as sharing information among employers and employees with disabilities.

During early ADA implementation, more than two thirds of employers (68 percent) reported that they were not aware of the passage of the ADA. Although this finding may reflect limited knowledge on the part of the responding managers, it is troubling, given the importance of the ADA and its high profile in the workplace. Studies have indicated a growing awareness of the ADA, but it is not clear that employers are fully informed about the complexities of the law.[36] To avoid disputes under the ADA, it is vital that employers understand the Act's provisions.

Of the employers reporting knowledge of the ADA, most (86 percent) believe that the law will not affect the way in which they employ individuals with disabilities. Moreover, all of these employers (100 percent) understand that under the ADA employers do not have to choose job applicants with disabilities over equally or more qualified applicants without disabilities.

The pattern of findings in the present investigation may be contrasted with those from

[36] Susan Harrigan, Business of Being Fair to Disabled, at 17 **Newsday** (Oct. 18, 1991) (discussing a study conducted during the summer of 1991 by Jackson, Lewis, a New York employment law firm, finding that 59 percent of the employers knew that they would be affected by the ADA and 45 percent had begun planning for compliance; discussing a study of 252 New York City employers in October finding that 87 percent knew they would be affected by the ADA and 62 percent had begun planning for compliance).

a survey conducted during meetings of the Society for Human Resource Management in 1990 soon after the passage of the ADA.[37] Of the human resource executives surveyed, 85 percent were aware of the ADA, and of these respondents, 87 percent said they were familiar with Title I. Most executives (89 percent) did not know how much it would cost to comply with the ADA. Consistent with the findings of the present investigation, the human resource executives surveyed did not perceive a relationship between firm size and the ability to comply with Title I.

11.10 Summary

The present findings, though encouraging, suggest that a good deal of educational work lies ahead to ensure effective ADA implementation. One study found that almost 150 human resource trainees rated persons with mental retardation least positively in employment potential, when compared to persons with other disabilities such as epilepsy, spinal cord injury, and blindness.[38] Persons with mental retardation were rated lower on dimensions of productivity, coworker relations, attendance, adaptability, and potential for workplace accommodation. Many unfounded attitudes remain with regard to the employment of persons with mental retardation.

Information about the employability of qualified persons with mental retardation must be coordinated with educational and job training efforts structured to improve outcomes for those joining the workforce.[39] The findings add to the view that the employment of persons with disabilities is a function of several domains, including job skill, competence, and social-vocational competence.[40] Success in work requires that qualified employees with disabilities master these domains.

The present findings suggest that skills not directly related to employment (such as independence in living, self-care abilities, social inclusion, and self-advocacy empowerment activities) play an important role in the successful employment of persons with mental retardation. As discussed in Chapters XIII and XIV, for persons with severe disabilities covered by the ADA, workplace accommodations may involve individualized employment training, job coaching, or job-related personal assistance services (PAS).

Increased attention must be focused on the interaction of job-related, individual, and workplace accessibility factors in enhancing equal employment opportunity under the ADA. Professors Kiernan and Schalock have listed a number of such variables capable of study, including analysis of state economic and political characteristics, educational and training initiatives, family and coworker supports, natural supports in the workplace, employee work attitudes, skill and social behavior, economic incentives and barriers to work and access to transportation to work.[41] The following chapters of this book examine the implications of these factors for the emerging workforce of persons with mental retardation.

---

[37] *See* J. Freedley Hunsicker, Jr., Ready or Not: The ADA, 69 **Personnel J.,** at 80, 86 (Aug. 1990) (discussing a survey conducted by *Personnel Journal* in which 63 percent of the firms familiar with Title I believed they were in compliance with the law and 59 percent of the firms had started steps to comply).

[38] Michele Cheri Chism, Human Resource Management Students' Perceptions of Persons with Disabilities, Univ. Alabama, Dissertation Abstracts International, 57/12-A (1996). *See also* Laura M. Rees, et al., Do Attitudes Towards Persons with Handicaps Really Shift over Time? Comparison Between 1975 and 1988, 29 **Mental Retardation** 81 (1991) (positive shift in public attitudes toward persons with mental retardation).

[39] *See* McDonnell, et al., **supra Ch. X § 10.5,** at 424.

[40] *See* G.L. McCuller, S.C. Moore, & C.L. Salzberg, Programming for Vocational Competence in Sheltered Workshops, 56(3) **J. Rehab.** 41 (1990) (social skills required for successful competitive employment).

[41] *See* Robert L. Schalock, Person-Environment Analysis: Short and Long-term Perspectives, *in* **Economics, Industry, and the Disabled: A Look Ahead** (William E. Kiernan & Robert L. Schalock, eds., 1989), 105–16.

PART V:

Implications and Future Directions

CHAPTER XII

Implications of the Investigation's Findings

Arguably, Mattel's introduction of a new pal for Barbie, "Share-a-Smile Becky," represents a new consciousness toward disabled people. The doll comes in a pink-and-purple wheelchair.

Douglas Martin, New York Times[1]

Postscript: Becky's house was not accessible to her wheelchair use. Mattel is studying the problem. Some wonder whether Mattel will alter Becky's house or Becky's body dimensions.

12.1 Introduction

This book has described a comprehensive investigation of employment integration and economic opportunity during the initial implementation period of ADA Title I. The investigation is exploratory, with the findings requiring ongoing analysis. The views of policy makers, employers, and the disabled community regarding the integration of persons with disabilities into the mainstream of society has influenced the scope of this longitudinal investigation.

The research has explored attitudes, beliefs, and behavior relevant to ADA Title I. It is based on a large sample of persons with mental retardation, many of whom have physical disabilities. The book has described a process for exploring these issues within the context of a research model or framework of study, and the implications of the research findings. The chapters in this final part offer reflections on the investigation and its findings, suggest additional issues related to the future study of employment integration under the ADA, and examine implications for future policy development in the area.[2]

Although the present findings have immediate implications for persons with mental retardation, their families, and employers, the findings are perhaps better perceived as a bridge to future study. For these participants with mental retardation, relationships were discovered and documented that may be useful to the developing research.

Researchers will need to replicate and refine the findings before conclusive statements may be made about the implications for the long-term implementation of the ADA.[3] Discussion of the research "process of study" illustrated how quantitative and qualitative methods may be a powerful combination for this exploration.

---

[1] Douglas Martin, Disability Culture: Eager to Bite the Hands That Would Feed Them, **N.Y. Times,** at § 4, 1 (June 1, 1997).

[2] For a review, *see* **ADA Mandate, supra Ch. VIII § 8.6.**

[3] Campbell, **supra Ch. I § 1.1,** at 428 (reality testing is necessary but once it has been decided that the social reform—the ADA—is to be adopted, then experimental evaluations are required).

12.2 Employment Integration

The findings show that from 1990 to 1996 almost half of the participants remain in the same type of employment category (47 percent), almost half (44 percent) move to more integrated employment settings, while approximately one tenth (9 percent) regress into less integrated employment. The findings highlight the development of an emerging workforce, as younger persons show relatively greater gains in integrated employment and earned income levels.

Men, relative to women, show gains in integrated employment. Relative unemployment levels for all participants decline substantially, with overall participant unemployment levels at 38 percent in 1990 and 13 percent in 1996. Likewise, the proportion of participants in competitive employment increase threefold, from 3 percent in 1990 to 9 percent by 1996. Higher job-related skills and capabilities, better health status, independence in living, involvement in self-advocacy, and increased levels of family and governmental supports predict greater integration in work in 1996.

In the United States, unemployment levels for persons with disabilities remain staggeringly high.[4] Estimates from the NCD's 1996 report *Achieving Independence* show that in 1995, almost three quarters (72 percent) of roughly 17 million working-age noninstitutionalized Americans with disabilities were unemployed.[5] Consistent with the present findings, unemployment rates of women with disabilities are found to be even higher.

The lack of access to integrated employment opportunities is a primary reason for discrimination against qualified persons with disabilities. As described in the first part of this book, although ADA implementation is an important step toward reducing chronic unemployment for millions of qualified persons with disabilities, the law does not mandate that employers hire persons with disabilities. Rather, the ADA is a tool that affords qualified individuals with disabilities the opportunity for job stability and advancement without experiencing unjustified employment discrimination or hitting a "glass ceiling."[6]

Professor Paul Wehman, a leader in developing research on supported employment programs for persons with mental retardation, argues that while the ADA cannot guarantee a job for every person with a disability, it can "provide a framework for improved employer attitudes [and] reduced discriminatory practices."[7] The present findings support this suggestion, showing that those participants attaining integrated employment in 1996 demonstrate a high degree of skill, independence, and involvement in self-advocacy activities. The findings also support those of other longitudinal studies, showing that persons with mental retardation in more integrated employment are significantly more satisfied with their work and daily lives.[8]

Yet the findings from the present investigation show that participants in more integrated employment settings are more likely to report limited accessibility to work and daily life activities. This result suggests that there may be differences in what policy makers, researchers, and others believe about ADA implementation, and what is actually or perceived to be happening in the disability community. Despite being subjected to the continued reality of structural and attitudinal discrimination, the post-ADA pioneers of the disability community may be even more likely to assert their civil rights in the future.

12.3 Economic Opportunity and Growth

The findings of this investigation show that from 1990 to 1996 the gross incomes of the participants increase significantly. Younger participants show particularly substantial increases in gross

---

[4] *See* **ADA Mandate, supra Ch. VIII § 8.6,** at 154 (providing estimate of unemployment levels).

[5] **Achieving Independence, supra Ch. VI § 6.7,** at 59.

[6] *See* Supported Employment: A Critical Analysis of Individual Placement Approaches, *in* **Supported Employment, supra Ch. VIII § 8.6,** at 49, 54–58 (discussing outcomes of the individual approach, including wages, integration, and ongoing support needs).

[7] *Id.* at 57.

[8] *See* Corporate Alternatives, Inc., Overview of the Second Year Longitudinal Study of Supported Employment in Illinois, Springfield, Ill. (1990), *cited in* **ADA Mandate, supra Ch. VIII § 8.6,** at 33.

and earned income. The strongest single and independent predictor of 1996 earned income is job skill level, which accounts for more than half of the predictive power of the regression model presented in Chapter X. These trends require further examination, as comparison is needed of the changes in the incomes of qualified persons without disabilities holding similar jobs.

When taking into account the other variables in the model, job skill level (i.e., a concept analogous to the assessment of the "qualifications" of an individual with a disability) is a stronger predictor of earned income than it is of the degree of integration in employment. This finding suggests that once qualified participants attain integrated employment, their job skills are linked to growth in their wage levels. The important leap for qualified persons with mental retardation is breaking the initial barrier to work, a topic discussed at length in Chapter XVI.

Inclusion factors, such as independence in living and job or life satisfaction, and empowerment factors, such as self-advocacy involvement and family support, help predict 1996 earned income levels. Participants with higher 1996 earned incomes report more limited accessibility to work, to governmental activities, and to daily life activities. This result reflects the barriers that many qualified persons with disabilities continue to face in daily life, even after they have attained integrated work.

A central goal of ADA Title I is to foster integrated employment opportunities that pay fair wages to qualified employees with disabilities. Professor Mitchell LaPlante and his colleagues have conducted a series of studies showing that people with disabilities affected in the major life activity of work are more likely to be poor compared to persons without disabilities.[9] LaPlante finds that 30 percent of people with work-related disabilities have incomes below the poverty level, compared to 10 percent of those without work disabilities. Consistent with the trends in this investigation, studies show that the poverty rate is higher for women with disabilities and other segments of the disability population.

The present findings support the conclusion of LaPlante and others that earned income is a critical factor affecting the satisfaction and quality of life for persons with disabilities.[10] A 1994 Harris poll finds that adults with disabilities perceive insufficient finances as their most serious problem (67 percent rate as a problem; 40 percent rate as a major problem). The next most frequently cited problems reported are lack of full social life (51 percent) and inadequate health insurance (26 percent).

Longitudinal studies by Professor Revell and his colleagues show that in moving from nonintegrated employment settings (e.g., sheltered workshop settings) to supported employment settings, the wages of qualified workers with mental retardation increase over 500 percent.[11] Consistent with the findings in this investigation that job skill levels are strongly predictive of earned income levels, Revell finds that increases in earned income for persons with mental retardation are greatest for those who retain employment over time. In addition, Revell finds that the single best predictor of future earned income is present income.

Other research shows significant wage disparities between people with and without disabilities in comparable jobs. LaPlante finds that people with disabilities earn one third less than people without disabilities in comparable jobs.[12] Over time, these income disparities act as disincentives for many qualified individuals with disabilities to continue work, particularly as other barriers to work—for instance, the ability to afford adequate health care coverage as discussed in Chapter XVI—become apparent. The present findings reflect this trend, showing that participants with higher 1996 earned incomes report more limited access to competitive work.

---

[9] Mitchell P. LaPlante, Jae Kennedy, H. Stephen Kaye, & Barbara L. Wenger, Disability and Employment, 11 **Disability Stat. Abstract,** at 2–3 (Jan. 1996).

[10] *Id.* at 53.

[11] *See* Frank Rusch, Laird W. Heal, & Robert E. Cimera, Predicting Earnings of Supported Employees with Mental Retardation: A Longitudinal Study, 101 **Am. J. Mental Retardation** 630–44 (1997), *citing* W.G. Revell, Paul Wehman, J. Kregel, M. West, & R. Rayfield, Supported Employment for Persons With Severe Disabilities: Positive Trends in Wages, Models, and Funding, *in* **Supported Employment, supra Ch. VIII § 8.6,** at 40–51. *See also* Stephen T. Murphy & Patricia M. Rogan, **Closing the Shop: Conversion from Sheltered to Integrated Work,** at 208 (1995) (supported employment compared to sheltered workshop outcomes superior in terms of income growth).

[12] LaPlante, **supra Ch. XII § 12.3,** at 2.

12.4 Individual Change and Growth over Time

From 1990 to 1996, the participants in this investigation improved in their job capabilities and qualifications, level of inclusion and empowerment in society, and level of accessibility to society. Several findings are of particular relevance to future study of ADA implementation:

1. the proportion of participants involved in self-advocacy programs increases, roughly twofold;
2. the degree of independent living increases substantially, almost twentyfold;[13]
3. reported satisfaction with work and daily life increases; and
4. accessibility to work and daily life, as defined by Titles I, II, and III of the Act, increases.

These findings illustrate encouraging trends on indicators related to the core goals of the ADA, such as equal opportunity, self-empowerment, and access to and satisfaction with work and daily life. Developments in the area of self-advocacy continue to reflect efforts by persons with mental retardation and their families and friends toward true integration in employment. Nancy Ward has written:

> By learning how to work together [through self-advocacy organizations], we are also learning that we can make a difference in politics. If you had all the people with a disability—no matter what type—banded together, you might have a majority....Issues that affect people with a disability would be heard and taken seriously. That is what the future should look like.[14]

In this way, disability policy and law, embodied in the ADA, is meant to eliminate the discrimination and segregation faced by qualified individuals with disabilities throughout society. As mentioned in Chapter V, even prior to the ADA, progress was made toward this goal. The number of persons with mental retardation living in segregated institutions declined from 195,000 in 1967 to 88,000 in 1989.[15] Braddock and his colleagues find that by the year 1992, 52 percent of the 347,000 persons with developmental disabilities in residential settings lived with 15 or fewer residents.[16]

While ADA implementation may accelerate the trend toward employment and community integration, the "black hole" findings in this investigation demonstrate that much work is needed. As discussed in Chapter XVII, qualified individuals with disabilities left behind in the black hole of nonintegrated settings may have a right under the ADA to equal opportunity to work and daily life activities.

In an important case decided by the United States Court of Appeals for the Third Circuit, *Helen L. v. DiDario*, the court concluded that the ADA defines unnecessary segregation in nonintegrated living settings as a form of illegal discrimination.[17] Similarly, in a 1997 case in Georgia, *L.C. v. Olmstead*, a federal district court concluded that under the ADA, unnecessary institutional segregation of persons with mental retardation constitutes discrimination which cannot be justified by a lack of state funding.[18]

In *L.C. v. Olmstead,* two persons with mental retardation had been institutionalized in a state mental hospital. There was no factual dispute that they were qualified individuals covered by the ADA who could live appropriately in the community. In fact, the state of Georgia had existing community programs to serve the individuals bringing the lawsuit. The court ordered the state to serve the two individuals with mental retardation in integrated community settings. The court noted: "The fact that it may be more convenient, either administratively or fiscally, to provide services in a segregated manner does not justify [the state's] failure to

---

[13] Much of this gain is attributable to the changes resulting from the Oklahoma deinstitutionalization effort in *Homeward Bound v. Hissom*, **supra Ch. VIII § 8.2.**

[14] Nancy A. Ward & Kenneth D. Keith, Self-Advocacy: Foundation for Quality of Life, *in* **Quality of Life, supra Ch. VII § 7.2,** at 10.

[15] For a review, *see* Steven J. Taylor & Robert Bogdan, Promises Made and Promises to Be Broken, *in* **ADA Mandate, supra Ch. VIII § 8.6,** at 255.

[16] David Braddock, Richard Hemp, & Glenn Fujiuar, **The State of the States in Developmental Disabilities** (2d ed. 1995).

[17] *Helen L. v. DiDario*, 46 F.3d 325 (3d Cir. 1995), *cert. denied*, 516 U.S. 813 (1995).

[18] *L.C. v. Olmstead*, 1997 WL 148674 (N.D. Ga. 1997) (*citing* in support *Helen L. v. DiDario*, 46 F.3d 325 (ADA defines unnecessary segregation as a form of illegal discrimination).

comply with the ADA."[19]

Based on the present findings that integrated living is a good predictor of employment integration and economic growth, integrated employment and living may be not only a civil right, but also cost-justified.[20] Yet almost half of the participants (43 percent) continue to live in nonintegrated settings. Study is needed of the quality of the participants' work and living arrangements.

12.5 The "Black Hole Effect"

In this investigation, more than three quarters (79 percent) of those participants not employed or employed in nonintegrated settings in 1990 *remained* in these settings in 1996. Over half (53 percent) of persons in integrated employment in 1990 *regressed* to nonintegrated settings by 1996. A much smaller proportion of the participants (21 percent) in nonintegrated settings in 1990 moved to integrated settings by 1996. Roughly half (47 percent) of those participants in integrated employment in 1990 remained in that setting in 1996.

The "black hole" findings reflect the problems of chronic unemployment and underemployment faced by qualified persons with mental retardation. Strategies are needed to assist the millions of qualified persons with mental retardation and other disabilities entering the workforce. Evaluation and placement services are needed not only to identify qualified individuals with disabilities, but also to help prepare them for competitive employment.[21] Chapter XIV discusses the emerging role of the staffing industry in the training and placement of qualified workers with mental retardation.

Harris survey data from 1994 indicate that a majority (52 percent) of employed adults with disabilities found employment through personal contacts. Only 12 percent found employment through employment placement services that are mainstreamed and specialized for people with disabilities. The discussion of the role of the staffing industry in Chapter XIV suggests that this disparity indicates the need for increased effort in improving employment placement services for qualified adults with disabilities.

Job retention, support, and advancement strategies are needed to help qualified workers with disabilities keep jobs and achieve their potential.[22] Effective input is required from individuals with disabilities, their families, employers, and researchers. To date, more than 110,000 people have been involved with supported employment programs, with an annual federal investment of $40 million.[23]

Despite these trends and the implementation of the ADA, the black hole effect for qualified people with mental retardation remains a national problem, as it has been for the last decade. In a critical reexamination of the supported employment movement, Mank sets forth five recommendations to recapture the promise of equal and meaningful job opportunity for persons with mental retardation:[24]

1. "Put more control of employment resources in the hands of people with disabilities and their significant others." Consistent with the ADA goals of empowerment and choice discussed in Chapter VIII of this book, follow a "customer-driven system" on behalf of individuals with disabilities, rather than a system driven by employment providers and state rehabilitation systems. This approach is consistent with trends toward increased involvement in self-advocacy activities for persons with mental retardation.
2. "Eradicate state and national policy confounds." Consistent with analysis of ADA litigation trends (i.e., the "judicial estoppel" conflict discussed in Chapter III), and policy reforms that eliminate "barriers to work" (i.e., identified in Chapter XVI), coordinate state and federal funding mechanisms, health insurance coverage programs, and incentives to work for qualified individuals with disabilities.

---

[19] *Id.* at *11.

[20] *See* William E. Kiernan, Robert L. Schalock, John Butterworth, & David Mank, The Next Steps, *in* **Integrated Employment, supra Ch. I § I.3,** at 134 (concluding that integrated employment is cost-effective).

[21] *See* Pamela S. Wolfe, Supported Employment: A Review of Group Models, *in* **Supported Employment, supra Ch. VIII § 8.6,** at 63, 64–65 (providing list of studies reviewed for group model analysis).

[22] *See* David Mank, The Underachievement of Supported Employment: A Call for Reinvestment, 5(2) **J. Disability Pol'y Stud.** 1–24 (1996), *cited in* **Achieving Independence, supra Ch. VI § 6.8,** at 63.

[23] *Id.*

[24] *Id.* at 16–19.

3. "Close the door of entry into segregated options." To eliminate the black hole trends found in the present investigation and discussed in Chapter XI, federal and state funding must support meaningful choices to work with individually tailored job supports and effective accommodations for qualified persons with disabilities who want to work.
4. "Expand investment with the community and employers." As discussed in Chapter XIV, studies show that communities and businesses that are effectively implementing disability law demonstrate an ability to look beyond the minimal requirements of the law in ways that both enhance individual dignity and capabilities, and result in successful investments in qualified workers by communities and businesses.
5. "Invest in such societal initiatives as the School to Work Opportunities Act." National and state legislation examined in Chapter XVI of this book create opportunities for the inclusion and empowerment of the emerging workforce of young adults with mental retardation and other disabilities. Chapter XI described profiles of this next generation of qualified workers with mental retardation and their employers.

12.6 Generalizing from the Present Findings

For the participants in this investigation, the individual factors in the research model set out in Figure 1.1, in combination and alone, predict aspects of employment integration and economic opportunity.[25] There is more to be learned about how the variables in the research model work together and how they independently predict employment integration and economic opportunity in the context of ADA implementation.[26] Additional information is needed, for instance, on the impact of class action institutional reform litigation on the employment rates of qualified persons with mental retardation. The means for addressing these questions is to replicate existing studies and to develop new ones.

The scientific and practical usefulness of the research model may be enhanced in future examinations of the quality of employment integration options and economic growth of the emerging workforce of persons with mental retardation. Mank has noted that although earned income may increase with integration in employment, corresponding quality of life may actually decline.[27] As the present findings suggest, this may be due, in part, to an increasing lack of access to and affordability of private health insurance and workplace training and education. These issues are addressed further in Chapter XVI.

For the relatively large group examined in this investigation, it was possible to explore findings that have implications not only for this sample, but also for other populations of individuals with disabilities covered under ADA Title I.[28] The issue of the generalizability of the present findings relates to the extent to which the results may hold true within the population of individuals with mental retardation and across the population of persons with other disabilities as defined by the ADA.

Given the large number of individuals covered by the ADA, it may not be possible for any single study to select randomly a representative cross-sampling of individuals with disabilities. Yet many of the issues faced by the participants in the present study likely are representative of concerns faced by millions of qualified persons covered by the ADA.[29] Nevertheless, caution must be exercised in generalizing from the conclusions in the present findings. The present findings cannot fully

---

[25] LaPlante, **supra Ch. XII § 12.3**, at 2–3 (arguing that one reason for reduced income and employment opportunity is related to the skills and education levels of persons with disabilities relative to persons without disabilities).

[26] *See* **Supported Employment, supra Ch. VIII § 8.6,** at 241, 245 (discussing model of vocational integration for persons with disabilities).

[27] David Mank, Systems Change Strategies for Integrated Employment: A Blueprint for the Future, *in* **Integrated Employment, supra Ch. I § 1.3,** at 112–14.

[28] *Cf.* Conroy & Bradley, **supra Ch. I § 1.1**, at 323 (calling for study in area but noting gains for Pennhurst population may generalize to other similar populations of persons with mental retardation).

[29] *Cf.* Burgdorf, **supra Ch. I § 1.4**, at 515–16 (noting generalizations based on ADA nondiscrimination standards must be viewed with caution, as application depends on the facts and circumstances in each situation).

inform policy makers, employers, the disability community, and others about many of the complex and ongoing issues related to the ADA's implementation. The individual measures in the research model are starting points for understanding the elements for the successful employment integration of persons with mental retardation.

The research also cannot address the potential for ADA backlash driven by widening attitudinal differences between the emerging generation of self-advocating individuals with disabilities and what Joseph Shapiro has referred to as "the stereotypical thinking of the rest of the country."[30] In this regard, analysis is required on stakeholders' perceptions of the law's effectiveness and trends in the filing of ADA charges.[31]

12.7 Aggregating Studies of Employment Integration and "Quality of Work Life"

In an important line of research that has aggregated findings from prior studies on employment integration for persons with mental retardation, Professors William Kiernan and Joseph Marrone have examined the concept of quality of work life (QWL) from the perspective of ADA stakeholders—persons with disabilities and their employers.[32] These researchers and others are concerned with ways effectively to measure consumer satisfaction, inclusion, and empowerment in the workplace.

Kiernan and Marrone write:

> QWL refers to the degree of an individual's satisfaction with his/her role, relationships, and duties in the workplace. This satisfaction is predicated on a variety of factors affecting the individual including, but not limited to, personality variables, family expectations, social cultural norms, workplace culture, and concrete facets of the job, within the setting where the duties are performed.[33]

There are at least three central components for assessing QWL: (1) worker satisfaction with and productivity in the workplace; (2) worker participation in the development of workplace functions; and, (3) correspondence of worker, company, and societal demands.

These factors are worthy of study. Future analysis of the present research model will address over time the relation of worker satisfaction, earned income, productivity, the provision of workplace accommodations, and job tenure. These and other examinations are needed to dispel myths about the capabilities of workers and job applicants with mental retardation and to document employment integration under the ADA.

The cumulative or aggregated findings from many research studies conducted in multiple disciplines is needed to explore fully the ramifications of disability law and employment policy. The present investigation and its findings yield a limited view of the broad areas related to concepts of employment integration and quality of life for persons with mental retardation. The effort embodied in this investigation may contribute to awareness of these issues and serve as a step toward developing a body of research useful for assessing ADA implementation.

The present findings must be qualified and amplified by researchers and persons with disabilities and their families. In this regard Chapter V discussed the importance of aggregating studies in the area of employment integration under the ADA. As the findings from more studies emerge, it will be necessary to summarize the resultant literature quantitatively and qualitatively.[34]

Professors Carolyn Hughes and Bogseon Hwang have developed a taxonomy of empirical measures used in research involving persons with mental retardation based on a summary of

---

[30] *See* Shapiro, **supra Ch. I § 1.1,** at 70–73, 328 (1994) (discussing backlash against disability rights movement).

[31] Donohue & Siegelman, **supra Ch. X § 10.5,** at 993 ("To raise a bona fide claim of employment discrimination, a worker must first perceive that discrimination has occurred.").

[32] William E. Kiernan & Joseph Marrone, Quality of Work Life for Persons with Disabilities: Emphasis on the Employee, *in* **Quality of Life, Vol. II, supra Ch. VII § 7.5,** at 63–77.

[33] *Id.* at 64–65.

[34] Meta-analysis is a set of concepts and procedures employed to summarize a domain of research to provide a more comprehensive understanding of the area. Peter David Blanck & Mollie Weighner Marti, Genetic Discrimination and the Employment Provisions of the Americans with Disabilities Act: Emerging Legal, Empirical, and Policy Implications, 14 **Behav. Sci. & L.** 411–32, 430 (1996).

87 studies conducted through the year 1995.[35] Their literature synthesis identifies measures useful for the future study of employment integration and economic study under the ADA.

Hughes and Bogseon's taxonomy describes the research measures, many employed in the present research, that may be used in the assessment of employment integration and economic opportunity under the ADA. The measures may prove to be useful in the determination of employee "qualifications" under the ADA. They include the quality of employee:

1. job initiative, work performance, and job-related interpersonal skills;
2. natural supports, and coworker interaction at the worksite;
3. work environment and accessibility; and
4. outside support services, vocational training, and education from private, governmental, and family sources.

The aggregation of research on these and other dimensions is needed to provide theoretical and practical benchmarks for consumers, program evaluators, employers, policy makers, courts, and others about the effects of the components of the present and other research models.[36] Knowledge gained from the aggregation of studies provide a basis for future interdisciplinary collaboration among social scientists, legal scholars, medical researchers, and members of the disability community and their families.

12.8 Summary

This chapter has described the implications of the present findings from the investigation of employment integration and economic opportunity during the initial ADA implementation. The investigation is exploratory, with the findings requiring ongoing analysis. The next chapter examines two areas that have been prominent in discussions about whether ADA implementation has been effective: analysis of labor force trends of qualified persons with disabilities during ADA implementation, and the impact of effective workplace accommodations on equal employment opportunities for workers with disabilities.

---

[35] Carolyn Hughes & Bogseon Hwang, Attempts to Conceptualize and Measure Quality of Life, *in* **Quality of Life, Vol. I, supra Ch. VII § 7.2,** at 51–61. *See also* Robert B. Edgerton, A Longitudinal-Ethnographic Research Perspective on Quality of Life, *in* **Quality of Life, Vol. I, supra Ch. VII § 7.2,** at 83–90 (discussing need for longitudinal study in the area).

[36] Hughes & Hwang, **supra Ch. XII § 12.7,** at 59–60; Carolyn Hughes, et al., Quality of Life in Applied Research: Conceptual Model and Analysis of Measures, 99 **J. Mental Retardation** 623–41 (1995).

CHAPTER XIII

Implications for the Emerging Workforce: Labor Force Trends and Workplace Accommodations

Some people seem to think that evaluating the impact of the ADA is irrelevant, given that its purpose is to establish certain rights and protections. But I believe that we have an obligation to make sure our laws are working. At the very least, we need to know that people affected by the ADA are aware of their rights and responsibilities and that its remedies are in fact available and effective.

Senator Bob Dole[1]

13.1 Introduction

This chapter addresses two ways in which effective ADA implementation may be assessed. First, the chapter examines the ways in which the law may foster employment integration and opportunity, in part, as reflected by changes in labor force participation of persons with disabilities. Second, it explores employers' increased use of workplace supports and accommodations as business strategies to attract and retain qualified workers with disabilities.

13.2 Labor Force Trends and the Emerging Workforce of Persons with Disabilities

Thirty years after the passage of the Civil Rights Act of 1964, scholars continue to assess whether positive changes in the employment integration of blacks and women may be attributable to that law.[2] In similar ways, researchers must begin to assess whether actual change or merely the appearance of change is occurring as a result of ADA implementation.[3] The findings from the present investigation illustrate that many factors are involved in understanding

---

[1] Bob Dole, Are We Keeping America's Promises to People with Disabilities?—Commentary on Blanck, 79 **Iowa L. Rev.** 927–28 (1994).

[2] *See* Richard A. Posner, The Efficiency and Efficacy of Title VII, 136 **U. Pa. L. Rev.** 513, 519–20 (1987) (arguing that the most responsible conclusion is that Title VII effects are unknown).

[3] *Id.* at 1539 (concluding that Title VII leaves open the possibility for covered entities to create the appearance of compliance without actual change to the composition of their workforce).

employment integration and economic opportunity for the participants with mental retardation.

As discussed in Chapter XII, the present findings suggest that for many qualified workers with mental retardation (for instance, the "improvers"), labor force participation is a function of experience in and attempts at competitive work. The findings show the high degree of unemployment and movement of qualified individuals in and out of the labor force.[4] At the same time, they illustrate the stagnation facing many qualified participant "stayers"—that is, young individuals with mental retardation, often who have high job skills, stuck in the black hole of nonintegrated work settings.

Professor Shafer and his colleagues report the results of a 24-month analysis of supported employment retention for a sample of 302 individuals, showing these employees experience regular movement in and out of the labor force. Shafer finds that, over time, 30 percent of the individuals studied were employed in their original employment, 20 percent employed in subsequent employment, and 31 percent lost employment and returned to the referral pool.[5] Other research suggests a declining trend in labor market opportunities for low-skilled workers with disabilities in the 1980s.[6]

Study addressing the economic factors and structural changes in the labor market that influence employment integration and economic opportunity for persons with and without disabilities is needed. These analyses may include factors such as:

1. types of jobs attained (entry level, service-related, or production);
2. geographic differences in job markets and seasonal hiring patterns;
3. turnover, retention, wage, and promotion rates;
4. availability of transportation to work;
5. provision of work-related benefits, such as health and life insurance, and pension plan participation;
6. availability of natural supports and mentoring in the workplace, such as from coworkers; and
7. availability and accessibility of adaptive equipment, computer, and technology at work.[7]

In this last regard, Professors Alan Krueger and Doug Kruse have investigated the labor market effects of computer skills held by people with severe disabilities, specifically by those with spinal cord injuries.[8] Their findings show that those individuals with disabilities who were proficient in the use of computer technology were more likely than those with disabilities without computer skills to attain and retain competitive employment and have higher earnings.[9]

In a similar vein, Professor Paul Wehman and his colleagues cite an eight-year study of 214 employees with mental retardation in competitive employment that showed the program generated public savings of almost $3 million, saving taxpayers approximately $1 million after subtracting project expenditures.[10] The savings are based on reductions in SSI payments and increases in taxes paid by the employed individuals.

The present findings support studies showing rising income levels for persons with disabilities since the mid-1980s.[11] Of interest, the findings

---

[4] *See* Shafer, et al., **supra Ch. X § 10.4,** at 106.

[5] *Id.* at 103.

[6] **Preliminary Status Report, supra Ch. I § 1.1,** at 109–10 (summarizing research using earnings levels of workers as a measure of the demand for their services, and concluding that "workers with limited skills who also have disabilities are doubly disadvantaged").

[7] Subsequent analyses in this project examine wage data of Oklahomans without disabilities in comparable jobs. *See* **Oklahoma Employment Sec. Comm'n, Oklahoma Wage Survey** (1996).

[8] *See* Alan Krueger & Douglas Kruse, Severe Disability, Disability, Employment, and Earnings in the Dawn of the Computer Age, 19 **Spine** 103 (1994).

[9] *Cf.* Steven J. Rubinsky, The Use of the McCarron-Dial Work Evaluation System to Predict Success in Sheltered, Supported, and Competitive Employment Settings, 24 **Voc. Eval. & Work Adjustment Bull.** 129 (1991) (finding a significant positive relation between intellectual abilities and degree of integration in employment).

[10] *See* Paul Wehman & Mark Hill, Competitive Employment for Persons with Mental Retardation, *in* **Economics, Industry, and Disability: A Look Ahead** 287–98 (William E. Kiernan & Robert L. Schalock, eds., 1989); John M. McNeil, Work Status, Earnings, and Rehabilitation of Persons with Disabilities, *in* **Disability in the United States: A Portrait from National Data** 133, 156 (Susan Thompson-Hoffman & Inez F. Storck, eds., 1991).

[11] *See* West, **supra Ch. I § 1.1,** at 4 (citing studies).

do not suggest income disparities based on ethnicity alone. Yet other studies have found gains in income for persons with disabilities are unevenly distributed, with minorities remaining relatively worse off. The NCD finds that individuals who are members of minority groups and who have disabilities experience double discrimination or even triple discrimination and that it is difficult to discern the causes of this discrimination.[12]

Study is required to determine relative rates of income growth for women, minorities, and other groups with disabilities.[13] Assessment must be made of the economic growth, or lack of growth, experienced by persons who are members of minority groups with and without disabilities.[14] A 1997 case study found important differences in the provision of workplace accommodations for men versus women with disabilities, which in turn affected job advancement opportunities and subsequent income.[15]

On a positive note, in 1996, the Census Bureau released data showing that the employment-to-population ratio for persons with severe disabilities has increased from roughly 23 percent in 1991 to 26 percent in 1994, reflecting an increase of approximately 800,000 additional people with severe disabilities in the labor force.[16] Professor Frederick Collignon has suggested that reductions on welfare dependency programs by persons with disabilities may be one important indicator of effective ADA implementation over time.[17]

Other studies suggest that from 1970 to 1992, there was no significant net change in the labor force participation rate among persons with disabilities.[18] Professor Murray Weidenbaum argues that negative trends in labor force participation of people with disabilities have less to do with ADA implementation than with inefficiencies in federal entitlement programs, such as the Supplemental Security Income program, which provide monetary incentives for persons with disabilities not to work.[19] The nature of current incentives and barriers to work for persons with disabilities is revisited in Chapter XVI.

Still others comment that the apparent decrease (or lack of growth) in labor force participation by persons with disabilities, combined with an increase in applications for entitlement benefits, suggests that the ADA may not be helping those it was intended to serve.[20] Additional examination is required of the labor force participation of qualified workers with disabilities, particularly in the context of reforms to welfare policy discussed in Chapter XVI later in the book. As discussed next, in addition to the analysis of labor force participation rates, other measures are needed to assess effective

---

[12] *See* **ADA Watch, supra Ch. I § 1.2,** at 63 (reporting that minorities with disabilities have higher unemployment rates, lower participation in disability programs, and tend not to know their rights under nondiscrimination laws).

[13] *See* Zirpoli, et al., **supra Ch. VIII § 8.6** (African-American women with disabilities are disproportionately disadvantaged in employment opportunities). In the present investigation, minority participants tended to be relatively younger, compared to nonminority participants ($r = -.07$, $p = .015$, n = 1095). Subgroup demographics and trends in employment integration need further study before any definitive conclusions can be drawn. *See* Philip G. Wilson, et al., Analysis of Minority-Status Supported Employees in Relation to Placement Approach and Selected Outcomes, 29 **Mental Retardation** 329, 331 (1991) (finding that minority-status supported employees were younger, had higher skill scores, and earned more wages per month than did nonminority supported employees).

[14] 29 C.F.R. § 1630 app. (1991) (stating that the ADA is about enabling all persons with disabilities to compete in the workplace based on performance standards and requirements identical to those that a covered entity expects of persons who do not have disabilities, subject to reasonable accommodation). There is debate as to whether people with disabilities, like those without disabilities, should have the "choice" to work. *See* **infra Ch. XVII § 17.2,** at 54.

[15] Jordan Jay Kaplan, Employer Compliance with the Reasonable Accommodation Provision of Title I of the Americans with Disabilities Act and Gender, Univ. Sarasota, Dissertation Abstracts International, 58/02-A (1997).

[16] "Six Years After Signing of Law, ADA Has Been Cited in More Than 1,000 Suits," **Disability Compliance Bull.** (Aug. 15, 1996) (data reflects a 27 percent increase of persons with severe disabilities in the workforce from 1991 to 1994).

[17] Collignon, *in* **Annals, supra Ch. IV § 4.4,** at 137–38.

[18] *See* Yelin, *in* **Annals, supra Ch. IV § 4.4,** at 124–25 (finding a disproportionate increase in persons with disabilities working part time).

[19] *Cf.* Murray Weidenbaum, Why the Disabilities Act Is Missing Its Mark, **Christian Sci. Mon.,** at 19 (Jan. 16, 1997).

[20] Rosen, **supra Ch. IV § 4.4,** at 28–29.

ADA implementation; prominent among them is assessment of the provision of workplace supports and accommodations for qualified workers with disabilities.

13.3 Workplace Supports and Accommodations

Prior chapters have suggested that study is needed of workers with mental retardation who are currently employed and who are not accommodated effectively under the ADA. Chapter IV discussed that for many persons with mental retardation, providing accommodations in the workplace is not a one-time initiative. The process requires an ongoing adjustment to the needs of the employee and the employer through the "interactive process" identified in the law.

The findings from the present investigation foreshadow the need for study of strategies that support job retention for qualified persons with disabilities, particularly strategies that transcend "mere compliance" with the law. These strategies are necessary because they provide employers with the economic incentive to supply workplace supports and accommodations and the ability to view qualified workers with disabilities as having the potential for long-term work associations.[21] In turn, this approach will improve the opportunities for employment integration that are available to persons with disabilities.[22]

Chapter XIV examines in greater detail information on the long-term economic value of ADA implementation. Information is emerging on the costs and benefits of accommodating persons with mental versus physical disabilities, given the stigma attached to those with mental disabilities.[23] This information has provided feedback to employers and employees about effective implementation in different business sectors, such as retail or production, reducing the likelihood of costly litigation on the subject.

Collignon has argued that it is crucial to establish baseline data and models of empirical study to help foster an informed dialogue about ADA implementation and the law's long-term effectiveness.[24] One area that is worthy of immediate attention, given the ability to quantify associated costs and benefits, is the economic implications to employers of workplace accommodations.[25]

As mentioned in Chapter III, perhaps the most common criticism of the ADA is that the costs of its mandated accommodations outweigh the benefits provided to employers and persons

---

[21] Elmer C. Bartels, Employment and the Public Vocational Rehabilitation Program, *in* **Rights and Responsibilities, supra Ch. I § 1.1,** at 75, 77 (rehabilitation programs assist people with severe mental disabilities to enter the workforce and to become economically independent); Paul Wehman, Supported Employment: Toward Equal Employment Opportunity for Persons with Severe Disabilities, 26 **Mental Retardation** 357–61 (1988) (urging greater emphasis on serving persons with severe disabilities); *cf.* Janet W. Hill, et al., Differential Reasons for Job Separation of Previously Employed Persons with Mental Retardation, 24 **Mental Retardation** 347–51 (1986) (reporting that, in a longitudinal review of 250 supported competitive employment placements, approximately 42 percent of all placements were terminated due to employee resignations, layoffs, or firings).

[22] *See* Shafer, et al., **supra Ch. X § 10.4,** at 109; Yelin, *in* **Annals, supra Ch. IV § 4.4,** at 146 (calling for research because "the EEOC must have a more contemporary model of work upon which to base its enforcement of ADA's employment provisions"); **Toward Independence, supra Ch. VI § 6.2,** at 3–4 (recommending that the Bureau of Census incorporate questions that assess numbers of persons with disabilities to provide a database for policy planning and service delivery).

[23] *See* Peter David Blanck, et al., Implementing Reasonable Accommodations Using ADR Under the ADA: A Case of a White Collar Employee with Bipolar Mental Illness, 18 **Mental & Physical Disability L. Rep.** 458 (1994) (analyzing an actual case).

[24] Collignon, **supra Ch. VI § 6.1,** at 130–32 (discussing various indicators of Title I implementation, including unemployment, poverty, and legal compliance rates); Corinne Kirchner, Looking Under the Street Lamp: Inappropriate Uses of Measures Because They Are There, 7 **J. Disability Pol'y Stud.** 77, 82–86 (1996) (critiquing prior researchers' overreliance on labor force participation measures as indicator of effective Title I implementation).

[25] *See* Rosen, **supra Ch. IV § 4.4,** at 18, 22; Weaver, **supra Ch. IV § 4.4,** at 5 ("The central flaw of the ADA...is in the imposition on employers of a duty to 'accommodate' the mental or physical limitations of the disabled worker or applicant without weighing the expected benefits of such accommodation.").

with disabilities.[26] Critics contend that the required provision of reasonable accommodations places financial burdens and administrative costs on the operation of businesses. Some argue that the costs of accommodations are especially high for large employers, who may be held accountable for extensive modifications due to their greater financial resources.[27]

A common thread in these critiques is that they are made without reliance on data. In the absence of such information, it is no surprise that the attitudes and behavior of many employers reflect the view that the costs of accommodations outweigh the benefits.[28] It is helpful to reiterate the prior discussions, in Chapters II and III, that the ADA does not require employers to hire individuals with disabilities who are not qualified, or to hire qualified individuals with disabilities over equally or more qualified individuals without disabilities.[29] Indeed, more than three quarters of all Title I charges filed with the EEOC have been dismissed because, among other reasons, the plaintiff alleging discrimination failed to show that he was qualified for the position.[30]

Many individuals with mental retardation currently in the workforce have appropriate job skills, that is, they are "qualified" for purposes of the law, and have their accommodation needs met in reasonable and effective ways.[31] Findings from the 1989 National Health Interview Survey show that roughly 60 percent of working-age adults with disabilities rate their health as good to excellent.[32] Yet at least one United States Court of Appeals has presumed that most impairments by definition impact an individual's "ability to perform up to the standards of the workplace" and increase the relative costs to employers of hiring the individual.[33]

In contrast to this view, the findings described

---

[26] *See* James Bovard, Disability Intentions Astray, **Wash. Times,** at A16 (May 20, 1996) (ADA is costly and economically inefficient); Richard A. Epstein, The Legal Regulation of Genetic Discrimination: Old Responses to New Technology, 74 **B.U. L. Rev.** 1 (1994) (when the absolute right to refuse employment or insurance is denied, without exception, the employer or insurer is forced into a losing economic position); Christopher J. Willis, Comment, Title I of the Americans with Disabilities Act: Disabling the Disabled, 25 **Cumb. L. Rev.** 715 (1994–1995) (same).

[27] Barnard, **supra Ch. VII § 7.2,** at 251–52.

[28] *See* Frederick C. Collignon, The Role of Reasonable Accommodation in Employing Disabled Persons in Private Industry, *in* **Disability and the Labor Market** (Monroe Berkowitz & M. Anne Hill, eds., 1986) 196 (arguing that economists' theorizing about the costly effects of accommodation often do not consider the actual experiences of businesses).

[29] Nevertheless, some scholars cast Title I's reasonable accommodation provision as "contrary to our understanding of equal treatment developed under other anti-discrimination statutes." *See* Deborah A. Calloway, Dealing with Diversity: Changing Theories of Discrimination, 10 **St. John's J. Leg. Comm.** 481, 492 (1995) (interpreting Title I to judge individuals on the basis of their group status and not on their individual merits).

[30] Lisa J. Stansky, Five Years After Its Passage, the Americans with Disabilities Act Has Not Fulfilled the Greatest Fears of Its Critics—or the Greatest Hopes of Its Supporters, 82 **A.B.A. J.** 66 (1996); 16 **Newsletter of the Great Lakes Disability and Business Technical Assistance Center, Region V News,** at 5 (Fall 1996) (as of Sept. 30, 1996, 46 percent of Title I charges filed with the EEOC were dismissed for having no reasonable cause; another 40 percent were closed for administrative reasons, including claims that they were withdrawn or were closed because the complaining parties failed to cooperate with the agency).

[31] *See* 2 **Successful Job Accommodations Strategies** (June 1996) (describing a study by the National Academy of Social Insurance finding that many qualified persons with disabilities prefer to work and use disability benefits only as a last resort). *See also* National Academy of Social Insurance, **Balancing Security and Opportunity: The Challenge of Disability Income Policy,** at 10 (Jan. 25, 1996) (about half of the 34 million working-age adults who experience mental illness over the course of a year are employed; about one third of the 16.8 million persons with work disabilities are in the labor force, either working or looking for work); Louis Harris & Associates, **Disabled Americans' Self-Perceptions: Bringing Disabled Americans into the Mainstream** (1986) (66 percent of persons with disabilities below the age of 65 who do not work report that they want to work).

[32] *See* **Disability Watch, supra Ch. II § 2.6,** at 12 (noting that in many cases, disability is the result of a past health problem or injury not currently requiring medical attention). For extensive analysis of factors related to the self-reported health status of persons with disabilities, see Mitchell P. LaPlante, **Disability, Health Insurance Coverage, and Utilization of Acute Health Services in the United States,** Disability Statistics Report No. 4: U.S. Dept. Ed., National Institute Disability Research (1993).

[33] *See Vande Zande v. State of Wisconsin Dept. Admin.*, 44 F.3d 538 (7th Cir. 1995).

in Chapter XI and those from other studies suggest that employers have favorable attitudes toward the employment and accommodation of qualified employees with mental retardation. Likewise, a 1995 Harris poll of business executives found that 79 percent of those surveyed believe that the employment of qualified people with disabilities is a boost to the economy, while only 2 percent believe it poses a "threat to take jobs" from people without disabilities.[34]

The developing empirical evidence does not reflect the view that the ADA's accommodation provision is a preferential treatment initiative that forces employers to ignore employee qualifications and economic efficiency. To the contrary, studies of accommodations suggest that companies that are effectively implementing the law reflect a "corporate culture" of going beyond minimal compliance of the law in ways that enhance economic value.

The low direct costs of accommodations for employees with mental retardation have been shown to produce substantial economic benefits to companies, in terms of increased work productivity, injury prevention, reduced workers' compensation costs, and workplace effectiveness and efficiency.[35] In their research, the late Elizabeth Boggs and her colleagues found that not only are workplace accommodations for persons with mental retardation cost effective, but they are also straightforward to implement.[36]

13.3 Workplace Accommodations at Sears, Roebuck & Co. and Elsewhere

In a series of studies conducted at Sears, Roebuck and Co. from 1978 to 1996, a time period before and after Title I's July 26, 1992, effective date, nearly all of the 500 accommodations sampled required little or no cost.[37] During the years 1993 to 1996, the average direct cost for accommodations was $45, and from 1978 to 1992, the average direct cost was $121. The Sears studies show that the direct costs of accommodating employees with hidden disabilities (e.g., emotional and neurological impairments comprising roughly 15 percent of the cases studied) is even lower than the overall average of $45.[38]

Other studies show that accommodations for employees with disabilities lead to direct and indirect benefits and cost-effective applications that increase the productivity of employees without disabilities. Studies by the Job Accommodation Network (JAN) demonstrate the benefits to employers of accommodations for qualified employees. More than two thirds of effective accommodations implemented as a result of a JAN consultation cost less than $500. In addition, almost two thirds of the accommodations studied result in savings to the company in excess of $5,000.[39]

---

[34] Louis Harris & Associates & National Organization on Disability, **1995 Survey of Corporate Executives on the ADA** (1995) [**hereinafter Harris Study**]; Mason-Dixon Poll, **Florida Chamber of Commerce Foundation's Disability Awareness Project** (Jan. 1995) (72 percent of businesses that hired persons with disabilities reported that the employment of people with disabilities had a favorable effect on their business and 87 percent said they would encourage other employers to hire persons with disabilities); OSHA Rules by Far Most Burdensome for Employer Chamber Survey Finds, 1996 **DLR** 124 d25 (June 27, 1996) (in rating the relative burden of requirements issued under various labor and employment laws on a scale of 1 (least) to 10 (most burdensome), small employers rated ADA requirements at 4.8 compared to a 6.2 for OSHA, and a 4.4 for the Fair Labor Standards Act).

[35] *See* **Sears II, supra Ch. IV § 4.1,** at 42–43; Francine S. Hall & Elizabeth L. Hall, The ADA: Going Beyond the Law, 8(1) **Acad. Mgmt. Executive Rev.** 17–26 (1994).

[36] *See* Thomas Baffuto & Elizabeth Boggs, What the ADA Has Meant and What It Can Mean for People with Mental Retardation, 1990–1991 **Am. Rehab.** 10–14 (Winter 1990–1991).

[37] *See* **Sears I, supra Ch. II § 2.3,** at 17 (finding 72 percent required no cost, 17 percent cost less than $100, 10 percent cost less than $500, and 1 percent cost more than $500, but not more than $1,000, noting that accommodations include assistive technology, physical access, changed schedules, assistance by others and changed job duties); Mary C. Daly & John Bound, Worker Adaptation and Employer Accommodation Following the Onset of a Health Impairment, 51B **J. Gerontology** S53 (1996).

[38] **Sears II, supra Ch. IV § 4.1,** at 20 (from 1993 to 1996, average cost for behavioral impairments was $0 and average cost for neurological impairments was $13).

[39] President's Committee on Employment of People with Disabilities, **Job Accommodation Network (JAN) Reports** (Oct.–Dec. 1994) (JAN provides information on accommodations for employees with disabilities).

The savings associated with accommodations include lower job training costs and insurance claims, increased worker productivity, and reduced rehabilitation costs after injury on the job. JAN reports that for every dollar invested in an effective accommodation, companies sampled realized an average of $50 in benefits. A 1995 Harris poll of more than 400 executives showed that more than three quarters of those surveyed report minimal increases in costs associated with the provision of accommodations (e.g., median direct cost for accommodations was $233 per covered employee), and from 1986 to 1995 the proportion of companies providing accommodations rose from 51 percent to 81 percent.

Several implications may be drawn from the existing findings. First, the degree to which many companies comply with the accommodation provisions of the ADA appears to have more to do with their corporate cultures, attitudes, and business strategies than with the actual demands of the law.

For many companies with a culture of workforce diversity and inclusion, implementation has resulted in economically effective business strategies that transcend minimal compliance with the law and produce economic value.[40] Studies of accommodation costs at Sears showed that the indirect cost of not retaining qualified workers is high, with an average administrative cost per employee replacement of $1,800 to $2,400—roughly 40 times the average of the direct costs of workplace accommodations.

Second, as discussed in Chapter XIV, although the direct costs of the accommodations for any disability tend to be low, many companies regularly make informal and undocumented accommodations that require minor and cost-free workplace adjustments that are implemented directly by an employee and his supervisor.[41] The trend toward the provision of accommodation in the workplace may suggest that employers are realizing positive economic returns on the accommodation investment; for instance, by enabling qualified workers with covered disabilities to return to or stay in the workforce, and reducing worker absenteeism.[42]

Professor Rosen suggests that where the benefits of accommodations exceed the costs "there is no inherent reason to expect that labor markets free of government intervention will fail to provide job accommodations in normal job situations."[43] Yet, as shown by the "black hole" findings, absent a truly competitive labor market, attitudinal discrimination against qualified individuals with disabilities alone may necessitate the required provision of accommodations, at least for a large segment of the labor force affected by this market failure.[44]

---

[40] *See* **Sears II, supra Ch. IV § 4.1,** at 24 (neither cost alone nor severity of disability determined Sears' strategy toward the provision of accommodations); Frederick C. Collignon, The Role of Reasonable Accommodation in Employing Disabled Persons in Private Industry, *in* **Disability and the Labor Market** 208 (Monroe Berkowitz & M. Anne Hill, eds.) (1986) ("firms saw accommodation as good business practice"); Peter David Blanck, **Transcending the Americans with Disabilities Act: Research, Policy, and Employment Strategies for the 21st Century** (*forthcoming* 1999) (when employers hire, work with, and accommodate qualified employees with disabilities, they enhance their customer bases, employee morale, and business goals); David A. Thomas & Robin J. Ely, Making Differences Matter: A New Paradigm for Managing Diversity, **Harv. Bus. Rev.** 79 (Sept.–Oct. 1996) (organizational culture stimulates worker skills).

[41] **Sears II, supra Ch. IV § 4.1,** at 19–24; **Sears I, supra Ch. II § 2.3,** at 12 (since 1972 fewer than 10 percent of Sears employees who self-identified as disabled through the company's Selective Placement Program require any kind of accommodation at the time of self-identification). *Cf.* Karlan & Rutherglen, **Ch. II § 2.2,** at 23 (without support of data, arguing that accommodation in any form requires employer to incur cost, and sometimes the "subsidy turns out to be a good investment" in terms of worker productivity or in attracting customers).

[42] *See* Collignon, *in* **Annals**, **supra Ch. VI § 6.1,** at 209 (businesses more likely to provide lower cost accommodations, particularly when current employee becomes disabled); Deborah Shalowitz Cowans, Employers Bear Millions in Elder Caregiving Costs, 29(30) **Bus. Insur.** 2 (1995) (study of large manufacturer with 87,000 employees estimates $5.5 million in lost productivity and time associated with employees providing personal care for elderly relatives, and accommodations such as flexible work schedules mitigate these costs); Weaver, **supra Ch. IV § 4.4,** at 9, 11–12 (Title I provides economic incentives to businesses to hire individuals requiring accommodations that have indirect benefits to the firm or to customers).

[43] Rosen, **supra Ch. IV § 4.4,** at 26.

[44] *See Bultemeyer*, **supra Ch. II § 2.2,** at 42 (bad faith in reasonable accommodation implementation process often reflective of irrational attitudinal bias by employer). Independent of the effects of the civil rights guaranteed by the law, the crux of the normative question is whether Title I is economically rational.

This is true given that the value of a worker with a disability often is contingent upon the worker's output and the employer's attitudes about the worker.[45] Over time,[46] with the lessening of prejudicial attitudes resulting from effective ADA implementation, and with increased knowledge from empirical study, employers who were formerly "economic discriminators" against qualified persons with disabilities may be less willing or less able to incur lost profits to satisfy their discriminatory tastes or preferences.[47]

Third, accommodations involving universally designed and advanced technology have been shown to enable groups of employees with and without disabilities to perform jobs productively, cost-effectively, and safely.[48] The studies at Sears show that the direct costs associated with many technologically based accommodations (e.g., computer voice synthesizers) enable qualified employees with disabilities to perform essential job functions and that these strategies create an economic "ripple effect" throughout the company, as related applications are developed that increase the productivity of employees without disabilities. Moreover, the direct costs attributed to technologically based accommodations may be lowered by companies when their fixed or sunk costs are amortized over time.[49]

Close examination is needed of direct and indirect costs and benefits of ADA implementation, and who bears the costs and receives the benefits associated with workplace accommodations for qualified persons with covered disabilities. A recent study based on more than 1,000 observations in the Canadian workforce examined the extent to which the costs of workplace accommodations are shifted by employers to injured workers through wage adjustments upon the injured worker's return to work after a workplace injury.[50]

These researchers found that injured workers did not incur the cost of workplace accommodations when they returned to their time-of-accident employer. Presumably, these workers were "qualified" to resume their essential or comparable job duties in ways that added economic value to the employer. Injured workers who returned to the workforce but to a different employer did "pay" for a portion of workplace accommodations by accepting substantially lower wages.[51]

Study is required of the extent to which accommodations for workplace injury enable qualified workers with covered disabilities to stay or return to work at their time-of-accident employer or to a different employer, who bears the associated costs, and how these costs vary with job type and other factors such as insur-

---

[45] *See* Donohue, **supra Ch. II § 2.9,** at 2584 (discussing concept of "contingent equality"). Research is needed on the extent to which contingent worker value varies across industries or with different labor markets.

[46] *Cf.* David L. Rose, Twenty-Five Years Later: Where Do We Stand on Equal Employment Opportunity Law Enforcement, *in* **Equal Employment Opportunity: Labor Market Discrimination and Public Policy,** at 39 (Paul Burstein, ed., 1994); John J. Donohue III & James Heckman, Continuous Versus Episodic Change: The Impact of Civil Rights Policy on the Economic Status of Blacks, *id.* at 183.

[47] *See* Weaver, **supra Ch. IV § 4.4,** at 6 ("Lost profits are the price an 'economic discriminator' pays to indulge his preferences."), *citing* Gary S. Becker, **The Economics of Discrimination** (2d ed.) (1971). Study is needed of the impact of the emerging consumer market of people with disabilities and the affect that this market will have on employers' preferences and economic ability to hire and retain qualified workers with disabilities. *See* **Sears I, supra Ch. II § 2.3,** at 8–9.

[48] S.F. Wilson, et al., **A Technical Assistance Report on Consumer and Ex-patient Roles in Supported Housing Services** (1991) (the effect of hiring people with psychiatric disabilities was to improve the level of individual attention and accommodation to all employees, thus creating a more positive working environment).

[49] *See* Collignon, **supra Ch. VI § 6.1,** at 205–06 (universally designed accommodations may reflect more efficient way to undertake production and improve productivity of coworkers); Donohue, **supra Ch. II § 2.9,** n.72 (suggesting that if accommodation costs for workers with disabilities are sunk, then the market incentive would be to retain the qualified disabled worker over an equally or less qualified nondisabled worker requiring no accommodation).

[50] *See* Morley Gunderson & Douglas Hyatt, Do Injured Workers Pay for Reasonable Accommodation?, 50(1) **Indus. & Lab. Rel. Rev.** 92 (1996).

[51] *See also* Karlan & Rutherglen, **supra Ch. II § 2.2,** at 23 (without support of data, suggesting that persons with disabilities face higher costs of searching for a job than do persons without disabilities, and that if costs to employer of accommodation by job transfer are greater than costs of worker job search then worker should bear that cost).

ance coverage rates. Some researchers have suggested that ADA accommodations may increase, or at least help maintain, employment rates by enabling newly disabled workers to retain employment.[52] Other studies show that accommodations for workers' health conditions extends their work life an average of five years.[53]

13.4 Summary

Examination is required of labor force trends, workplace accommodations, and employment discrimination faced by individuals with disabilities.[54] Information is needed to help assess the labor force participation by individuals with disabilities and to lessen the negative economic and societal impact of employment discrimination. These negative effects may be strongest for vulnerable populations of persons with disabilities in society, such as children, patients, persons in poverty, and others disenfranchised from society with little voice in research or regulation.[55]

Many economic and social benefits and challenges associated with the ADA implementation remain to be discovered and need to be documented.[56] United Cerebral Palsy's 1996 "Snapshot of America" reported that almost all (96 percent) individuals with disabilities and their friends and family members surveyed said the ADA had made a difference in their lives, and almost half (46 percent) perceived more acceptance by their communities.[57]

The present investigation highlights an emerging labor force of qualified participants with mental retardation, members of a new generation who have experienced mainstreamed education and who have advocated for their rights.[58] More information is needed on the effect of the ADA on the population of young, qualified persons with disabilities able to join the labor force.[59]

---

[52] *See* Nancy R. Mudrick, Employment Discrimination Laws for Disability: Utilization and Outcome, *in* **Annals, supra Ch. IV § 4.4,** at 53, 68–70 (citing stud ies showing majority of persons injured in the workplace maintain their labor force attachment).

[53] Burkhauser, **supra Ch. X § 10.1,** at 80–81 (range of work life extension from accommodations was found to be from 2.6 to 7.5 years, but authors suggest that range is affected by severity of condition and expected prognosis rates).

[54] Dole, **supra Ch. XIII § 13.1,** at 927–28 (concluding that society has an obligation to know how the ADA is working and whether people covered are aware of rights).

[55] President's Committee on Employment of People with Disabilities, **Disability and Diversity: New Leadership for a New Era** (Jan. 1995) (implications of disability for minority populations); Susan M. Vazakas, Genetic Discrimination and the Americans with Disabilities Act, Ph.D. Dissertation, Boston University, Dissertation Abstracts International, 54/02-A, at 662 (1993) (suggesting risk for "biological underclass" susceptible to genetic discrimination).

[56] Jack A. Stark & Tammi L. Goldsbury, Analysis of Labor and Economics: Needs for the Next Decade, 26 **Mental Retardation** 363 (1988).

[57] *See* United Cerebral Palsy Associations, **1996 ADA "Snapshot of America" Shows Change in Lives of Americans with Disabilities** (July 26, 1996).

[58] *See* Paul Wehman & Wendy Parent, Critical Issues in Planning Vocational Services in the 1990s, *in* **Mental Retardation in the Year 2000,** at 258 (Louis Rowitz, ed., 1992) (discussing research involving workers with mental retardation).

[59] *See* Kathleen Teltsch, As the Labor Pool Dwindles, Doors Open for the Disabled, **N.Y. Times,** at A1 (June 22, 1989) (quoting Senator Harkin's estimate that the ADA would help find jobs for 8.2 million persons with disabilities); **ADA Watch, supra Ch. 1 § 1.2,** at 65–67 (data collected by the Social Security Administration, such as the Survey of Disability and Work and the Survey of Income and Program Participation (SIPP), are inadequate); National Council on Disability, **Meeting the Unique Needs of Minorities with Disabilities: A Report to the President and to Congress** 17, 49 (1993) (finding lack of "hard data" on minority persons with disabilities and recommending research with sampling techniques that allow analysis of smaller samples). *See also* Jon Fortune, et al., Job Placement Results of a Profoundly Rural State Using Job Training and Partnership Act and a Sheltered Workshop, 9 **Int'l J. Rehab. Res.** 269 (1986); John M. McNeil, Work Status, Earnings, and Rehabilitation of Persons With Disabilities, *in* **Disability in the United States: A Portrait from National Data** 133, 156 (Susan Thompson-Hoffman & Inez F. Storck, eds., 1991).

CHAPTER XIV

Implications for the Emerging Workforce: Economic Study

Civil Rights and free enterprise are not in conflict; they are two sides of the same cultural currency. Working in combination, they have powered American democracy to miracles of productivity, self-realization, and quality of life that have revolutionalized the political, economic, and cultural processes of the world.

Justin Dart[1]

14.1 Introduction

This chapter builds on the discussion in Chapter XIII by examining in greater detail the economic implications associated with ADA implementation. A premise of this chapter is that the existing empirical evidence does not reflect the view that the ADA's accommodation provision is a preferential treatment initiative that forces employers to ignore employee qualifications and economic efficiency.

To the contrary, as described in Chapter XIII, studies of accommodations suggest that companies that are effectively implementing the law demonstrate the ability to look beyond minimal compliance of the law in ways that enhance economic value. This ability, as discussed in the next section, often is reflected in "corporate cultures."

Chapter XIII described the findings from the studies at Sears of the workplace accommodations sampled, including those involving assistive technology, physical access, changed schedules, assistance by others, and changed job duties. Other studies previously discussed show that accommodations for employees with disabilities lead to direct and indirect benefits and cost-effective applications that increase the productivity of employees without disabilities. As mentioned, the trend toward the provision of accommodations suggests that employers are realizing positive returns on the accommodation investment by enabling qualified workers with mental retardation to return to or stay in the workforce.[2]

Although many of the accommodations studied at Sears involve simple and common

---

[1] Dart, *in* **Rights and Responsibilities, supra Ch. I § 1.1,** at xxv.

[2] Collignon, *in* **Annals, supra Ch. VI § 6.1,** at 209 (businesses likely to provide lower cost accommodations when current employee becomes disabled); Deborah Shalowitz Cowans, Employers Bear Millions in Elder Caregiving Costs, 29(30) **Bus. Insur.** 2 (1995) (study of large manufacturer with 87,000 employees estimates $5.5 million in lost productivity and time associated with employees' providing personal care for elderly relatives, accommodations such as flexible work schedules mitigate these costs); Weaver, **supra Ch. IV § 4.4,** at 9, 11–12 (Title I provides incentives to businesses to hire individuals requiring accommodations that have indirect benefits to the firm or to customers).

sense strategies, these same accommodation requests in other settings have been the subject of costly litigation at other organizations.[3] Workplace accommodations involving universally designed and assistive technology enable groups of employees with and without disabilities to perform jobs productively, cost-effectively, and safely.[4] The Sears findings support those of organizational researchers showing that many traditional jobs increasingly require workers to use or monitor computers that control equipment performing work tasks, and that workers with disabilities may increasingly perform such essential job functions.[5]

Examination is needed of the type, effectiveness, and net cost of accommodations at large and small organizations, using standardized means for gathering and analyzing information.[6] Study must be conducted on the fears and stigmas associated with disclosure of actual and hidden disabilities and the resulting employment consequences. There is limited information on the extent to which qualified job applicants and employees with hidden disabilities forgo the benefits of accommodations due to fear of disclosure, thereby potentially depriving the labor market and employers of a source of value.[7]

14.2 Corporate Culture and the Benefits of Workplace Accommodations

Chapter XI of this book discusses findings from the present investigation of employers' attitudes toward their employees with mental retardation. Employment integration is fostered by an employer's organizational culture toward the inclusion of qualified workers with disabilities. Systematic study may address the impact of corporate cultures on the availability of workplace supports, particularly those that influence employment opportunity for persons with and without different disabilities. Study is needed, given that many nondisabled individuals or members of their families will experience a disabling condition during the course of their lifetime, possibly a workplace injury, that will affect their employment activities.[8]

Cary Griffen and Katherine Carol have developed a training model for organizations to improve their ability and their corporate culture in the recruiting and hiring of workers with disabilities using "total quality management principles."[9] A first component of their model includes development of an organizational values and mission statement that identifies the value of integrated and diversified employment.

Second, examination of corporate culture is needed. This component includes analysis of decision-making practices and coworker interaction styles. As discussed in Chapter III, increasingly courts have considered as essential job functions under the ADA the ability to interact with others and as part of a work team.[10] Examination of corporate culture also enables assessment of natural supports (e.g., coworker mentoring) in the workplace that have proven important to the successful employment of workers with mental retardation.

A third component of Griffen and Carol's model involves assessment of management and

---

[3] *See Kuehl v. Wal-Mart Stores, Inc.*, 909 F. Supp. 794 (D. Colo. 1995) (Title I litigation involving requested accommodation of periodic sitting on stool while on work duty).

[4] *See* **Sears I, supra Ch. II § 2.3,** at 14–17, 26–29; **Sears II, supra IV § 4.1,** at 35–36; Wilson, et al., **supra Ch. XIII § 13.3** (the effect of hiring people with psychiatric disabilities was to improve the level of individual attention and accommodation to all employees, thus creating a more positive working environment); Deborah Kaplan, et al., **Telecommunications for Persons with Disabilities: Laying the Foundation**, World Institute on Disability Reports (1992).

[5] *See* Edward H. Yelin, The Employment of People with and Without Disabilities in an Age of Insecurity, *in* **Annals, supra Ch. IV § 4.4**, at 117, 128; Shoshana Zuboff, **In the Age of the Smart Machine: The Future of Work and Power** (1988).

[6] *See* Mary T. Giliberti, Implementation of the Reasonable Accommodation Provisions of the ADA by the EEOC and the Courts, 6 **J. Cal. Alliance Mentally Ill** 19–20 (1995).

[7] *See* Collignon, *in* **Annals, supra IV § 4.4,** at 231 (noting a need for studies on those accommodations requested by job applicants who subsequently are not hired).

[8] Tom Harkin, The Americans with Disabilities Act: Four Years Later—Commentary on Blanck, 79 **Iowa L. Rev.** 935, 936 (1994) (disability is a natural part of the human experience). *See also* Zwerling, **supra Ch. III § 3.6** (research on prevalence of workplace injury for workers with disabilities).

[9] Cary Griffen & Katherine Carol, Organizational Change: Key to the Future, *in* **Integrated Employment, supra Ch. I § 1.1,** at 121–23.

[10] *See* **supra Ch. III § 3.4**.

leadership training and supports available to supervisors to foster integrated employment activities.

A fourth component integrates values, culture, and skills to develop an organizational approach to workplace and job design, workplace accommodations, problem solving, and dispute resolution.[11]

Finally, a fifth component identifies the desired outcomes and rewards for achieving organizational goals.

Mank and his colleagues have demonstrated the importance of corporate culture—as reflected by a company's willingness to provide disability and diversity awareness training programs—to the inclusion of qualified persons with mental retardation into a workforce.[12] Mank's findings show that company size alone is not a strong predictor of its "culture" toward workers with mental retardation. Factors such as coworker attitudes, training of coworkers, and disability and diversity training may be better predictors of corporate culture toward disability than company size alone.

In addition to the study of corporate culture and the provision of workplace accommodations, analysis is needed of related corporate policies that affect all workers, such as employee wellness programs, flexible hours for workers with young children, employer-sponsored child care centers, job sharing strategies for workers with limited time availability and employee assistance programs (EAPs).[13] In a 1996 survey of 3,200 worksites, one third (33 percent) of employers with 50 or more employees offered EAPs, with median cost per eligible employee of $20, commonly addressing worker substance abuse and family and emotional problems.[14]

Martin Gerry suggests that many companies already expend large sums of money "accommodating" the needs of workers without disabilities, which in the aggregate may be substantially greater than the costs associated with accommodations for qualified workers with covered disabilities.[15] Large companies are employing universal workplace and job site design and access to efficiently include qualified individuals with and without disabilities into productive workforce participation in ways that add economic value to the company.[16] Analysis of these strategies show that they complement accommodations required by qualified workers with disabilities.

In-depth case study also is required of organizational reponses to ADA implementation over time. Patricia Scott has examined in-depth the response of four companies to ADA implementation for their workers with mental disabilities.[17] Consistent with the discussion in Chapter XV, Scott finds that in these organizations workers with mental disabilities tend not

---

[11] *See* **infra Ch. XV § 15.2** (discussing effective dispute resolution of ADA claims).

[12] *See* Mank, et al., **supra Ch. IV § 4.9,** at 446.

[13] *Cf.* Karlan & Rutherglen, **supra Ch. II § 2.2,** at 39-40 (casting accommodation as "an individualized form of affirmative action" that may have applications for deterring employment discrimination based on gender and race); Joan C. Williams, Restructuring Work and Family Entitlements Around Family Values, 19 **Harv. J. L. & Pub. Pol'y** 753, 756 (1996) (flexible work hours may accommodate needs of workers with children in child-care).

[14] *See* Tyler D. Hartwell, Paul Steele, et al., Aiding Troubled Employees: The Prevalence, Cost, and Characteristics of Employee Assistance Programs in the United States, 86(6) **J. Pub. Health** 804–08 (1996).

[15] *See* Martin H. Gerry, Disability and Self-Sufficiency, *in* **Disability and Work, supra Ch. IV § 4.4** (suggesting that large businesses are increasingly investing in attracting and retaining qualified employees "in a more holistic way" with disability as only one component of the measure of potential productivity and value). *See also* Burgdorf, **supra Ch. II § 2.7,** at 530-33 (suggesting that accommodations for workers with disabilities are a more general subclass of accommodations routinely provided to workers without disabilities); U.S. Dept. of Health & Human Services, 1992 National Survey of Worksite Health Promotion Activities, 7 **Am. J. Health Promotion** 452-64 (1993) (1992 survey of 1507 worksites found that 81 percent of companies offered employee health promotion activity).

[16] *See* **Sears II, supra Ch. IV § 4,1,** at 6; Daniel Stokols, Kenneth R. Pelletier, & Jonathan E. Fielding, Integration of Medical Care and Worksite Health Promotion, 273 **JAMA** 1136 (1995) (new technologies relate to cost-effective worksite wellness and health care programs); Susan J. Olson, Worksite Health Promotion: An Investment Beyond Health Care Cost Containment, *in* **Driving Down Health Care Costs** 470 (1996).

[17] Patricia J. Scott, Organizational Responses to Employment under the ADA of Workers with Psychiatric Diabilities: Four Case Studies, Florida International University, Ph.D. Dissertation, Dissertation Abstracts International, Vol. 58/03-A, at 1086 (1997).

to disclose their impairments or request accommodations due to fear of adverse actions by their employers. Scott's analysis suggests that study of organizational responses to ADA implementation must focus on means to enhance communications among employees with disabilities, their supervisors, and human resource professionals.

14.3 Economic and Noneconomic Benefits of Workplace Supports

Studies show that accommodation strategies enhance the productivity and job tenure of those large numbers of qualified workers without disabilities who are injured on the job or who may become impaired in the future.[18] A 1996 survey of 251 employers showed that companies using an integrated approach to disability management, workplace accommodations, and "return-to-work" programs reported annual reductions of 14 percent in their total costs associated with worker disability and showed corresponding increases in productivity and employee morale.[19] These employers reported that the primary problem in establishing effective disability management programs was the lack of adequate empirical information about the costs and benefits of such programs.

In an eight-year study of Coors Brewing Company's health screening program covering almost 4,000 employees, the company realized net and direct savings of roughly $2.5 million, in terms of saved payments in short-term disability, temporary worker replacement, and direct medical costs.[20] Given a conservative estimate of $100 average direct cost per employee for accommodations based on the Sears findings, the savings generated by the Coors study could fund accommodations for 25,000 qualified workers.[21] Another study of Coors Brewing Company's wellness initiatives (e.g., health screening and education, exercise, stress, and smoking cessation programs) found that the company saves up to eight dollars for every dollar invested in these programs.[22]

A nine-year study of 28,000 Union Pacific Railroad employees found that their wellness program resulted in net savings of $1.3 million to the company.[23] These findings suggest the huge economic implications associated with cost-effective accommodation strategies designed to prevent workplace injury and to help retain the increasing numbers of qualified employees with and without disabilities. Considering that by the year 2000, the employers' costs associated with back injury alone in the workplace are estimated to approach $40 billion, examination of the economic savings related to accommodation strategies, injury prevention, and wellness programs is warranted.[24]

The educational side-effects associated with Title I implementation and accommodation strategies may enhance employee moral and productivity.[25] These side-effects may produce positive coworker attitudes about qualified

---

[18] *See* Hal Clifford, The Perfect Chemistry: DuPont's Work-Life Program, **Hemispheres** 33, 34 (1996) (claiming a 637 percent return on expenditures for its LifeWorks program, a program designed to help employees deal with job and life pressures, based on estimated value of resulting increased performance, employee retention, stress reduction, and reduced absenteeism).

[19] **Staying @ Work: Value Creation Through Integration**, Watson Wyatt Worldwide, Survey on Integration in Disability Plans (1997).

[20] Henritze J. Greenwood, Coorscreen—A Low Cost, On-site Mammography Screening-Program, 10(5) **Am. J. Health Promotion** 364–70 (1996) (breast cancer screening provided for roughly 4,000 employees, cost savings of program was $3,110,080, procedural costs for program were $668,690, with net savings of $2,441,190).

[21] In 1995, it is estimated that companies spent over $100 billion rehabilitating 3.5 million employees with work-related injuries. *See* Shelly Reese, Building an Express Lane Back to Work, 14(11) **Business & Health** 24–29 (1996) (arguing that return-to-work programs and accommodation strategies may ease worker rehabilitation costs).

[22] *See* Martha McDonald, Valuing Experience: How to Keep Older Workers Healthy, 8(1) **Bus. & Health** 35–38 (1990) (for older workers, stress control program estimated to save company $100,000 over a five-year period).

[23] *See* Catherine Carythers, Will Wellness Ever Really Catch On?, **Business & Health: State of Health Care in America Supplement** 55–58 (1996) (wellness programs on stress, exercise and eating habits).

[24] *See* Blanck, **supra Ch. III § 3.8**, at 103–07 (citing studies estimating that in 1990, the cost to society of back-related disability included an estimated $16 billion in workers' compensation costs, lost productivity, and other intangible costs).

individuals or about those who are members of other protected groups.[26] In a series of studies, Professor Frank Rusch and his colleagues find that coworkers without disabilities serve as important mentors (natural supports) for qualified workers with mental retardation in comparable jobs.[27]

Issues related to employment hiring are another topic for study, given the substantial percentage of qualified people with disabilities who are not working and who are seeking jobs or seeking to return to work after a disability.[28] A recent survey of human resource professionals at large organizations found that more than 90 percent report that substantially more workers are returning to work after a disability due to the increased availability of workplace accommodations.[29] Almost half of those surveyed reported that 95 percent or more of their employees returned to work after a disability and cited an average savings of $15,000 per returned employee.

Analysis of harassment and hostile work environment hiring cases also may implicate underlying biased attitudes toward disability.[30] Cases involving the failure to provide accommodations, as illustrated by the *Wilson* case discussed in Chapter III, reflect individual or corporate attitudes toward employment of persons with disabilities, and create or contribute to a hostile work environment or disability harassment.[31]

14.4 The Staffing Industry and the Employment of People with Disabilities

Systematic study has not addressed the emerging role of the staffing (i.e., temporary employment agency) industry supporting the employment of qualified persons with disabilities.[32] In 1997 my colleagues and I began an in-depth case study of Manpower, Inc., the world's

---

[25] Andrew I. Batavia, Ideology and Independent Living: Will Conservatism Harm People with Disabilities?, 549 **Annals, supra Ch. IV § 4.4,** 10, 20 (Jan. 1997) (arguing that Title I may be interpreted to require employers to accommodate the needs of employees with and without disabilities, rather than an infringement on business objectives).

[26] Lisa E. Key, Co-Worker Morale, Confidentiality, and the Americans with Disabilities Act, 46 **DePaul L. Rev.** 1003–42 (1997) (ADA confidentiality provisions may lead to worker morale problems in context of accommodation process); Rose A. Daly-Rooney, Designing Reasonable Accommodations Through Co-worker Participation: Therapeutic Jurisprudence and the Confidentiality Provisions of the Americans with Disabilities Act, 8 **J. L. & Health** 89, 90 (1993-94) (suggesting that ADA's confidentiality provisions may impair worker interaction).

[27] Frank R. Rusch, Philip G. Wilson, Carolyn Hughes, & Laird Heal, Matched-Pairs Analysis of Coworker Interactions in Relation to Opportunity, Type of Job, and Placement Approach, 32 **Mental Retardation** 113–22 (1994).

[28] *See* **Sears II, supra Ch. IV § 4.1,** at 14 (discussing a hiring case involving a charging party who uses a wheelchair and who filed 7 applications with a retail store during a period when that particular store filled 108 positions, contending the retail store discriminated in failing to hire the applicant and failing to provide him with reasonable accommodations). *See also* **Disability Watch, supra Ch. II § 2.6,** at 16 (58 percent of Americans with disabilities are of working age). By some estimates three quarters of working-age Americans with disabilities do not have jobs. *Id.* at 19 (citing data from 1995 Current Population Survey showing that 72.2 percent of Americans with disabilities of working age do not have jobs).

[29] Mike Norton, Survey: "More Workers Are Returning to Jobs After a Disability Today Than Five Years Ago—Employer Accommodations Cited as Main Reason," **Unum News** (Oct. 10, 1997) (describing survey results of 50 human resource professionals).

[30] *See* **supra, Ch. V § 5.10** (discussing harassment and retaliation claims under the ADA). *See also* Jerome L. Holzbauer & Norman L. Berven, Disability Harassment: A New Term for a Long-Standing Problem, 74(5) **J. Couns. & Dev.** 478–83 (May 1996) (no systematic study of psychological consequences of disability harassment available); Ravitch, **supra, Ch. V § 5.10,** at 1506 n.157 (study needed of employees' with disabilities perceptions of harassing conduct); Deborah Epstein, Can a "Dumb Ass Woman" Achieve Equality in the Workplace?: Running the Gauntlet of Hostile Environment Harassing Speech, 84 **Geo. L.J.** 339 (review of impact of hostile work environment cases).

[31] *See* Ravitch, **supra Ch. V § 5.10,** at 1509 (providing example of qualified employee with covered psychiatric disability who requires accommodation of sensitivity from employer to perform essential job functions, but employer ridicules condition and unfairly disciplines employee without providing appropriate supervision). *See James v. Frank*, 772 F. Supp. 984 (S.D. Ohio 1991) (ineffectual accommodation process contributes to hostile work environment for qualified person with a disability).

[32] The ADA applies to individuals working in the staffing industry. *See* **EEOC Enforcement Guidance on Contingent Workers** (Dec. 3, 1997).

largest employer.[33] Manpower annually provides employment to more than 800,000 people in the United States and more than 1,500,000 people worldwide, maintaining 2,500 offices in 43 countries.

The Manpower study examines emerging employment opportunities available to qualified persons with disabilities within the staffing industry. The study explores the importance of these opportunities to welfare reform strategies that provide a bridge to full-time employment, a topic discussed in Chapter XVI. Preliminary interviews with Manpower employees suggest that a critical element of the company's success in hiring and retaining workers with disabilities has been its investment in individualized training, worker assessment, and job-matching tools.

The size of the contingent workforce—including self-employed, temporary, and part-time workers—has been estimated to range from 34 million to 42 million individuals, roughly 25 to 31 percent of the American labor force in 1996.[34] Economist Richard Belous finds that, from 1980 to 1996, the contingent workforce grew faster than the economy as a whole.[35] Supplemental staffing—staffing with temporary workers—is the fastest growing component of the contingent workforce. The U.S. Bureau of Labor Statistics estimates that between the years 1994 and 2005, temporary employment opportunities will grow by 55 percent.[36]

Manpower's business mix is approximately 40 percent light industrial, 40 percent office, and 20 percent technical or professional assignments. The company provides workers with opportunities in positions at different skill levels. Manpower has expanded its services to include the provision of on-site staff to support a client company's supplemental staffing needs (this may include the provision of job training coaches for qualified persons with disabilities), programs that transition temporary workers to permanent jobs, and job skills assessment and training services.

Manpower's role as a provider of short-term workers has evolved into a more sophisticated human resources function. The expanded functions serve as a bridge for qualified workers with disabilities seeking to enter the labor force. The Manpower study identifies aspects of its corporate culture that foster equal employment of qualified persons with disabilities under ADA implementation, including: a belief that there are no unskilled workers, that every individual has skills and aptitudes that can be measured, and every job may be broken down into essential tasks; a training focus on what workers can do, rather than on what they cannot do, and on identifying as many potential jobs as possible for each employee; and an empirically based process of matching employee essential job skills and customer company needs.[37]

In addition, Manpower assesses the customer company's skill needs and work environment. The company's Work Environment Service Call Report gathers information from company representatives and from personal worksite tours. The report covers customer expectations, physical details of the work area, work pace, dress requirements, hours, breaks, safety issues, parking, and accessibility issues. Manpower customers complete assignment requests that include job descriptions and the equipment, software, and machinery to be used. This assessment is consistent with analysis of essential and marginal work functions, a concept discussed in Chapter III that is central to determining a "qualified" worker under the ADA.

Manpower's applicant intake and skills assessment procedures are individualized.

---

[33] *See* Peter David Blanck, **Communicating the Americans With Disabilities Act: The Role of the Staffing Industry in the Employment of Persons with Disabilities—A Case Report on Manpower, Inc.** (1998) (describing the study).

[34] *See* Richard S. Belous, The Rise of the Contingent Workforce: Growth of Temporary, Part-Time, and Subcontracted Employment, 19(1) **Looking Ahead,** at 2–24 (1997); Richard Belous, **The Rise of the Contingent Workforce** (1997).

[35] *Id.*

[36] *See* Contingent Workers Said to Comprise 25% of U.S. Workforce, 8 **Staffing Indus. Rep.,** at 9–10 (Aug. 22, 1997).

[37] Additionally, the Manpower study examines myths about the staffing industry's ability to work with people with disabilities, including that: (1) individualized training and job placement are not available; (2) minimum wages and inadequate health insurance benefits are provided; (3) there is no opportunity for career advancement; (4) there is little opportunity for transition to full-time competitive employment; and (5) there are limited opportunities for self-advancement and self-learning.

Intake begins with an interview that gathers information on work history, job skills, and preferences. Applicants describe the work environment and job responsibilities that interest them. Applicants then complete diagnostic skills assessments selected according to their abilities and interests. These assessments use actual work samples to give workers a preview of what they may do on the job as well as ways to measure their skills or the need for accommodation.

In addition to skills assessment, Manpower offers its employees skill enhancement through work training programs. Skills training is individualized depending on the employee's job abilities and interests. When the skills assessment and training process is complete, Manpower uses its databases of customer needs and employee information to make a match. In this way, as economist Richard Belous writes, "the temporary help industry has become a key source of training and human resource development and is beginning to be viewed more as an industry that trains experts than one that represents unskilled labor."[38]

Manpower anticipates the company will continue to serve as a gateway to the workforce for greater numbers of qualified workers with disabilities. Increasingly, businesses view their supplemental workforce as a source of candidates for permanent positions. More than 40 percent of Manpower's workforce accepts permanent jobs offered to them as a result of Manpower assignments. Chapter XV discusses additional ways in which economic and noneconomic barriers to full-time work for qualified persons with mental retardation may be alleviated.

14.5 Emerging Research Questions

Adequate information is not available on the growing economic impact of the emerging workforce of persons with mental retardation. In 1990 alone almost 15,000 persons with severe disabilities were employed under the National Industries for the Severely Handicapped (NISH) programs and earned almost $50 million in wages.[39] Many long-term questions for future economic study may be suggested:

1. How to assess in economic and noneconomic terms whether a person with mental retardation has equal opportunity to employment for which he or she is qualified?
2. How to assess the economic impact of employment for qualified persons with mental retardation in large and small firms covered by Title I?
3. What subgroups of persons with developmental disabilities who are not "substantially limited" in major life activities are excluded from coverage under Title I?
4. How to delineate essential job functions for persons with different degrees of mental retardation?
5. How to measure employers' perceived and actual Title I compliance and its impact on their economic bottomlines?
6. What is the effect of private and state job training and coaching programs designed to foster equal employment opportunity, independence, and income growth for qualified persons with mental retardation?
7. How to assess systematically wage disparities among persons with and without disabilities in various jobs?
8. How will an increasingly global economy affect employment integration and the rights of persons with mental retardation in this country and abroad?[40]
9. How to assess in economic and noneconomic terms the impact of the policies set forth in the ADA?
10. What will be the economic benefits and costs of ADA implementation not anticipated when the law was passed?

One attempt to address the last question listed above is reflected in a recent study conducted by Heidi Berven and me. We have examined the unintended economic benefits of the ADA by focusing on developments in the

---

[38] Belous, **Rise of the Contingent Workforce, supra Ch. XIV § 14.4.**

[39] New Directions, **NISH Update,** (21)6 Pub. Nat. Ass'n State Mental Retardation Program Directors 1, 8 (June 1991).

[40] Issues related to labor force organizations are relevant to the emerging workforce of qualified Americans with disabilities, as well as those related to union growth and membership. *See* Guy Stubblefield, Organized Labor's Role in Implementing the ADA, *in* **Rights and Responsibilities, supra Ch. I § 1.1,** at 81–85 (reviewing union perspectives on ADA implementation).

assistive technology market.[41] The research was guided by several propositions:

> The ADA recognizes that to achieve inclusion and equal participation of individuals with disabilities, society must be accessible architecturally and structurally.
>
> To support independence and self-determination, many individuals with severe disabilities require assistive technology devices and services.
>
> Monetary benefits associated with inventive activity in the assistive technology market must be factored into cost-benefit models of the ADA because the law has helped to increase demand for assistive devices and has created economic opportunities for assistive device inventors and manufacturers.

The research investigates how ADA implementation created unintended economic opportunities for assistive technology inventors and manufacturers—stakeholders not mentioned in the literature as beneficiaries of the law. The study examines patenting trends for assistive technology devices, whereby patents are used as a proxy to gauge the unintended economic effects of ADA implementation.

The findings of the patent study suggest that ADA implementation is impacting assistive technology inventive activity in positive economic ways. Assistive technology patent numbers have shown annual increases since 1976, and since 1990 the number of patents citing the ADA has increased.

During the years 1991 to 1997, patents were granted for a wide range of assistive devices. In turn, these devices are reflective of an expanding consumer market for goods that improve accessibility to work and daily life. The study illustrates how ADA implementation may spur technological innovation, which in turn gives rise to benefits to employees with disabilities and their employers.

14.6 Summary

The findings from studies of Sears, Manpower, and other companies suggest that, in the years to come, many of the protections first afforded by the ADA may become standard practice for employers in the hiring and retention of qualified workers with disabilities, workers who add economic value to their employers' bottomlines. Study is needed to reinforce the forward-looking employment practices in place by many employers of persons with mental retardation and other disabilities.[42]

Empirical verification of ADA implementation may help to accelerate knowledge and reveal myths and misconceptions about persons with disabilities. There is a need for analysis of microeconomic variables, such as individual, coworker and staff education, and job skill levels.[43] Study of corporate and industry downsizing patterns, and their relation to the labor force participation of qualified workers with disabilities, is required. Likewise, macroeconomic variables need to be studied, such as labor force trends and composition (for instance, the aging of the workforce and the prevalence of worker disability), community attitudes, and the impact of state and federal changes to health and welfare policies.

[41] Heidi Berven & Peter David Blanck, The Economics of the Americans with Disabilities Act: Patents and Economic Development, **Notre Dame J. L. Ethics & Pub. Pol'y** (*forthcoming* 1998).

[42] *See* C.A. Powell, The Americans with Disabilities Act: The Effect of Title I on Employer/Employee Relations, 15 **Law & Psychology Rev.** 313, 321 (1991).

[43] *See* **Working with Disability: Employment Statistics and Policy,** at 2 (H. Stephen Kaye, ed., Mar. 1996) (calling for improved data on characteristics of people with disabilities); **The Future of Disability Statistics,** at 3 (H. Stephen Kaye, ed., Mar. 1996) (noting relation of data needs and disability policy).

CHAPTER XV

Implications for the Emerging Workforce: Study of Workplace Disputes and of Medical and Genetic Testing

We have seen more than once that the public welfare may call upon the best citizens for their lives. It would be strange if it could not call upon those who already sap the strength of the state for these lesser sacrifices, ...in order to prevent our being swamped with incompetence. It is better for all the world, if instead of waiting to execute degenerate offspring for their imbecility, society can prevent those who are manifestly unfit from continuing their kind.

Oliver Wendell Holmes, U.S. Supreme Court Justice[1]

15.1 Introduction

This chapter examines two distinct areas related to ADA implementation that have important implications for the emerging workforce of persons with mental retardation: the effective resolution of workplace disputes involving the ADA, and the use of medical and genetic testing in employment.

Analysis of these two areas may help formulate educational programs for ADA stakeholders.[2] Education plays a central role in eliminating employment discrimination facing people with mental retardation.[3] One study showed that less than 50 percent of the general population with disabilities reported being aware of the ADA, four years after the law's enactment.[4] In another study, only one third of individuals who reported experiencing genetic discrimination knew of the existence of state commissions designated to combat discrimination.[5] Research

---

[1] *Buck v. Bell*, 274 U.S. 200, 207 (1927).

[2] *See* Dole, **supra Ch. XIII § 13.1,** at 927–28 (1994) (suggesting society has obligation to know how ADA is working and whether people covered are aware of rights); Laura L. Mancuso, ADA Fact or Fiction?, 6 **J. Cal. Alliance Mentally Ill** 6–9 (1995) (discussing role of education in changing one journalist's views on ADA).

[3] *See* Martha J. McGaughey, et al., **Implementation of the Americans with Disabilities Act: Perceptions and Experiences of Individuals with Disabilities** 14 (1996) (reporting that 98 percent of highly educated sample of persons with disabilities, but only 58 percent of less educated sample, were aware of ADA; two thirds of the highly educated sample reported that they knew how to file an ADA-related discrimination complaint, compared with only 8 percent of the less educated sample).

[4] National Organization on Disability and Louis Harris & Associates, **1994 Survey of Americans with Disabilities** (1994).

and education are needed to help prevent unjustified attitudes and discriminatory behavior toward persons with mental retardation.[6]

15.2 The Nature of Workplace Disputes

When ADA Title I was passed, critics predicted the law would foster extensive and costly litigation.[7] Some commentators continue to make these claims.[8] The view of one federal court is illustrative:

> [T]he ADA as it [is] being interpreted [has] the potential of being the greatest generator of litigation ever...[it is doubtful] whether Congress, in its wildest dreams or wildest nightmares, intended to turn every garden variety workers' compensation claim into a federal one....The court doubts that the ultimate result of this law will be to provide substantial assistance to persons for whom it was obviously intended....[9]

The greatest source of indirect costs alleged by critics to be associated with ADA implementation is related to expenses for administrative, compliance, and legal actions.[10] The Sears study described in earlier chapters examined all 138 Title I charges filed with the EEOC against Sears from 1990 to mid-1995.[11] The findings shows that almost all of the EEOC charges (98 percent) were resolved without resort to trial litigation, and many through informal dispute processes at low costs that enabled qualified employees with disabilities to return to productive work.[12] A 1997 study of nationwide trends in Title I charges filed with the EEOC shows that 94 percent of beneficial outcomes were obtained by the charging parties before full EEOC investigations and formal litigation were initiated.[13]

---

[5] *See* Lisa N. Geller, et al., Individual, Family, and Societal Dimensions of Genetic Discrimination: A Case Study Analysis, 2 **Sci. & Engineering** 71, 80 (1996) (surveying more than 900 individuals regarding genetic discrimination); Jean E. McEwen, et al., A Survey of State Insurance Commissioners Concerning Genetic Testing and Life Insurance, 51 **Am. J. Hum. Genetics** 785, 790 (1992) (finding only 2 of every 42 insurance commissioners reported receiving formal complaints about genetic discrimination).

[6] Research must be devoted to attitudes involving vulnerable populations, such as children, patients, persons with other disabilities, persons in poverty and those disenfranchised from society with little voice in research or regulation. *See* Peter David Blanck & Mollie Weighner Marti, Genetic Discrimination and the Employment Provisions of the Americans with Disabilities Act: Emerging Legal, Empirical, and Policy Implications, 14 **Behav. Sci. & L.** 411, 432 (1997) (discussing legal and ethical dilemmas related to genetic testing involving vulnerable populations); Susan M. Vazakas, Ph.D. Dissertation, Genetic Discrimination and the Americans with Disabilities Act (Ph.D. dissertation, Boston University), *in* 54/02-A **Dissertation Abstracts Int'l** 662 (1993) (suggesting risk for "biological underclass" susceptible to genetic discrimination); **Disability and Diversity, supra Ch. XIII § 13.4,** at 17 (discussing implications of disability for minority populations).

[7] 135 **Cong. Rec.** 510,741 (daily ed. Sept. 7, 1989) (statement of Sen. Pryor).

[8] David Frum, Oh, My Aching Back (Head), **Forbes,** at 64 (Nov. 8, 1993) (arguing that the ADA is doing little for people with disabilities and "a great deal for lawyers and malingerers"). *Cf.* ABA Commission on Mental and Physical Disability Law and Commission on Legal Problems of the Elderly, **Targeting Disability Needs: A Guide to the Americans With Disabilities Act for Dispute Resolution Programs** 3 (1994) (suggesting that the ADA presents significant opportunities for informal dispute resolution).

[9] *Fussell v. Georgia Ports Authority*, 906 F. Supp. 1561, 1577 (S.D. Ga. 1995) (*quoting Pedigo v. P.A.M. Transport, Inc.*, 891 F. Supp. 482, 485–86 (W.D. Ark. 1994) (citing studies in support of claim that ADA generates litigation)).

[10] Peter David Blanck, Transcending Title I of the Americans with Disabilities Act: A Case Report on Sears, Roebuck and Co., 20 **Mental & Physical Disability L. Rep.** 278, 283–84 (1996) (discussion of direct and indirect costs associated with Title I implementation).

[11] **Sears II, supra Ch. IV § 4.1,** at 33–34.

[12] *Id.* at 35–37 (in addition, of the cases studied, the average settlement cost to Sears, exclusive of attorney fees, was $6,193). *See also* Karlan & Rutherglen, **supra Ch. II § 2.2,** at 23 (arguing there is an advantage of settlement over litigation in Title I context for persons with disabilities compared to other protected groups, due to factors such as hypothesized limitations in job search ability of persons with disabilities).

[13] *See* Kathryn Moss, Matthew Johnsen, & Michael Ullman, Assessing Employment Discrimination Charges Filed Under the Americans with Disabilities Act, **J. Disability Pol'y Stud.** (*forthcoming* 1998) (suggesting that presence of Title I motivates parties to resolve disputes informally without resort to costly trial litigation, also finding that variation in a charging party's likelihood of receiving a benefit based on party's type of disability, race, and gender).

Analysis is needed on a national scale of the patterns and magnitude of the costs and benefits associated with Title I implementation, compliance, and related litigation.[14] Professors Pamela Karlan and George Rutherglen have suggested a variety of factors involving Title I implementation and compliance that may help guide future study.[15] They hypothesize that, given the low cost of many accommodations and high costs attendant to litigation, employers and employees with disabilities create a "bargaining range" within which they negotiate the costs and benefits associated with accommodation.[16]

Analysis of the magnitude of the costs and benefits associated with the accommodation process, for different employers and for workers with and without disabilities in similar jobs, may enable an accurate assessment over time of the economic impact of Title I.[17] Broadly defined, indirect costs and benefits may include the impact of effective accommodations on employee morale, perceptions of the business and its reputation by customers and the community, or relationship to effective implementation of other laws such as the Family Medical Leave Act or workers' compensation laws.[18]

15.3 ADA Title I Charges Filed with the EEOC

In contrast to the implementation history of Title VII, litigation need not be the primary means to define "the boundaries of compliance" under the ADA.[19] Analysis of ADA Title I charges filed by persons with mental retardation with the EEOC from July 26, 1992, through March 1997 supports this suggestion.

Of the approximately 82,000 Title I charges filed, only 0.4 percent (approximately 320) involved persons with mental retardation.[20] Two thirds (67 percent) of the charges filed by persons with mental retardation involved discharge from employment, while 17 percent involved complaints related to workplace accommodations, and 21 percent involved complaints related to workplace harassment.

From July 26, 1992, to March 31, 1997, analysis of ADA Title I cases involving charging parties with mental retardation shows that approximately 10 percent of the cases were either settled or conciliated by the parties, resulting in $622,000 in monetary benefits to the charging parties. Half of the charges (50 percent) were determined by the EEOC to be without reasonable cause and 8 percent were withdrawn before they were investigated fully.

---

[14] *See* **1995 Harris Survey, supra Ch. XIII § 13.2** (survey of employers finding that 66 percent report that litigation has not increased as a result of the ADA, 82 percent report that ADA is worth the cost of implementation, 27 percent report that it costs more to employ a person with a disability than a person without a disability); President's Committee on Employment of People with Disabilities, 5(2) **Washington Fax** 1 (Nov.–Dec. 1996) (*citing* EEOC records showing that Title I charge filings decreased by 10 percent during 1996 as compared to 1995).

[15] *See* Karlan & Rutherglen, **supra Ch. II § 2.2,** at 30.

[16] *See* Blanck, **ADA and ADR, supra Ch. I § 1.1,** at 259, 263–64, 270–71 (1992) (discussion of the benefits of alternative dispute resolution practices in cases involving persons with disabilities, including the development of a "settlement framework" and "dynamic" relationships among the parties).

[17] *See* Collignon, **supra Ch. VI § 6.1,** at 208 (discussing economic benefits of accommodation, and reviewing study of accommodation costs under Rehabilitation Act of 1973); Oi, **supra Ch. III § 3.2,** at 39 (suggesting the need for study comparing the average productivity and the costs and benefits of accommodations for a random sample of persons with and without disabilities, in and out of the workforce).

[18] *See* Peter David Blanck, **Communicating the Americans with Disabilities Act, Transcending Compliance: 1997 Report on Direct and Indirect Costs and Benefits of Workplace Accommodations at Sears, Roebuck & Co.** (*forthcoming,*1998) (preliminary findings showing low direct and indirect costs and high direct and indirect benefits of workplace accommodations at Sears).

[19] *See* Junda Woo, Self-Policing Can Pay Off for Companies, **Wall St. J.,** at B5 (Sept. 8, 1993) (suggesting that proactive attempts at compliance with laws like the ADA are advantageous to many businesses); Wendy S. Tien, Note, Compulsory Arbitration of ADA Claims: Disabling the Disabled, 77 **Minn. L. Rev.** 1443, 1445–47 (1993) (discussing the role of arbitration in resolving ADA claims).

[20] Statistics dervied from EEOC National Database on ADA Title I, from July 26, 1992, to Mar. 31, 1997. *See also* Miller, **supra Foreword** (discussing ADA litigation and persons with mental retardation).

Of all the Title I charges filed with the EEOC through March 1997, the most common type involved the discharge or termination of individuals with back and spine impairments. Roughly 13 percent involved a mental or neurologic disability.[21] Of the complaints filed with the EEOC through March 1997, roughly 52 percent involved employee discharge, 28 percent involved an accommodation, and 9 percent involved a hiring decision. Only a small percentage of the Title I claims involved issues of workforce entry and integration.[22]

These trends suggest areas worthy of future study. First, perhaps optimistically, during initial Title I implementation large numbers of qualified but unemployed or underemployed individuals with mental retardation may have pursued methods other than litigation to attain and retain integrated employment. Alternative methods for gaining access to jobs involve programs on supported employment, self-advocacy, mediation, and informal dispute resolution.

Second, and less optimistically, the pattern of Title I filings suggests that the majority of individuals with mental retardation did not or may not have been able to avail themselves of their rights.[23] Either they failed to perceive or chose not to report many of the barriers the ADA was designed to eliminate. A general lack of awareness of the ADA among adults with disabilities may worsen this situation.

Critics of the ADA continue to charge that the Act may be a "nightmare" for employers and a "dream" for plaintiffs' lawyers.[24] Others question the lack of clarity of the provisions of Title I.[25] Nevertheless, as described in Chapter XI, survey of the present participants' employers show favorable attitudes toward the employment and accommodation of qualified employees with mental retardation.[26] As mentioned, a 1995 Harris poll of business executives found that 79 percent of those surveyed believe that the employment of qualified people with disabilities is a boost to the economy, while only 2 percent believe it poses a "threat to take jobs" from people without disabilities.[27]

Study limited to the EEOC charges associated with ADA Title I implementation focuses discussion on the failures of the system, as opposed to economically efficient strategies that enhance a productive workforce. Analysis of Title I cases alone present a skewed picture of accommodation costs and benefits, particularly when they involve situations where accommodation costs are high and job availability is limited.[28]

The emerging research suggests that starting from a base of ADA compliance, companies can look beyond minimal legal compliance to "transcendence of the law," in ways that make economic sense and that prevent employment-related disputes from arising. One way to avoid potential ADA disputes is through adoption of universal design and access strategies to workplaces. As discussed in Chapter XIV, study has shown how innovative and cost-effective corporate solutions for providing accommodations have universal applications to workers with and without disabilities.

Other companies have found that self-analytic study, such as that performed in the Sears and Manpower studies described in this book, provides a process and structure to educate management and employees about Title I compliance, reducing costly litigation on the subject. Companies adopting proactive approaches to implementation have not experienced the explosion of litigation that critics predicted.

---

[21] *See* EEOC, National Database Charge Receipt Listing, at 55 (Aug. 8, 1993) (outlining breakdown of 1993 Title filings. Approximately 73 complaints involved persons with mental retardation, resulting in 49 EEOC charges).

[22] Statistics derived from EEOC National Database on ADA Title I, from July 26, 1992, to Mar. 31, 1997.

[23] *See* Miller, **supra Foreword** (reaching similar conclusion).

[24] *See* Barnard, **supra Ch. VII § 7.2,** at 229; Lavelle, **supra Ch. I § 1.7,** at 1135–36 (*citing* related articles).

[25] Walter Olson, **The Excuse Factory: How Employment Law Is Paralyzing the American Workplace,** at 134 (1997) (stating that "[f]ew laws have done as much as the Americans with Disabilities Act to make a note from your doctor something you can take to the bank.").

[26] *See* **supra Ch. XI § 11.7** (discussing survey findings). *Cf.* Crespi, Efficiency Rejected: Evaluating "Undue Hardship" Claims Under the Americans with Disabilities Act, 26 **Tulsa L. J.** 1, 33 (1990).

[27] **1995 Harris Survey, supra Ch. XIII § 13.2**.

[28] *See* Karlan & Rutherglen, **supra Ch. II § 2.2,** at 30–31.

Employers adopting a framework for effective dispute avoidance and resolution have reduced litigation and created an environment of cooperation, rather than hostility and confrontation, in managing disability issues in the workplace.[29] In the Sears studies approximately 80 percent of the informal disputes sampled were resolved successfully without resort to formal legal mechanisms.[30]

Another study found that individuals with disabilities are less likely to perceive employment discrimination when they informally negotiate job-related problems successfully.[31] The study asked respondents with a disability whether they had resolved a problem related to alleged employment discrimination without filing a Title I charge.

Respondents reported resolving problems substantially more times than they reported experiencing discrimination.[32] Moreover, more than half (59 percent) of those who attempted informal negotiation activities resolved the problem successfully.[33] Effective dispute resolution processes foster attitudes of responsibility by employees with disabilities and their supervisors, facilitating problem solving at appropriate corporate levels.[34]

15.4 Study of Workplace Medical Testing

Chapter V of this book described how persons with mental retardation and others with mental disabilities sometimes are alleged to be "unqualified" for a job when they are believed to pose a direct safety or health threat to themselves or others in the workplace. Cases in which a direct threat defense is used by an employer have tended to implicate underlying and unfounded attitudinal biases about mental impairments.[35]

Employers are required to make an individualized determination of direct threat, based on the employee's present ability to safely perform essential job functions.[36] Often, this determination is made on the basis of medical or psychological

---

[29] Robin Talbert & Naomi Karp, Collaborative Approaches: Aging, Disability, and Dispute Resolution, 29 **Clearinghouse Rev.** 638 (1995).

[30] *Id.* at 30. One example of informal dispute resolution in the Sears study involved alleged disability harassment (e.g., rude comments and inappropriate work assignments) against a deaf employee. *See* **Sears II, supra Ch. IV § 4.1,** at 63.

[31] McGaughey, et al., **supra Ch. XV § 15.1,** at 16.

[32] *Id.* at 16–17 (depending on type of job discrimination, between 5.4 percent and 11.4 percent report job discrimination and between 8.7 percent and 18.6 percent report problem resolution).

[33] *See* Lorraine Rovig, Negotiation Principles for Reasonable Accommodation, 20 **Employment in the Mainstream** 22–24 (Sept.–Oct. 1995).

[34] The ADA expressly encourages alternative forms of dispute resolution, such as mediation and arbitration. *See* 42 U.S.C. § 12212. Litigants are permitted to waive their rights to a judicial forum for review of ADA claims and resolve their disputes in alternative forums. *See Bercovitch v. Baldwin School, Inc.*, 133 F.3d 141 (1st Cir. 1998) (finding plaintiff waived right to judicial forum and must submit to binding arbitration); Wright V. Universal Maritime Serv. Corp., 121 F.3d 702 (4th Cir. 1997), *cert. granted,* 1998 U.S. LEXIS (U.S. Mar. 2, 1998) (same). However, the waiver of remedial rights must be scrutinized closely by courts to ensure that the release was knowing and voluntary. *See Bledsoe v. Palm Beach County Soil and Water Conservation District,* 133 F.3d 816 (11th Cir. 1998).

[35] *See Doe v. University of Md. Med. Sys. Corp.*, 50 F.3d 1261, 1266 (4th Cir. 1995) (holding hospital did not violate ADA when it suspended HIV-positive surgical resident because of threat to patients); *Judice v. Hospital Serv. Dist. No. 1*, 919 F. Supp. 978 (E.D. La. 1996) (holding hospital did not violate ADA by requesting recovering alcoholic surgeon to undergo medical evaluation before reinstatement of staff privileges); *Scoles v. Mercy Health Corp.*, 887 F. Supp. 765, 770 (E.D. Pa. 1994) (finding that hospital did not violate ADA by suspending clinical privileges of HIV-positive surgeon because of safety threat to patients). *See* Peter D. Blanck, Students with Hearing Disabilities, Reasonable Accommodations, and the Rights of Institutions of Higher Education to Establish and Enforce Academic Standards: *Guckenberger v. Boston Univ.*, 21 **Mental & Physical Disability L. Rep.** 679–86 (1997) (reviewing accommodation case); James J. McDonald, Jr., et al., Mental Disabilities Under the ADA: A Management Rights Approach, **Employer Rel. L. J.,** at 541–69, 557–58 (Spring 1995) (reviewing cases involving direct threat defense); Phillip L. McIntosh, When the Surgeon Has HIV: What to Tell Patients About the Risk of Exposure and the Risk of Transmission, 44 **U. Kan. L. Rev.** 315, 315–64 (1996) (examining legal issues raised by HIV infection of health care workers); Pope L. Moseley, et al., Hospital Privileges and the Americans with Disabilities Act, 21 **Spine** 2288, 2290–93 (1996) (reviewing cases involving direct threat defense); Mary E. Sharp, The Hidden Disability That Finds Protection Under the Americans with Disabilities Act: Employing the Mentally Impaired, 12 **Ga. St. U. L. Rev.** 889, 921–26 (1996) (same).

[36] *See* 29 C.F.R. § 1630.2(r).

tests in the workplace.[37]

The ADA prohibits disability-related *pre-employment* inquiries and medical tests. Medical examinations are permitted after a conditional job offer has been made.[38] Medically related employment tests, if used by an employer, must be administered to all employees regardless of disability, and, with limited exceptions, the information and records obtained must be treated as confidential.[39]

The unauthorized dissemination of an individual's medical records or test results may constitute a per se (that is, automatic) violation of the ADA's provisions. In such circumstances, a plaintiff does not have to make a showing of harm beyond the violation to state a viable ADA charge.[40] Although the ADA prohibits the dissemination of confidential medical records, supervisors and managers may be informed at the prehire or posthire stage about necessary restrictions on an employee's work duties and potential accommodations.[41]

Medical test results obtained during employment or after a conditional offer of employment is made may not be used to exclude a qualified individual from a job unless the exclusion is "job related." A job-related determination is consistent with business necessity (e.g., business objectives) and not amenable to reasonable accommodation.[42] If an employee meets the threshold showing of discrimination by alleging that an employer unfairly used a medical test to screen out individuals with disabilities, the employer may rebut the claim by proving that the test accurately measured job skills that are consistent with business necessity, such as workplace health, safety, productivity, or security requirements.[43]

Employment decisions based on unjustified attitudes about the usefulness and predictability of medical tests deny employment or employment-related benefits (e.g., health insurance) to currently qualified individuals solely on the basis of their perceived status.[44] The following

---

[37] *See Grenier v. Cyanamid Plastics, Inc.*, 70 F.3d 667, 674–75 (1st Cir. 1995) (finding employer did not violate ADA when it inquired into ability of job applicant, former employee with known psychological disability, to function effectively in workplace and get along with coworkers and supervisor, or where employer required that applicant provide medical information as to ability to return to work with or without accommodation and as to type of accommodation necessary).

[38] 42 U.S.C. § 12112(d)(3) (1994). *See also* Susan Alexander, Preemployment Inquiries and Examination: What Employers Need to Know About the New EEOC Guidelines, 45 **Lab. L. J.** 667–78 (1994) (summarizing EEOC guidelines); Robert B. Fitzpatrick, Employer's Screening Procedures Under the Americans with Disabilities Act: What's Legal? What's Debatable?, **A.L.I.–A.B.A.**, at 285 (Mar. 2, 1995) (surveying ADA in practical context); David M. Katz, Disability Queries Okay After Offering Job, **Nat'l Underwriter Prop. & Casualty-Risk & Benefit Mgmt.**, at 31 (June 17, 1996) (discussing window of opportunity for employers to ask about job applicants' disabilities after offers are made).

[39] *See* 42 U.S.C. § 12112(d)(3)(A), (B). *Cf. Prado v. Continental Air Transport Co., Inc.*, 982 F. Supp. 1304 (N.D. Ill. E. Div. 1997) (finding that an employer's decision to require a medical exam before making a conditional offer of employment to a job applicant is not necessarily a *per se* violation of the ADA and that medical examinations are sometimes necessary to determine if the job applicant satisfies job qualifications); *Bloodsaw et al., v. Lawrence Berkeley Laboratory et al.*, 135 F.3d 1260 (9th Cir. 1998) (finding that the ADA imposes no restriction on the scope of post-offer medical examinations but only guarantees the confidentiality of the information gathered).

[40] *Valle v. Runyon*, 1997 EEOPUB LEXIS 3288 (Sept. 5, 1997) (finding *per se* violation under applicable sections of the Rehabilitation Act of 1973 as amended in 1992 where plaintiff's medical records were handed out at a meeting of the agency with union representatives).

[41] *See* 29 C.F.R. § 1630.14(c).

[42] *See id.* § 12112(c)(4)(A); 29 C.F.R. § 1630.14(b)(3) (1997).

[43] *See* 42 U.S.C. § 12113(a); Kimberli R. Black, Personality Screening in Employment, 32 **Am. Bus. L. J.** 69, 113–15 (1994) (discussing methods to satisfy job-relatedness requirement that scored test validly relates to job at issue); **supra Ch. V § 5.2** (discussing burdens of proof in ADA cases). *See also Padilla v. Tingstol Co.*, 1997 U.S. Dist. LEXIS 20018 (N.D. Ill., E.D. 1997) (finding that a plaintiff's adverse reaction to employment-related medical tests itself is not a covered disability under the ADA because of its temporary nature, and therefore plaintiff not entitled to reasonable accommodation).

[44] *See* Paul R. Billings, et al., Discrimination as a Consequence of Genetic Testing, 50 **Am. J. Hum. Genetics** 476, 477 (1992) (noting that consequences of genetic testing and discrimination are not understood); **Office of Technology Assessment, U.S. Congress, Medical Monitoring and Screening in the Workplace** 3 (1991) (finding that 42 percent of corporate respondents considered job applicants' health insurance risk factors in determining employability and 36 percent engaged in insurance risk assessments of job applicants); Velida Starcevich,

sections examine potential issues of dispute arising from the use and misuse of genetic and psychological testing in the workplace.

15.5 Genetic Testing in the Workplace

In the past five years, more than 50 genetic tests have been identified as having the potential for discovering the causes of inheritable but often hidden diseases.[45] The availability and low cost of these medical tests has increased the possibility of test misapplication, resulting in stigmatization and discrimination against many qualified individuals with mental retardation and other disabilities.

Confirming Justice Holmes' stereotypic views set out at the beginning of the chapter, studies of genetic testing suggest that the likelihood of developing a genetic condition is perceived differently than the probability of contracting an illness not produced by genetic factors.[46] Attitudinal bias has been demonstrated in studies of the faulty prediction of future disease onset.[47]

Qualitative studies suggest that people with genetic markers, such as those with mental retardation, who are currently healthy and asymptomatic are denied health insurance and employment opportunities on the basis of predictions that they may become "unhealthy" in the future. Target individuals report being treated as if they were currently disabled or chronically ill. One study of the perceptions of members of genetic support groups found that, as a result of a genetic disorder in the family, one quarter of the respondents believed that they were denied life insurance, 22 percent believed they were refused health insurance, and 13 percent believed they were denied employment opportunity.[48]

Discussion is needed of the effectiveness of the ADA prohibitions that prevent medical testing during the application process and of the improper use of test results for other purposes.[49] Employment discrimination based on misinformation precludes qualified people from being hired, holds employees hostage to their current employment, serves as a basis for firing, or results in the denial or unwarranted limitation of health coverage for particular conditions.[50]

Study is lacking on the extent to which individuals who undergo testing understand their privacy rights,[51] as well as issues concern-

---

Workplace: Designer Genes Only, Please, **Observer,** at 8 (June 2, 1996) (discussing EEOC estimate that 5 percent of companies test their employees' genes).

45 *See* Wendy McGoodwin, Genie Out of the Bottle: Genetic Testing and the Discrimination It's Creating, **Wash. Post,** at C3 (May 5, 1996) (discussing Human Genome Project).

46 *See* Billings, et al., **supra Ch. XV § 15.4,** at 480 (discussing stigmatization of individuals diagnosed with genetic disease, but asymptomatic).

47 *See* Amos Tversky & Daniel Kahneman, Evidential Impact of Base Rates, *in* **Judgment Under Uncertainty: Heuristics and Biases** 153–60 (Daniel Kahneman, et al., eds., 1982) (discussing base-rate phenomenon); Ward Casscells, et al., Interpretation by Physicians of Clinical Laboratory Results, 299 **New Eng. J. Med.** 999–1000 (1978) (reporting that less than 20 percent of responding students and staff at Harvard Medical School gave correct answer of 2 percent to question about prevalence rate given base-rate information; almost half of respondents gave incorrect answer of 95 percent).

48 *See* E. Virginia Lapham, et al., Genetic Discrimination: Perspectives of Consumers, 274 **Sci.** 621 (1996) (finding that fear of genetic discrimination resulted in 9 percent of respondents refusing to be tested for genetic conditions, 18 percent not revealing genetic conditions to insurers and 17 percent not revealing information to employers).

49 *See* McGoodwin, **supra Ch. XV § 15.5,** at C3. Some states have enacted genetic information privacy laws to prevent the unapproved release of information and employment discrimination on the basis of genetic information. *See* Illinois Statutes, H.B. 8 adding 410 Ill. Comp. Stat. 513/1 *et seq.* (1997); Texas Laws, H.B. No. 39 adding Tex. Lab. Code Ann. § 21.401 *et seq.* (1997). *See also* Mark S. Dichter & Sarah E. Sutor, The New Genetic Age: Do Our Genes Make Us Disabled Individuals Under the Americans with Disabilities Act? 42 **Vill L. Rev.** 613–33 (1997) (suggesting that courts exercise caution in applying ADA to persons with asymptomatic genetic disorders).

50 *See* Joseph S. Alper, et al., Genetic Discrimination and Screening for Hemochromatosis, 15 **J. Pub. Health Pol'y** 345, 354 (1994); Prepared Statement of Dr. Collins, **Fed. News Service** (Apr. 23, 1996) (lack of health insurance often precludes fighting genetic risks with the necessary level of surveillance or surgery and discussing consequences).

51 *See* Genetic Testing for Cancer Susceptibility ASCO Statement Published, **PR Newswire** (May 1, 1996) (American Society of Clinical Oncology recommends counseling be provided for individuals at risk for inheriting a cancer susceptibility gene, and patients and their families be informed about the potential for genetic discrimination by insurers or employers).

ing informed consent and confidentiality in related research, diagnosis, and therapy.[52] Ethical issues surrounding medical testing in employment increasingly are implicated, as medical and other records are placed in computer databases that are accessible to individuals and companies.[53]

There are other potential biases associated with the provision of genetic testing in the workplace for workers with mental retardation. First, many genetic conditions and diseases are variable in expressivity and not all individuals with the genotype will develop the disease.[54] Professor Patrick Brockett and his colleagues comment that although Phenylketonuria (PKU) is a severe inherited genetic condition that may result in mental retardation, a target individual who is never exposed to Phenylanine in his diet may never develop PKU.[55]

Second, when decisions regarding health insurance and employment are based solely on a diagnostic label, the severity or range of the individual's condition is disregarded. Research shows that genotype alone does not necessarily predict the onset or severity of a disabling condition.[56] Nevertheless, low base-rate occurrences (for instance, predicting the most severe scenario) often are used as the benchmark for decisions regarding the employment of persons with genetic and other hidden conditions.

Third, few genetic conditions are caused by a single gene.[57] Health conditions, such as mental retardation and developmental disabilities, have many causes. Focusing solely on the role of genetics minimizes the impact of other social conditions, such as poverty or environmental conditions, that relate to poor health and higher mortality rates.[58] Unfounded emphasis on genetic test information diverts employers from considering the underlying economic and social mediating factors of workplace health and injury prevention. Uninformed uses of genetic testing also reinforce biases associated with a "blame the victim" mindset, condemning people with "faulty" genes solely on the basis of that status.[59]

Another common misconception is that a genetic condition indicates the end of a person's present productive work life. Professors Mary Daly and John Bound examined the extent to which workers, through their own actions or their employers' accommodations, adjust to their health limitations and continue working. The results show that only about one quarter of those who become impaired while employed exited the labor force on a permanent basis.[60]

In addition, Daly and Bound find that over half of the individuals who continued working remained with their employer, and the remaining individuals continued to work for different employers. Significantly more employees who remained with their employer after the onset of their impairment reported receiving accommodations from their employer. Study is needed on

---

[52] *See* Julie Holland, Should Parents Be Permitted to Authorize Genetic Testing for Their Children?, 31 **Fam. L. Q.** 321 (1997) (discussing genetic testing and legal rights of children and parents).

[53] Lori B. Andrews & Ami S. Jaeger, Confidentiality of Genetic Information in the Workplace 17 **Am. J. L. & Med.** 75 (1991). *See also* Elaine A. Draper, Social Issues of Genome Innovation and Intellectual Property, 7 **Risk: Health Safety & Env't** 201 (Summer 1996) (analysis of information and data banks on job applicant and employee genetic conditions); On-Line Service Checks Job Applicant Histories, **Charleston Newspapers** (Apr. 18, 1996) (employers access online information about a job applicant's previous workers' compensation claims and health-related information even though it violates ADA).

[54] *See* Joseph S. Alper, et al., Genetic Discrimination and Screening for Hemochromastosis, 15 **J. Pub. Health Pol'y** 345, 353 (1994) (noting that at least 25 percent of those with genotype for hemochromatosis, common recessive iron storage disorder, do not develop symptoms of disease).

[55] Patrick L. Brockett & Susan E. Tankersley, The Genetics Revolution, Economics, Ethics and Insurance, 16 **J. Business Ethics** 161–67 (1997).

[56] *See* Billings, et al., **supra Ch. XV § 15.4,** at 479–80.

[57] *See* Abigail Trafford, Ethics and Genetics, **Wash. Post,** at Z6 (Apr. 16, 1996).

[58] *See* McGoodwin, **supra Ch. XV § 15.5,** at C3 ("[O]veremphasis on the role of genes in human health neglects environmental and social factors.").

[59] *Id.* at C03 (reporting that fear of discrimination causes people to avoid genetic testing); Paul Steven Miller, Statement of EEOC Commissioner, at 3 (May 24, 1996) (referring to *EEOC v. Hertz* case, **supra Ch. V § 5.8,** involving individuals with mental retardation as "a particularly egregious case of blaming the victim").

[60] *See* Mary C. Daly & John Bound, Worker Adaptation and Employer Accommodation Following the Onset of a Health Impairment, 51 **J. Gerontology** 53 (1996) (respondents who reported that they had "any impairment or health problem that limits the kind or amount of paid work" were classified as disabled).

the social and economic consequences of genetic testing by employers for persons with mental retardation entering the workforce.[61]

15.6 Psychological Testing in the Workplace

A second major area requiring study involves psychological testing of qualified individuals with mental retardation. Chapter IV of this book described that an employer covered by Title I must provide accommodations for a qualified employee or job applicant with a mental impairment in circumstances where the employer knows of the condition and the individual can perform the essential job functions.[62]

Not all personality-oriented employment tests constitute medical tests for purposes of the ADA. Employers may assess a broad set of personality characteristics during pre- and post-employment screening as long as the purpose is to predict necessary, job-related functions, rather than to screen out qualified individuals with disabilities.[63] The determination of whether a test is medical in nature is made on a case-by-case basis.

Failure to disclose a mental disability may prevent an individual from receiving accommodations at the time of hiring or subsequent to that time. While the decision to disclose a mental disability is complex,[64] open disclosure may promote equal employment opportunity by assisting the employee in obtaining workplace accommodations.[65] Nevertheless, fear of negative attitudes and discriminatory behavior often prevents qualified workers from disclosing their disabilities or submitting to medical testing.[66]

Studies suggest that employers attach greater stigma to employees with mental disabilities

---

[61] *See* Diane Eicher, Genetic Tests: A Catch-22 Life-Saving Information Might Easily Be Misused, **Denv. Post**, at G1 (May 29, 1996) (fears about health, insurance and employment are based on genetic testing for risk of cancer); Mark A. Rothstein, Preventing the Discovery of Plaintiff Genetic Profiles by Defendants Seeking to Limit Damages in Personal Injury Litigation, 71 **Ind. L. J.** 877, 878 (1996) (reviewing ethical and public policy issues in genetic testing).

[62] Accommodations for psychiatric disabilities include flexible scheduling, reasonable time off, restructuring jobs and work environments, educating coworkers. *See* U.S. Office of Tech. Assessment, Rep. No. OTA-BP-BBS-124, **Psychiatric Disabilities, Employment, and the Americans with Disabilities Act** 9–11 (1994) (discussing employers' obligation to provide accommodations to qualified individuals with disabilities); Conference Report: Mainstream Conference Speaker Addresses Accommodations for Mental Disabilities, *in* 5 **Americans with Disabilities Act Manual** 73 (1996) (same); Laura L. Mancuso, Reasonable Accommodation for Persons with Psychiatric Disabilities, 14 **Psychosocial Rehab. J.** 3–19 (1990) (discussing barriers to employment for people with psychiatric disabilities and suggesting types of accommodations); John W. Parry, Mental Disabilities Under the ADA: A Difficult Path to Follow, 17 **Mental & Physical Disability L. Rep.** 100, 104–05 (1993) (same).

[63] *See, e.g.*, Jane C. Duckworth, The Minnesota Multiphasic Personality Inventory-2: A Review, **J. Counseling & Dev.**, at 564–65 (July–Aug. 1991) (describing revised instrument and its advantages and disadvantages).

[64] *See* Laura Mancuso, **Cal. Dep't Mental Health, Case Studies of Reasonable Accommodations for Workers with Psychiatric Disabilities** (1993).

[65] *See Taylor v. Principal Fin. Group*, 93 F.3d 155, 157 (5th Cir. 1996) (finding plaintiff failed to disclose to employer any limitations resulting from his disability and any need for reasonable accommodation), *cert. denied*, 117 S. Ct. 586 (1996); Disclosure, 6 **J. Cal. Alliance Mentally Ill** 32, 33 (1995) (stating disclosure is step toward exercising rights by workers with psychiatric disabilities; without disclosure, employer has no obligation to accommodate and potential of ADA to promote equal employment opportunity is curtailed).

[66] *See* Deborah Zuckerman, et al., **The ADA and People with Mental Illness: A Resource Manual for Employers** 9 (1993) (stating that media portrayals of persons with mental illness as dangerous and unpredictable reinforce negative stereotypes); Daniel B. Fisher, Disclosure, Discrimination and the ADA, 6 **J. Cal. Alliance Mentally Ill** 55 (1995) (advising prudent disclosure of psychiatric history in face of stigma and discrimination); Ann Nelson Marshall, A Hope Not Yet Fulfilled: People with Psychiatric Disabilities and the ADA, 6 **J. Cal. Alliance Mentally Ill** 41, 42 (1995) (discussing barriers of stigma, misunderstanding and lack of information about individuals with psychiatric disabilities).

[67] *See* **1995 Harris Study, supra Ch. XIII § 13.3** (finding that 19 percent of respondents reported being "very comfortable" when meeting someone known to have mental illness, compared with 22 percent for someone who has mental retardation, 47 percent for someone who is blind and 59 percent for someone who uses wheelchair); John B. Allen, Jr., Don't Judge a Book by Its Cover: Qualified Employees Under the ADA, 6 **J. Cal. Alliance Mentally Ill** 29–30 (1995) (stating ADA makes it possible for persons with disabilities to become employed, but negative attitudes are barrier to employment); Ira H.

than to those with physical disabilities.[67] Fueled by prejudice toward mental impairments, employers and coworkers interpret work and personal difficulties or symptoms experienced by an individual with a mental condition as related directly to the individual's ability to perform a job. This tendency may be especially true if the employee previously requested an accommodation for a known mental disability.[68] Chapter V discussed that it is difficult to predict how employers and coworkers will respond to individuals with mental disabilities who self-disclose or whose condition is divulged from medical tests.[69]

Analysis is required of the psychological, organizational, and economic impact of psychological and genetic testing on qualified job applicants and employees with disabilities.[70] Professors Leslie Boden and Howard Cabral examined the relative impact of company characteristics—such as company size, labor market, and whether the company has a self-funded insurance plan—on the prevalence of the use of medical testing.[71] Their findings show that the economic characteristics of companies help predict the prevalence of their medical testing. They suggest that ADA implementation may have substantial economic benefits to society in curtailing overly broad medical testing policies that disproportionately shift the costs of workplace illness to workers.

Effective testing in the workplace must balance employers' legitimate goals of maximizing worker productivity, health, and safety, with equal employment opportunity for qualified workers.[72] The prior discussion of psychological and genetic testing is not meant to suggest that employers, insurance companies, and others do not have an important interest in promoting medical testing to identify, place, and assess employees with disabilities.[73]

Identifying health risks or heightened

Combs & Clayton P. Omvig, Accommodation of Disabled People into Employment: Perceptions of Employers, 52 **J. Rehabilitation** 42–45 (1986) (reporting that mental illness ranked 13th out of 16 severe disabilities surveyed for employability and ease of accommodations); Brian J. Jones, et al., A Survey of Fortune 500 Corporate Policies Concerning the Psychiatrically Handicapped, 57 **J. Rehabilitation** 31–35 (1991) (reporting employers perceive employees with physical disabilities more desirable than those with psychiatric disabilities); Marshall, **supra Ch. XV § 15.6,** at 41 (stating myths and stereotypes about mental illness and violence encourage employers to request medical information about "job fitness").

[68] *See* George Howard, The Ex-Mental Patient as an Employee, 45 **Am. J. Orthopsychiatry** 479 (1975) (maintaining that employees with history of psychiatric problems are indistinguishable from randomly selected employees in job performance and human relations); J. Mintz, et al., Treatments of Depression and Functional Capacity to Work, 49 **Archives Gen. Psych.** 761, 766 (1992) ("Behavioral impairments, including missed time, decreased performance, and significant interpersonal problems are common features of depression that appear to be highly responsive to symptomatically effective treatment given adequate time.").

[69] Craig Haney, Employment Tests and Employment Discrimination: A Dissenting Psychological Opinion, 5 **Indus. Rel. L. J.** 1, 60 (1982) (recognizing personality tests discount situational factors in employee behavior); Donald H. J. Hermann III, Privacy, the Prospective Employee, and Employment Testing: The Need to Restrict Polygraph and Personality Testing, 47 **Wash. L. Rev.** 73, 75 (1971) (listing invasion of individual privacy among criticisms of personality screening); Daniel Sommer & Jean-Claude Lasry, Personality and Reactions to Stressful Life Events, **Canada's Mental Health** 19 (Sept. 1984) (stating personality tests overlook impact of stress-related factors); G. Stephen Taylor & Thomas W. Zimmerer, Personality Tests for Potential Employees: More Harm Than Good, 67 **Personnel J.** 60 (1988) (stating personality tests fail to measure individual motivation in job performance).

[70] *See* M. A. Nester, Employment Testing for Handicapped People, 13 **Pub. Personnel Mgmt.** 417–34 (1984) (discussing testing for persons with various disabilities).

[71] *See* Leslie I. Boden & Howard Cabral, Company Characteristics and Workplace Medical Testing, **J. Pub. Health,** at 1070–75 (Aug. 1995) (analysis controlled for variance by firms in employee exposure to workplace hazards); Michelle A. Travis, Psychological Health Tests for Violence-Prone Police Officers: Objectives, Shortcomings, and Alternatives, 46 **Stan. L. Rev** 1719–29 (1994) (discussing policy goals of psychological testing).

[72] *See Varnagis v. Chicago*, 1997 U.S. Dist. LEXIS 903 1 (N.D. Ill. 1997) (finding that an individual who did not have a disability covered by the ADA could not challenge the use of MMPI test on the grounds that it violated ADA prohibition against preoffer medical inquiries).

[73] *See* Billings, et al., **supra Ch. XV § 15.4,** at 476 ("Insurance companies, private employers, governments and educational institutions all have an immediate or potential interest in promoting large-scale genetic screening to identify individuals carrying disease-associated genes.").

susceptibility to injury from workplace exposures is another valid goal of medical testing.[74] Courts recognize that there are situations in which an employer concerned about workplace health, security, and injury prevention would be justified in requiring employees to undergo physical or mental examinations or testing that is job-related and consistent with business needs.[75] Work-related examinations may be allowed under the ADA even if they disclose the nature or extent of an employee's disability when potential health problems have a substantial or injurious impact on an employee's job performance.[76]

Yet caution is warranted to the extent that biased attitudes about the predictability and usefulness of medical tests may lead to increased discrimination against qualified people and their relatives.[77] In the employment realm, discrimination based on misinformation from medical tests may preclude qualified people from being hired or promoted, serve as a basis for firing, or result in the denial or unwarranted limitation of health coverage for particular conditions.[78]

15.7 Summary

This chapter examined two prominent issues related to ADA implementation. First, the prevalence and resolution of ADA disputes was discussed. Second, the growing use of medical testing (genetic and psychological) in the employment context was examined. These areas require careful attention to prevent employment discrimination based on unjustified attitudes toward qualifed workers.

---

[74] *See* Marne E. Brom, Note, Insurers and Genetic Testing: Shopping for the Perfect Pair of Genes, 40 **Drake L. Rev.** 121, 138 (1990) ("Faced with concerns of an employee's job performance, co-workers' safety, and the public's safety, employers have considerable incentive to predict who might be susceptible to occupational exposure.").

[75] *See Duda v. Board of Education of Franklin Park Public School District No. 84*, 133 F.3d 1054 (7th Cir. 1998) (*citing* 42 U.S.C. § 12112(b)(1), that the ADA includes "segregating" a job applicant or worker among its definitions of discrimination). *See also* **infra Ch. IV § 4.10** (discussing job reassignment as a workplace accommodation); 42 U.S.C. § 12112(d)(4)(A) (stating that ADA prohibits disability-related inquiries unless information requested is "job-related and consistent with business necessity").

[76] *See Yin v. State of California*, 95 F.3d 864, 867–68 (9th Cir. 1996), *cert. denied*, 117 S. Ct. 955 (1997).

[77] *See also* David T. Wiley, If You Can't Fight 'Em, Join 'Em: Class Actions Under Title I of the Americans with Disabilities Act, 13 **Lab. Law.** 197 (1997) (arguing that blanket psychological testing in the employment context may violate the ADA against a class of individuals).

[78] *See* Peggy R. Mastroianni & Carol R. Miaskoff, Coverage of Psychiatric Disorders Under the Americans with Disabilities Act, 42 **Vill. L. Rev.** 723–40 (1997) (suggesting that understanding of psychiatric conditions and ADA provisions may help to reduce employment discrimination); Alper, et al., **supra Ch. XV § 15.5,** at 354 (stating that advances in genetic tests and pressures on insurance companies and employers to use tests are increasing frequency of genetic discrimination).

CHAPTER XVI

Implications for Policy Development and Reform: Health Care and Welfare Reform

There has never been a clear articulation of the goals and underlying values of policy affecting disabled people. This lack of a framework for policy development and implementation is in large part responsible for the patchwork nature of disability policy.

Judith Heumann[1]

16.1 Introduction

One long-term goal of the present investigation is to refine the research model to include persons with other disabilities, living in rural and urban settings, and participating in different types of employment and preemployment training. It is clear from the experience with the 1964 Civil Rights Act that laws, such as the ADA, alone cannot guarantee integration.[2] As illustrated by the outcome in *EEOC v. Hertz* case described in Chapter V, researchers must explore the extent to which qualified individuals with mental retardation are forced to assume a victim status, rather than the one of empowerment and inclusion envisioned by the law.[3]

A second long-term goal is to further evaluation of the implications associated with antidiscrimination laws and policy affecting the emerging and existing workforce of qualified persons with mental retardation.[4] The relationship among the requirements of other ADA Titles, such as those affecting the provision of public transportation[5] or integrated living arrangements, have important implications for employment opportunities for qualified persons with mental retardation. This chapter examines current policy issues associated with ADA Title II and Title III implementation and with health care, education, and welfare reform.

---

[1] Heumann, *in* **Rights and Responsibilities, supra Ch. I § 1.1,** at 252.

[2] Shapiro, **supra Ch. I § 1.1,** at 180–81. *See also* Burgdorf, **supra Ch. II § 2.7,** at 582–84 (discussing judicial narrowing of the ADA).

[3] *Cf.* Bumiller, **supra Ch. II § 2.2,** at 433 (discussing the need for individuals who suffer discrimination to assume the role of victim before filing a claim).

[4] *See* David Braddock, Richard Hemp, Susan Parish, & James Westrich, **The State of the States in Developmental Disabilities** (5th ed. 1998) (discussing the growth and development of services and funding for persons with developmental disabilities and mental retardation in the United States).

[5] *See* Wehman, *in* **ADA Mandate, supra Ch. VIII § 8.6,** at 35.

16.2 State and Local Governmental Activities and ADA Title II

The Congressional findings in the ADA recognize that persons with disabilities are a "discrete and insular minority" who have been subjected to "a history of purposeful unequal treatment."[6] ADA Title II prevents unjustified discrimination against qualified persons in all areas of state and local governmental activities, such as in public employment, or in the provision of building permits for treatment centers, group home or individual housing treatment centers, or the provision of accessible recreational programs by a local municipality.[7]

ADA Title II prohibits discrimination by state and local governments in much the same way Section 504 of the Rehabilitation Act of 1973 prohibits discrimination by programs receiving federal financial assistance.[8] As mentioned, Title II applies to the employment actions of state and local governments. It protects public employees from employment discrimination in the same manner as set forth under ADA Title I.[9]

ADA Title II also applies in cases in which a qualified individual with mental retardation faces the unnecessary segregation of residing in an institution primarily because of state funding requirements. In such a case an individual cannot enjoy the social and economic benefits of independent living and work.[10] In *L.C. v. Olmstead*,[11] discussed in Chapter XII, a federal district court in Georgia determined that ADA Title II was violated when state mental health officials institutionalized two persons with mental retardation who could be served effectively in community-based programs. This state action was held to be a per se violation of the law.

In another 1997 case, *Innovative Health Systems v. City of White Plains*,[12] decided by the United States Court of Appeals for the Second Circuit, it was held that ADA Title II prohibits discrimination against people with disabilities that may be reflected in city zoning ordinances. In that case the City of White Plains had denied a health care provider the necessary permit to build an out-patient drug and alcohol treatment center. The court concluded that both the ADA and the Rehabilitation Act encompass claims of discrimination in zoning decisions by a city because these decisions are part of the normal functioning of governmental entities covered by these laws.[13]

Professor Stanley Herr has described the importance of ADA Title II to the rights of persons with mental retardation and developmental disabilities.[14] Herr notes that prior to the passage of the ADA, persons with mental retardation had limited legal redress in the face of discrimination by state and local governments because of the U.S. Supreme Court's decision in *Cleburne Living Center v. City of Cleburne*.[15] In the *Cleburne* decision, the Supreme Court refused to treat persons with mental retardation as a "suspect class" subject to higher scrutiny

---

[6] 42 U.S.C. § 1210[a][7].

[7] *See Concerned Parents to Save Dreher Park Center v. West Palm Beach*, 884 F. Supp. 487 (S.D. Fla. 1994) (finding that a city's decision to eliminate recreational programs only for people with physical and mental disabilities, and not for nondisabled citizens, violated ADA Title II, despite the city's purported budget crisis).

[8] *See* Stanley S. Herr, The ADA in International and Developmental Diabilities Perspectives, *in* **Rights and Responsibilities, supra Ch. I § 1.1,** at 229–49.

[9] *See Bledsoe v. Palm Beach County Soil and Water Conservation District*, 133 F.3d 816 n.4 (11th Cir. 1998) (finding that ADA Title II encompasses employment discrimination and reviewing cases in accord with this interpretation). Unlike the requirements for filing an ADA Title I employment discrimination charge, *see* **supra Ch V § 5.6,** plaintiffs are not required to exhaust their administrative remedies before filing an ADA Title II charge, so they may proceed directly in federal district court. *Bledsoe*, **supra** (*citing* cases in support).

[10] *See L.C. v. Olmstead*, 1997 WL 148674 (N.D. Ga. 1997) (*citing* in support *Helen L. v. DiDario*, 46 F.3d 325 (3d Cir., *cert. denied*, 516 U.S. 813 (1995) affirmed, 1998 WL 163707 (11th cir.1998). *See also Kathleen S. v. Department of Public Welfare,* 1998 WL 83973 (E.D. Pa. 1998) (court certifying class of institutionalized persons in state psychiatric hospital to bring ADA claim).

[11] *Id.*

[12] 117 F.3d 37 (2d Cir. 1997).

[13] In *Innovative Health Sys., Inc.*, the Second Circuit applied the association provision of discrimination under ADA Titles I and III to a case arising under ADA Title II. *See* **supra Ch. II § 2.2** (discussing association provision of discrimination under the ADA); *Den Hartog v. Wasatch Academy*, 129 F.3d 1076 (10th Cir. 1997) (same).

[14] *See* Herr, *in* **Rights and Responsibilities, supra Ch. I § 1.1,** at 229–49.

[15] 473 U.S. 432 (1985).

analysis for disadvantaged groups under the equal protection clause of the U.S. Constitution.[16]

The findings from the present investigation and from other studies illustrate the strong trends toward movement into integrated community living settings. ADA Title II increasingly may become an important tool to address unjustified discrimination against people with mental retardation in the areas of employment, housing, recreational services, and the provision of state and local governmental services.

16.3 Public Accommodations and ADA Title III

ADA Title III prohibits discrimination in public accommodations (for instance, inaccessibility to retail stores, doctors' offices, private hospitals) on the basis of disability. Herr reports that some of the most "glaring examples of discrimination" have involved access to public accommodations by persons with mental retardation. In one example in the legislative hearings on the ADA, an owner of a private zoo refused to admit children with Down syndrome "because he feared they would upset the chimpanzees."[17]

Bragdon v. Abbott,[18] the first ADA case to be reviewed by the U.S. Supreme Court, involved a suit brought under ADA Title III. In *Bragdon*, Ms. Abbott, an individual with asymptomatic HIV disease, claimed that defendant Bragdon, a dentist, violated ADA Title III by refusing to treat her—filling her dental cavity—in his office. Dr. Bragdon offered to treat Abbott at a hospital that was a several-hour drive from her home and which would have forced her to incur considerable expense for the procedure.

In affirming the lower court ruling, the First Circuit ruled that the defendant violated Title III by not providing Abbott routine dental care at his office of public accommodation. The court determined that Bragdon's dental office constituted a place of public accommodation under Title III, Abbott had a disability for purposes of the ADA, and treatment of Abbott in Bragdon's office did not pose a direct health or safety threat.

Title III requires accommodations and commercial facilities (for instance, hotels, retail stores, and restaurants) to be physically accessible to persons with disabilities.[19] In addition, it covers transportation provided by public and private entities (for example, employee shuttle bus services operated by private companies or by employers).[20] The provisions require the operators of public accommodations, like employers, to make employment decisions based on facts, not on presumptions about individuals with disabilities.

A qualified employee with mental retardation who lacks accessible public transportation, adequate housing, or appropriate state-provided services will not have the opportunity to take advantage of effective workplace accommodations and achieve employment integration. Professor Mank has called for a "blueprint for

---

[16] In *Cleburne*, the U.S. Supreme Court held that discrimination against persons with disabilities is a form of discrimination protected under the Equal Protection Clause of the Fourteenth Amendment to the U.S. Constitution. 473 U.S. at 450. However, in *Cleburne* the Supreme Court found that "rational basis" analysis (i.e., as opposed to "strict scrutiny" analysis) was appropriate for reviewing cases involving persons with mental retardation and mental illness. *See also Welsh v. City of Tulsa*, 977 F.2d 1415, 1420 (10th Cir. 1992) (finding that for purposes of equal protection analysis, persons with disabilities do not constitute a "suspect class"). *Cf.* William Christian, Normalization as a Goal: The Americans with Disabilities Act and Individuals with Mental Retardation, 73 **Tex. L. Rev.** (1994) (arguing that persons with mental retardation are a "quasi-suspect class").

In recent cases, individual states as defendants in lawsuits involving the rights of persons with developmental disabilities and other impairments have claimed the ADA is not within the scope of legislation protected under the Equal Protection Clause. These states claim, therefore, that they are entitled to legal immunity under the Eleventh Amendment to the Constitution from suits brought against them under the ADA. In *Clark v. State of California*, 123 F.3d 1267 (9th Cir. 1997), the Ninth Circuit rejected this contention, ruling that a class of individuals with developmental disabilities may proceed with their ADA suit because of the articulated goal of the law to prohibit discrimination against the disabled and its language, set forth in 42 U.S.C. § 12202, stating that a state is not immune under the Eleventh Amendment. *See also Coolbaugh v. State of Louisiana,* 136 F.3d 430 (5th Cir. 1998) (same).

[17] *Id.* at 236 (*citing* U.S. Senate Committee on Labor and Human Resources Aug. 30, 1989 Hearings, Sen. Rep. No. 101–116).

[18] 118 S. Ct. 554 (1997). *See* **supra Ch. II § 2.6** (discussing implications of the case in the employment context).

[19] 28 C.F.R. § 36 (1991).

[20] *See* **infra Appendix A** (setting forth ADA Title II).

the future" to coordinate policy, legal, educational, and funding initiatives *and* incentives to support employment integration for the emerging workforce of persons with mental retardation.[21]

Mank argues that systems change toward integrated employment "requires an affirmation of community and a rejection of segregation as the predominant approach" in society.[22] A blueprint for change thus requires examination of national, state, and local policies and related funding in the areas of health insurance, welfare benefits, education and training reform, and legal dispute resolution reform.

ADA Title III's definition of a public accommodation is not limited to issues involving physical accessibility to structures. In a 1997 case, *Lewis v. Aetna Life Insurance Co.*,[23] a federal district court found that a long-term disability plan that entitled employees with physical disabilities to receive benefits for a longer period of time than employees with mental disabilities violated ADA Title III.

In concluding that ADA Title III protections covered the employer's insurance policies, the court commented:

> Both a decision to deny coverage on the basis of mental disability and to provide inferior coverage for mental disabilities target the mentally disabled for inferior treatment. In both cases, an insurer has subjected the mentally disabled individual to treatment inferior to that accorded to others solely on the basis of that individual's disability.[24]

ADA Title III implementation is an important area worthy of empirical and economic study.[25] The ARC, through a grant received from the U.S. Department of Justice, has developed educational materials to further the understanding by ADA stakeholders—businesses, insurance companies, and persons with mental retardation—of the social and economic issues surrounding accessibility to public accommodations faced by persons with mental retardation.[26]

Likewise, a recent study by the U.S. General Accounting Office finds that the implementation of ADA Title III access provisions has increased revenues in the hotel and hospitality industry by 12 percent.[27] Tony Cohelo, chairman of the President's Committee on Employment of People with Disabilities, notes that the millions of Americans with disabilities currently control twice as much income as the teen market, representing a largely untapped consumer market. Chapter XIV discussed how this vast consumer market may be courted by companies, entrepreneurs, inventors, and others whose services and products are made accessible and usable by people with different disabilities.[28]

16.4 Health Care, Health Insurance Reform, and the ADA

Study of the emerging labor force of persons with mental retardation will aid in long-term ADA implementation, as well as in interpretation of policy initiatives in related areas of health care and health insurance reform.[29] Persons with disabilities account for the majority of medical expenditures in the United States.[30]

Researchers find that persons with disabilities spend more than four times as much on health care services as do persons without disabili-

---

21 Mank, Systems Change Strategies for Integrated Employment: A Blueprint for the Future, *in* **Integrated Employment**, **supra Ch. 1 § 1.1**, at 107.

22 *Id.*

23 982 F. Supp. 1158 (E.D. Va. 1997).

24 *Id.* (court also finding that plaintiff, as a "qualified individual with a disability," was entitled to sue under ADA Title I to redress the effects of related employment discrimination).

25 *See* Ellen D. Cook, et al., Tax Incentives for Complying with Title III of the Americans with Disabilities Act, **Taxes,** at 63 (Feb. 1994) (discussing relation of ADA to tax code).

26 *See* The ARC, **Access ADA: Free Assistance to Help Your Business Comply with Title III of the Americans with Disabilities Act** (1992) (*cited in* Herr, **supra Ch. XVI § 16.2,** at 237).

27 *See* Tony Cohelo, Companies Discovering Lucrative New Market, 20 **Newsletter of the Great Lakes Disability & Business Technical Center** 1 (1997) (discussing GAO study).

28 *See* **supra Ch. XIV § 14.5** (for instance, discussing study of patents for assistive technology devices since ADA implementation).

29 Johnson, *in* **Annals, supra Ch. II § 2.4,** at 160–62 (arguing that ADA must be evaluated in context of other social welfare programs, for instance, with regard to economic incentives to work or return to work).

30 Wendy Max, Dorothy P. Rice, & Laura Trupin, Medical Expenditures for People with Disabilities, 12 **Disability Stat. Ab.** (Mar. 1996).

ties.[31] The delivery of health care services in the United States exceeds 10 percent of our gross national product.[32] People with mental retardation and developmental disabilities account for a substantial portion of all Medicaid spending.[33]

ADA Title V[34] allows insurance companies to administer medical tests[35] that are consistent with state law practice and based on sound actuarial data.[36] Although the results of medical tests conducted as part of a postoffer examination may not be used to withdraw an offer of employment to a qualified applicant, third-party insurers or employers self-funding their insurance plans may classify employees with regard to health insurance coverage on the basis of their medical histories.[37]

Chapter XV described that limitations on health insurance coverage or exclusions of hidden disabilities, such as genetic or psychological conditions, are permitted under the ADA as long as they are not a pretext for disability-based discrimination.[38]

Lack of access to adequate health care and insurance remains a significant problem for persons with disabilities, especially for those qualified individuals who seek or attempt to retain integrated employment.[39] McNeil's analysis of Census Bureau information shows that 80 percent of people with no disability ages 22 to 64 were covered by a private health insurance plan. In contrast, only 44 percent of people with severe disabilities in the same age category had private insurance coverage, while another 40 percent of this group had coverage through governmental programs.[40]

The American public may be ready to address the difficult choices in the area of health insurance reform. A 1997 Harris poll found that 82 percent of those surveyed believed that the federal government should provide health insurance coverage to children who are currently uninsured.[41] In addition, two

---

[31] *Id.*

[32] For a review, *see* Jack Stark & Earl Faulkner, Quality of Life Across the Life Span, in **Quality of Life, supra Ch. VII § 7.2,** at 27 (1996).

[33] *See* Theodore A. Kastner, Kevin K. Walsh, & Teri Criscione, Overview and Implications of Medicaid Managed Care for People with Developmental Disabilities, 35 **Mental Retardation** 257–69 (1997) (discussing of spending on Medicaid services for people with mental retardation); Theodore A. Kastner, Kevin K. Walsh, & Teri Criscione, Technical Elements, Demonstration Projects, and Fiscal Models in Medicaid Managed Care for People with Developmental Disabilities, 35 **Mental Retardation** 270–85 (1997) (discussing trends in spending and utilization of services for people with mental retardation). *See also* David Braddock & Richard Hemp, Medicaid Spending Reductions and Developmental Disabilities, 7 **J. Disability Pol'y Stud.** 1–32 (1996) (concluding that Congressional proposals to reduce Medicaid spending would place program enrollment restrictions on thousands of affected individuals with developmental disabilities).

[34] 42 U.S.C. § 12201.

[35] *See id.* § 12201(c)(1); EEOC Compliance Manual (CCH) ¶ 6903 (Oct. 10, 1995) (defining medical examination as "a procedure or test that seeks information about an individual's physical or mental impairments or health").

[36] 29 C.F.R. § 1630.16(f) (1997).

[37] Although the ADA's legislative history generally addresses health insurance issues, it does not address the extent to which Title I may affect employees' life and disability insurance coverage. *See* **S. Rep. No.** 101–116, at 29 (1989); Marvin R. Natowicz, et al., Genetic Discrimination and the Law, 50 **Am. J. Hum. Genetics** 465, 471 (1992) (discussing effect of new technologies on insurance coverage); *see also* Health Insurance Portability and Accountability Act of 1996, **Pub. L.** 104–191 (1996) (including provisions prohibiting denial of insurance coverage based on mental or physical disability); Can Benefits for Mental Illness Be Limited to Two Years Under the ADA?, **Law. Wkly. USA,** at 512 (June 3, 1996) (discussing EEOC position on mental illness benefits as extending beyond health insurance plan to disability plan).

[38] *See* 42 U.S.C. § 12112(a). A self-funded employer may offer a health insurance policy to employees. An employer may offer a policy that does not cover experimental treatment for Huntington's disease, but may not withdraw dependent coverage for an employee whose child develops cystic fibrosis or bipolar mental illness solely on the basis of that disability. In cases where companies self-fund, in effect acting as an insurer, attitudinal biases and economic considerations provide incentives to use genetic or psychological testing to avoid future insurance costs and compensation claims. *Cf. Parker v. Metropolitan Life Ins. Co.*, 121 F.3d 1006 (6th Cir. 1997) (holding ADA does not prohibit disparate coverage in disability plan for physical and mental conditions).

[39] Mitchell P. LaPlante, Dorothy P. Rice, & Juliana K. Cyril, Health Insurance Coverage of People with Disabilities in the U.S., 7 **Disability Stat. Ab.** (Sept. 1994).

[40] McNeil, **supra Ch. I § 1.2,** at 6.

[41] **Harris Poll,** No. 29 (June 23, 1997).

thirds of those surveyed favored raising taxes to spend on expanded health care coverage for children.

With a similar goal in mind, the Health Insurance Reform Act of 1996 was written to ensure access to portable health insurance for employees with chronic illness or disabilities who lose or change their jobs.[42] Under the law, group health plan premium charges may not be based on disability status or the severity of an individual's illness.[43]

The Mental Health Parity Act of 1996 also may enhance employment integration for qualified persons with mental retardation by prohibiting discrimination in the area of health insurance on the basis of physical and mental disability.[44] Yet the Act applies only to group health plans and not to employer self-funded initiatives, and it does not require employers to provide health insurance coverage.[45] Some courts have rejected the view that ADA Title I requires parity among physical and mental health benefits provided by employers.[46] The economic impact of the health insurance reform and Title I on reducing employment discrimination facing qualified persons with covered disabilities is a promising area for study.

Increasing public pressure is being brought to bear for the provision of quality health care services. With the advent of managed care health services and an aging labor force, other areas related to access, equity, and quality in health insurance and care will emerge.[47]

Professor Theodore Kastner and his colleagues have argued that elements of managed health care services are particularly important to enhance health outcomes for people with mental retardation and developmental disabilities.[48] Managed care systems emphasize the "management of costs by controlling access through primary care provider[s]," often referred to as gatekeepers.[49] Fees for services per patient are preset or "capitated."

Kastner suggests five system components of privatized managed care services that have important implications for people with mental retardation and other developmental disabilities:[50]

1. "disability specific interventions"—certain disease categories, such as mental retardation, may be subject to reduced utilizations, due to a lower prevalence in the general population, therefore, the availability of services used more frequently by people with mental retardation is crucial;
2. "care coordination"—providing linkages across various service providers (e.g., employing the use of independent case managers or care coordinators) has been shown to be important for successful care for people with developmental disabilities;
3. "quality of care"—outcome measures of the quality of care of health services for persons with developmental disabilities are needed, and quality assurance programs must be available to managed care services;
4. "individual and family supports"—should be included in managed care service packages as essential components of health care suports for persons with mental retardation and developmental disabilities; and
5. "interdisciplinary assessment and long-term tracking"— are cornerstones of service planning and delivery for persons with developmental disabilities, as reflected by the use of Individual Habilitation Plans (IHPs), Individual Education Plans (IEPs), and other coordinated measures.

Kastner's five areas of inquiry are related to many of the issues examined in the present research model—including health status, family and governmental supports, and adaptive skill

---

[42] *See* Health Insurance Protability and Accountability Act of 1996, **Pub. L.** 104–191 (1996) (this antidiscrimination provision does not apply to individual insurance plans).

[43] *See* John V. Jacobi, The Ends of Health Insurance, 30 **U.C. Davis Law Rev.** 311, 366 (1997).

[44] Title VII of **Pub. L.** 104–204 (1996).

[45] For a review of the act, *see* Tucker, **supra Ch. I § 1.4,** at 927–28.

[46] *See EEOC v. CNA Insurance Co.*, 96 F.3d 1039 (7th Cir. 1996).

[47] *See* John V. Jacobi, Patients at a Loss: Protecting Health Care Consumers Through Data Driven Quality Assurance, 45 **Kan. L. Rev.** 705, 722 (1997).

[48] Kastner, et al., **supra Ch. XVI § 16.4,** at 258–66; David Braddock, Medicaid and Persons with Developmental Disabilities, 34 **Mental Retardation** 331 (1996).

[49] Kastner, et al., **supra Ch. XVI § 16.4,** at 258–66.

[50] *Id.*

levels. Other issues addressed in prior chapters related to managed care services for persons with mental retardation include protection of individual privacy rights, informed consent, and the prevention of discrimination on the basis of medical tests.[51] Increased attention must be given to preventing and resolving disputes involving managed care plans and their enrollees with disabilities in the areas of health care treatment and reimbursement for services.[52]

The immediate challenge is how best to serve the health care needs of individuals with mental retardation in ways that support their equal employment opportunity as well as other areas of their lives. A 1997 Harris poll found that physicians practicing in states with participation in managed care services reported more serious problems in caring for their patients.[53] In states with high HMO enrollments, physicians reported more limitations on the referral of patients to specialists and on ordering diagnostic tests.

Meaningful involvement by persons with mental retardation, their families, and advocates in the design of managed care systems is an important goal. In the present research model, examination of self-advocacy activities in the area of the provision of health care services is a topic worthy of future study. Examination of these issues may further the quality and affordability of health care for qualified workers with mental retardation in full-time and part-time employment.[54]

16.5 Part- and Full-Time Employment, Health Benefits, and ADA Implementation

Issues involving the relation of ADA implementation to the provision of health, disability, and life insurance benefits for workers with mental retardation require attention. As mentioned earlier in this chapter and as reflected in the present findings, increasingly workers with disabilities are choosing to work part time.

The Manpower case study described in Chapter XIV and other studies suggest that, over the past 25 years, while there has been limited net change in the labor force participation rate among persons with disabilities, there has been a disproportionate increase in the number of persons with disabilities working part time.[55]

As discussed in prior sections of this chapter, ADA Title IV does not require employers to alter their insurance benefit plans for employees with disabilities in relation to employees without disabilities. Some courts have concluded that under ADA Title I, an employer is not in violation of the law when providing health benefits only to full-time workers, even if this requirement results in a reduction in benefits for workers with disabilities who are accommodated with part-time schedules.[56]

The EEOC has taken a similar position, concluding that employers may require their employees (regardless of having a disability or not) to work a certain number of hours to receive health insurance benefits.[57] But Professor Bonnie Tucker has commented "employees

---

[51] *See* Jacobi, **supra Ch. XVI § 16.4,** at 345 (discussing ADA and risk selection in employment-based insurance).

[52] *See* American Bar Association, **Resolution of Consumer Disputes in Managed Care: Insights from an Interdisciplinary Roundtable** (1997) (discussing methods of addressing disagreements between enrollees and private health plans, Medicaid, and Medicare programs, and noting that the Balanced Budget Amendment of 1997 sets out regulations for appeals procedures for Medicare beneficiaries).

[53] **U.S. Physicians Report More Serious Problems Caring for Patients in States with High HMO Enrollment,** Harris Poll No. 58 (Nov. 24, 1997).

[54] The debate on physician-assisted suicide has implications for the provision of health care services for persons with disabilities, *see* Peter David Blanck, Kristi Kirschner, & Leigh Bienen, The Right to Die and Persons with Disabilities, 21 **Mental & Physical Disability L. Rep.** 538–43 (1997); Paul Steven Miller, The Impact of Assisted Suicide on Persons with Disabilities—Is It a Right Without Freedom, 9 **Issues Law & Med.** 47 (1993).

[55] *See* Yelin, *in* **Annals, supra Ch. IV § 4.4,** at 117, 124–25; *see also* **supra Ch. XIV § 14.7** (discussing Manpower study findings).

[56] *See Tenbrink v. Federal Home Loan Bank*, 920 F. Supp. 1156, 1162 (D. Kan. 1996).

[57] *See Letter Re: Health Insurance*, 8 NDLR § 181 (EEOC June 6, 1995) (*cited in* Tucker, **supra Ch. I § 1.4,** at 916.

with disabilities may not be able to avail themselves of a requisite reasonable accommodation of part-time hours since to do so may mean they have to forfeit necessary insurance coverage."[58] Proposed legislation, such as the Medicaid Community Attendant Services Act of 1997 (MiCASA) discussed in Chapter IV, may enhance employment opportunities for workers with severe disabilities by enabling them the option of spending longer hours at the worksite.[59]

16.6 Welfare Reform and the ADA

According to the most recent U.S. Census Bureau data, roughly half (51 percent) of the 13 million Americans ages 22 to 64 who participate in means-tested assistance programs for cash, food, or rent coverage have either a severe or nonsevere disability.[60] McNeil finds that the disability rates among the 133 million Americans in the 22 to 64 age category who did not participate in a government sponsored assistance program were 17 percent. Thus, a high percentage of working age Americans with disabilities participate in government assistance programs.[61]

According to studies by Professor David Braddock and his associates, total public spending for mental retardation/developmental disability services in the U.S. has grown from $3.457 billion in 1977 to $22.862 billion in 1996.[62] Braddock attributes the increase in public spending to the growth in integrated community services, deinstitutionalization efforts, and the growth of self-advocacy activities during the time period.[63]

Monitoring is needed of public funding trends, ADA implementation, trends in employment integration, and resultant reforms in welfare law and policy.[64] Critics of recent changes in welfare programs argue that the changes make it more difficult for families, particularly those with members with disabilities, to escape poverty and be self-sufficient. The Personal Responsibility and Work Opportunity Reconciliation Act of 1996 (PRWOR welfare reform law) ends the Aid to Families with Dependent Children (AFDC) program and replaces it with welfare block grant funding administered by the states.[65]

PRWOR modifies the standards for children to qualify for the Supplemental Security Income (SSI) program, which provides monetary funds to families with children with disabilities. Some policy analysts suggest that those children most likely to lose benefits are those with multiple disabilities (for instance, with mental retardation and a physical disability), but with no single impairment that meets the law's severity threshold.[66]

In addition, the law modifies access to job training programs that are important to attaining and retaining employment for many persons with mental retardation. It ends the Job Opportunities and Basic Skills Training (JOBS) program, which was aimed at preventing discrimination against participants on the basis of

---

[58] Tucker, **supra Ch. I § 1.4,** at 917.

[59] In addition, Sen. Feingold has sponsored the Long-Term Care Reform and Deficit Reduction Act of 1997 (S. 879, June 11, 1997) to support home and community-based services for persons with disabilities including certain Medicaid services under Title XIX of the Social Security Act.

[60] McNeil, **supra Ch. I § 1.2,** at 6 (finding 40 percent of means-tested assistance program participants had a severe disability).

[61] Among people with severe disabilities, only 37 percent of those betwen the ages of 22 and 64 received benefits from a government assistance program. *See* McNeil, **supra Ch. I § 1.2,** at 7.

[62] Braddock, et al., **supra Ch. XVI § 16.1,** at 22, 393–401 (summarizing the Oklahoma State profile for MR/DD services).

[63] *Id.* (other reasons for the growth in community services are related to the growth of deinstitutionalization strategies during the period and the growth of the Home and Community-Based Waiver (HCBS Waiver Program). The HCBS Waiver Program supports services such as case management, supported employment, adaptive equipment, and occupational therapists.

[64] *See* The Personal Responsibility and Work Opportunity Reconciliation Act, **Pub. L.** 104-193 (1996) ("Welfare Reform" Law).

[65] *Id.*

[66] *See* Jocelyn Frye, Joan Entmacjer, & Susan Baruch, Building Bridges—or Barriers? Ending Welfare As We Know It, *in* Corrine M. Yu & William L. Taylor, eds., **The Continuing Struggle: Civil Rights and the Clinton Administration**, Report of the Citizen's Commission on Civil Rights, at 127–37 (1997).

disability.[67] Participating individuals currently are limited by the law to 12 months of vocational education training and to 60 months in their lifetime to funds from state block grant programs.

Despite these changes, PRWOR requires states to have rising work participation rates. To be eligible for program benefits, individuals must participate in specified work activities for a minimum number of hours. Joyce Frye and her colleagues have argued that as a result of the welfare reform law, "individuals who need the most help, including participants with certain learning disabilities, may not be able to participate in a program for its full duration."[68]

Analysis is needed of the relation among welfare reform, Social Security regulations, changes in the labor force participation of persons with mental retardation, ADA implementation, and supported employment and vocational training programs. Longitudinal assessments of employment integration (types of jobs) and economic growth (wage levels) for this emerging workforce are required to assess the long-term impact of welfare reform.

Moreover, federal and state entities implementing welfare reform laws will need to coordinate their efforts with programs that enable qualified workers with disabilities to maintain adequate health insurance coverage and to receive appropriate, individualized, and effective workplace accommodations and job training required by the ADA. Job coaching, vocational training, and workplace accommodations strategies will be required to enable welfare recipients with mental retardation to achieve self-sufficiency and attain and retain competitive employment.

Unfortunately, as the NCD has commented in its 1997 report *National Disability Policy: A Progress Report*, the rhetoric of welfare reform has emphasized that "able-bodied" people on welfare should work, suggesting that disabled recipients of welfare "need not apply."[69] However, given the large number of individual with disabilities receiving welfare benefits, "the success or failure of welfare reform will likely turn on the ability of states to meet the needs of welfare recipients with disabilities."[70]

Study and assessment of the federal and state implementation plans are required, therefore, to facilitate the goals of welfare reform—that is, to increase the rates of integrated employment for qualified persons with mental retardation.[71] Professor Paul Wehman and his colleagues have argued that improved access to competitive employment for persons with mental retardation serves as an important means for reducing SSI expenditures.[72] Future analysis of the research model with the present cohort of persons with mental retardation will be needed to assess changes over time in SSI and SSDI payments to qualified individuals with mental retardation as they transition into supported and competitive employment programs.

16.7 Breaking Down Barriers to Work

Governmental support programs such as Medicaid provide health care coverage to persons with mental retardation and other disabilities who meet certain eligibility criteria. Historically, these programs have tended to support individuals living in large aggregate care settings, as opposed to those in community living programs. At a minimum, these programs require careful evaluation, given the present investigation's findings of the central relation of independence in living to the ability to attain and retain integrated work.[73]

---

[67] 42 U.S.C. § 684 (1988 Family Support Act amendments).

[68] *See* Frye, **supra Ch. XVI § 16.6,** at 27.

[69] *See* **National Disability Policy, supra Ch. VI § 6.8,** at 11.

[70] *Id.* (*citing* a 1997 U.S. Dept. of Health and Human Services report that approximately 50 percent of the Aid to Families with Dependent Children (AFDC) program recipients are individuals with disabilities or parents of disabled children).

[71] Dana S. Gilmore, Robert L. Schalock, William E. Kiernan, & John Butterworth, National Comparisons and Critical Findings in Integrated Employment, *in* **Integrated Employment, supra Ch. I § 1.3,** at 62–63.

[72] Paul Wehman, et al., Improving Access to Competitive Employment for Persons with Disabilities as a Means of Reducing Social Security Expeditures, 12(1) **Focus on Autism and Other Developmental Disabilities** 23–30 (1997) (discussing relation of competitive work to SSI expenditures).

[73] *See* **supra Ch X** (discussing the simple and complex relationships found in the test of the research model).

Chapter IV discussed MiCASA, the bill proposed by House Speaker Gingrich that would allow states to use Medicaid funds to support personal assistant services (PAS) for people with disabilities, as an initiative to facilitate employment for qualified indivduals.[74] In addition to the important role that PAS may play as a workplace accommodation for persons with severe disabilities, MiCASA may help to provide the financial incentives necessary for employers to hire and retain many qualified individuals.[75]

McNeil finds that the proportion of individuals needing personal assistance increases substantially with age.[76] Nine million Americans over 15 years of age received personal assistance in daily life activities during the years 1994 to 1995. Approximately half of these individuals (4.1 million) needing personal assistance were of working age. Professor Margaret Nosek argues that until adequate research is conducted on the use of PAS by people with disabilities, in the work setting and elsewhere, the majority of individuals who may benefit from PAS will continue not to receive these services.[77]

Increased coordination among Medicaid, Medicare, other entitlement programs, PAS, and the incentives to work for persons with disabilities requires attention. In late 1997, the NCD, in its report *Removing Barriers to Work*,[78] focused on the reforms needed to remove barriers preventing SSI recipients and SSDI beneficiaries from becoming self-sufficient through meaningful employment. The NCD writes:

> The proposals reflect the emerging bipartisan emphasis on personal responsibility by removing some of the complex and burdensome federal requirements that prevent many people with disabilities from taking charge of their own lives and becoming employed.

The 1997 NCD report presents its fact-finding and reform proposals as part of the effort to empower qualified individuals with disabilities to achieve equal employment opportunity consistent with the goals of the ADA. The NCD finds that although more than 3.5 million people with disabilities between the ages of 16 and 64 receive SSI benefits, only 2 percent of these individuals are working and earning more than $500 per month.[79] These findings are comparable to the results of the present investigation showing the relatively low proportion of individuals in competitive employment and the large numbers stuck in the "black hole" of segregated work.

In its report, the NCD identifies three major barriers to work and proposals to address each barrier:[80]

> *Barrier 1.* "Many people would be worse off financially if they worked and earned to their potential than if they did not work"
>
> *Proposals to Make Work Pay*:
>
> - provide adequate medical coverage for workers with disabilities;
> - eliminate $500 "income cliff" faced by disability income beneficiaries;
> - ensure that people with, permanent, episodic, or currently asymptomatic disabilities do not lose SSI or DI benefits because they work;[81]
> - establish a tax-credit to reimburse persons with disabilities for disability-related work expenses.
>
> *Barrier 2.* "People with disabilities cannot choose their own vocational rehabilitation program"

---

[74] *See* **supra Ch. IV § 4.8** (discussing MiCASA bill). *See also* Chandra M. Hayslett, Disabled to Push for Personal Attendants, **Com. Appeal,** Sunday Edition, at Metro, B8 (June 15, 1997) (bill sponsored by House Speaker Gingrich).

[75] *See* 20 **Newsletter of the Great Lakes Disability & Business Technical Center** 2 (1997) (noting that in 1997 President Clinton discussed the establishment of a task force at the U.S. Dept. Health and Human Services on funding programs for PAS).

[76] McNeil, **supra Ch. I § 1.2,** at 7.

[77] Margaret A. Nosek, Personal Assistance Services: A Review of the Literature and Analysis of Policy Implications, 2 **J. Disability Pol'y Stud.** 1–17 (1991). *See also* Simi Litvak, Financing Personal Assistance Services 3 **J. Disability Pol'y Stud.** 93–105 (1992) (suggesting financing options for PAS at state and federal levels).

[78] **Removing Barriers to Work, supra Ch. III § 3.1.** *See also* **National Disability Policy, supra Ch. VI § 6.8,** at 8–13 (discussing removing barriers to work and welfare reform).

[79] *Id.* The NCD finds that of the more than 4 million persons receiving SSDI, only 0.3 percent earn more than $500 per month after their 12-month trial work period.

[80] **Removing Barriers to Work, supra Ch. III § 3.1,** at 2–7.

Proposals to Increase Access and Choice:

- create an equitable voucher program that enables SSI and DI recipients to purchase a range of services, such as job coaching and assistive technology;
- retain means for SSI and DI recipients to invest in training, equipment, and assets needed for employment.

Barrier 3. "People with disabilities lack employment opportunities"

Proposals to Increase Employer Incentives:

- reimburse employers for disability-related expenses, such as for braille printers, on-the-job personal assistants, job coaches, and workplace accommodations;
- establish a tax credit for employers to conduct disability and diversity training and education for all employees.

Research strategies are needed to examine these and other barriers and proposals for reform in ways that are consistent with ADA implementation.[82] The present research project begins the broad task of assessing labor force trends associated with workplace support and training strategies.

Outcome measures, other than employment integration and economic opportunity, will be needed to assess whether proposals such as those set forth by the NCD result in effective entitlement reform, strengthen Medicaid and related programs, and enable qualified persons with disabilities to attain and retain competitive employment.

16.8 Reforms in Education, Training, and Job Placement

Work-related education, training, placement, and career development programs are needed for qualified persons with mental retardation with differing degrees of job skills and capabilities.[83] Family and career support programs help prepare this emerging workforce for employment opportunities. The President's Committee on Employment of People with Disabilities has initiated a program called High School/High Tech to promote career development for students with disabilities interested in technology, science, and related areas.

In the area of workplace training, an employer's positive corporate culture and attitudes toward worker education has been shown to generate a productive effect through out the company. Complementary workplace strategies mentioned earlier—flexible scheduling, job sharing, supported employment, telecommuting, and PAS—enhance workplace productivity for employees with and without disabilities.[84] Positive outcomes may reflect attitudes and corporate cultures that encourage and help qualified employees to pursue productive careers.

The proposed reauthorization and amendment of the Rehabilitation Act of 1973, The Employment, Training, and Literacy Enhance-

---

[81] One of the objectives of the SSI program is to provide incentives for those with disabilities who are able and want to work. Plans to Achieve Self-Support (PASS) are intended to expand employment opportunities for recipients of SSI by permitting individuals to work and earn income without losing their SSI benefits. *See* 42 U.S.C. §§ 1382a(b)(4) & (a)(4). Legal challenges to the ways in which states administer PASS under the Medicaid Act to persons with different disabilities have been raised under ADA Title II. *See Vaughn v. Sullivan*, 83 F.3d 907 (7th Cir. 1996) (finding the ADA does not prohibit distinctions in the administration of the PASS to persons who are blind and to sighted persons with physical disabilities).

[82] *See also* Douglas A. Martin, Ronald W. Conley, & John H. Noble, Jr., The ADA and Disability Benefits Policy, 6 **J. Disability Pol'y Stud.** 1–15 (1995) (suggesting that despite passage of the ADA there are major impediments to integrated employment for people with disabilities due to SSI and SSDI regulations); Tony Young, Prepared Statement Before the House Ways and Means Committee, Social Security Subcommittee on Behalf of the Consortium for Citizens with Disabilities Vocational Working Group (July 24, 1997) (arguing that there are five principal barriers to employment for persons with disabilities—loss of health benefits, complexities of work incentives, financial penalties of working, lack of choice in employment services and providers, and inadequate work opportunities). In March of 1998, The Work Incentives Improvement Act of 1998 (S. 1858) was introduced as bipartisan work incentive legislation to help remove barriers to work for persons with disabilities by restructuring existing disability programs.

[83] *See* Wehman, *in* **ADA Mandate, supra Ch. VIII § 8.6,** at 45.

[84] Hall & Hall, **supra Ch. I § 1.4,** at 17; Kristen M. Ludgate, Telecommuting and the Americans with Disabilities Act: Is Working at Home a Reasonable Acommodation?, 81 **Minn. L. Rev.** 1309 (1997) (discussing telecommuting as an effective accommodation).

ment Act of 1997, would consolidate federal job training programs by establishing three block grant programs to the states.[85] The training components would include adult employment training, disadvantaged youth job training, and adult education and literacy training.

As highlighted by the federal district court's decision in the *EEOC v. Hertz* case discussed in Chapter V, examination is needed of an employer's obligation under the ADA to provide workplace accommodations in light of the availability of job training and coaching, placement, and retention services from public and private employment agencies. For qualified workers with mental retardation, frequently employment agencies provide job coaches and other assistance in vocational rehabilitation.[86] At a minimum, the ADA requirement to provide workplace accommodations to qualified workers with disabilities may include a good faith effort on the part of an employer to consider using free assistance from employment provider agencies.[87]

In addition, the Rehabilitation Act of 1973 provides funding for states to provide job assistance to persons with disabilities, which may lessen a potential decision by an employer that providing workplace accommodations imposes an economic "undue hardship." The 1992 amendments to the Rehabilitation Act of 1973 place a burden on state vocational rehabilitation systems to show that a person with a disability is not capable of employment.[88] They also reflect the view that qualified persons with mental retardation and other disabilities are underutilized in the workforce.[89] Stewart Hakola argues that the Congressional findings accompanying the 1992 amendments highlight the untapped economic potential of qualified persons with mental retardation.[90]

A related area requiring study involves educational reform. The Reauthorization of the Individuals with Disabilities Education Act (IDEA 1997), signed June 4, 1997,[91] guarantees a "free and appropriate" education to millions of children with disabilities in the United States. In making integrated education available to children with disabilities, IDEA 1997 is an important tool fostering employment integration of the workforce of the 21st century.

IDEA 1997 includes improvements in educational policy to enable students with disabilities to transition in to higher educational programs and to competitive employment. One central goal of the 1997 amendments to the law was to improve the educational links between special education and the regular curriculum.[92] IDEA 1997 requires that a disabled student's Individual Education Plan (IEP), establishing educational and instructional goals, must more closely follow the regular curriculum of the student's school.

IDEA 1997 mandates the strengthening of parental involvement in the educational process and in the development of appropriate accommodations and technical assistance. The law reflects a significant attempt to improve educational policy through the fostering of individual empowerment and inclusion strategies that lead to increased educational and work-related opportunities for more than 5 million children with disabilities covered by the law.

Transition programs from school to the

---

[85] H.R. 1385, passed on May 19, 1997 (referred to the Senate Committee on Labor and Human Resources).

[86] *See* **infra Appendix D** (amicus Brief in *EEOC v. Hertz*, prepared by Stewart Hakola, for Michigan Protection & Advocacy Service discussing these issues). *Cf.* **Appendix E** (decision in *EEOC v. Hertz*).

[87] *Id.* at 7–9. *See also* **supra Ch. IV § 4.5** (discussing "interactive process" and workplace accommodations under the ADA).

[88] *See* 29 U.S.C. 722(a)(4)(A). *See also* **infra Appendix E** (concluding that the 1992 amendments of the Rehabilitation Act were designed to strengthen the relation between the Rehabilitation Act and the ADA).

[89] Congress has found that persons with mental retardation are capable of competitive employment and are entitled to employment rehabilitation services and workplace accommodations. 29 U.S.C. 720(a)(3)(A) and (B).

[90] *See* **infra Appendix D,** at 8 (noting the findings that: "Individuals with disabilities, including individuals with the most severe disabilities, have demonstrated their ability to achieve gainful employment in integrated settings if appropriate services and supports are provided... [T]he reasons for the significant number of individuals with disabilities not working... include... discrimination... [and] lack of education, training, and supports to meet job qualification standards." 29 U.S.C. 720(a)(1)(C) and (D)).

[91] **Pub. L.** 102-569.

[92] *See* **National Disability Policy, supra Ch. VI § 6.8,** at 21–24.

workplace also are needed to foster integrated employment opportunity. As Professor Pamela Luft and her colleagues have written: "School departure and work-force entry are the transitions of most consequence in shaping work careers today."[93] Examination of national efforts embodied in *America 2000* and *Goals 2000* are needed to reach millions of children with disabilities and to prepare them for integrated and meaningful work oppotunities.[94]

Other national laws, such as the School-to-Work Opportunities Act of 1994,[95] reflect efforts to foster opportunities for integrated employment for persons with disabilities. The 1994 Act stresses the important relation of education, career counseling, work-based training, and work. The Carl D. Perkins Vocational and Technology Act of 1990 provides funding for vocational training for students with and without disabilities.[96]

The Technology-Related Assistance Act of 1988, as reformed in 1994, fosters opportunities for using new technologies in support of educational and workplace design for persons with disabilities. Developing concepts of "universal design" in the workplace emphasize that accessibility must be built into computer programs, the national information infrastructure (e.g., the Internet), and telecommuting work relationships. The success of such initiatives is critical to the employment integration for the more than 300,000 high school graduates with disabilities who enter the workforce each year.

Still other national and state efforts are designed to further the universal design of technology so that employers may have access to the emerging workforce of qualified persons with disabilities. The Telecommunications Act of 1996 requires telecommunications equipment to be accessible to individuals with disabilities.[97] Under the law, the Federal Communications Commission is to issue proposed regulations on the accessibility of telecommunications services. In 1997 the Web Accessibility Initiative (WAI) was organized to promote Internet access for millions of people with disabilities.[98] WAI is a partnering effort among the World Wide Web Consortium, U.S. governmental agencies, and others.

As technology becomes more important, concepts such as accessibility and universal design become more important. Technology has the potential to make education and job training vastly more inclusive for people with mental retardation through individualized curricula and supported communications with classmates and coworkers. Accessible technology has implications also for health care reform (telemedicine will bring doctors to geographically isolated people) and for welfare reform (telecommuting will reduce chronic unemployment and underemployment among people with disabilities).

Additional dialogue and research are needed on emerging technological accessibility issues, not only for people with disabilities, but for all underrepresented individuals in society—the poor, the isolated, and the vulnerable. A profound question lies ahead: Will the developing national information infrastructure help people with disabilities and others move closer to full participation in society? Or will it further isolate them from the mainstream?

16.9 Summary

Areas of policy reform relevant to the emerging workforce of persons with mental retardation have been discussed in the areas of health care and health insurance reform, welfare reform, and related education and vocational training. Integration of these and emerging policy initiatives will be required to empower all qualified individuals and their families to

---

93 Pamela Luft, Frank R. Rusch, Teresa Dais, & Nancy Meier-Kronick, Schools and Employment: Forging New Links, in **Integrated Employment, supra Ch. I § 1.13,** at 86.

94 *Id.* at 87–88; U.S. Dept. Education, **America 2000: An Educational Strategy** (1991); U.S. Dept. Education, **Goals 2000: Educate America: Building Bridges from School to Work** (1993).

95 **Pub. L.** 103-239.

96 **Pub. L.** 101-392.

97 *See* **National Disability Policy, supra Ch. VI § 6.8,** at 26–27 (discussing the importance of the Telecommunications Act of 1996 to people with disabilities); Peter David Blanck, Celebrating Communications Technology for Everyone, 47 **Fed. Comm. L. J.** 185–91 (1994) (arguing the importance of accessible communications technology to the emerging workforce of persons with disabilities).

98 *See* **National Disability Policy, supra Ch. VI § 6.8,** at 27 (discussing this initiative and related efforts in making technology accessible).

achieve equal employment opportunity. Loss of adequate health insurance is a primary concern for qualified people with disabilities who want to work.[99]

A reexamination of policy, educational, legal, and other reforms are needed from the perspective of those impacted by these initiatives. Input in policy formation is required from consumers with disabilities and their families, from employers, educators, and others committed to employment integration as a right of all qualified persons with less and more severe disabilities.[100]

This dialogue is needed to tailor services and programs to the needs of consumers, rather than the converse; to empower consumers and enhance their options in employment in their local communities; and to prevent a backlash against the evolving disability policy and law that may be driven by misinformation, misconceptions, and paternalistic sentiments.

---

[99] **Removing Barriers to Work, supra Ch. III § 3.1,** at 17.

[100] Mank, *in* **Integrated Employment, supra Ch. I § 1.3,** at 107 (discussing "blue print" for the future).

CHAPTER XVII

Conclusion

Faced with a lack of education, residential, and economic opportunities; a service system that frequently fails to meet actual needs, and exclusion from mainstream society, individuals with developmental disabilities are often left powerless.

Alison Miller and Christopher Keys[1]

Until both the disability community and public policymakers take the risk of shifting from a disability policy primarily based on transfers to one based on the proposition that people with disabilities can and should be expected to work, young people with disabilities can look forward to a life of dependency.

Richard Burkhauser[2]

17.1 Introduction

This book has examined issues of employment integration and economic growth for the emerging workforce of persons with mental retardation. Historically, persons with mental retardation have been excluded from employment and society.[3] Persons with mental retardation continue to face prejudice, myths, and stereotypes about their needs and abilities.

In the past two decades, however, there has been a shift in public attitudes toward persons with mental retardation.[4] Changing attitudes in turn affect society's behavior toward persons with mental retardation and persons with disabilities generally. It is crucial to investigate how society's views of persons with disabilities and of itself change over time so that the vision of the ADA may develop into reality for all citizens. This book has ventured to explore the

[1] Alison B. Miller & Christopher B. Keys, Awareness, Action, and Collaboration: How the Self-Advocacy Movement Is Empowering for Persons with Developmental Disabilities, 34 **Mental Retardation** 312–19 (1996).

[2] Burkhauser, *in* **Annals, supra Ch. X § 10.1,** at 71.

[3] *See* Robert E. Rains, A Pre-History of the Americans with Disabilities Act and Some Initial Thoughts as to Its Constitutional Implications, 11 **St. Louis U. Pub. L. Rev.** 185, 202 (1992) ("Whether or not the Supreme Court ultimately decides that Congress [through the ADA] has now mandated heightened judicial scrutiny in cases of discrimination on the basis of disability brought under the fourteenth amendment, there can be no question that the A.D.A. will provide, when fully effective, powerful avenues of redress for Americans with disabilities who are subjected to discrimination."); Michael A. Rebell, Structural Discrimination and the Rights of the Disabled, 74 **Geo. L. J.** 1435, 1436–37 (1986) (discussing the history of invidious discrimination against the handicapped).

[4] *See* L.M. Rees, O. Spreen, & M. Harnadek, Do Attitudes Towards Persons with Handicaps Really Shift Over Time?—Comparison Between 1975 and 1988, 29 **Mental Retardation** 81 (1991) (results show a positive shift over time in public attitudes toward persons with mental retardation).

law in action; that is, to explore the legal and social interpretation of the reform legislation embodied in the ADA during the initial period of implementation.

In 1986 the report *Toward Independence* was hailed by many as a revolutionary effort to develop a national policy toward persons with disabilities. Twelve years later, with ADA implementation underway, the report's major recommendation remains unfulfilled: Disability policy continues to reflect "an over-emphasis on income support and an under-emphasis on initiatives for equal opportunity" and independence.[5]

Professors Pat Rogan and Stephen Murphy have argued that integration goes beyond mere physical or economic accommodation of persons with disabilities.[6] True integration involves attitudinal change as well.

Justin Dart, a long-time advocate and former chair of the NCD, has written:

> Our society still is infected by an insidious, now almost subconscious, assumption that people with disabilities are less than fully human and therefore are not entitled to the respect, the opportunities, and the services and support systems that are available to other people as a matter of right.[7]

The present investigation highlights that the passage of the ADA alone cannot change attitudes about employment integration and empowerment for people with disabilities.[8] In a study conducted by Professor Pauline Graham and her colleagues, attitudes about employment integration were assessed by examining almost 200 employers' responses to two fictitious applicants with identical job qualifications, capabilities, background characteristics, and education, with the only difference being that one was disabled and one not.[9] These researchers found that the applicants without disabilities were one and one half times more successful in receiving a positive response from an employer, as compared to applicants with disabilities.

In addition to overcoming attitudinal bias, two other factors stand out as necessary for qualified adults with mental retardation to obtain and retain equal employment: access to adequate health insurance and medical treatment, and access to education or job-skill support and vocational training.

As a result, eight years after the enactment of the ADA—the "emancipation proclamation" for people with disabilities—at least two thirds of working-age Americans with disabilities remain unemployed. In spite of encouraging advances in education and training, and the employment trends reported in this investigation, the unemployment problem facing Americans with disabilities remains unresolved, the "black hole" of the segregated worksite is still a reality.

17.2 Future of the "Right to Work"

This book has emphasized that study is needed to address the economic, cultural, attitudinal, and symbolic aspects of inclusion and empowerment for citizens with mental retardation in all aspects of society. Understanding of the interaction among disability law and policy and developing social, economic, and cultural norms is needed to foster employment integration for the emerging workforce. Professor Richard Burkhauser has said that unless these issues are addressed, the emerging generation of persons with disabilities will look toward a life of dependency and not employment integration well into the next millennium.[10]

The economic cost-benefit approach to the fashioning of social policy has yet to demonstrate empirically the hypothesized labor market inefficiencies associated with emerging disability policy and law. And yet, as this book has

---

[5] **Toward Independence, supra Ch. VI § 6.2,** at vi.

[6] Rogan & Murphy, **supra Ch. X § 10.4,** at 41; *Trautz v. Weisman*, 819 F. Supp. 282, 294 (S.D.N.Y. 1993) (stating in dicta that the ADA has identified people with disabilities as "a discrete and insular minority" now able to bring a claim under 42 U.S.C. § 1985(3)).

[7] Dart, *in* **Rights and Responsibilities, supra Ch. I § 1.1,** at xxi (disability rights must be guaranteed as a matter of law).

[8] Professor LaPlante estimates that approximately 38 million Americans with disabilities report a total of 61 million disabling conditions. Mitchell LaPlante, Health Conditions and Impairments Causing Disability, 16 **Disability Stat. Ab.** 1 (Sept. 1996).

[9] Pauline Graham, Antoinette Jordan, & Brian Lamb, An Equal Chance? Or No Chance?, **Spastics Soc'y** (Nov. 1997) (discussing findings from study of employers in the United Kingdom).

[10] Burkhauser, *in* **Annals, supra Ch. X § 10.1,** at 71.

emphasized throughout, independent of economic analysis, the legal, social, and moral policies underlying the equal employment of qualified persons with disabilities must be defined for effective implementation of the law to continue.[11]

The late Professor Gregory Kavka has written about the foundations for a legal "right to work," defined as a moral and economic right of persons with disabilities.[12] Kavka writes: "The 'right to work' [for persons who want to work]...is the right to participate as an active member in the productive processes of one's society, insofar as such participation is reasonably feasible."[13]

The right to work is a right to earn income at or above minimum levels of basic human maintenance. It is not an entitlement to receive state funded supports. The position taken in the Rehabilitation Act Amendments of 1992, like Kavka's, is that all persons with disabilities are capable of meaningful employment.[14]

Despite claims to the contrary,[15] small gains in economic efficiency should not be strong enough to override an individual's basic right to meaningful work. The ADA sends this message, that society has accepted its obligation to empower qualified individuals with disabilities by supporting equal employment opportunity. The law requires no more, but certainly no less.

As illustrated by the findings of the present investigation, support for the right to meaningful work may take several forms. First, societal assistance may involve a right of nondiscrimination in employment, consistent with the principles of the ADA.[16] A 1997 *Harvard Law Review* article argues that social assistance in the form of a broad right of nondiscrimination—with a focus on disability, race, gender, and other protected categories—should apply to the large class of individuals in our society without jobs.[17]

In many instances, economic and social discrimination against people is a result of their membership in a "jobless class."[18] This aspect of discrimination is particularly true for persons with disabilities, given the unconscionably high numbers of those individuals who are unemployed and living in poverty.

Professor Peter Blau, the distinguished sociologist, commented more than 30 years ago that social status and position are determined most directly by the employment an individual holds.[19] Professor Michael Oliver has described the deep moral stigma attached to those who are receiving public support and are not working.[20] Kavka's notion of assistance includes a right to training and fair compensation for one's work. This right requires accessibility to education, public services, and to equal employment.

Kavka would extend the right to work further than the boundaries of the ADA. Social assistance, he argues, should involve a right of preferential treatment for qualified individuals with disabilities who are in competition for jobs with equally qualified persons without disabilities.[21] He argues that a "weak form" of affirmative action is justified—perhaps as a tie breaker—for equally qualified individuals with disabilities over those without disabilities.[22] It is through this process, Kavka argues, that persons

---

[11] *See* Karlan & Rutherglen, **supra Ch. II § 2.2,** at 25 (concluding that "[t]he prohibitions against discrimination and the requirements of accommodation... require more than efficiency and less than charity."); Richard K. Scotch & Kay Schriner, Disability as Human Variation: Implications for Policy, *in* **Annals, supra Ch. IV § 4.4,** at 148, 157 (arguing that disability implicates social issues beyond those associated with discrimination and stigma).

[12] Gregory S. Kavka, Disability and the Right to Work, 9(1) **Soc. Phil. & Pol.** 262, 288 (1992) (concluding that economic analysis should not be sole criterion for defining social policy toward employment for qualified persons with disabilities).

[13] *Id.* at 264. *See also* Weihe Huang & Sanford E. Rubin, Equal Access to Employment for People with Mental Retardation: An Obligation of Society, 63 **J. Rehab.** 27 (1997) (discussing "right" to employment and obligation of society to persons with mental retardation).

[14] *See* Kiernan & Schalock, *in* **Integrated Employment, supra Ch. I § 1.3,** at vii.

[15] *Cf.* Judge Posner's opinion in *Vande Zande,* **supra Ch. IV § 4.3.**

[16] Kavka, **supra Ch. XVII § 17.2,** at 264.

[17] Note, Finding a Place For the Jobless in Discrimination Theory, 110 **Har. L. Rev.** 1609 (1997).

[18] *Id.*

[19] Peter M. Blau & Otis Dudley Duncan, **The American Occupational Structure** (1967).

[20] Michael Oliver, **The Politics of Disablement: A Sociological Approach** (1990).

[21] Kavka, **supra Ch. XVII § 17.2,** at 265.

[22] *Id.* at 289. *Cf. Terrell v. USAIR,* 132 F.3d 621 (11th Cir. 1998) (concluding that the ADA does not grant preferential treatment to disabled workers).

with disabilities will move toward employment integration and advancement within employment without hitting a "glass ceiling."

Kavka believes that as long as there is prejudice facing qualified workers with disabilities, the free market alone cannot provide for equal employment opportunity. Chapter III discussed that the ADA does not require an employer to give preference to individuals with disabilities who are less qualified than individuals without disabilities. So, too, employers are not discouraged from searching for the most qualified individuals with or without disabilities.[23] Workers with disabilities are not deemed "equal" to others without disabilities solely by their disability status. Views about whether the ADA is an expression of the failed affirmative action policies of the past misdirect the true purposes of the law.[24]

17.3 Future Policy and Legal Questions About the Emerging Workforce

Many creative and equitable employment strategies have yet to emerge in support of the goals of the ADA. Tax benefits for employers hiring, retaining, and accommodating qualified workers with disabilities support the goals of ADA implementation.[25] Innovations in new products that generate expanded consumer markets may be the norm of the next century. Tax credits to disabled workers in low income families may enable millions to break the barrier to work, escape the black hole of continued segregation, and become viable consumers in the marketplace.

Analysis of proposals to provide disabled workers a tax credit to low income families—with payments based on work productivity and not as an entitlement—have been estimated to cost $3 billion per year. Cost reductions resulting from these proposals are estimated to be in the range of $51 billion SSDI payments or $21 billion in SSI paid in 1994 to disabled workers and their families.[26]

Professor Frank Bowe, a leading researcher in the area, has expressed the magnitude of the complex policy challenges facing America in the area of disability policy and law. Bowe writes:

> What combination of education, training, civil rights, and SSI work incentives will appeal enough to SSI recipients that they will make genuine good-faith efforts to become and remain employed? That way, those whose disabilities really do not prevent employment would identify themselves by entering the labor force....Such a strategy encourages those who can work to leave SSI roles voluntarily. As they do, they'll benefit from the nondiscrimination provisions of the ADA's Title I.[27]

Like Kavka's views discussed above, Bowe recognizes that the success of this strategy depends on macroeconomic factors, such as a growing labor market and companies' needs for qualified workers. The findings from the present investigation illustrate both encouraging labor force growth and stagnation in the "black hole" of segregated and governmental subsidized work.

Other policy questions persist, prominent among them: "How many adults who say their 'disabilities' prevent them from working, cannot work?"[28] Answers to such questions were examined in Chapter II of this book in relation to analysis of "qualified" persons with "disabilities" covered by the ADA. Future study and dialogue are needed, given the diverging definitions of disability for purposes of ADA law and policy, Social Security benefit payments, and Census Bureau tabulations.

Additional questions regarding interpretation of ADA law need to be addressed. The more controversial issues discussed in this book include interpretation of whether:[29]

---

[23] *Cf.* Oi, **supra Ch. III § 3.2,** at 112.

[24] Under other laws, such as the Rehabilitation Act of 1973, workers with disabilities are given preferences in hiring by federal contractors, companies who are recipients of federal grants, and those employed by the federal government. For a discussion of affirmative action laws toward the hiring of persons with disabilities in other countries, *see* Peter David Blanck, Comparative Study of the ADA, *in* **International Perspectives on Disability Law and Policy** (Stanley Herr, ed., *forthcoming* 1999).

[25] Burkhauser, *in* **Annals, supra Ch. X § 10.1,** at 80–82.

[26] *Id.* at 83.

[27] Frank G. Bowe, Statistics, Politics, and Employment of People with Disabilities—Commentary, 4 **J. Dis. Pol'y Stud.** 84–91, at 88 (1993).

[28] *Id.* at 89.

[29] For discussion of these and other emerging questions of ADA interpretation, *see* Burgdorf, **supra Ch. II § 2.7,** at 572–85; Mayerson, **supra Ch. II § 2.10,** at 591–612.

1. the definition of disability under the ADA applies to asymptomatic individuals and to those whose impairments are controlled by medication;
2. the "substantially limiting" phrase in the first prong of the ADA definition of disability applies to an individual's ability to perform a class of jobs or a single job;
3. the definition of disability is affected by the representations of impairments to other courts or agencies (e.g., the application of the doctrine of judicial estoppel);[30]
4. the definition of disability under the "regarded as" prong requires proof of an underlying impairment that, if it existed, would qualify as "substantially limiting" under the first prong of the definition; and
5. the definition of disability under the "record of" prong results in an employer's obligation to accommodate an employee based on a history of a substantially limiting impairment, even if that individual's current limitations are not substantial.[31]

One effort to help address such questions and assess the capabilities of persons with disabilities and their employment opportunities has been undertaken by The Council on Quality and Leadership in Supports for People with Disabilities. Through a grant from the U.S. Department of Health's Administration on Developmental Disabilities, the Council has established the National Center for Outcomes Research.

The goals of the National Center include longitudinal data collection and dissemination of information on employment and daily living outcomes for people with disabilities.[32] The investigation described in this book, anchored by its research model and empirical findings, attempts to help stimulate that discussion as well.

The President's Committee on Mental Retardation also has undertaken a comprehensive effort to identify policy, legal, and research questions facing the emerging workforce of persons with mental retardation.[33] The policy challenges identified by the President's Committee include enhancing incentives for inclusion and empowerment in work, fairness in managed health care and governmental entitlement programs, and developments in assistive technology.

Consistent with the present investigation, the research challenges identified by the President's Committee include collaborative and informed involvement by persons with mental retardation in research projects and the development of comprehensive models of research that explore aspects of work, individual capabilities and qualifications, educational and training supports, and integrated daily living supports.

17.4 Closing

The empirical investigation described in this book provides a springboard for discussion about evolving disability law and policy for researchers, legal scholars, employers, policy makers, and persons with mental retardation, their families, and their advocates. More dialogue and information is needed to achieve the inclusion and empowerment envisioned by the ADA. But the movement for individual inclusion and empowerment, and toward the development of adequate empirical information to inform policy, must be driven by people with mental retardation, their families, and advocates.

Similarly, discussion of true employment

---

[30] For a discussion of The Disabled, Work at Home, the SSA, and the ADA, *see Harris v. Chater*, 1998 U.S. Dist. LEXIS 425, at *11 (E.D. N.Y. 1998) (discussing "catch-22" situation facing many capable persons with disabilities who want to work but who have received SSI compensation). *See also* **supra Ch. II § 2.7** (discussing judicial estoppel doctrine as applied to the ADA definition of disability).

[31] *See Davidson v. Midelfort Clinic, LTD*, 133 F.3d 499 (7th Cir. 1998) (discussing whether the "record of" prong applies to those who may require some accommodation from their employer, despite their inability to demonstrate a present impairment that would qualify as a disability under the ADA). *Cf. School Bd. Of Nassau County, Fla. v. Arline,* 480 U.S. 273 (1987) (in Rehabilitation Act case, suggesting that a person with recurring condition such as tuberculosis may be able to show that she is disabled under the ADA based on previous hospitalization for that disease, and therefore may be entitled to a workplace accommodation related to the possibility of recurrence).

[32] *See* The Council Launches the National Center for Outcomes Research, 14 **The Council** 1 (Dec. 1997).

[33] *See* **Voices and Visions: Building Leadership For the 21st Century—1996 Report to the President,** President's Committee on Mental Retardation (Aug. 1, 1997).

integration under the ADA must be driven by views of the important noneconomic values related to the sense of individual worth, identity, and self-respect.[34] The definition of these values will shape the lives of the next generation of children with mental retardation and other disabilities, those who experienced integrated education and who will become part of the competitive workforce of the next century.[35]

Definition of the values of individual self-worth, identity, and self-respect will enable a better understanding of the culture of disability. Professor Carol Gill has commented that an understanding of the concept of "disability culture" will serve to unify people with disabilities and enable others without disabilities to better understand the social meaning embodied in laws like the ADA.[36] Professor Sharon Barnartt goes a step further, arguing that a "collective consciousness" better describes the social movement and actions of the disability community in the past 25 years than does a static concept of disability culture.[37]

However defined, the culture and consciousness of the emerging labor force of people with disabilities will need to be evaluated through interdisciplinary research, and through dialogue on society's moral underpinnings and values. Professor H. Rutherford Turnbull and his colleagues have said that future generations will assess the quality of life for citizens with mental retardation through *their* attainment of empowerment as full and equal members of the democratic process.[38] Measures of empowerment, work integration, and quality of life for people with mental retardation include citizenship participation, self-determination, and personal autonomy.[39]

Change is needed to fulfill the pledge embodied in the ADA to the emerging workforce of Americans with mental retardation and with other disabilities.

Justin Dart has written of the work to be done:

> [N]o matter how well we enforce civil rights laws, [people with disabilities] will not be equal in real life until [they] communicate the simple message of [their] equality to the more than 240 million Americans who will never read any law, but whose thoughts and actions will define our humanity every hour of every day.[40]

---

[34] Kavka, **supra Ch. XVII § 17.2,** at 271 (arguing that the key mediating concept for true employment integration for persons with disabilities is self-respect).

[35] Burkhauser, *in* **Annals, supra Ch. X § 10.1,** at 77.

[36] Carol Gill, A Psychological View of Disability Culture, 15 **Disability Stud. Q.** 16–19 (1995). *See also* Paul Longmore, The Second Phase: From Disability Rights to Disability Culture, **Disability Rag** 4–11 (Sept.–Oct. 1995).

[37] Sharon N. Barnartt, Disability Culture or Disability Consciousness, 7 **J. Disability Pol'y Stud.** 1–19 (1996).

[38] H. Rutherford Turnbull III & Gary L. Brunk, Quality of Life and Public Policy, *in* **Quality of Life, Vol. II, supra Ch. VII § 7.5,** at 201–209.

[39] *Id.* at 203–04.

[40] Dart, *in* **Rights and Responsibilities, supra Ch. I § 1.1,** at xxvii.

Appendices

Appendix A:
Americans with Disabilities Act of 1990

Appendix B:
Civil Rights Act of 1991

Appendix C:
EEOC v. Hertz, Amicus Brief in Support of Plaintiff EEOC

Appendix D:
EEOC v. Hertz, Amicus Brief in Support of Plaintiff EEOC, Michigan Protection & Advocacy Service

Appendix E:
EEOC v. Hertz, United States District Court Opinion

Appendix F:
EEOC Enforcement Guidance on the Americans with Disabilities Act and Psychiatric Disabilities

APPENDIX A

Americans with Disabilities Act of 1990

The Americans with Disabilities Act of 1990, codified as 42 USC § 12101 et seq.

AMERICANS WITH DISABILITIES ACT

Table of Contents

SUBCHAPTER III - PUBLIC ACCOMMODATIONS AND SERVICES OPERATED BY PRIVATE ENTITIES

SUBCHAPTER IV - MISCELLANEOUS PROVISIONS

Sec. 12101. Findings and Purposes

(a) Findings

The Congress finds that-

(1) Some 43,000,000 Americans have one or more physical or mental disabilities, and this number is increasing as the population as a whole is growing older;

(2) historically, society has tended to isolate and segregate individuals with disabilities, and, despite some improvements, such forms of discrimination against individuals with disabilities continue to be a serious and pervasive social problem;

(3) discrimination against individuals with disabilities persists in such critical areas as employment, housing, public accommodations, education, transportation, communication, recreation, institutionalization, health services, voting, and access to public services;

(4) unlike individuals who have experienced discrimination on the basis of race, color, sex, national origin, religion, or age, individuals who have experienced discrimination on the basis of disability have often had no legal recourse to redress such discrimination;

(5) individuals with disabilities continually encounter various forms of discrimination, including outright intentional exclusion, the discriminatory effects of architectural, transportation, and communication barriers, overprotective rules and policies, failure to make notifications to existing facilities and practices, exclusionary qualification standards and criteria, segregation, and relegation to lesser services, programs, activities, benefits, jobs, or other opportunities;

(6) census data, national polls, and other studies have documented that people with disabilities, as a group, occupy an inferior status in our society, and are severely disadvantaged socially, vocationally, economically, and educationally;

(7) individuals with disabilities are a discrete and insular minority who have been faced with restrictions and limitations, subjected to a history of purposeful unequal treatment, and relegated to a position of political powerlessness in our society, based on characteristics that are beyond the control of such individuals and resulting from stereotypic assumptions not truly indica-

tive of the individual ability of such individuals to participate in, and contribute to, society;

(8) the Nation's proper goals regarding individuals with disabilities are to assure equality of opportunity, full participation, independent living, and economic self-sufficiency for such individuals; and

(9) the continuing existence of unfair and unnecessary discrimination and prejudice denies people with disabilities the opportunity to compete on an equal basis and to pursue those opportunities for which our free society is justifiably famous, and costs the United States billions of dollars in unnecessary expenses resulting from dependency and nonproductivity.

(b) Purpose

It is the purpose of this chapter-

(1) to provide a clear and comprehensive national mandate for the elimination of discrimination against individuals with disabilities;

(2) to provide clear, strong, consistent, enforceable standards addressing discrimination against individuals with disabilities;

(3) to ensure that the Federal Government plays a central role in enforcing the standards established in this Act on behalf of individuals with disabilities; and

(4) to invoke the sweep of congressional authority, including the power to enforce the fourteenth amendment and to regulate commerce, in order to address the major areas of discrimination faced day-to-day by people with disabilities.

Sec. 12102. Definitions

As used in this Act:

(1) Auxiliary aids and services

The term "auxiliary aids and services" includes-

(A) qualified interpreters or other effective methods of making aurally delivered materials available to individuals with hearing impairments;

(B) qualified readers, taped texts, or other effective methods of making visually delivered materials available to individuals with visual impairments;

(C) acquisition or modification of equipment or devices; and

(D) other similar services and actions.

(2) Disability

The term "disability" means, with respect to an individual-

(A) a physical or mental impairment that substantially limits one or more of the major life activities of such individual;

(B) record of such an impairment; or

(C) being regarded as having such an impairment.

(3) State

The term "State" means each of the several States, the District of Columbia, the Commonwealth of Puerto Rico, Guam, American Samoa, the Virgin Islands, the Trust Territory of the Pacific Islands, and the Commonwealth of the Northern Mariana Islands.

SUBCHAPTER I - EMPLOYMENT

Sec. 12111. Definitions

As used in this subchapter:

(1) Commission

The term "Commission" means the Equal Employment Opportunity Commission established by section 705 of the Civil Rights Act of 1964 (42 U.S.C. 2000e-4).

(2) Covered entity

The term "covered entity" means an employer, employment agency, labor organization, or joint labor-management committee.

(3) Direct Threat

The term "direct threat" means a significant risk to the health or safety of others that cannot be eliminated by reasonable accommodation.

(4) Employee

The term "employee" means an individual employed by an employer. With respect to

employment in a foreign country, such term includes an individual who is a citizen of the United States.
[Section 12111 (4) amended by the Civil Rights Act of 1991. S. 1745]

(5) Employer

(A) In general

The term "employer" means a person engaged in an industry affecting commerce who has 15 or more employees for each working day in each of 20 or more calendar weeks in the current or preceding calendar year, and any agent of such person, except that, for two years following the effective date of this title, an employer means a person engaged in an industry affecting commerce who has 25 or more employees for each working day in each of 20 or more calendar weeks in the current or preceding year, and any agent of such person.

(B) Exceptions

The term "employer" does not include-

(i) the United States, a corporation wholly owned by the government of the United States, or an Indian tribe; or

(ii) a bona fide private membership club (other than a labor organization) that is exempt from taxation under section 501(c) of the Internal Revenue Code of 1986.

(6) Illegal use of drugs

(A) In general

The term "illegal use of drugs" means the use of drugs, the possession or distribution of which is unlawful under the Controlled Substances Act (21 U.S.C. 812). Such term does not include the use of a drug taken under supervision by a licensed health care professional, or other uses authorized by the Controlled Substances Act or other provisions of Federal law.

(B) Drugs

The term "drug" means a controlled substance, as defined in schedules I through V of section 202 of the Controlled Substances Act [21 USC § 812].

(7) Person, etc.

The terms "person", "labor organization", "employment agency", "commerce", and "industry affecting commerce", shall have the same meaning given such terms in section 701 of the Civil Rights Act of 1964 (42 U.S.C. 2000e).

(8) Qualified individual with a disability

The term "qualified individual with a disability" means an individual with a disability who, with or without reasonable accommodation, can perform the essential functions of the employment position that such individual holds or desires. For the purposes of this title, consideration shall be given to the employer's judgment as to what functions of a job are essential, and if an employer has prepared a written description before advertising or interviewing applicants for the job, this description shall be considered evidence of the essential functions of the job.

(9) Reasonable accommodation

The term "reasonable accommodation" may include-

(A) making existing facilities used by employees readily accessible to and usable by individuals with disabilities; and

(B) job restructuring, part-time or modified work schedules, reassignment to a vacant position, acquisition or modification of equipment or devices, appropriate adjustment or modifications of examinations, training materials or policies, the provision of qualified readers or interpreters, and other similar accommodations for individuals with disabilities.

(10) Undue hardship

(A) In general

The term "undue hardship" means an action requiring significant difficulty or expense, when considered in light of the factors set forth in subparagraph (B).

(B) Factors to be considered

In determining whether an accommodation would impose an undue hardship on a covered entity, factors to be considered include-

(i) the nature and cost of the accommodation needed under this Act;

(ii) the overall financial resources of the facility or facilities involved in the provision of the reasonable accommodation; the number of persons employed at such facility; the effect on expenses and resources, or the impact otherwise of such accommodation upon the operation of the facility;

(iii) the overall financial resources of the covered entity; the overall size of the business of a covered entity with respect to the number of its employees; the number, type, and location of its facilities; and

(iv) the type of operation or operations of the covered entity, including the composition, structure, and functions of the workforce of such entity; the geographic separateness, administrative, or fiscal relationship of the facility or facilities in question to the covered entity.

Sec. 12112. Discrimination

(a) General rule

No covered entity shall discriminate against a qualified individual with a disability because of the disability of such individual in regard to job application procedures, the hiring, advancement, or discharge of employees, employee compensation, job training, and other terms, conditions, and privileges of employment.

(b) Construction

As used in subsection (a), the term "discriminate" includes-

(1) limiting, segregating, or classifying a job applicant or employee in a way that adversely affects the opportunities or status of such applicant or employee because of the disability of such applicant or employee;

(2) participating in a contractual or other arrangement or relationship that has the effect of subjecting a covered entity's qualified applicant or employee with a disability to the discrimination prohibited by this subchapter (such relationship includes a relationship with an employment or referral agency, labor union, an organization providing fringe benefits to an employee of the covered entity, or an organization providing training and apprenticeship programs);

(3) utilizing standards, criteria, or methods of administration-

(A) that have the effect of discrimination on the basis of disability; or

(B) that perpetuate the discrimination of others who are subject to common administrative control;

(4) excluding or otherwise denying equal jobs or benefits to a qualified individual because of the known disability of an individual with whom the qualified individual is known to have a relationship or association;

(5)(A) not making reasonable accommodations to the known physical or mental limitations of an otherwise qualified individual with a disability who is an applicant or employee, unless such covered entity can demonstrate that the accommodation would impose an undue hardship on the operation of the business of such covered entity; or

(B) denying employment opportunities to a job applicant or employee who is an otherwise qualified individual with a disability, if such denial is based on the need of such covered entity to make reasonable accommodation to the physical or mental impairments of the employee or applicant;

(6) using qualification standards, employment tests or other selection criteria that screen out or tend to screen out an individual with a disability or a class of individuals with disabilities unless the standard, test or other selection criteria, as used by the covered entity, is shown to be job-related for the position in question and is consistent with business necessity; and

(7) failing to select and administer tests concerning employment in the most effective manner to ensure that, when such test is administered to a job applicant or employee who has a disability that impairs sensory, manual, or speaking skills, such test results accurately reflect the skills, aptitude, or whatever other factor of such applicant or employee that such test purports to measure, rather than reflecting the impaired sensory, manual, or speaking skills of such employee or applicant (except where such skills are the factors that the test purports to measure).

(c) Covered Entities in Foreign Countries-

(1) In general.- It shall not be unlawful under this section for a covered entity to take any action that constitutes discrimination under this section with respect to an employee in a workplace in a foreign country if compliance with this section would cause such covered entity to violate the law of the foreign country in which such workplace is located.

(2) Control of corporation -

(A) Presumption. - If an employer controls a corporation whose place of incorporation is a foreign country, any practice that constitutes discrimination under this section and is engaged in by such corporation shall be presumed to be engaged in by such employer.

(B) Exception. - This section shall not apply with respect to the foreign operations of an employer that is a foreign person not controlled by an American employer.

(C) Determination. - For purposes of this paragraph, the determination of whether an employer controls a corporation shall be based on-

(i) the interrelation of operations;

(ii) the common management;

(iii) the centralized control of labor relations; and

(iv) the common ownership or financial control, of the employer and the corporation.

[Section 12112 amended by the Civil Rights Act of 1991. S. 1745]

(d) Medical examinations and inquiries

(1) In general

The prohibition against discrimination as referred to in subsection (a) of this section shall include medical examinations and inquiries.

(2) Pre-employment

(A) Prohibited examination or inquiry

Except as provided in paragraph (3), a covered entity shall not conduct a medical examination or make inquiries of a job applicant as to whether such applicant is an individual with a disability or as to the nature or severity of such disability.

(B) Acceptable inquiry

A covered entity may make pre-employment inquiries into the ability of an applicant to perform job-related functions.

(3) Employment entrance examination

A covered entity may require a medical examination after an offer of employment has been made to a job applicant and prior to the commencement of the employment duties of such applicant, and may condition an offer of employment on the results of such examination, if -

(A) all entering employees are subjected to such an examination regardless of disability;

(B) information obtained regarding the medical condition or history of the applicant is collected and maintained on separate forms and in separate medical files and is treated as a confidential medical record, except that -

(i) supervisors and managers may be informed regarding necessary restrictions on the work or duties of the employee and necessary accommodations;

(ii) first aid and safety personnel may be informed, when appropriate, if the disability might require emergency treatment; and

(iii) government officials investigating compliance with this Act shall be provided relevant information on request; and

(C) the results of such examination are used only in accordance with this title.

(4) Examination and inquiry

(A) Prohibited examinations and inquiries

A covered entity shall not require a medical examination and shall not make inquiries of an employee as to whether such employee is an individual with a disability or as to the nature or severity of the disability, unless such examination or inquiry is shown to be job-related and consistent with business necessity.

(B) Acceptable examinations and inquiries

A covered entity may conduct voluntary medical examinations, including voluntary medical histories, which are part of an employee health program available to employees at that work site. A covered entity may make inquiries into the ability of an employee to perform job-related functions.

(C) Requirement

Information obtained under subparagraph (B) regarding the medical condition or history of any employee are subject to the requirements of subparagraphs (B) and (C) of paragraph (3).

Sec. 12113. Defenses

(a) In general

It may be a defense to a charge of discrimination under this Act that an alleged application of qualification standards, tests, or selection criteria that screen out or tend to screen out or otherwise deny a job or benefit to an individual with a disability has been shown to be job-related and consistent with business necessity, and such performance cannot be accomplished by reasonable accommodation, as required under this title.

(b) Qualification standards

The term "qualification standards" may include a requirement that an individual shall not pose a direct threat to the health or safety of other individuals in the workplace.

(c) Religious entities

(1) In general

This title shall not prohibit a religious corporation, association, educational institution, or society from giving preference in employment to individuals of a particular religion to perform work connected with the carrying on by such corporation, association, educational institution, or society of its activities.

(2) Religious tenets requirement

Under this title, a religious organization may require that all applicants and employees conform to the religious tenets of such organization.

(d) List of infectious and communicable diseases

(1) In general

The Secretary of Health and Human Services, not later than 6 months after the date of enactment of this Act, shall -

(A) review all infectious and communicable diseases which may be transmitted through handling the food supply;

(B) publish a list of infectious and communicable diseases which are transmitted through handling the food supply;

(C) publish the methods by which such diseases are transmitted; and

(D) widely disseminate such information regarding the list of diseases and their modes of transmissibility to the general public. Such list shall be updated annually.

(2) Applications

In any case in which an individual has an infectious or communicable disease that is transmitted to others through the handling of food, that is included on the list developed by the Secretary of Health and Human Services under paragraph (1), and which cannot be eliminated by reasonable accommodation, a covered entity may refuse to assign or continue to assign such individual to a job involving food handling.

(3) Construction

Nothing in this Act shall be construed to preempt, modify, or amend any State, county, or local law, ordinance, or regulation applicable to food handling which is designed to protect the public health from individuals who pose a significant risk to the health or safety of others, which cannot be eliminated by reasonable accommodation, pursuant to the list of infectious or communicable diseases and the modes of transmissibility published by the Secretary of Health and Human Services.

Sec. 12114. Illegal Use of Drugs and Alcohol

(a) Qualified individual with a disability

For purposes of this title, the term "qualified individual with a disability" shall not include any employee or applicant who is currently engaging in the illegal use of drugs, when the covered entity acts on the basis of such use.

(b) Rules of construction

Nothing in subsection (a) shall be construed to exclude as a qualified individual with a disability an individual who -

(1) has successfully completed a supervised drug rehabilitation program and is no longer engaging in the illegal use of drugs, or has otherwise been rehabilitated successfully and is no loner engaging in such use;

(2) is participating in a supervised rehabilitation program and is no longer engaging in such use; or

(3) is erroneously regarded as engaging in such use, but is not engaging in such use, except that it shall not be a violation of this Act for a covered entity to adopt or administer reasonable policies or procedures, including but not limited to drug testing, designed to ensure that an

individual described in paragraph (1) or (2) is no longer engaging in the illegal use of drugs.

(c) Authority of covered entity

A covered entity -

(1) may prohibit the illegal use of drugs and the use of alcohol at the workplace by all employees;

(2) may require that employees shall not be under the influence of alcohol or be engaging in the illegal use of drugs at the workplace;

(3) may require that employees behave in conformance with the requirements established under the Drug-Free Workplace Act of 1988 (41 U.S.C. 701 et seq.);

(4) may hold an employee who engages in the illegal use of drugs or who is an alcoholic to the same qualification standards for employment or job performance and behavior that such entity holds other employees, even if any unsatisfactory performance or behavior is related to the drug use or alcoholism of such employee; and

(5) may, with respect to Federal regulations regarding alcohol and the illegal use of drugs, require that -

(A) employees comply with the standards established in such regulations of the Department of Defense, if the employees of the covered entity are employed in an industry subject to such regulations, including complying with regulations (if any) that apply to employment in sensitive positions in such an industry, in the case of employees of the covered entity who are employed in such positions (as defined in the regulations of the Department of Defense);

(B) employees comply with the standards established in such regulations of the Nuclear Regulatory Commission, if the employees of the covered entity are employed in an industry subject to such regulations, including complying with regulations (if any) that apply to employment in sensitive positions in such an industry, in the case of employees of the covered entity who are employed in such positions (as defined in the regulations of the Nuclear Regulatory Commission); and

(C) employees comply with the standards established in such regulations of the Department of Transportation, if the employees of the covered entity are employed in a transportation industry subject to such regulations, including complying with such regulations (if any) that apply to employment in sensitive positions in such an industry, in the case of employees of the covered entity who are employed in such positions (as defined in the regulations of the Department of Transportation).

(d) Drug testing

(1) In general

For purposes of this title, a test to determine the illegal use of drugs shall not be considered a medical examination.

(2) Construction

Nothing in this title shall be construed to encourage, prohibit, or authorize the conducting of drug testing for the illegal use of drugs by job applicants or employees or making employment decisions based on such test results.

(e) Transportation employees

Nothing in this subchapter shall be construed to encourage, prohibit, restrict, or authorize the otherwise lawful exercise by entities subject to the jurisdiction of the Department of Transportation of authority to -

(1) test employees of such entities in, and applicants for, positions involving safety-sensitive duties for the illegal use of drugs and for on-duty impairment by alcohol; and

(2) remove such persons who test positive for illegal use of drugs and on-duty impairment by alcohol pursuant to paragraph (1) from safety-sensitive duties in implementing subsection (c).

Sec. 12115. Posting Notices

Every employer, employment agency, labor organization, or joint labor-management committee covered under this title shall post notices in an accessible format to applicants, employees, and members describing the applicable provisions of this Act, in the manner prescribed by section 711 of the Civil Rights Act of 1964 (42 U.S.C. 2000e-10).

Sec. 12116. Regulations

Not later than 1 year after July 26, 1990, the Commission shall issue regulations in an accessible format to carry out this title in accordance with subchapter II of chapter 5 of title 5, United States Code.

Sec. 12117. Enforcement

(a) Powers, remedies, and procedures

The powers, remedies, and procedures set forth in sections 705, 706, 707, 709, and 710 of the Civil Rights Act of 1964 (42 U.S.C. 2000e-4, 2000e-5, 2000e-6, 2000e-8, and 2000e-9) shall be the powers, remedies, and procedures this title provides to the Commission, to the Attorney General, or to any person alleging discrimination on the basis of disability in violation of any provision of this chapter, or regulations promulgated under section 12116, concerning employment.

(b) Coordination

The agencies with enforcement authority for actions which allege employment discrimination under this title and under the Rehabilitation Act of 1973 shall develop procedures to ensure that administrative complaints filed under this title and under the Rehabilitation Act of 1973 are dealt with in a manner that avoids duplication of effort and prevents imposition of inconsistent or conflicting standards for the same requirements under this title and the Rehabilitation Act of 1973. The Commission, the Attorney General, and the Office of Federal Contract Compliance Programs shall establish such coordinating mechanisms (similar to provisions contained in the joint regulations promulgated by the Commission and the Attorney General at part 42 of title 28 and part 1691 of title 29, Code of Federal Regulations, and the Memorandum of Understanding between the Commission and the Office of Federal Contract Compliance Programs dated January 16, 1981 (46 Fed. Reg. 7435, January 23, 1981) in regulations implementing this title and Rehabilitation Act of 1973 not later than 18 months after July 26, 1990.

Effective Date

This title shall become effective 24 months after July 26, 1990.

SUBCHAPTER II - PUBLIC SERVICES

Subtitle A - Prohibition Against Discrimination and Other Generally Applicable Provisions

Sec. 12131. Definition

As used in this title:

(1) Public entity

The term "public entity" means -

(A) any State or local government;

(B) any department, agency, special purpose district, or other instrumentality of a State or States or local government; and

(C) the National Railroad Passenger Corporation, and any commuter authority (as defined in section 103(8) of the Rail Passenger Service Act).

(2) Qualified individual with a disability

The term "qualified individual with a disability" means an individual with a disability who, with or without reasonable modifications to rules, policies, or practices, the removal of architectural, communication, or transportation barriers, or the provision of auxiliary aids and services, meets the essential eligibility requirements for the receipt of services or the participation in programs or activities provided by a public entity.

Sec. 12132. Discrimination

Subject to the provisions of this subchapter, no qualified individual with a disability shall, by reason of such disability, be excluded from participation in or be denied the benefits of the services, programs, or activities of a public entity, or be subjected to discrimination by any such entity.

Sec. 12133. Enforcement

The remedies, procedures, and rights set forth in section 505 of the Rehabilitation Act of 1973 (29 U.S.C. 794a) shall be the remedies, procedures and rights this title provides to any person alleging discrimination on the basis of disability in violation of section 12132 of this title.

Sec. 12134. Regulations

(a) In general

Not later than 1 year after July 26, 1990, the Attorney General shall promulgate regulations in an accessible format that implement this subtitle. Such regulations shall not include any matter within the scope of the authority of the Secretary of Transportation under section 12143, 12149, or 12164.

(b) Relationship to other regulations

Except for "program accessibility, existing facilities", and "communications", regulations under subsection (a) shall be consistent with this chapter and with the coordination regulations under part 41 of title 28, Code of Federal Regulations (as promulgated by the Department of Health, Education, and Welfare on January 13, 1978), applicable to recipients of Federal financial assistance under section 504 of the Rehabilitation Act of 1973 (29 U.S.C. 794). With respect to "program accessibility, existing facilities", and "communications", such regulations shall be consistent with regulations and analysis as in part 39 of title 28 of the Code of Federal Regulations, applicable to federally conducted activities under such section 794 of Title 29.

(c) Standards

Regulations under subsection (a) shall include standards applicable to facilities and vehicles covered by this subtitle, other than facilities, stations, rail passenger cars, and vehicles covered by subtitle B. Such standards shall be consistent with the minimum guidelines and requirements issued by the Architectural and Transportation Barriers Compliance Board in accordance with section 12204(a) of this title.

Effective Date

(a) General rule

Except as provided in subsection (b), this subtitle shall become effective 18 months after July 26, 1990.

(b) Exception

Section 12134 shall become effective on July 26, 1990.

Subtitle B - Actions Applicable to Public Transportation Provided by Public Entities Considered Discriminatory

Part I - PUBLIC TRANSPORTATION OTHER THAN BY AIRCRAFT OR CERTAIN RAIL OPERATIONS

Sec. 12141. Definitions

As used in this part:

(1) Demand responsive system

The term "demand responsive system" means any system of providing designated public transportation which is not a fixed route system.

(2) Designated public transportation

The term "designated public transportation" means transportation (other than public school transportation) by bus, rail, or any other conveyance (other than transportation by aircraft or intercity or commuter rail transportation (as defined in section 12161 of this title) that provides the general public with general or special service (including charter service) on a regular and continuing basis.

(3) Fixed route system

The term "fixed route system" means a system of providing designated public transportation on which a vehicle is operated along a prescribed route according to a fixed schedule.

(4) Operates

The terms "operates", as used with respect to a fixed route system or demand responsive system, includes operation of such system by a person under a contractual or other arrangement or relationship with a public entity.

(5) Public school transportation

The term "public school transportation" means transportation by schoolbus vehicles of schoolchildren, personnel, and equipment to and from a public elementary or secondary school and school-related activities.

(6) Secretary

The term "Secretary" means the Secretary of Transportation.

Sec. 12142. Public Entities Operating Fixed Route Systems

(a) Purchase and lease of new vehicles

It shall be considered discrimination for purposes of section 12132 of this title and section 504 of the Rehabilitation Act of 1973 (29 U.S.C. 794) for a public entity which operates a fixed route system to purchase or lease a new bus, a new rapid rail vehicle, a new light rail vehicle, or any other new vehicle to be used on such system, if the solicitation for such purchase or lease is made after the 30th day following the effective date of this subsection and if such bus, rail vehicle, or other vehicle is not readily accessible to and usable by individuals with disabilities, including individuals who use wheelchairs.

(b) Purchase and lease of used vehicles

Subject to subsection (c)(1), it shall be considered discrimination for purposes of section 12132 of this title and section 504 of the Rehabilitation Act of 1973 (29 U.S.C. 794) for a public entity which operates a fixed route system to purchase or lease, after the 30th day following the July 26, 1990, effective date, a used vehicle for use on such system unless such entity makes demonstrated good faith efforts to purchase or lease a used vehicle for use on such system that is readily accessible to and usable by individuals with disabilities, including individuals who use wheelchairs.

(c) Remanufactured vehicles

(1) General rule

Except as provided in paragraph (2), it shall be considered discrimination for purposes of section 202 of this Act and section 504 for the Rehabilitation Act of 1973 (29 U.S.C. 794) for a public entity which operates a fixed route system -

(A) to remanufacture a vehicle for use on such system so as to extend its usable life for 5 years or more, which remanufacture begins (or for which the solicitation is made) after the 30th day following July 26, 1990; or

(B) to purchase or lease for use on such system a remanufactured vehicle which has been remanufactured so as to extend its usable life for 5 years or more, which purchase or lease occurs after such 30th day and during the period in which the usable life is extended; unless, after remanufacture, the vehicle is, to the maximum extent feasible, readily accessible to and usable by individuals with disabilities, including individuals who use wheelchairs.

(2) Exception for historic vehicles

(A) General rule

If a public entity operates a fixed route system any segment of which is included on the National Register of Historic Places and if making a vehicle of historic character to be used solely on such segment readily accessible to and usable by individuals with disabilities would significantly alter the historic character of such vehicle, the public entity only has to make (or to purchase or lease a remanufactured vehicle with) those modifications which are necessary to meet the requirements of paragraph (1) and which do not significantly alter the historic character of such vehicle.

(B) Vehicles of historic character defined by regulations

For purposes of this paragraph and section 12148(b), a vehicle of historic character shall be defined by the regulations issued by the Secretary to carry out this subsection.

Sec. 12143. Paratransit as a Complement to Fixed Route Service

(a) General rule

It shall be considered discrimination for purposes of section 12132 of this title and section 504 of the Rehabilitation Act of 1973 (29 U.S.C. 794) for a public entity which operates a fixed route system (other than a system which provides solely commuter bus services) to fail to provide with respect to the operations of its fixed route system, in accordance with this section, paratransit and other special transportation services to individuals with disabilities, including individuals who use wheelchairs, that are sufficient to provide to such individuals a level of service (1) which is comparable to the level of designated public transportation services provided to individuals without disabilities using such system; or (2) in the case of response time, which is comparable, to the extent practicable, to the level of designated public transportation services provided to individuals without disabilities using such system.

(b) Issuance of regulations

Not later than 1 year after the effective date of this subsection, the Secretary shall issue final regulations to carry out this section.

(c) Required contents of regulations

(1) Eligible recipients of service

The regulations issued under this section shall require each public entity which operates a fixed route system to provide the paratransit and other special transportation services required under this section -

(A)(i) to any individual with a disability who is unable, as a result of a physical or mental impairment (including a vision impairment) and without the assistance of another individual (except an operator of a wheelchair lift or other boarding assistance device), to board, ride, or disembark from any vehicle on the system which is readily accessible to and usable by individuals with disabilities.

(ii) to any individual with a disability who needs the assistance of a wheelchair lift or other boarding assistance device (and is able with such assistance) to board, ride, and disembark from any vehicle which is readily accessible to and usable by individuals with disabilities if the individual wants to travel on a route on the system during the hours of operation of the system at a time (or within a reasonable period of such time) when such a vehicle is not being used to provide designated public transportation on the route; and

(iii) to any individual with a disability who has a specific impairment-related condition which prevents such individual from traveling to a boarding location or from a disembarking location on such system;

(B) to one other individual accompanying the individual with the disability; and

(C) to other individuals, in addition to the one individual described in subparagraph (B), accompanying the individual with a disability provided that space for these additional individuals is available on the paratransit vehicle carrying the individual with a disability and that the transportation of such additional individuals will not result in a denial of service to individuals with disabilities.

For purposes of clauses (i) and (ii) of subparagraph (A), boarding or disembarking from a vehicle does not include travel to the boarding location or from the embarking location.

(2) Service area

The regulations issued under this section shall require the provision of paratransit and special transportation services required under this section in the service area of each public entity which operates a fixed route system, other than any portion of the service area in which the public entity solely provides commuter bus service.

(3) Service criteria

Subject to paragraphs (1) and (2), the regulations issued under this section shall establish minimum service criteria for determining the level of services to be required under this section.

(4) Undue financial burden limitation

The regulations issued under this section shall provide that, if the public entity is able to demonstrate to the satisfaction of the Secretary that the provision of paratransit and other special transportation services otherwise required under this section would impose an undue financial burden on the public entity, the public entity, notwithstanding any other provision of this section (other than paragraph (5), shall only be required to provide such services to the extent that providing such services would not impose such a burden.

(5) Additional services

The regulations issued under this section shall establish circumstances under which the Secretary may require a public entity to provide, notwithstanding paragraph (4), paratransit and other special transportation services under this section beyond the level of paratransit and other special transportation services which would otherwise be required under paragraph (4).

(6) Public participation

The regulations issued under this section shall require that each public entity which operates a fixed route system hold a public hearing, provide an opportunity for public comment, and consult with individuals with disabilities in preparing its plan under paragraph (7).

(7) Plans

The regulations issued under this section shall require that each public entity which operates a fixed route system -

(A) within 18 months after July 26, 1990, submit to the Secretary, and commence implementation of, a plan for providing paratransit and other special transportation services which meets the requirements of this section; and

(B) on an annual basis thereafter, submit to the Secretary, and commence implementation of, a plan for providing such services.

(8) Provision of services by others

The regulations issued under this section shall -

(A) require that a public entity submitting a plan to the Secretary under this section identify in the plan any person or other public entity which is providing a paratransit or other special transportation service for individuals with disabilities in the service area to which the plan applies; and

(B) provide that the public entity submitting the plan does not have to provide under the plan such service for individuals with disabilities.

(9) Other provisions

The regulations issued under this section shall include such other provisions and requirements as the Secretary determines are necessary to carry out the objectives of this section.

(d) Reviews of plan

(1) General rule

The Secretary shall review a plan submitted under this section for the purpose of determining whether or not such plan meets the requirements of this section, including the regulations issued under this section.

(2) Disapproval

If the Secretary determines that a plan reviewed under this subsection fails to meet the requirements of this section, the Secretary shall disapprove the plan and notify the public entity which submitted the plan of such disapproval and the reasons therefor.

(3) Modification of disapproved plan

Not later than 90 days after the date of disapproval of a plan under this subsection, the public entity which submitted the plan shall modify the plan to meet the requirements of this section and shall submit to the Secretary, and commence implementation of, such modified plan.

(e) Discrimination defined

As used in subsection (a), the term "discrimination" includes -

(1) a failure of a public entity to which the regulations issued under this section apply to submit, or commence implementation of, a plan in accordance with subsections (c)(6) and (c)(7);

(2) a failure of such entity to submit, or commence implementation of, a modified plan in accordance with subsection (d)(3);

(3) submission to the Secretary of a modified plan under subsection (d)(3) which does not meet the requirements of this section; or

(4) a failure of such entity to provide paratransit or other special transportation services in accordance with the plan or modified plan the public entity submitted to the Secretary under this section.

(f) Statutory construction

Nothing in this section shall be construed as preventing a public entity -

(1) from providing paratransit or other special transportation services at a level which is greater than the level of such services which are required by this section,

(2) from providing paratransit or other special transportation services in addition to those paratransit and special transportation services required by this section, or

(3) from providing such services to individuals in addition to those individuals to whom such services are required to be provided by this section.

Sec. 12144. Public Entity Operating a Demand Responsive System

If a public entity operates a demand responsive system, it shall be considered discrimination, for purposes of section 12132 of this title and section 504 of the Rehabilitation Act of 1973 (29 U.S.C. 794), for such entity to purchase or lease a new vehicle for use on such system, for which a solicitation is made after the 30th day following the effective date of this section, that is not readily accessible to and usable by individuals with disabilities, including individuals who use wheelchairs, unless such system, when viewed in its entirety, provides a level of service to such individuals equivalent to the level of service such system provides to individuals without disabilities.

Sec. 12145. Temporary Relief Where Lifts are Unavailable

(a) Granting

With respect to the purchase of new buses, a public entity may apply for, and the Secretary may temporarily relieve such public entity from the obligation under section 12143(a) or 12144 of this title to purchase new buses that are readily accessible to and usable by individuals with disabilities if such public entity demonstrates to the satisfaction of the Secretary -

(1) that the initial solicitation for new buses made by the public entity specified that all new buses were to be lift-equipped and were to be otherwise accessible to and usable by individuals with disabilities;

(2) the unavailability from any qualified manufacturer of hydraulic, electromechanical, or other lifts for such new buses;

(3) that the public entity seeking temporary relief has made good faith efforts to locate a qualified manufacturer to supply the lifts to the manufacturer of such buses in sufficient time to comply with such solicitation; and

(4) that any further delay in purchasing new buses necessary to obtain such lifts would significantly impair transportation services in the community served by the public entity.

(b) Duration and notice to Congress

Any relief granted under subsection (a) shall be limited in duration by a specified date, and the appropriate committees of Congress shall be notified of any such relief granted.

(c) Fraudulent application

If, at any time, the Secretary has reasonable cause to believe that any relief granted under subsection (a) was fraudulently applied for, the Secretary shall -

(1) cancel such relief if such relief is still in effect; and

(2) take such other action as the Secretary considers appropriate.

Sec. 12146. New Facilities

For purposes of section 12132 of this title and section 504 of the Rehabilitation Act of 1973 (29 U.S.C. 794), it shall be considered discrimination for a public entity to construct a new facility to be used in the provision of designated public transportation services unless such facility is readily accessible to and usable by individuals with disabilities, including individuals who use wheelchairs.

Sec. 12147. Alteration of Existing Facilities

(a) General rule

With respect to alterations of an existing facility or part thereof used in the provision of designated public transportation services that affect or could affect the usability of the facility or part thereof, it shall be considered discrimination, for purposes of section 12132 of this title and section 504 of the Rehabilitation Act of 1973 (29 U.S.C. 794), for a public entity to fail to make such alterations (or to ensure that the alterations are made) in such a manner that, to the maximum extent feasible, the altered portions of the facility are readily accessible to and usable by individuals with disabilities, including individuals who use wheelchairs, upon the completion of such alterations. Where the public entity is undertaking an alteration that affects or could affect usability of or access to an area of the facility containing a primary function, the entity shall also make the alterations in such a manner that, to the maximum extent feasible, the path of travel to the altered area and the bathrooms, telephones, and drinking fountains serving the altered area, are readily accessible to and usable by individuals with disability, including individuals who use wheelchairs, upon completion of such alterations, where such alterations to the path of travel or the bathrooms, telephones, and drinking fountains serving the altered area are not disproportionate to the overall alterations in terms of cost and scope (as determined under criteria established by the Attorney General).

(b) Special rule for stations

(1) General rule

For purposes of section 12132 of this title and section 504 of the Rehabilitation Act of 1973 (29 U.S.C. 794), it shall be considered discrimination for a public entity that provides designated public transportation to fail, in accordance with the provisions of this subsection, to make key stations (as determined under criteria established by the Secretary by regulation) in rapid rail and light rail systems readily accessible to and usable by individuals with disabilities, including individuals who use wheelchairs.

(2) Rapid rail and light rail key stations

(A) Accessibility

Except as otherwise provided in this paragraph, all key stations (as determined under criteria established by the Secretary by regulation) in rapid rail and light rail systems shall be made readily accessible to and usable by individuals with disabilities, including individuals who use wheelchairs as soon as practicable but in no event later than the last day of the 3-year period beginning on the effective date of this paragraph.

(B) Extension for extraordinarily expensive structural changes. - The Secretary may extend the 3-year period under subparagraph (A) up to a 30-year period for key stations in a rapid rail or light rail system which stations need extraordinarily expensive structural changes to, or replacement of, existing facilities; except that by the last day of the 20th year following July 26, 1990, the enactment of this title at least 2/3 of such key stations must be readily accessible to and usable by individuals with disabilities.

(3) Plans and milestones

The Secretary shall require the appropriate public entity to develop and submit to the Secretary a plan for compliance with this subsection -

(A) that reflects consultation with individuals with disabilities affected by such plan and the results of a public hearing and public comments on such plan, and

(B) that establishes milestones for achievement of the requirements of this subsection.

Sec. 12148. Public Transportation

Programs and Activities in Existing Facilities and One Car Per Train Rule

(a) Public transportation programs and activities in existing facilities

(1) In general

With respect to existing facilities used in the provision of designated public transportation services, it shall be considered discrimination, for purposes of section 12132 of this title and section 504 of the Rehabilitation Act of 1973 (29 U.S.C. 794), for a public entity to fail to operate a designated public transportation program or activity conducted in such facilities so that, when viewed in the entirety, the program or activity is readily accessible to and usable by individuals with disabilities.

(2) Exception

Paragraph (1) shall not require a public entity to make structural changes to existing facilities in order to make such facilities accessible to individuals who use wheelchairs, unless and to the extent required by section 12147(a) (relating to alterations) or section 12147(b) (relating to key stations).

(3) Utilization

Paragraph (1) shall not require a public entity to which paragraph (2) applies, to provide to individuals who use wheelchairs services made available to the general public at such facilities when such individuals could not utilize or benefit from such services provided at such facilities.

(b) One car per train rule

(1) General rule

Subject to paragraph (2), with respect to 2 or more vehicles operated as a train by a light or rapid rail system, for purposes of section 12132 of this title and section 504 of the Rehabilitation Act of 1973 (29 U.S.C. 794), it shall be considered discrimination for a public entity to fail to have at least 1 vehicle per train that is accessible to individuals with disabilities, including individuals who use wheelchairs, as soon as practicable but in no event later than the last day of the 5-year period beginning on the effective date of this section.

(2) Historic trains

In order to comply with paragraph (1) with respect to the remanufacture of a vehicle of historic character which is to be used on a segment of a light or rapid rail system which is included on the National Register of Historic Places, if making such vehicle readily accessible to and usable by individuals with disabilities would significantly alter the historic character of such vehicle, the public entity which operates such system only has to make (or to purchase or lease a remanufactured vehicle with) those modifications which are necessary to meet the requirements of section 12142(c)(1) and which do not significantly alter the historic character of such vehicle.

Sec. 12149. Regulations

(a) In general

Not later than 1 year after July 26, 1990, the Secretary of Transportation shall issue regulations, in an accessible format, necessary for carrying out this part (other than section 12143 of this title).

(b) Standards

The regulations issued under this section and section 12143 shall include standards applicable to facilities and vehicles covered by this subtitle. The standards shall be consistent with the minimum guidelines and requirements issued by the Architectural and Transportation Barriers Compliance Board in accordance with section 12204 of this title.

Sec. 12150. Interim Accessibility Requirements

If final regulations have not been issued pursuant to section 12149, for new construction or alterations for which a valid and appropriate State or local building permit is obtained prior to the issuance of final regulations under such section, and for which the construction or alteration authorized by such permit begins within one year of the receipt of such permit and is completed under the terms of such permit, compliance with the Uniform Federal Accessibility Standards in effect at the time the building permit is issued shall suffice to satisfy the requirement that facilities be readily accessible to and usable by persons with disabilities as required under sections of 12146 ad 12147, except that, if such final regulations have not been issued one year after the Architectural and Transportation Barriers Compliance Board has issued the supplemental minimum guidelines required under section 12204(a) of this title, compliance with such supplemental minimum guidelines shall be necessary to satisfy the requirement that facilities be readily accessible to and usable by persons with disabilities prior to issuance of the final regulations.

Effective Date

(a) General rule

Except as provided in subsection (b), this part shall become effective 18 months after July 26, 1990.

(b) Exception

Sections 222, 223 (other than subsection (a)), 12144, 12145, 12147(b), 12148(b), and 2149 shall become effective on the date of enactment of this Act.

PART II - PUBLIC TRANSPORTATION BY INTERCITY AND COMMUTER RAIL

Sec. 12161. Definitions

As used in this part:

(1) Commuter authority

The term "commuter authority" has the meaning given such term in section 103(8) of the Rail Passenger Service Act (45 U.S.C. 502(8)).

(2) Commuter rail transportation

The term "commuter rail transportation" has the meaning given the term "commuter service" in section 103(9) of the Rail Passenger Service Act (45 U.S.C. 502(9)).

(3) Intercity rail transportation

The term "intercity rail transportation" means transportation provided by the National Railroad Passenger Corporation.

(4) Rail passenger car

The term "rail passenger car" means, with respect to intercity rail transportation, single-level and bi-level coach cars, single-level and bi-level dining cars, single-level and bi-level dining cars, single-level and bi-level lounge cars, and food service cars.

(5) Responsible person

The term "responsible person" means -

(A) in the case of a station more than 50 percent of which is owned by a public entity, such public entity;

(B) in the case of a station more than 50 percent of which is owned by a private party, the persons providing intercity or commuter rail transportation to such station, as allocated on an equitable basis by regulation by the Secretary of Transportation; and

(C) in a case where no party owns more than 50 percent of a station, the persons providing intercity or commuter rail transportation to such station and the owners of the station, other than private party owners, as allocated on an equitable basis by regulation by the Secretary of Transportation.

(6) Station

The term "station" means the portion of a property located appurtenant to a right-of-way on which intercity or commuter rail transportation is operated, where such portion is used by the general public and is related to the provision of such transportation, including passenger platforms, designated waiting areas, ticketing areas, restrooms, and, where a public entity providing rail transportation owns the property, concession areas, to the extent that such public entity exercises control over the selection, design, construction, or alteration of the property, but such term does not include flag stops.

Sec. 12162. Intercity and Commuter Rail Actions Considered Discriminatory

(a) Intercity rail transportation

(1) One car per train rule

It shall be considered discrimination for purposes of section 12132 of this title and section 504 of the Rehabilitation Act of 1973 (29 U.S.C. 794) for a person who provides intercity rail transportation to fail to have at least one passenger car per train that is readily accessible to and usable by individuals with disabilities, including individuals who use wheelchairs, in accordance with regulations issued under section 12164, as soon as practicable, but in no event later than 5 years after July 26, 1990.

(2) New intercity cars

(A) General rule

Except as otherwise provided in this subsection with respect to individuals who use wheelchairs, it shall be considered discrimination for purposes of section 12132 of this title and section 504 of the Rehabilitation Act of 1973 (29 U.S.C. 794) for a person to purchase or lease any new rail passenger cars for use in intercity rail transportation, and for which a solicitation is made later than 30 days after July 26, 1990, unless all such rail cars are readily accessible to and usable by individuals with disabilities, including individuals who use wheelchairs, as prescribed by the Secretary of Transportation in regulations issued under section 12164 of this title.

(B) Special rule for single-level passenger coaches for individuals who use wheelchairs

Single-level passenger coaches shall be required to -

(i) be able to be entered by an individual who uses a wheelchair;

(ii) have space to park and secure a wheelchair;

(iii) have a seat to which a passenger in a wheelchair can transfer, and a space to fold and store such passenger's wheelchair; and

(iv) have a restroom usable by an individual who uses a wheelchair, only to the extent provided in paragraph (3).

(C) Special rule for single-level dining cars for individuals who use wheelchairs

Single-level dining cars shall not be required to-

(i) be able to be entered from the station platform by an individual who uses a wheelchair; or

(ii) have a restroom usable by an individual who uses a wheelchair if no restroom is provided in such car for any passenger.

(D) Special rule for bi-level dining cars for individuals who use wheelchairs

Bi-level dining cars shall not be required to -

(i) be able to be entered by an individual who uses a wheelchair;

(ii) have space to park and secure a wheelchair;

(iii) have a seat to which a passenger in a wheelchair can transfer, or a space to fold and store such passenger's wheelchair; or

(iv) have a restroom usable by an individual who uses a wheelchair.

(3) Accessibility of single-level coaches

(A) General rule

It shall be considered discrimination for purposes of section 12132 of this title and section 504 of the Rehabilitation Act of 1973 (29 U.S.C. 794) for a person who provides intercity rail transportation to fail to have on each train which includes one or more single-level rail passenger coaches -

(i) a number of spaces -

(I) to park and secure wheelchairs (to accommodate individuals who wish to remain in their wheelchairs) equal to not less than one-half of the number of single-level rail passenger coaches in such train; and

(II) to fold and store wheelchairs (to accommodate individuals who wish to transfer to coach seats) equal to not less than one-half of the number of single-level rail passenger coaches in such train, as soon as practicable, but in no event later than 5 years after July 26, 1990; and

(ii) a number of spaces -

(I) to park and secure wheelchairs (to accommodate individuals who wish to remain in their wheelchairs) equal to not less than the total number of single-level rail pasenger coaches in such train; and

(II) to fold and store wheelchairs (to accommodate individuals who wish to transfer to coach seats) equal to not less than the total number of single-level rail passenger coaches in such train, as soon as practicable, but in no event later than 10 years after July 26, 1990.

(B) Location

Spaces required by subparagraph (A) shall be located in single-level rail passenger coaches or food service cars.

(C) Limitation

Of the number of spaces required on a train by subparagraph (A), not more than two spaces to park and secure wheelchairs nor more than two spaces to fold and store wheelchairs shall be located in any one coach or food service car.

(D) Other accessibility features

Single-level rail passenger coaches and food service cars on which the spaces required by subparagraph (A) are located shall have a restroom usable by an individual who uses a wheelchair and shall be able to be entered from the station platform by an individual who uses a wheelchair.

(4) Food service

(A) Single-level dining cars

On any train in which a single-level dining car is used to provide food service -

(i) if such single-level dining car was purchased after the date of enactment of this title, table service in such car shall be provided to a passenger who uses a wheelchair if -

(I) the car adjacent to the end of the dining car through which a wheelchair may enter is itself accessible to a wheelchair;

(II) such passenger can exit to the platform from the car such passenger occupies, move down the platform, and enter the adjacent accessible car described in subclause (I) without the necessity of the train being moved within the station; and

(III) space to park and secure a wheelchair is available in the dining car at the time such passenger wishes to eat (if such passenger wishes to remain in a wheelchair), or space to store and fold a wheelchair is available in the dining car at the time such passenger wishes to eat (if such passenger wishes to transfer to a dining car seat); and

(ii) appropriate auxiliary aids and services, including a hard surface on which to eat, shall be provided to ensure that other equivalent food service is available to individuals with disabilities, including individuals who use wheelchairs, and to passengers traveling with such individuals.

Unless not practicable, a person providing intercity rail transportation shall place an accessible car adjacent to the end of a dining car described in clause (i) through which an individual who uses a wheelchair may enter.

(B) Bi-level dining cars

On any train in which a bi-level dining car is used to provide food service-

(i) if such train includes a bi-level lounge car purchased after July 26, 1990, table service in such lounge car shall be provided to individuals who use wheelchairs and to other passengers; and

(ii) appropriate auxialiary aids and services, including a hard surface on which to eat, shall be provided to ensure that other equivalent food service is available to individuals with disabilities, including individuals who use wheelchairs, and to passengers traveling with such individuals.

(b) Commuter rail transportation

(1) One car per train rule

It shall be considered discrimination for purposes of section 12132 of this title and section 504 of the Rehabilitation Act of 1973 (29 U.S.C. 794) for a person who provides commmuter rail transportation to fail to have at least one passenger car per train that is readily accessible to and usable by individuals with disabilities, including individuals who use wheelchairs, in accordance with regulations issued under section 12164, as soon as practicable, but in no event later than 5 years after July 26, 1990.

(2) New commuter rail cars

(A) General rule

It shall be considered discrimination for purposes of section 12132 of this title and section 504 of the Rehabilitation Act of 1973 (29 U.S.C. 794) for a person to purchase or lease any new rail passenger cars for use in commuter rail transportation, and for which a solicitation is made later than 30 days after July 26, 1990, unless all such rail cars are readily accessible to and usable by individuals with disabilities, including individuals who use wheelchairs, as prescribed by the Secretary of Transportation in regulations issued under section 12164 of this title.

(B) Accessibility

For purposes of section 12132 of this title and section 504 of the Rehabilitation Act of 1973 (29 U.S.C. 794), a requirement that a rail passenger car used in commuter rail transportation be accessible to or readily accessible to and usable by individuals with disabilities, including individuals who use wheelchairs, shall not be construed to require -

(i) a restroom usable by an individual who uses a wheelchair if no restroom is provided in such car for any passenger;

(ii) space to fold and store a wheelchair; or

(iii) a seat to which a passenger who uses a wheelchair can transfer.

(c) Used rail cars

It shall be considered discrimination for purposes of section 12132 of this title and section 504 of the Rehabilitation Act of 1973 (29 U.S.C. 794) for a person to purchase or lease a used rail passenger car for use in intercity or commuter rail transportation, unless such person makes demonstrated good faith efforts to purchase or lease a used rail car that is readily accessible to and usable by individuals with disabilities, including individuals who use wheelchairs, as prescribed by the Secretary of Transportation in regulations issued under section 12164.

(d) Remanufactured rail cars

(1) Remanufacturing

It shall be considered discrimination for purposes of section 12132 of this title and section 504 of the Rehabilitation Act of 1973 (29 U.S.C. 794) for a person to remanufacture a rail passenger car for use in intercity or commuter rail transportation so as to extend its usable life for 10 years or more, unless the rail car, to the maximum extent feasible, is made readily accessible to and usable by individuals with disabilities, including individuals who use wheelchairs, as prescribed by the Secretary of Transportation in regulations issued under section 12164 of this title.

(2) Purchase or lease

It shall be considered discrimination for purposes of section 12132 of this title and section 504 of the Rehabilitation Act of 1973 (29 U.S.C. 794) for a person to purchase or lease a remanufactured rail passenger car for use in intercity or commuter rail transportation unless such car was remanufactured in accordance with paragraph (1).

(e) Stations

(1) New stations

It shall be considered discrimination for purposes of section 12132 of this title and section

504 of the Rehabilitation Act of 1973 (29 U.S.C. 794) for a person to build a new station for use in intercity or commuter rail transportation that is not readily accessible to and usable by individuals with disabilities, including individuals who use wheelchairs, as prescribed by the Secretary of Transportation in regulations issued under section 12164 of this title.

(2) Existing stations

(A) Failure to make readily accessible

(i) General rule

It shall be considered discrimination for purposes of section 12132 of this title and section 504 of the Rehabilitation Act of 1973 (29 U.S.C. 794) for a responsible person to fail to make existing stations in the intercity rail transportation system, and existing key stations in commuter rail transportation systems, readily accessible to and usable by individuals with disabilities, including individuals who use wheelchairs, as prescribed by the Secretary of Transportation in regulations issued under section 12164 of this title.

(ii) Period for compliance

(I) Intercity rail - All stations in the intercity rail transportation system shall be made readily accessible to and usable by individuals with disabilities, including individuals who use wheelchairs, as soon as practicable, but in no event later than 20 years after July 26, 1990.

(II) Commuter rail - Key stations in commuter rail transportation systems shall be made readily accessible to and usable by individuals with disabilities, including individuals who use wheelchairs, as soon as practicable but in no event later than 3 years after July 26, 1990, except that the time limit may be extended by the Secretary of Transportation up to 20 years after July 26, 1990, in a case where the raising of the entire passenger platform is the only means available of attaining accessibility or where other extraordinarily expensive structural changes are necessary to attain accessibility.

(iii) Designation of key stations

Each commuter authority shall designate the key stations in its commuter rail transportation system, in consultation with individuals with disabilities and organizations representing such individuals, taking into consideration such factors as high ridership and whether such station serves as a transfer or feeder station. Before the final designation of key stations under this clause, a commuter authority shall hold a public hearing.

(iv) Plans and milestones

The Secretary of Transportation shall require the appropriate person to develop a plan for carrying out this subparagraph that reflects consultation with individuals with disabilities affected by such plan and that establishes milestones for achievement of the requirements of this subparagraph.

(B) Requirement when making alterations

(i) General rule

It shall be considered discrimination, for purposes of section 12132 of this title and section 504 of the Rehabilitation Act of 1973 (29 U.S.C. 794), with respect to alterations of an existing station or part thereof in the intercity or commuter rail transportation systems that affect or could affect the usability of the station or part thereof, for the responsible person, owner, or person in control of the station to fail to make the alterations in such a manner that, to the maximum extent feasible, the altered portions of the station are readily accessible to and usable by individuals with disabilities, including individuals who use wheelchairs, upon completion of such alterations.

(ii) Alterations to a primary function area

It shall be considered discrimination, for purposes of section 12132 of this title and section 504 of the Rehabilitation Act of 1973 (29 U.S.C. 794), with respect to alterations that affect or could affect the usability of or access to an area of the station containing a primary function, for the responsible person, owner, or person in control of the station to fail to make the alterations in such a manner that, to the maximum extent feasible, the path of travel to the altered area, and the bathrooms, telephones, and drinking fountains serving the altered area, are readily accessible to and usable by individuals with disabilities, including individuals who use wheelchairs, upon completion of such alterations, where such alterations to the path of travel or the bathrooms, telephones, and drinking fountains serving the altered area are not disproportionate to the overall alterations in terms of cost and scope (as determined under criteria established by the Attorney General).

(C) Required cooperation

It shall be considered discrimination for purposes of section 12132 of this title and section of 504 of the Rehabilitation Act of 1973 (29 U.S.C. 794) for an owner, or person in control, of a station governed by subparagraph (A) or (B) to fail to provide reasonable cooperation to a responsible person with respect to such station in that responsible person's efforts to comply with such subparagraph. An owner, or person in control, of a station shall be liable to a responsible person for any failure to provide reasonable cooperation as required by this subparagraph. Failure to receive reasonable cooperation required by this subparagraph shall not be a defense to a claim of discrimination under this title.

Sec. 12163. Conformance of Accessibility Standards

Accessibility standards included in regulations issued under this part shall be consistent with the minimum guidelines issued by the Architectural and Transportation Barriers Compliance Board under section 12204(a) of this title.

Sec. 12164. Regulations

Not later than 1 year after July 26, 1990, the Secretary of Transportation shall issue regulations, in an accessible format, necessary for carrying out this part.

Sec. 12165. Interim Accessibility Requirements

(a) Stations

If final regulations have not been issued pursuant to section 12164, for new construction or alterations for which a valid and appropriate State or local building permit is obtained prior to the issuance of final regulations under such section, and for which the construction or alteration authorized by such permit begins within one year of the receipt of such permit and is completed under the terms of such permit, compliance with the Uniform Federal Accessibility Standards in effect at the time the building permit is issued shall suffice to satisfy the requirement that stations be readily accessible to and usable by persons with disabilities as required under section 12162(e), except that, if such final regulations have not been issued one year after the Architectural and Transportation Barriers Compliance Board has issued the supplemental minimum guidelines required under section 12204(a) of this title, compliance with such supplemental minimum guidelines shall be necessary to satisfy the requirement that stations be readily accessible to and usable by persons with disabilities prior to issuance of the final regulations.

(b) Rail passenger cars

If final regulations have not been issued pursuant to section 12164, a person shall be considered to have complied with the requirements of section 12162(a) through (d) that a rail passenger car be readily accessible to and usable by individuals with disabilities, if the design for such car complies with the laws and regulations (including the Minimum Guidelines and Requirements for Accessible Design and such supplemental minimum guidelines are issued under section 12204(a) of this title) governing accessibility of such cars, to the extent that such laws and regulations are not in effect at the time such design is substantially completed.

Effective Date

(a) General rule

Except as provided in subsection (b), this part shall become effective 18 months after July 26, 1990.

(b) Exception

Sections 12162 and 12164 shall become effective July 26, 1990.

SUBCHAPTER III - PUBLIC ACCOMMODATIONS AND SERVICES OPERATED BY PRIVATE ENTITIES

Sec. 12181. Definitions

As used in this title:

(1) Commerce

The term "commerce" means travel, trade, traffic, commerce, transportation or communication -

(A) among the several States;

(B) between any foreign country or any territory or possession and any State; or

(C) between points in the same State but through another State or foreign country.

(2) Commercial facilities

The term "commercial facilities" means facilities -

(A) that are intended for nonresidential use; and

(B) whose operations will affect commerce.

Such term shall not include railroad locomotives, railroad freight cars, railroad cabooses, railroad cars described in section 12162 or covered under this title, railroad rights-of-way, or facilities that are covered or expressly exempted from coverage under the Fair Housing Act of 1968 (42 U.S.C. 3601 et seq.).

(3) Demand responsive system

The term "demand responsive system" means any system of providing transportation of individuals by a vehicle, other than a system which is a fixed route system.

(4) Fixed route system

The term "fixed route system" means a system of providing transportation of individuals (other than by aircraft) on which a vehicle is operated along a prescribed route according to a fixed schedule.

(5) Over-the-road bus

The term "over-the-road bus" means a bus characterized by an elevated passenger deck located over a baggage compartment.

(6) Private entity

The term "private entity" means any entity other than a public entity (as defined in section 12131(1)).

(7) Public accommodation

The following private entities are considered public accommodations for purposes of this title, if the operations of such entities affect commerce -

(A) an inn, hotel, motel, or other place of lodging, except for an establishment located within a building that contains not more than five rooms for rent or hire and that is actually occupied by the proprietor of such establishment as the residence of such proprietor;

(B) a restaurant, bar, or other establishment serving food or drink;

(C) a motion picture house, theater, concert hall, stadium, or other place of exhibition or entertainment;

(D) an auditorium, convention center, lecture hall, or other place of public gathering;

(E) a bakery, grocery store, clothing store, hardware store, shopping center, or other sales or rental establishment;

(F) a laundromat, dry-cleaner, bank, barber shop, beauty shop, travel service, shoe repair service, funeral parlor, gas station, office of an accountant or lawyer, pharmacy, insurance office, professional office of a health care provider, hospital, or other service establishment;

(G) a terminal, depot, or other station used for specified public transportation;

(H) a museum, library, gallery, or other place of public display or collection;

(I) a park, zoo, amusement park, or other place of recreation;

(J) a nursery, elementary, secondary, undergraduate, or postgraduate private school, or other place of education;

(K) a day care center, senior citizen center, homeless shelter, food bank, adoption agency, or other social service center establishment; and

(L) a gymnasium, health spa, bowling alley, golf course, or other place of exercise or recreation.

(8) Rail and railroad

The terms "rail" and "railroad" have the meaning given the term "railroad" in section 202(e) of the Federal Railroad Safety Act of 1970 (45 U.S.C. 431(e)).

(9) Readily achievable

The term "readily achievable" means easily accomplishable and able to be carried out without much difficulty or expense. In determining whether an action is readily achievable, factors to be considered include -

(A) the nature and cost of the action needed under this chapter;

(B) the overall financial resources of the facility or facilities involved in the action; the number of persons employed at such facility; the effect on expenses and resources, or the impact otherwise of such action upon the operation of the facility;

(C) the overall financial resources of the covered entity; the overall size of the business of a covered entity with respect to the number of its employees; the number, type, and location of its facilities; and

(D) the type of operation or operations of the covered entity, including the composition, structure, and functions of the workforce of such entity; the geographic separateness, administrative or fiscal relationship of the facility or facilities in question to the covered entity.

(10) Specified public transportation

The term "specified public transportation" means transportation by bus, rail, or any other conveyance (other than by aircraft) that provides the general public with general or special service (including charter service) on a regular and continuing basis.

(11) Vehiclc

The term "vehicle" does not include a rail passenger car, railroad locomotive, railroad freight car, railroad caboose, or a railroad car described in section 12162 of this title or covered under this subchapter.

Sec. 12182. Prohibition of Discrimination by Public Accommodations

(a) General rule

No individual shall be discriminated against on the basis of disability in the full and equal enjoyment of the goods, services, facilities, privileges, advantages, or accommodations of any place of public accommodation by any person who owns, leases (or leases to), or operates a place of public accommodation.

(b) Construction

(1) General prohibition

(A) Activities

(i) Denial of participation

It shall be discriminatory to subject an individual or class of individuals on the basis of a disability or disabilities of such individual or class, directly, or through contractual, licensing, or other arrangements, to a denial of the opportunity of the individual or class to participate in or benefit from the goods, services, facilities, privileges, advantages, or accommodations of an entity.

(ii) Participation in unequal benefit

It shall be discriminatory to afford an individual or class of individuals, on the basis of a disability or disabilities of such individual or class, directly, or through contractual, licensing, or other arrangements with the opportunity to participate in or benefit from a good, service, facility, privilege, advantage, or accommodation that is not equal to that afforded to other individuals.

(iii) Separate benefit

It shall be discriminatory to provide an individual or class of individuals, on the basis of a disability or disabilities of such individuals or class, directly, or through contractual, licensing, or other arrangements with a good, service, facility, privilege, advantage, or accommodation that is different or separate from that provided to other individuals, unless such action is necessary to provide the individual or class of individuals with a good, service, facility, privilege, advantage, or accommodation, or other opportunity that is as effective as that provided to others.

(iv) Individual or class of individuals

For purposes of clauses (i) through (iii) of this subparagraph, the term "individual or class of individuals" refers to the clients or customers of the covered public accommodation that enters into the contractual, licensing or other arrangement.

(B) Integrated settings

Goods, services, facilities, privileges, advantages, and accommodations shall be afforded to an individual with a disability in the most integrated setting appropriate to the needs of the individual.

(C) Opportunity to participate

Notwithstanding the existence of separate or different programs or activities provided in accordance with this section, an individual with a disability shall not be denied the opportunity to participate in such programs or activities that are not separate or different.

(D) Administrative methods

An individual or entity shall not, directly or through contractual or other arrangements, utilize standards or criteria or methods of administration -

(i) that have the effect of discriminating on the basis of disability; or

(ii) that perpetuate the discrimination of others who are subject to common administrative control.

(E) Association

It shall be discriminatory to exclude or otherwise deny equal goods, services, facilities, privileges, advantages, accommodations, or other opportunities to an individual or entity because of the known disability of an individual with whom the individual or entity is known to have a relationship or association.

(2) Specific prohibitions

(A) Discrimination

For purposes of subsection (a), discrimination includes -

(i) the imposition of application of eligibility criteria that screen out or tend to screen out an individual with a disability or any class of individuals with disabilities from fully and equally enjoying any goods, services, facilities, privileges, advantages, or accommodations, unless such criteria can be shown to be necessary for the provision of the goods, services, facilities, privileges, advantages, or accommodations being offered;

(ii) a failure to make reasonable modifications in policies, practices, or procedures, when such modifications are necessary to afford such goods, services, facilities, privileges, advantages, or accommodations to individuals with disabilities, unless the entity can demonstrate that making such modifications would fundamentally alter the nature of such goods, services, facilities, privileges, advantages, or accommodations;

(iii) a failure to take such steps as may be necessary to ensure that no individual with a disability is excluded, denied services, segregated or otherwise treated differently than other individuals because of the absence of auxiliary aids and services, unless the entity can demonstrate that taking such steps would fundamentally alter the nature of the good, service, facility, privilege, advantage, or accommodation being offered or would result in an undue burden;

(iv) a failure to remove architectural barriers, and communication barriers that are structural in nature, in existing facilities, and transportation barriers in existing vehicles or rail passenger cars used by an establishment for transporting individuals (not including barriers that can only be removed through the retrofitting of vehicles or rail passenger cars by the installation of a hydraulic or other lift), where such removal is readily achievable; and

(v) where an entity can demonstrate that the removal of a barrier under clause (iv) is not readily achievable, a failure to make such goods, services, facilities, privileges, advantages, or accommodations available through alternative methods if such methods are readily achievable.

(B) Fixed Route System

(i) Accessibility

It shall be considered discrimination for a private entity which operates a fixed route system and which is not subject to section 12184 of this title to purchase or lease a vehicle with a seating capacity in excess of 16 passengers (including the driver) for use on such system, for which a solicitation is made after the 30th day following the effective date of this subparagraph, that is not readily accessible to and usable by individuals with disabilities, including individuals who use wheelchairs.

(ii) Equivalent service

If a private entity which operates a fixed route system and which is not subject to section 12184 purchases or leases a vehicle with a seating capacity of 16 passengers or less (including the driver) for use on such system after the effective date of this subparagraph that is not readily accessible to or usable by individuals with disabilities, it shall be considered discrimination for such entity to fail to operate such system so that, when viewed in its entirety, such system ensures a level of service to individuals with disabilities, including individuals who use wheelchairs, equivalent to the level of service provided to individuals without disabilities.

(C) Demand Responsive System

For purposes of subsection (a), discrimination includes -

(i) a failure of a private entity which operates a demand responsive system and which is not subject to section 304 to operate such system so that, when viewed in its entirety, such system ensures a level of service to individuals with disabilities, including individuals who use wheelchairs, equivalent to the level of service provided to individuals without disabilities; and

(ii) the purchase or lease by such entity for use on such system of a vehicle with a seating capacity in excess of 16 passengers (including the driver), for which solicitations are made after the 30th day following the effective date of this paragraph, that is not readily accessible to and usable by individuals with disabilities (including individuals who use wheelchairs) unless such entity can demonstrate that such system, when viewed in its entirety, provides a level of service to individuals with disabilities equivalent to that provided to individuals without disabilities.

(D) Over-the-road buses

(i) Limitation on applicability

Subparagraphs (B) and (C) do not apply to over-the-road buses.

(ii) Accessibility requirements

For purposes of subsection (a), discrimination includes (I) the purchase or lease of an over-the-road bus which does not comply with the regulations issued under section 12186(a)(2) of this title by a private entity which provides transportation of individuals and which is not primarily engaged in the business of transporting people, and (II) any other failure of such entity to comply with such regulations.

(3) Specific construction

Nothing in this subchapter shall require an entity to permit an individual to participate in or benefit from the goods, services, facilities, privileges, advantages and such accommodations of such entity where such individual poses a direct threat to the health or safety of others. The term "direct threat" means a significant risk to the health or safety of others that cannot be eliminated by a modification of policies, practices, or procedures or by the provision of auxiliary aids or services.

Sec. 12183. New Construction and Alterations in Public Accommodations and Commercial Facilities

(a) Application of term

Except as provided in subsection (b), as applied to public accommodations and commercial facilities, discrimination for purposes of section 12182(a) of this title includes -

(1) a failure to design and construct facilities for first occupancy later than 30 months after July 26, 1990, that are readily accessible to and usable by individuals with disabilities, except where an entity can demonstrate that it is structurally impracticable to meet the requirements of such subsection in accordance with standards set forth or incorporated by reference in regulations issued under this title; and

(2) with respect to a facility or part thereof that is altered by, on behalf of, or for the use of an establishment in a manner that affects or could affect the usability of the facility or part thereof, a failure to make alterations in such a manner that, to the maximum extent feasible, the altered portions of the facility are readily accessible to and usable by individuals with disabilities, including individuals who use wheelchairs. Where the entity is undertaking an alteration that affects or could affect usability of or access to an area of the facility containing a primary function, the entity shall also make the alterations in such a manner that, to the maximum extent feasible, the path of travel to the altered area and the bathrooms, telephones, and drinking fountains serving the altered area, are readily accessible to and usable by individuals with disabilities where such alterations to the path of travel or the bathrooms, telephones, and drinking fountains serving the altered area are not disproportionate to the overall alterations in terms of cost and scope (as determined under criteria established by the Attorney General).

(b) Elevator

Subsection (a) of this section shall not be construed to require the installation of an elevator for facilities that are less than three stories or have less than 3,000 square feet per story unless the building is a shopping center, a shopping mall, or the professional office of a health care provider or unless the Attorney General determines that a particular category of such facilities requires the installation of elevators based on the usage of such facilities.

Sec. 12184. Prohibition of Discrimination in Specified Public Transportation Services Provided by Private Entities

(a) General rule

No individual shall be discriminated against on the basis of disability in the full and equal enjoyment of specified public transportation services provided by a private entity that is primarily engaged in the business of transporting people and whose operations affect commerce.

(b) Construction

For purposes of subsection (a), discrimination includes -

(1) the imposition or application by an entity described in subsection (a) of eligibility criteria that screen out or tend to screen out individuals with disabilities from fully enjoying the specified public transportation services provided by the entity, unless such criteria can be shown to be necessary for the provision of the services being offered;

(2) the failure of such entity to -

(A) make reasonable modifications consistent with those required under section 12182(b)(2)(A)(ii) of this title;

(B) provide auxiliary aids and services consistent with the requirements of section 12182(b)(2)(A)(iii) of this title; and

(C) remove barriers consistent with the requirements of section 12182(b)(2)(A) of this title and with the requirements of section 12183(a)(2) of this title;

(3) the purchase or lease by such entity of a new vehicle (other than an automobile, a van with a seating capacity of less than 8 passengers, including the driver, or an over-the-road bus) which is to be used to provide specified public transportation and for which a solicitation is made after the 30th day following the effective date of this section, that is not readily accessible to and usable by individuals with disabilities, including individuals who use wheelchairs; except that the new vehicle need not be readily accessible to and usable by such individuals if the new vehicle is to be used solely in a demand responsive system and if the entity can demonstrate that such system, when viewed in its entirety, provides a level of service to such individuals equivalent to the level of service provided to the general public;

(4)(A) the purchase or lease by such entity of an over-the-road bus which does not comply with the regulations issued under section 12186(a)(2) of this title; and

(B) any other failure of such entity to comply with such regulations; and

(5) the purchase or lease by such entity of a new van with a seating capacity of less than 8 passengers, including the driver, which is to be used to provide specified public transportation and for which a solicitation is made after the 30th day following the effective date of this section that is not readily accessible to or usable by individuals with disabilities, including individuals who use wheelchairs; except that the new van need not be readily accessible to and usable by such individuals if the entity can demonstrate that the system for which the van is being purchased or leased, when viewed in its entirety, provides a level of service to such individuals equivalent to the level of service provided to the general public;

(6) the purchase or lease by such entity of a new rail passenger car that is to be used to provide specified public transportation, and for which a solicitation is made later than 30 days after the effective date of this paragraph, that is not readily accessible to and usable by individuals with disabilities, including individuals who use wheelchairs; and

(7) the remanufacture by such entity of a rail passenger car that is to be used to provide specified public transportation so as to extend its usable life for 10 years or more, or the purchase or lease by such entity of such a rail car, unless the rail car, to the maximum extent feasible, is made readily accessible to and usable by individuals with disabilities, including individuals who use wheelchairs.

(c) Historical or antiquated cars

(1) Exception

To the extent that compliance with subsection (b)(2)(C) or (b)(7) of this section would significantly alter the historic or antiquated character of a historical or antiquated rail passenger car, or a rail station served exclusively by such cars, or would result in violation of any rule, regulation, standard, or order issued by the Secretary of Transportation under the Federal Railroad Safety Act of 1970 [45 USC § 431 et seq.], such compliance shall not be required.

(2) Definition

As used in this subsection, the term "historical or antiquated rail passenger car" means a rail passenger car -

(A) which is not less than 30 years old at the time of its use for transporting individuals;

(B) the manufacturer of which is no longer in the business of manufacturing rail passenger cars; and

(C) which -

(i) has a consequential association with events or persons significant to the past; or

(ii) embodies, or is being restored to embody, the distinctive characteristics of a type of rail passenger car used in the past, or to represent a time period which has passed.

Sec. 12185. Study

(a) Purposes

The Office of Technology Assessment shall undertake a study to determine -

(1) the access needs of individuals with disabilities to over-the-road buses and over-the-road bus service; and

(2) the most cost-effective methods for providing access to over-the-road buses and over-the-road bus service to individuals with disabilities, particularly individuals who use wheelchairs, through all forms of boarding options.

(b) Contents

The study shall include, at a minimum, an analysis of the following:

(1) The anticipated demand by individuals with disabilities for accessible over-the-road buses and over-the-road bus service.

(2) The degree to which such buses and service, including any service required under sections 12184(b)(4) and 12186(a)(2), are readily accessible to and usable by individuals with disabilities.

(3) The effectiveness of various methods of providing accessibility to such buses and service to individuals with disabilities.

(4) The cost of providing accessible over-the-road buses and bus service to individuals with disabilities, including consideration of recent technological and cost saving developments in equipment and devices.

(5) Possible design changes in over-the-road buses that could enhance accessibility, including the installation of accessible restrooms which do not result in a loss of seating capacity.

(6) The impact of accessibility requirements on the continuation of over-the-road bus service, with particular consideration of the impact of such requirements on such service to rural communities.

(c) Advisory committee

In conducting the study required by subsection (a), the Office of Technology Assessment shall establish an advisory committee, which shall consist of -

(1) members selected from among private operators and manufacturers of over-the-road buses;

(2) members selected from among individuals with disabilities, particularly individuals who use wheelchairs, who are potential riders of such buses; and

(3) members selected for this technical expertise on issues included in the study, including manufacturers of boarding assistance equipment and devices.

The number of members selected under each of paragraphs (1) and (2) shall be equal, and the total number of members selected under paragraphs (1) and (2) shall exceed the number of members selected under paragraph (3).

(d) Deadline

The study required by subsection (a) of this section, along with recommendations by the Office of Technology Assessment, including any policy options for legislative action, shall be submitted to the President and Congress within 36 months after July 26, 1990. If the President determines that compliance with the regulations issued pursuant to section 12186(a)(2)(B) of this title on or before the applicable deadlines specified in section 12186(a)(2)(B) of this title will result in a significant reduction in intercity over-the-road bus service, the President shall extend each such deadline by 1 year.

(e) Review

In developing the study required by subsection (a) of this section, the Office of Technology Assessment shall provide a preliminary draft of such study to the Architectural and Transportation Barriers Compliance Board established under section 502 of the Rehabilitation Act of 1973 (29 U.S.C. 792). The Board shall have an opportunity to comment on such draft study, and any such comments by the Board made in writing within 120 days after the Board's receipt of the draft study shall be incorporated as part of the final study required to be submitted under subsection (d) of this section.

Sec. 12186. Regulations

(a) Transportation provisions

(1) General rule

Not later than 1 year after July 26, 1990, the Secretary of Transportation shall issue regulations in an accessible format to carry out sections 12182(b)(2)(B) and (C) and to carry out section 12184 (other than subsection (b)(4)).

(2) Special rules for providing access to over-the-road buses

(A) Interim requirements

(i) Issuance

Not later than 1 year after July 26, 1990, the Secretary of Transportation shall issue regulations in an accessible format to carry out sections 12184(b)(4) and 12182(b)(2)(D)(ii) of this title that require each private entity which uses an over-the-road bus to provide transportation of individuals to provide accessibility to such bus; except that such regulations shall not require any structural changes in over-the-road buses in order to provide access to individuals who use wheelchairs during the effective period of such regulations and shall not require the purchase of boarding assistance devices to provide access to such individuals.

(ii) Effective Period

The regulations issued pursuant to this subparagraph shall be effective until the effective date of the regulations issued under subparagraph (B).

(B) Final requirement

(i) Review of study and interim requirements

The Secretary shall review the study submitted under section 12185 and the regulations issued pursuant to subparagraph (A).

(ii) Issuance

Not later than 1 year after the date of the submission of the study under section 12185 of this title, the Secretary shall issue in an accessible format new regulations to carry out sections 12184(b)(4) and 12182(b)(2)(D)(ii) of this title that require, taking into account the purposes of the study under section 12185 of this title and any recommendations resulting from such study, each private entity which uses an over-the-road bus to provide transportation to individuals to provide accessibility to such bus to individuals with disabilities, including individuals who use wheelchairs.

(iii) Effective period

Subject to section 12185(d) of this title, the regulations issued pursuant to this subparagraph shall take effect -

(I) with respect to small providers of transportation (as defined by the Secretary), 7 years after July 26, 1990; and

(II) with respect to other providers of transportation, 6 years after July 26, 1990.

(C) Limitation on requiring installation of accessible restrooms

The regulations issued pursuant to this paragraph shall not require the installation of accessible restrooms in over-the-road buses if such installation would result in a loss of seating capacity.

(3) Standards

The regulations issued pursuant to this subsection shall include standards applicable to facilities and vehicles covered by sections 12182(b)(2) and 12184 of this title.

(b) Other provisions

Not later than 1 year after July 26, 1990, the Attorney General shall issue regulations in an accessible format to carry out the provisions of this title not referred to in subsection (a) that include standards applicable to facilities and vehicles covered under section 12182 of this title.

(c) Consistency with ATBCB guidelines

Standards included in regulations issued under subsection (a) and (b) shall be consistent with the minimum guidelines and requirements issued by the Architectural and Transportation Barriers Compliance Board in accordance with section 12204 of this title.

(d) Interim accessibility standards

(1) Facilities

If final regulations have not been issued pursuant to this section, for new construction or alterations for which a valid and appropriate State or local building permit is obtained prior to the issuance of final regulations under this section, and for which the construction or alteration authorized by such permit begins within one year of the receipt of such permit and is completed under the terms of such permit, compliance with the Uniform Federal Accessibility Standards in effect at the time the building permit is issued shall suffice to satisfy the requirement that facilities be readily accessible to and usable by persons with disabilities as required under section 12183 of this title, except that, if such final regulations have not been issued one year after the Architectural and Transportation Barriers Compliance Board has issued the supplemental minimum guidelines required under section 12204(a) of this title, compliance with such supplemental minimum guidelines shall be necessary to satisfy the requirement that facilities be readily accessible to and usable by persons with disabilities prior to issuance of the final regulations.

(2) Vehicles and rail passenger cars

If final regulations have not been issued pursuant to this section, a private entity shall be considered to have complied with the requirements of this title, if any, that a vehicle or rail passenger car be really accessible to and usable by individuals with disabilities, if the design for such vehicle or car complies with the laws and regulations (including the Minimum Guidelines and Requirements for Accessible Design and such supplemental minimum guidelines as are issued under section 12204(a) of this title) governing accessibility of such vehicles or cars, to the extent that such laws and regulations are not inconsistent with this title and are in effect at the time such design is substantially completed.

Sec. 12187. Exemptions for Private Clubs and Religious Organizations

The provisions of this title shall not apply to private clubs or establishments exempted from coverage under title II of the Civil Rights Act of 1964 (42 U.S.C. 2000a (e)) or to religious organizations or entities controlled by religious organizations, including places of worship.

Sec. 12188. Enforcement

(a) In general

(1) Availability of remedies and procedures

The remedies and procedures set forth in section 204(a) of the Civil Rights Act of 1964 (42 U.S.C. 2000a-3(a)) are the remedies and procedures this subchapter provides to any person who is being subjected to discrimination on the basis of disability in violation of this title or who has reasonable grounds for believing that such person is about to be subjected to discrimination in violation of section 12183. Nothing in this section shall require a person with a disability to engage in a futile gesture if such person has actual notice that a person or organization covered by this title does not intend to comply with its provisions.

(2) Injunctive relief

In the case of violations of sections 12182(b)(2)(A)(iv) and section 12183(a) of this title, injunctive relief shall include an order to alter facilities to make such facilities readily accessible to and usable by individuals with disabilities to the extent required by this title. Where appropriate, injunctive relief shall also include requiring the provision of an auxiliary aid or service, modification of a policy, or provision of alternative methods, to the extent required by this title.

(b) Enforcement by the attorney general

(1) Denial of rights

(A) Duty to investigate

(i) In general

The Attorney General shall investigate alleged violations of this title, and shall undertake periodic reviews of compliance of covered entities under this subchapter.

(ii) Attorney general certification

On the application of a State or local government, the Attorney General may, in consultation with the Architectural and Transportation Barriers Compliance Board, and after prior notice and a public hearing at which persons, including individuals with disabilities, are provided an opportunity to testify against such certification, certify that a State law or local building code or similar ordinance that establishes accessibility requirements meets or exceeds the minimum requirements of this chapter for the accessibility and usability of covered facilities under this title. At any enforcement proceeding under this section, such certification by the Attorney General shall be rebuttable evidence that such State law or local ordinance does meet or exceed the minimum requirements of this chapter.

(B) Potential violation

If the Attorney General has reasonable cause to believe that -

(i) any person or group of persons is engaged in a pattern or practice of discrimination under this subchapter; or

(ii) any person or group of persons has been discriminated against under this subchapter and such discrimination raises an issue of general public importance,

the Attorney General may commence a civil action in any appropriate United States district court.

(2) Authority of court

In a civil action under paragraph (1)(B), the court -

(A) may grant any equitable relief that such court considers to be appropriate, including, to the extent required by this subchapter -

(i) granting temporary, preliminary, or permanent relief;

(ii) providing an auxiliary aid or service, modification of policy, practice, or procedure, or alternative method; and

(iii) making facilities readily accessible to and usable by individuals with disabilities;

(B) may award such other relief as the court considers to be appropriate, including monetary damages to persons aggrieved when requested by the Attorney General; and

(C) may, to vindicate the public interest, assess a civil penalty against the entity in an amount -

(i) not exceeding $50,000 for a first violation; and

(ii) not exceeding $100,000 for any subsequent violation.

(3) Single violation

For purposes of paragraph (2)(C), in determining whether a first or subsequent violation has occurred, a determination in a single action, by judgment or settlement, that the covered entity has engaged in more than one discriminatory act shall be counted as a single violation.

(4) Punitive damages

For purposes of subsection (b)(2)(B) of this section, the term "monetary damages" and "such other relief" does not include punitive damages.

(5) Judicial consideration

In a civil action under paragraph (1)(B), the court, when considering what amount of civil penalty, if any, is appropriate, shall give consideration to any good faith effort or attempt to comply with this Act by the entity. In evaluating good faith, the court shall consider, among other factors it deems relevant, whether the entity could have reasonably anticipated the need for an appropriate type of auxiliary aid needed to accommodate the unique needs of a particular individual with a disability.

Sec. 12189. Examinations and Courses

Any person that offers examinations or courses related to applications, licensing, certification, or credentialing for secondary or postsecondary education, professional, or trade purposes shall offer such examinations or courses in a place and manner accessible to persons with disabilities or offer alternative accessible arrangements for such individuals.

Effective Date

(a) General rule

Except as provided in subsections (b) and (c), this subchapter shall become effective 18 months after July 26, 1990.

(b) Civil actions

Except for any civil action brought for a violation of section 12183 of this title, no civil action shall be brought for any act or omission described in section 12182 of this title which occurs -

(1) during the first 6 months after the effective date, against businesses that employ 25 or fewer employees and have gross receipts of $1,000,000 or less; and

(2) during the first year after the effective date, against businesses that employ 10 or fewer employees and have gross receipts of $500,000 or less.

(c) Exception

Sections 12182(a) for purposes of section 12182(b)(2)(B) and (C) only, 12184(a) for purposes of section 12184(b)(3) only, 12184(b)(3), 12185, and 12186 of this title shall take effect July 26, 1990.

SUBCHAPTER IV - MISCELLANEOUS PROVISIONS

Sec. 12201. Construction

(a) In general

Except as otherwise provided in this chapter, nothing in this Act shall be construed to apply a lesser standard than the standards applied under title V of the Rehabilitation Act of 1973 (29 U.S.C. 790 et seq.) or the regulations issued by Federal agencies pursuant to such title.

(b) Relationship to other laws

Nothing in this chapter shall be construed to invalidate or limit the remedies, rights, and procedures of any Federal law or law of any State or political subdivision of any State or jurisdiction that provides greater or equal protection for the rights of individuals with disabilities than are afforded by this Act. Nothing in this chapter shall be construed to preclude the prohibition of, or the imposition of restrictions on, smoking in places of employment covered by subchapter I, in transportation covered by subchapter II or III of this chapter, or in places of public accommodation covered by subchapter III of this chapter.

(c) Insurance

Subchapters I through III of this chapter and title IV of this Act shall not be construed to prohibit or restrict -

(1) an insurer, hospital or medical service company, health maintenance organization, or any agent, or entity that administers benefit plans, or similar organizations from underwriting risks, classifying risks, or administering such risks that are based on or not inconsistent with State law; or

(2) a person or organization covered by this Act from establishing, sponsoring, observing or administering the terms of a bona fide benefit plan that are based on underwriting risks, classifying risks, or administering such risks, or administering such risks that are based on or not inconsistent with State law; or

(3) a person or organization covered by this Act from establishing, sponsoring, observing or administering the terms of a bona fide benefit plan that is not subject to State laws that regulate insurance.

Paragraphs (1), (2), and (3) shall not be used as a subterfuge to evade the purposes of subchapters I and III.

(d) Accommodations and services

Nothing in this chapter shall be construed to require an individual with a disability to accept an accommodation, aid, service, opportunity, or benefit which such individual chooses not to accept.

Sec. 12202. State Immunity

A State shall not be immune under the eleventh amendment to the Constitution of the United States from an action in Federal or State court of competent jurisdiction for a violation of this Act. In any action against a State for a violation of the requirements of this Act, remedies (including remedies both at law and in equity) are available for such a violation to the same extent as such remedies are available for such a violation in an action against any public or private entity other than a State.

Sec. 12203. Prohibition Against Retaliation and Coercion

(a) Retaliation

No person shall discriminate against any individual because such individual has opposed any act or practice made unlawful by this chapter or because such individual made a charge, testified, assisted, or participated in any manner in an investigation, proceeding, or hearing under this chapter.

(b) Interference, coercion, or intimidation

It shall be unlawful to coerce, intimidate, threaten, or interfere with any individual in the exercise or enjoyment of, or on account of his or her having exercised or enjoyed, or on account of his or her having aided or encouraged any other individual in the exercise or enjoyment of, any right granted or protected by this chapter.

(c) Remedies and procedures

The remedies and procedures available under sections 12117, 1213, and 12188 of this title shall be available to aggrieved persons for violations of subsections (a) and (b) of this section, with respect to subchapter I, subchapter II and subchapter III, respectively.

Sec. 12204. Regulations by the Architectural and Transportation Barriers Compliance Board

(a) Issuance of guidelines

Not later than 9 months after July 26, 1990, the Architectural and Transportation Barriers Compliance Board shall issue minimum guidelines that shall supplement the existing Minimum Guidelines and Requirements for Accessible Design for purposes of subchapters II and III of this chapter.

(b) Contents of guidelines

The supplemental guidelines issued under subsection (a) shall establish additional requirements, consistent with this Act, to ensure that buildings, facilities, rail passenger cars, and vehicles are accessible, in terms of architecture and design, transportation, and communication, to individuals with disabilities.

(c) Qualified historic properties

(I) In general

The supplemental guidelines issued under subsection (a) shall include procedures and requirements for alterations that will threaten or destroy the historic significance of qualified historic buildings and facilities as defined in 4.1.7(1)(a) of the Uniform Federal Accessibility Standards.

(2) Sites eligible for listing in national register

With respect to alterations of buildings or facilities that are eligible for listing in the National Register of Historic Places under the National Historic Preservation Act (16 U.S.C. 470 et seq.), the guidelines described in paragraph (1) shall, at a minimum, maintain the procedures and requirements established in 4.1.7(1) and (2) of the Uniform Federal Accessibility Standards.

(3) Other sites

With respect to alterations of buildings or facilities designated as historic under State or local law, the guidelines described in paragraph (1) shall establish procedures equivalent to those established by 4.1.7(1)(b) and (c) of the Uniform Federal Accessibility Standards, and shall require, at a minimum, compliance with the requirements established in 4.1.7(2) of such standards.

Sec. 12205. Attorney's Fees

In any action or administrative proceeding commenced pursuant to this Act, the court or agency, in its discretion, may allow the prevailing party, other than the United States, a reasonable attorney's fee, including litigation expenses, and costs, and the United States shall be liable for the foregoing the same as a private individual.

Sec. 12206. Technical Assistance

(a) Plan for assistance

(1) In general

Not later than 180 days after July 26, 1990, the Attorney General, in consultation with the Chair of the Equal Employment Opportunity Commission, the Secretary of Transportation, the Chair of the Architectural and Transportation Barriers Compliance Board, and the Chairman of the Federal Communications Commission, shall develop a plan to assist entities covered under this chapter, and other Federal agencies, in understanding the responsibility of such entities and agencies under this chapter.

(2) Publication of plan

The Attorney General shall publish the plan referred to in paragraph (1) for public comment in accordance with subchapter II of chapter 5 of title 5, United States Code (commonly known as the Administrative Procedure Act).

(b) Agency and public assistance

The Attorney General may obtain the assistance of other Federal agencies in carrying out subsection (a), including the National Council on Disability, the President's Committee on Employment of People with Disabilities, the Small Business Administration, and the Department of Commerce.

(c) Implementation

(1) Rendering assistance

Each Federal agency that has responsibility under paragraph (2) for implementing this chapter may render technical assistance to individuals with institutions that have rights or duties under the respective title or titles for which such agency has responsibility.

(2) Implementation of subchapter I, II, and III of this chapter and title IV of this Act

(A) Subchapter I

The Equal Employment Opportunity Commission and the Attorney General shall implement the plan for assistance developed under subsection (a), for subchapter I of this chapter.

(B) Subchapter II

(i) Division A

The Attorney General shall implement such plan for assistance for division A of subchapter II.

(ii) Division B

The Secretary of Transportation shall implement such plan for assistance for division B of subchapter II of this chapter.

(C) Subchapter III

The Attorney General, in coordination with the Secretary of Transportation and the Chair of the Architectural Transportation Barriers Compliance Board, shall implement such plan for assistance for subchapter III, except for section 12184, the plan for assistance for which shall be implemented by the Secretary of Transportation.

(D) Title IV

The Chairman of the Federal Communications Commission, in coordination with the Attorney General, shall implement such plan for assistance for title IV.

(3) Technical Assistance Manuals

Each Federal agency that has responsibility under paragraph (2) for implementing this chapter shall, as part of its implementation responsibilities, ensure the availability and provision of appropriate technical assistance manuals to individuals or entities with rights or duties under this Act no later than six months after applicable final regulations are published under subchapters I, II, III of this chapter and title IV of this Act.

(d) Grants and contracts

(1) In General

Each Federal agency that has responsibility under subsection (c)(2) for implementing this chapter may make grants or award contracts to effectuate the purposes of this section, subject to the availability of appropriations. Such grants and contracts may be awarded to individuals, institutions not organized for profit and no part of the net earnings of which inures to the benefit of any private shareholder or individual (including educational institutions), and associations representing individuals who have rights or duties under this chapter. Contracts may be awarded to entities organized for profit, but such entities may not be the recipients of grants described in this paragraph.

(2) Dissemination of information

Such grants and contracts, among other uses, may be designed to ensure wide dissemination of information about the rights and duties established by this chapter and to provide information and technical assistance about techniques for effective compliance with this chapter.

(e) Failure to receive assistance

An employer, public accommodation, or other entity covered under this chapter shall not be excused from compliance with the requirements of this chapter because of any failure to receive technical assistance under this section, including any failure in the development of dissemination of any technical assistance manual authorized by this section.

Sec. 12207. Federal Wilderness Areas

(a) Study

The National Council on Disability shall conduct a study and report on the wilderness land management practices have on the ability of individuals with disabilities to use and enjoy the National Wilderness Preservation System as established under the Wilderness Act (16 U.S.C. 1131 et seq.).

(b) Submission of report

Not later than 1 year after the enactment of this Act, the National Council on Disability shall submit the report required under subsection (a) to Congress.

(c) Specific wilderness access

(1) In general

Congress reaffirms that nothing in the Wilderness Act is to be construed as prohibiting the use of a wheelchair in a wilderness area by an individual whose disability requires use of a wheelchair, and consistent with the Wilderness Act no agency is required to provide any form of special treatment or accommodation, or to construct any facilities or modify any conditions of lands within a wilderness area in order to facilitate such use.

(2) Definition

For purposes of paragraph (1), the term "wheelchair" means a device designed solely for use by a mobility-impaired person for locomotion, that is suitable for use in an indoor pedestrian area.

Sec. 12208. Transvestites

For the purpose of this chapter, the term "disabled" or "disability" shall not apply to an individual solely because that individual is a transvestite.

Sec. 12209. Instrumentalities of the Congress

(c) The General Accounting Office, the Government Printing Office, and the Library of Congress shall be covered as follows:

(1) In general

The rights and protections under this chapter, shall subject to paragraph (2), apply with respect to the conduct of each instrumentality of the Congress.

(2) Establishment of remedies and procedures by instrumentalities

The chief official of each instrumentality of the Congress shall establish remedies and procedures to be utilized with respect to the rights and protections provided pursuant to paragraph (1).

[Section 12209 amended by the Civil Rights Act of 1991. S. 1745]

(3) Report to Congress

The chief official of each instrumentality of the Congress shall, after establishing remedies and procedures for purposes of paragraph (2), submit to the Congress a report describing the remedies and procedures.

(4) Definition of instrumentalities

For purposes of this section, the term "instrumentality of the Congress" means the General Accounting Office, the Government Printing Office, and the Library of Congress.

(5) Enforcement of employment rights—The remedies and procedures set forth in section 717 of the Civil Rights Act of 1964 (42 U.S.C. 2000e-16) shall be available to any employee of an instrumentality of the Congress who alleges a violation of the rights and protections under sections 102 through 104 of this Act that are made applicable by this section, except that the authorities of the Equal Employment Opportunity Commission shall be exercised by the chief official of the instrumentality of the Congress.

(6) Enforcement of rights to public services and accommodations.— The remedies and procedures set forth in section 717 of the Civil Rights Act of 1964 (42 U.S.C. 2000e-16) shall be available to any qualified person with a disability who is a visitor, guest, or patron of an instrumentality of Congress and who alleges a violation of the rights and protections under sections 201 through 230 or section 302 or 303 of this Act that are made applicable by this section, except that the authorities of the Equal Employment Opportunity Commission shall be exercised by the chief official of the instrumentality of the Congress.

(7) Construction

Nothing in this section shall alter the enforcement procedures for individuals with disabilities provided in the General Accounting Office Personnel Act of 1980 and regulations promulgated pursuant to that Act.

Sec. 12210. Illegal Use of Drugs

(a) In general

For purposes of this chapter, the term "individual with a disability" does not include an individual who is currently engaging in the illegal use of drugs, when the covered entity acts on the basis of such use.

(b) Rules of construction

Nothing in subsection (a) shall be construed to exclude as an individual with a disability an individual who -

(1) has successfully completed a supervised drug rehabilitation program and is no longer engaging in the illegal use of drugs, or has otherwise been rehabilitated successfully and is no longer engaging in such use;

(2) is participating in a supervised rehabilitation program and is no longer engaging in such use; or

(3) is erroneously regarded as engaging in such use, but is not engaging in such use; except that it shall not be a violation of this chapter for a covered entity to adopt or administer reasonable policies or procedures, including but not limited to drug testing, designed to ensure that an individual described in paragraph (1) or (2) is no longer engaging in the illegal use of drugs; however, nothing in this section shall be construed to encourage, prohibit, restrict, or authorize the conducting of testing for the illegal use of drugs.

(c) Health and other services

Notwithstanding subsection (a) of this section and section 12211(b)(3) of this title, an individual shall not be denied health services, or services provided in connection with drug rehabilitation, on the basis of the current illegal use of drugs if the individual is otherwise entitled to such services.

(d) Definition of illegal use of drugs

(1) In general

The term "illegal use of drugs" means the use of drugs, the possession or distribution of which is unlawful under the Controlled Substances Act (21 U.S.C. 812). Such term does not include the use of a drug taken under supervision by a licensed health care professional, or other uses authorized by the Controlled Substances Act or other provisions of Federal law.

(2) Drugs

The term "drug" means a controlled substance, as defined in schedules I through V of section 202 of the Controlled Substances Act.

Sec. 12211. Definitions

(a) Homosexuality and bisexuality

For purposes of the definition of "disability" in section 12102(2), homosexuality and bisexuality are not impairments and as such are not disabilities under this chapter.

(b) Certain conditions

Under this chapter, the term "disability" shall not include -

(1) transvestism, transsexualism, pedophilia, exhibitionism, voyeurism, gender identity disorders not resulting from physical impairments, or other sexual behavior disorders;

(2) compulsive gambling, kleptomania, or pyromania; or

(3) psychoactive substance use disorders resulting from current illegal use of drugs.

Sec. 12212. Alternative Means of Dispute Resolution

Where appropriate and to the extent authorized by law, the use of alternative means of dispute resolution, including settlement negotiations, conciliation, facilitation, mediation, fact finding, minitrials, and arbitration, is encouraged to resolve disputes arising under this chapter.

Sec. 12213. Severability

Should any provision in this chapter be found to be unconstitutional by a court of law, such provision shall be served from the remainder of the chapter, and such action shall not affect the enforceability of the remaining provisions of the chapter.

APPENDIX B

Civil Rights Act of 1991

The Civil Rights Act of 1991 (P.L. 102-166), effective Nov. 7, 1991, amended by P.L. 103-283, effective July 22, 1994; codified as 42 U.S.C. § 1981a.

SECTION 1. SHORT TITLE.

This Act may be cited as the "Civil Rights Act of 1991".

SEC. 2. FINDINGS.

The Congress finds that -

(1) additional remedies under Federal law are needed to deter unlawful harassment and intentional discrimination in the workplace;

(2) the decision of the Supreme Court in Wards Cove Packing Co. v. Antonio, 490 U.S. 642 (1989) has weakened the scope and effectiveness of Federal civil rights protections; and

(3) legislation is necessary to provide additional protections against unlawful discrimination in employment.

SEC. 3. PURPOSES.

The purposes of this Act are -

(1) to provide appropriate remedies for intentional discrimination and unlawful harassment in the workplace;

(2) to codify the concepts of "business necessity" and "job related" enunciated by the Supreme Court in Griggs v. Duke Power Co., 401 U.S. 424 (1971), and in the other Supreme Court decisions prior to Wards Cove Packing Co. v. Antonio, 490 U.S. 642 (1989):

(3) to confirm statutory authority and provide statutory guidelines for the adjudication ofdisparate impact suits under title VII of the Civil Rights Act of 1964 (42 U.S. C. 2000e et seq.); and

(4) to respond to recent decisions of the Supreme Court by expanding the scope of relevant civil rights statutes in order to provide adequate protection to victims of discrimination.

TITLE I - FEDERAL CIVIL RIGHTS REMEDIES

SEC. 101. PROHIBITION AGAINST ALL RACIAL DISCRIMINATION IN THE MAKING AND ENFORCEMENT OF CONTRACTS.

Section 1977 of the Revised Statutes (42 U.S.C. 1981) is amended -

(1) by inserting "(a)" before "All persons within"; and

(2) by adding at the end the following new subsections;

"(b) For purposes of this section, the term 'make and enforce contracts' includes the making, performance, modification, and termination of contracts, and the enjoyment of all benefits, privileges, terms, and conditions of the contractual relationship.

"(c) The rights protected by this section are protected against impairment by nongovernmental discrimination and impairment under color of State law."

SEC. 102. DAMAGES IN CASES OF INTENTIONAL DISCRIMINATION.

The Revised Statutes are amended by inserting after section 1977 (42 U.S.C. 1981) the following new section:

"SEC. 1977A. DAMAGES IN CASES OF INTENTIONAL DISCRIMINATION IN EMPLOYMENT. [42 U.S.C. 1981a.]

"(a) **Right of Recovery.** -

"(1) **Civil rights.** - In an action brought by a complaining party under section 706 or 717 of the Civil Rights Act of 1964 (42 U.S.C. 2000e-5) against a respondent who engaged in unlawful intentional discrimination (not an employment practice that is unlawful because of its disparate impact) prohibited under section 703, 704, or 717 of the Act (42 U.S.C. 2000e-2 or 2000e-3), and provided that the complaining party cannot recover under section 1977 of the Revised Statutes (42 U.S.C. 1981), the complaining party may recover compensatory and punitive damages as allowed in subsection (b), in addition to any relief authorized by section 706(g) of the Civil Rights Act of 1964, from the respondent.

"(2) **Disability.** - In an action brought by a complaining party under the powers, remedies, and procedures set forth in section 706 or 717 of the Civil Rights Act of 1964 (as provided in section 107(a) of the Americans with Disabilities Act of 1990 (42 U.S.C. 12117(a)), and section 505(a)(1) of the Rehabilitation Act of 1973 (29 U.S.C. 794a(a)(1)), respectively) against a respondent who engaged in unlawful intentional discrimination (not an employment practice that is unlawful because of its disparate impact) under section 501 of the Rehabilitation Act of 1973 (29 U.S.C. 791) and the regulations implementing section 501, or who violated the requirements of section 501 of the Act or the regulations implementing section 501 concerning the provision of a reasonable accommodation, or section 102 of the Americans with Disabilities Act of 1990 (42 U.S.C. 12112), or committed a violation of section 102(b)(5) of the Act, against an individual, the complaining party may recover compensatory and punitive damages as allowed in subsection (b), in addition to any relief authorized by section 706(g) of the Civil Rights Act of 1964, from the respondent.

"(3) **Reasonable accommodation and good faith effort.** - In cases where a discriminatory practice involves the provision of a reasonable accommodation pursuant to section 102(b)(5) of the Americans with Disabilities Act of 1990 or regulations implementing section 501 of the Rehabilitation Act of 1973, damages may not be awarded under this section where the covered entity demonstrates good faith efforts, in consultation with the person with the disability who has informed the covered entity that accommodation is needed, to identify and make a reasonable accommodation that would provide such individual with an equally effective opportunity and would not cause an undue hardship on the operation of the business.

"(b) **Compensatory and Punitive Damages.** -

"(1) **Determination of punitive damages.** - A complaining party may recover punitive damages under this section against a respondent (other than a government, government agency or political subdivision) if the complaining party demonstrates that the respondent engaged in a discriminatory practice or discriminatory practices with malice or with reckless indifference to the federally protected rights of an aggrieved individual.

"(2) **Exclusions from compensatory damages.** - Compensatory damages awarded under this section shall not include backpay, interest on backpay, or any other type of relief authorized under section 706(g) of the Civil Rights Act of 1964.

"(3) **Limitations.** - The sum of the amount of compensatory damages awarded under this section for future pecuniary losses, emotional pain, suffering, inconvenience, mental anguish, loss of enjoyment of life, and other nonpecuniary losses, and the amount of punitive damages awarded under this section, shall not exceed, for each complaining party -

"(A) in the case of a respondent who has more than 14 and fewer than 101 employees in each of 20 or more calendar weeks in the current or preceding calendar year, $50,000;

"(B) in the case of a respondent who has more than 100 and fewer than 201 employees in each of 20 or more calendar weeks in the current or preceding calendar year, $100,000; and

"(C) in the case of a respondent who has more than 200 and fewer than 501 employees in each of 20 or more calendar weeks in the current or preceding calendar year, $200,000; and

"(D) in the case of a respondent who has more than 500 employees in each of 20 or more calendar weeks in the current or preceding calendar year, $300,000.

"(4) **Construction.** - Nothing in this section shall be construed to limit the scope of, or the relief available under, section 1977 of the Revised Statutes (42 U.S.C. 1981).

"(c) **Jury Trial.** - If a complaining party seeks compensatory or punitive damages under this section -

"(1) any party may demand a trial by jury; and

"(2) the court shall not inform the jury of the limitations described in subsection (b)(3).

"(d) Definitions. - As used in this section:

"(1) Complaining party. - The term 'complaining party' means -

"(A) in the case of a person seeking to bring an action under subsection (a)(1), the Equal Employment Opportunity Commission, the Attorney General, or a person who may bring an action or proceeding under title VII of the Civil Rights Act of 1964 (42 U.S.C. 2000e et seq.); or

"(B) in the case of a person seeking to bring an action under subsection (a)(2), the Equal Employment Opportunity Commission, the Attorney General, a person who may bring an action or proceeding under section 505(a)(1) of the Rehabilitation Act of 1973 (29 U.S.C. 794a(a)(1), or a person who may bring an action or proceeding under title I of the Americans with Disabilities Act of 1990 (42 U.S.C. 12101 et seq.).

"(2) Discriminatory practice. - The term 'discriminatory practice' means the discrimination described in paragraph (1), or the discrimination or the violation described in paragraph (2), of subsection (a)."

SEC. 103. ATTORNEY'S FEES.

The last sentence of section 722 of the Revised Statutes (42 U.S.C. 1988) is amended by inserting, "1977A" after "1977".

SEC. 104. DEFINITIONS.

Section 701 of the Civil Rights Act of 1964 (42 U.S.C. 2000e) is amended by adding at the end the following new subsections:

"(l) The term 'complaining party' means the Commission, the Attorney General, or a person who may bring an action or proceeding under this title.

"(m) The term 'demonstrates' means meets the burdens of production and persuasion.

"(n) The term 'respondent' means an employer, employment agency, labor organization, joint labor-management committee controlling apprenticeship or other training or retraining program, including an on-the-job training program, or Federal entity subject to section 717."

SEC. 105. BURDEN OF PROOF IN DISPARATE IMPACT CASES.

(a) Section 703 of the Civil Rights Act of 1964 (42 U.S.C. 2000e-2) is amended by adding at the end the following new subsection:

"(k)(1)(A) An unlawful employment practice based on disparate impact is established under this title only if -

"(i) a complaining party demonstrates that a respondent uses a particular employment practice that causes a disparate impact on the basis of race, color, religion, sex, or national origin and the respondent fails to demonstrate that the challenged practice is job related for the position in question and consistent with business necessity; or

"(ii) the complaining party makes the demonstration described in subparagraph (C) with respect to an alternative employment practice and the respondent refuses to adopt such alternative employment practice.

"(B)(i) With respect to demonstrating that a particular employment practice causes a disparate impact as described in subparagraph (A)(i), the complaining party shall demonstrate that each particular challenged employment practice causes a disparate impact, except that if the complaining party can demonstrate to the court that the elements of a respondent's decisionmaking process are not capable of separation for analysis, the decisionmaking process may be analyzed as one employment practice.

"(ii) If the respondent demonstrates that a specific employment practice does not cause the disparate impact, the respondent shall not be required to demonstrate that such practice is required by business necessity.

"(C) The demonstration referred to by subparagraph (A)(ii) shall be in accordance with the law as it existed on June 4, 1989, with respect to the concept of 'alternative employment practice'.

"(2) A demonstration that an employment practice is required by business necessity may not be used as a defense against a claim of intentional discrimination under this title.

"(3) Notwithstanding any other provision of this title, a rule barring the employment of an individual who currently and knowingly uses or possesses a controlled substance, as defined in schedules I and II of section 102(6) of the Controlled Substances Act (21 U.S.C. 802(6)), other than the use or possession of a drug taken under the supervision of a licensed health care professional, or any other use or possession authorized by the Controlled Substances Act or any other provision of Federal law, shall be considered an unlawful employment practice under this title only if such rule is adopted or applied with an intent to discriminate because of race, color, religion, sex, or national origin.".

(b) No statements other than the interpretative memorandum appearing at Vol. 137 Congressional Record S 15276 (daily ed. Oct. 25, 1991) shall be considered legislative history of, or relied upon in any way as legislative history in construing or applying, any provision of this Act that relates to Wards Cove - Business necessity/cumulation/alternative business practice.

SEC. 106. PROHIBITION AGAINST DISCRIMINATORY USE OF TEST SCORES.

Section 703 of the Civil Rights Act of 1964 (42 U.S.C. 2000e-2) (as amended by section 105) is further amended by adding at the end the following new subsection:

"(l) It shall be an unlawful employment practice for a respondent, in connection with the selection or referral of applicants or candidates for employment or promotion, to adjust the scores of, use different cutoff scores for, or otherwise alter the results of, employment related tests on the basis of race, color, religion, sex, or national origin.".

SEC. 107. CLARIFYING PROHIBITION AGAINST IMPERMISSIBLE CONSIDERATION OF RACE, COLOR, RELIGION, SEX, OR NATIONAL ORIGIN IN EMPLOYMENT PRACTICES.

(a) In General. - Section 703 of the Civil Rights Act of 1964 (42 U.S.C. 2000e-2) (as amended by sections 105 and 106) is further amended by adding at the end the following new subsection:

"(m) Except as otherwise provided in this title, an unlawful employment practice is established when the complaining party demonstrates that race, color, religion, sex, or national origin was a motivating factor for any employment practice, even though other factors also motivated the practice.".

(b) Enforcement Provisions. - Section 706(g) of such Act (42 U.S.C. 2000e-5(g)) is amended-

(1) by designating the first through third sentences as paragraph (1);

(2) by designating the fourth sentence as paragraph (2)(A) and indenting accordingly; and

(3) by adding at the end the following new subparagraph:

"(B) On a claim in which an individual proves a violation under section 703(m) and a respondent demonstrates that the respondent would have taken the same action in the absence of the impermissible motivating factor, the court -

"(i) may grant declaratory relief, injunctive relief (except as provided in clause (ii)), and attorney's fees and costs demonstrated to be directly attributable only to the pursuit of a claim under section 703(m); and

"(ii) shall not award damages or issue an order requiring any admission, reinstatement, hiring, promotion, or payment, described in subparagraph (A).".

SEC. 108. FACILITATING PROMPT AND ORDERLY RESOLUTION OF CHALLENGES TO EMPLOYMENT PRACTICES IMPLEMENTING LITIGATED OR CONSENT JUDGMENTS OR ORDERS.

Section 703 of the Civil Rights Act of 1964 (42 U.S.C. 2000e-2) (as amended by sections 105, 106, and 107 of this title) is further amended by adding at the end the following new subsection:

"(n)(1)(A) Notwithstanding any other provision of law, and except as provided in paragraph (2), an employment practice that implements and is within the scope of a litigated or consent judgment or order that resolves a claim of employment discrimination under the Constitution or Federal civil rights laws may not be challenged under the circumstances described in subparagraph (B).

"(B) A practice described in subparagraph (A) may not be challenged in a claim under the Constitution or Federal civil rights laws -

"(i) by a person who, prior to the entry of the judgment or order described in subparagraph (A), had -

"(I) actual notice of the proposed judgment or order sufficient to apprise such person that such judgment or order might adversely affect the interests and legal rights of such person and that an opportunity was available to present objections to such judgment or order by a future date certain; and

"(II) a reasonable opportunity to present objections to such judgment or order; or

"(ii) by a person whose interests were adequately represented by another person who had previously challenged the judgment or order on the same legal grounds and with a similar factual situation, unless there has been an intervening change in law or fact.

"(2) Nothing in this subsection shall be construed to -

"(A) alter the standards for intervention under rule 24 of the Federal Rules of Civil Procedure or apply to the rights of parties who have successfully intervened pursuant to such rule in the proceeding in which the parties intervened;

"(B) apply to the rights of parties to the action in which a litigated or consent judgment or order was entered, or of members of a class represented or sought to be represented in such action, or of members of a group on whose behalf relief was sought in such action by the Federal Government;

"(C) prevent challenges to a litigated or consent judgment or order on the ground that such judgment or order was obtained through collusion or fraud, or is transparently invalid or was entered by a court lacking subject matter jurisdiction; or

"(D) authorize or permit the denial to any person of the due process of law required by the Constitution.

"(3) Any action not precluded under this subsection that challenges an employment consent judgment or order described in paragraph (1) shall be brought in the court, and if possible before the judge, that entered such judgment or order. Nothing in this subsection shall preclude a transfer of such action pursuant to section 1404 of title 28, United States Code.".

SEC. 109. PROTECTION OF EXTRATERRITORIAL EMPLOYMENT.

(a) Definition of Employee. - Section 701(f) of the Civil Rights Act of 1964 (42 U.S.C. 2000e(f)) and section 101(4) of the Americans with Disabilities Act of 1990 (42 U.S.C. 12111(4)) are each amended by adding at the end the following: "With respect to employment in a foreign country, such term includes an individual who is a citizen of the United States.".

(b) Exemption. -

(1) Civil rights act of 1964. - Section 702 of the Civil Rights Act of 1964 (42 U.S.C. 2000e-1) isamended -

(A) by inserting "(a)" after "Sec. 702"; and

(B) by adding at the end the following:

"(b) It shall not be unlawful under section 703 or 704 for an employer (or a corporation controlled by an employer), labor organization, employment agency, or joint labor-management committee controlling apprenticeship or other training or retraining (including on-the-job training programs) to take any action otherwise prohibited by such section, with respect to an employee in a workplace in a foreign country if compliance with such section would cause such employer (or such corporation), such organization, such agency, or such committee to violate the law of the foreign country in which such workplace is located.

"(c)(1) If an employer controls a corporation whose place of incorporation is a foreign country, any practice prohibited by section 703 or 704 engaged in by such corporation shall be presumed to be engaged in by such employer.

"(2) Sections 703 and 704 shall not apply with respect to the foreign person not controlled by an American employer.

"(3) For purposes of this subsection, the determination of whether an employer controls a corporation shall be based on -

"(A) the interrelation of operations;

"(B) the common management;

"(C) the centralized control of labor relations; and

"(D) the common ownership or financial control, of the employer and the corporation.".

(2) Americans with disabilities act of 1990. - Section 102 of the Americans with Disabilities Act of 1990 (42 U.S.C. 12112) is amended -

(A) by redesignating subsection (c) as subsection (d); and

(B) by inserting after subsection (b) the following new subsection:

"(c) Covered Entities in Foreign Countries. -

"(I) In general. - It shall not be unlawful under this section for a covered entity to take any action that constitutes discrimination under this section with respect to an employee in a workplace in a foreign country if compliance with this section would cause such covered entity to violate the law of the foreign country in which such workplace is located.

"(2) Control of corporation. -

"(A) Presumption. - If an employer controls a corporation whose place of incorporation is a foreign country, any practice that constitutes discrimination under this section and is engaged in by such corporation shall be presumed to be engaged in by such employer.

"(B) Exception. - This section shall not apply with respect to the foreign operations of an employer that is a foreign person not controlled by an American employer.

"(C) Determination. - For purposes of this paragraph, the determination of whether an employer controls a corporation shall be based on -

"(i) the interrelation of operations;

"(ii) the common management;

"(iii) the centralized control of labor relations; and

"(iv) the common ownership or financial control, of the employer and the corporation.".

(c) Application of Amendments. - The amendments made by this section shall not apply with respect to conduct occurring before the date of the enactment of this Act.

SEC. 110. TECHNICAL ASSISTANCE TRAINING INSTITUTE.

(a) Technical Assistance. - Section 705 of the Civil Rights Act of 1964 (42 U.S.C. 2000e-4) is amended by adding at the end the following new subsection:

"(i)(1) The Commission shall establish a Technical Assistance Training Institute, through which the Commission shall provide technical assistance and training regarding the laws and regulations enforced by the Commission.

"(2) An employer or other entity covered under this title shall not be excused from compliance with the requirements of this title because of any failure to receive technical assistance under this subsection.

"(3) There are authorized to be appropriated to carry out this subsection such sums as may be necessary for fiscal year 1992.".

(b) Effective Date. - The amendment made by this section shall take effect on the date of the enactment of this Act.

SEC. 111. EDUCATION AND OUTREACH.

Section 705(h) of the Civil Rights At of 1964 (42 U.S.C. 2000e-4(h) is amended -

(1) by inserting "(1)" after "(h)"; and

(2) by adding at the end the following new paragraph:

"(2) In exercising its powers under this title, the Commission shall carry out educational and outreach activities (including dissemination of information in languages other than English) targeted to -

"(A) individuals who historically have been victims of employment discrimination and have not been equitably served by the Commission; and

"(B) individuals on whose behalf the Commission has authority to enforce any other law prohibiting employment discrimination, concerning rights and obligations under this title or such law, as the case may be.".

SEC. 112. EXPANSION OF RIGHT TO CHALLENGE DISCRIMINATORY SENIORITY SYSTEMS.

Section 706(e) of the Civil Rights Act of 1964 (42 U.S.C. 2000e-5(e)) is amended -

(1) by inserting "(1)" before "A charge under this section"; and

(2) by adding at the end the following new paragraph:

"(2) For purposes of this section, an unlawful employment practice occurs, with respect to a seniority system that has been adopted for an intentionally discriminatory purpose in violation of this title (whether or not that discriminatory purpose is apparent on the face of the seniority provision), when the seniority system is adopted, when an individual becomes subject to the seniority system, or when a person aggrieved is injured by the application of the seniority system or provision of the system.".

SEC. 113. AUTHORIZING AWARD OF EXPERT FEES.

(a) Revised Statutes. - Section 722 of the Revised Statutes is amended -

(1) by designating the first and second sentences as subsections (a) and (b), respectively, and indenting accordingly; and

(2) by adding at the end the following new subsection:

"(c) In awarding an attorney's fee under subsection (b) in any action or proceeding to enforce a provision of sections 1977 or 1977A of the Revised Statutes, the court, in its discretion, may include expert fees as part of the attorney's fee.".

(b) Civil Rights Act of 1964. - Section 706(k) of the Civil Rights Act of 1964 (42 U.S.C. 2000e-5(k)) is amended by inserting "(including expert fees)" after "attorney's fee".

SEC. 114. PROVIDING FOR INTEREST AND EXTENDING THE STATUTE OF LIMITATIONS IN ACTIONS AGAINST THE FEDERAL GOVERNMENT.

Section 717 of the Civil Rights Act of 1964 (42 U.S.C. 2000e-16) is amended -

(1) in subsection (c), by striking "thirty days" and inserting '90 days'; and

(2) in subsection (d), by inserting before the period ", and the same interest to compensate for delay in payment shall be available as in cases involving nonpublic parties.".

SEC. 115. NOTICE OF LIMITATIONS PERIOD UNDER THE AGE DISCRIMINATION IN EMPLOYMENT ACT OF 1967.

Section 7(e) of the Age Discrimination in Employment Act of 1967 (29 U.S.C. 626(e)) is amended -

(1) by striking paragraph (2);

(2) by striking the paragraph designation in paragraph (1);

(3) by striking "Sections 6 and" and inserting "Section"; and

(4) by adding at the end the following: "If a charge filed with the Commission under this Act is dismissed or the proceedings of the Commission are otherwise terminated by the Commission, the Commission shall notify the person aggrieved. A civil action may be brought under this section by a person defined in section 11(a) against the respondent named in the charge within 90 days after the date of the receipt of such notice.".

SEC. 116. LAWFUL COURT-ORDERED REMEDIES, AFFIRMATIVE ACTION, AND CONCILIATION AGREEMENTS NOT AFFECTED.

Nothing in the amendments made by this title shall be construed to affect court-ordered remedies, affirmative action, or conciliation agreements, that are in accordance with the law.

SEC. 117. COVERAGE OF HOUSE OF REPRESENTATIVES AND THE AGENCIES OF THE LEGISLATIVE BRANCH.

(a) Coverage of the House of Representatives. -

(1) In general. - Notwithstanding any provision of title VII of the Civil Rights Act of 1964 (42 U.S.C. 2000e et seq.) or of other law, the purposes of such title shall, subject to paragraph (2), apply in their entirety to the House of Representatives.

(2) Employment in the house.-

(A) Application. - The rights and protections under title VII of the Civil Rights Act of 1964 (42 U.S.C. 2000e et seq.) shall, subject to subparagraph (B), apply with respect to any employee in an employment position in the House of Representatives and any employing authority of the House of Representatives.

(B) Administration. -

(i) In general. - In the administration of this paragraph, the remedies and procedures made applicable pursuant to the resolution described in clause (ii) shall apply exclusively.

(ii) Resolution. - The resolution referred to in clause (i) is the Fair Employment Practices Resolution (House Resolution 558 of the One Hundredth Congress, as agreed to October 4, 1988), as incorporated into the Rules of the House of Representatives of the One Hundred Second Congress as Rule LI, or any other provision that continues in effect the provisions of such resolution.

(C) Exercise of rulemaking power. - The provisions of subparagraph (B) are enacted by the House of Representatives as an exercise of the rulemaking power of the House of Representatives, with full recognition of the right of the House to change its rules, in the same manner, and to the same extent as in the case of any other rule of the House.

(b) Instrumentalities of Congress.-

(1) In general. - The rights and protections under this title and title VII of the Civil Rights Act of 1964 (42 U.S.C. 2000e et seq.) shall, subject to paragraph (2), apply with respect to the conduct of each instrumentality of the Congress.

(2) Establishment of remedies and procedures by instrumentalities. - The chief official of each instrumentality of the Congress shall establish remedies and procedures to be utilized with respect to the rights and protections provided pursuant to paragraph (1). Such remedies and procedures shall apply exclusively, except for the employees who are defined as Senate employees, in section 301(c)(1).

(3) Report to Congress. - The chief official of each instrumentality of the Congress shall, after establishing remedies and procedures for purposes of paragraph (2), submit to the Congress a report describing the remedies and procedures.

(4) Definition of instrumentalities. - For purposes of this section, instrumentalities of the Congress include the following: The Architect of the Capitol, the Congressional Budget Office, the General Accounting Office, the Government Printing Office, the Office of Technology Assessment, and the United States Botanic Garden.

(5) Construction. - Nothing in this section shall alter the enforcement procedures for individuals protected under section 717 of title VII for the Civil Rights Act of 1964 (42 U.S.C. 2000e-16).

SEC. 118. ALTERNATIVE MEANS OF DISPUTE RESOLUTION.

Where appropriate and to the extent authorized by law, the use of alternative means of dispute resolution, including settlement negotiations, conciliation, facilitation, mediation, fact finding, minitrials, and arbitration, is encouraged to resolve disputes arising under the Acts or provisions of Federal law amended by this title.

APPENDIX C

EEOC v. Hertz, Amicus Brief in Support of Plaintiff EEOC

PETER DAVID BLANCK (Mass. Bar No. 548686)
Professor of Law, Preventive Medicine, and Psychology, University of Iowa.
Director of Law, Health Policy and Disability Center.
(319) 335-9043

SID WOLINSKY (Cal. Bar No. 33716)
Director of Litigation
Disability Rights Advocates
1999 Harrison Street; Suite 1760
Oakland, CA 94612
(510) 273-8644

Assisted by Noah D. Lebowitz
Admitted in New York and New Jersey

UNITED STATES DISTRICT COURT
EASTERN DISTRICT OF MICHIGAN
SOUTHERN DIVISION

EQUAL EMPLOYMENT OPPORTUNITY COMMISSION,

Plaintiff,

v.

THE HERTZ CORPORATION,

Defendant,

and

THE HERTZ CORPORATION
Third-Party Plaintiff,

v.

ARKAY, INC.,

Third-Party Defendant
________________________________/

CASE NO. 96-CV-72421 DT

HONORABLE JOHN FEIKENS

MAGISTRATE JUDGE TOMAS A. CARLSON

AMICUS BRIEF IN SUPPORT OF PLAINTIFF EEOC

TABLE OF CONTENTS

TABLE OF AUTHORITIES

CASES:

Circuit Court Cases:

Supreme Court Cases:

I. Introduction

The importance of this case cannot be overstated. Supported employment in this country has led people with mental retardation from the nightmare of state-funded institutionalization to the freedom and efficiency of the private-sector workplace. This transformation of people from tax burdens to tax payers has resulted in dramatically enhancing the quality of life for people with mental retardation. At the same time, countless employers in both small businesses and large corporations have benefitted from their efficient, dedicated, and hard-working employees with disabilities. Accordingly, ruling in favor of the defendant Hertz Corporation ("Hertz") in the context of a summary judgment motion would effectively set back some of the most important gains made by men and women with mental retardation in the last two decades.

To place this case in perspective, it is important to remember the history of people with mental retardation in this country. With the blessing of the courts, people with mental retardation were once routinely institutionalized and sterilized. Oliver Wendell Holmes even endorsed the notion of sterilizing people with mental retardation for the "good of society."

> We have seen more than once that the public welfare may call upon the best citizens for their lives. It would be strange if it could not call upon those who already sap the strength of the state for these lesser sacrifices, often not felt to be such by those concerned, in order to prevent our being swamped with incompetence. It is better for all the world, if instead of waiting to execute degenerate offspring for their imbecility, society can prevent those who are manifestly unfit from continuing their kind.

Buck v. Bell, 274 U.S. 200, 207 (1927).

As one historian noted, "Viewed in professional circles and in the popular media as incompetent, child-like potential parents, morons and high-grade imbeciles were sterilized to make them ready for community placement or parole, a new policy to relieve the crowded conditions of public institutions..."[1] James W. Trent, Jr., *Inventing the Feeble Mind, A History of the Mental Retardation in the United States* 202 (1994). Slowly, and only after the horrors of life inside institutions were finally brought to the public's and the judiciary's attention in the period of 1965 to 1975, the walls of custodial institutions have crumbled in favor of assisted and independent living. *See* Stanley S. Herr, *Rights and Advocacy for Retarded People* 5, 45-48 (1983). With this development came community-supported work programs.

Supported employment programs, which have evolved and been tested over many years and hundreds of job sites, create a mutually-beneficial relationship between employers and people with mental retardation. They have received positive evaluations from employers and have provided documented positive outcomes for participating employees. Paul Wehman et al., *Supported Employment: A Decade of Rapid Growth and Impact, in Supported Employment Research: Expanding Competitive Employment Opportunities for Persons with Significant Disabilities*[1] (Paul Wehman et al. eds., 1997). Accordingly, the popularity of such programs has risen steadily since their inception. *Id.* The results have been remarkable: supported employment programs have provided work opportunities to over 140,000 individuals with severe disabilities who were previously excluded from the workforce. John Kregel et al., *Introduction—The Myths & Realities of Supported Employment, in Supported Employment Research,* at i.

A. Employers Receive Substantial Benefit from Supported Employment

Numerous studies of employers participating in supported employment programs demonstrate that employers view the programs and participating employees very favorably. An Oklahoma survey of 47 firms of varying sizes found that "employers maintain very positive views of the contributions and abilities of their employees with disabilities." Peter D. Blanck, *The Emerging Work Force: Empirical Study of the Americans with Disabilities Act,* 16 J. Corp. L. 693, 773

---

[1] Obviously the terms "incompetent," "moron," and "imbecile" are outdated and offensive to modern society. Trent used these terms in this excerpt because they "reveal in their honesty the sensibilities of the people who used them and the meanings they attached to mental retardation." Trent, *Inventing the Feeble Mind,* at 5.

(1991). Specifically, employers report high levels of satisfaction with their employees with mental retardation on work attendance, productivity, dedication and initiative. *Id.* at 775. The Oklahoma survey also showed that the employers have high levels of satisfaction with employee interactions with co-workers and with customers. *Id.* The majority of employers indicated that employees with mental retardation did not exhibit higher turnover rates or higher absenteeism rates than non-disabled employees. *Id.* at 778. Overall, most of the employers in the study rated their employees with mental retardation as "excellent or good in their overall job performance, willing to work hard and take the initiative, as punctual, and as productive." *Id.* at 775-76. Further research indicates that the vast majority of supported employment participants achieve acceptable work performance standards. John Kregel et al., *The Impact of Behavioral Deficits on Employment Retention: An Illustration from Supported Employment, in New Directions in Supported Employment,* (Paule Wehman & John Kregel eds., 1994) at 69, 76. Moreover, very large well-known corporations such as Marriott, Burger King, and McDonalds have used supported employment to good effect. These corporations report lower rates of turnover, less need for retraining, and other substantial benefits because of their employees who utilize supported employment.

Job coaches are crucial to the success of supported employment programs. The provision of job coaches may form the central component of most such programs. Blanck, *The Emerging Work Force,* at 777. Employment providers, such as vocational services managers, directors of community services, and project directors of supported employment programs, consider the availability of job coaches to be a significant factor for the success of integrated employment programs. Peter David Blanck, *Empirical Study of the Employment Provisions of the Americans with Disabilities Act: Methods, Preliminary Findings, and Implications,* 22 N.M. L. Rev. 119, 232 (1992). Specifically, supported employment provides benefits to both employers and employees without incurring higher costs. For example, 91% of the employers surveyed in Oklahoma did not believe that making workplace accommodations for employees with disabilities was too expensive. Blanck, *The Emerging Work Force,* at 778. Additionally, a state-by-state comparison of supported employment services to other day service options, including sheltered workshops or activity centers, indicates that the cost for supported employment services is 20% to 60% less than the costs of the other options. John Kregel et al., *Introduction—The Myths & Realities of Supported Employment, in Supported Employment Research,* at i, ii.

B. Supported Employment Provides Numerous Benefits to the Employees

"[M]ost needs of people labeled mentally retarded are the same as those of people not labeled mentally, retarded: meaningful work and economic security, fulfilling personal and community relations, dignity and a measure of control over one's life." Trent, *Inventing the Feeble Mind,* at 274. It is difficult to overstate the benefits provided to the society of individuals with mental retardation; some such benefits cannot easily be quantified. The transformation of self-esteem that occurs in a person who, once regarded as an outcast by society, becomes a productive, contributing member of that society has profound consequences. Even being able to perform some of the daily tasks found mundane by most people, like paying bills, brings feelings of self-worth to people who have never been allowed to do so in the past. The income that supported employment brings to people with mental retardation enables them to participate in the economy, be consumers, and experience the rights and privileges of citizenship.

Supported employment has significantly increased the wages and earning power of people with disabilities. W. Grant Revell et al., *Supported Employment for Persons with Severe Disabilities: Positive Trends in Wages, Models, and Funding, in New Directions,* at 30, 32-35; *see also* John Kregel et al., *The Impact of Behavioral Deficits on Employment Retention: An Illustration from Supported Employment, in New Directions,* at 69, 71. In addition to the significant economic benefits, research indicates that supported employment greatly enhances participants' overall quality of life. Employees participating in supported employment report that they like their jobs and are highly satisfied both with their work experiences and the assistance provided by their job coaches. Wendy Parent et al, *The Role of the Job Coach: Orchestrating Community & Workplace Supports, in New Directions,* at 40. Studies of adults with mental retardation living in Oklahoma from

1990 to 1993 found that employed participants experienced significant improvement in their capabilities, qualifications, and level of inclusion and empowerment in society. Peter D. Blanck, *Employment Integration, Economic Opportunity, and The Americans with Disabilities Act: Empirical Study from 1990-1993,* 79 Iowa L. Rev. 853, 860 (1994). Additionally, supported employment programs create beneficial employment outcomes for individuals with disabilities in the areas of consumer satisfaction, job placements, favorable employer perceptions, and effective support strategies. Wehman et. al, *Supported Employment: A Decade of Rapid Growth, in Supported Employment Research,* at 2. Indeed, "[g]oing to a real job, getting paid, having coworkers, and getting into a normal daily work routine are critical aspects of life. Too many persons with significant disabilities are needlessly left out of the experience. Supported employment is an approach with the demonstrated ability to definitely reverse this unnecessary lack of employment." *Id.* at 16.

In sum, supported employment is an all-around success. It benefits employers and employees alike, and thus, society as a whole. Moreover, supported employment has been a documented success model for continuing our national policy of moving people from the welfare rolls to the workforce. Hertz' approach to this entire matter, from the hiring of Klem and Miller to the filing of this motion for summary judgment, has been completely out of step with modern society and sound public policy as well as applicable statutes.

II. The Analysis Presented by Hertz Is Erroneous and Inapplicable; This Action Is Based on a Failure to Accommodate, Not on Disparate Treatment

The analysis presented to the Court by Hertz is thoroughly misleading. Hertz has both misstated and misapplied the relevant substantive law governing this case. This case does *not* involve a disparate treatment claim. This case *does* involve a claim of failure to accommodate. These constitute two distinct types of claims. The EEOC guidelines also make this clear. In explaining disparate treatment, the regulations provide the following analysis.

> Disparate treatment means, with respect to title I of the ADA, that an individual was treated differently on the basis of his or her disability. For example, disparate treatment has occurred where an employer excludes an employee with a severe facial disfigurement from staff meetings because the employer does not like to look at the employee. The individual is being treated differently because of the employer's attitude towards his or her perceived disability.

29 C.F.R. pt. 1630, app. § 1630.15(a). In explaining the notion of reasonable accommodation, the regulations state:

> The reasonable accommodation requirement is best understood as a means by which barriers to the equal employment opportunity of an individual with a disability are removed or alleviated. These barriers may, for example, be physical or structural obstacles. . . . Or they may be rigid work schedules that permit no flexibility as to when work is performed or when breaks may be taken, or inflexible job procedures that unduly limit the modes of communication that are used on the job, or the way in which particular tasks are accomplished.

29 C.F.R. pt. 1630, app. § 1630.9. Moreover, under section 1613.15 "Defenses," the regulations set forth separate subsections for "Disparate treatment charges" and "Charges of not making a reasonable accommodation." *See* 29 C.F.R. § 1630.15(a),(d). The section explaining the defenses to a disparate treatment charge incorporates the familiar *McDonnell Douglas / Burdine* burden shifting framework. In contrast, the section explaining the defenses to not making a reasonable accommodation details only the defense of undue hardship. Thus, the burden-shifting framework articulated by Hertz is not the controlling law and any application of such law would lead to reversible error.

The case law interpreting the above regulations reaches the same conclusion. Hertz correctly cites the case of *Monette v. Electronic Data Systems Corp.,* 90 F.3d 1173 (6th Cir. 1996), as stating the burden-shifting framework in a disparate treatment claim in the disability context. However, Hertz fails to disclose to the Court that the *Monette* case, and others cited by Hertz, involve claims where plaintiffs argue that they were treated differently from other employees. The Hertz analysis ignores the critical fact that Donald Klem and Kenneth Miller are arguing that Hertz discriminated against them by failing to accommodate their known disabilities.

Specifically, Klem and Miller argue that Hertz violated the Americans with Disabilities Act by

> not making reasonable accommodations to the known physical or mental limitations of an otherwise qualified individual with a disability who is an applicant or an employee, unless [the employer] can demonstrate that the accommodation would impose an undue hardship on the operation of the business of such covered entity; or
>
> denying employment opportunities to a job applicant or employee who is an otherwise qualified individual with a disability, if such denial is based on the need of such covered entity to make reasonable accommodation to the physical or mental impairments of the employee or applicant.

42 U.S.C. § 12112(b)(5)(A),(B); *see* Complaint ¶ 8. As the Seventh Circuit recognized, "[i]f it is true that [the employer] should have reasonably accommodated [the plaintiff's] disability and did not, [the employer] has discriminated against him. *There is no need for indirect proof or burden shifting.*" *Bultemeyer v. Fort Wayne Community Schools,* 100 F.3d 1281, 1283 (7th Cir. 1996) (emphasis added).

Thus, to ultimately prevail in this case, the plaintiffs must demonstrate that:

(1) Klem and Miller were each qualified individuals with a disability;
(2) Klem and Miller were each able to perform the essential functions of their positions with or without reasonable accommodation; and
(3) Klem and Miller were each denied a reasonable accommodation.

See Bultemeyer, 100 F.3d at 1284; *Roush v. WEASTEC, Inc.,* 96 F.3d 840, 843 (6th Cir. 1996); *see also Borkowski v. Valley Central Sch. Dist.,* 63 F.3d 131, 135 (2d Cir. 1995) (Calabresi, J.).

III. Numerous Major Genuine Issues of Material Fact Remain in Dispute, Rendering Summary Judgment Wholly Inappropriate for this Case

Summary judgment is only appropriate in those rare instances where there exist no genuine issues of material fact. Fed.R.Civ.P. 56(c); *Anderson v. Liberty Lobby, Inc.,* 477 U.S. 242 (1986). This case presents not one, but several genuine issues of material fact which remain in dispute. Any single one of these issues would require denial of a motion for summary judgment; taken together, these issues make summary judgment completely inappropriate at this stage of the litigation.

Additionally, as this is a motion brought by Hertz, this Court must examine the facts in the light most favorable to Klem and Miller. *Hartsel v. Keys,* 87 F.3d 795, 799 (6th Cir. 1996), cert. den., — U.S. —, 117 S.Ct. 683 (1997) (citing *Matsushita Elec. Indus. Co., Ltd. v. Zenith Radio Corp.,* 475 U.S. 574, 587 (1986)); *Anderson,* 477 U.S. at 255. As a result, this Court also should construe the lack of disciplinary action or complaint against Klem or Miller as further evidence that they adequately performed the essential functions of their jobs.

A. Determining Whether a Particular Accommodation Is Reasonable in a Particular Job Setting Is a Question of Fact, Not Properly Decided on Summary Judgment When, as Here, the Facts Are in Dispute.

Numerous courts have found that the question of whether a particular accommodation is reasonable is a question of fact. In a motion for summary judgment, if a question of fact cannot be firmly established by the moving party, the motion must be denied. Each element of Klem and Miller's ADA claim is a question of fact. *Feliberty v. Kemper Corp.,* 98 F.3d 274, 277 (7th Cir. 1996); *Borkowski,* 63 F.3d at 138; *Pandazides v. Virginia Bd. of Educ.,* 13 F.3d 823, 833 (4th Cir. 1994). As one court articulated, whether a handicapped person is otherwise qualified, and consequently whether the accommodations are reasonable, are questions of fact. So we can affirm the lower court's findings only if reasonable men could not differ from the conclusions that the [plaintiff's school] provided reasonable accommodations and McGregor was not otherwise qualified.

McGregor v. Louisiana State Univ. Bd. of Supervisors, 3 F.3d 850, 855 (5th Cir. 1993), cert. den., — U.S. —, 114 S.Ct. 1103 (1994).[2] More-

---

[2] Although this case dealt with Section 504 in the education context, the terminology is identical to the ADA and is meant to be interpreted alike.

The genuine issues of material fact which remain in dispute include:

PLAINTIFF'S CONTENTIONS	DEFENDANT'S CONTENTIONS
1) With the reasonable accommodation of their job coach, Klem and Miller performed the essential functions of their jobs and were gradually given increasing responsibility. *Plaintiff's Brief,* at 1, 3-4.	1) Klem and Miller could not perform the essential functions of their job, even with a reasonable accommodation. **Defendant's Brief,** at 6, 9-10.
2) Klem and Miller were employees of Hertz Corporation. *Id.* at 2.	2) Klem and Miller were under the auspices of Arkay, Inc. at all times. *Id.* at 3.
3) Hertz failed to engage in the "interactive process" mandated by the ADA's implementing regulations, and case law. *Id.* at 14-16.	3) Hertz acted in good faith in its accommodation of Klem and Miller and Arkay frustrated the process by demanding the accommodation of its choice. *Id.* at 3-4, 15-17.
4) Wellman had personal experience from which he knew that other job support organizations existed. *Id.* at 6.	4) Hertz did not know of any other supported employment provider. Id. at 5-6.
5) Klem and Miller's duties were previously performed by other "casual" employees. *Id.* at 1.	5) Hertz never employed people to do trash pick-up. *Id.* at 1.
6) No criticism was ever directed towards either Klem or Miller's job performance. *Id.* at 3.	6) Klem's disabilities resulted in his engaging in misconduct for which other employees would have been disciplined. *Id.* at 4.
7) Hertz acted in bad faith. *Id.* at 19.	7) Hertz acted charitably and in good faith. *Id.* at 1.
8) A full-time job coach, provided at no cost to Hertz, is a reasonable accommodation. *Id.* at 16-18.	8) Applicable case law and regulations establish that a full-time job coach is not a reasonable accommodation. *Id.* at 12-15.
9) Klem and Miller were employed for a period beyond any temporary trial period and met Hertz' expectations and their duties were expanding. *Id.* at 3, 11.	9) Klem and Miller were employed for an indeterminate trial period. *Id.* at 2-3.

over, "the question of whether an employer has provided a 'reasonable accommodation' is ordinarily a question of fact." *Frye v. Aspin,* 997 F.2d 426, 428-29 (8th Cir. 1993).

The Second Circuit, in the *Borkowski* case, engaged in a thoughtful and thorough analysis of summary judgment standards in a failure to accommodate case. In reversing a district court's grant of summary judgment to the employer, the court elaborated on the terms "reasonable" accommodation, essential job functions, and undue hardship. That court first recognized that "'Reasonable' is a relational term: it evaluates the desirability of a particular accommodation according to the consequences that the accommodation will produce." 63 F.3d at 138. The plaintiff in *Borkowski* was a school teacher who, due to her disability, experienced difficulty controlling her classroom. *Id.* at 134. To enable performance of the essential functions of her job, the plaintiff proposed the accommodation of allocating a teacher's aide to assist her in the classroom. *Id.* at 140. The court found that "once the plaintiff has introduced evidence that an accommodation exists that permits her to perform the job at the same level as a non-disabled employee, *a fact question has been created.*" *Id.* at 141 (citation omitted) (emphasis added). Applying this standard, the Second Circuit held:

> Ms. Borkowski has introduced evidence that an accommodation — provision of an aide — is available and would allow her to perform the essential functions of a tenured library teacher. Ms. Borkowski therefore has established, as a *prima facie* matter, that an effective accommodation exists. The School District to date has not brought in any evidence that would permit a court to rule as a matter of law that Ms. Borkowski's performance would be inadequate even with the proposed accommodation or that the accommodation would eliminate the essential functions of the job. Accordingly, an issue of fact remains as to whether Ms. Borkowski's proposed accommodation would render her otherwise qualified.

Id. at 141-42.

The case here presents an even more convincing scenario for the plaintiffs than in *Borkowski*. In *Borkowski,* the court was forced to speculate as to whether the plaintiff's proposed accommodation would enable her to perform the essential functions of her job. By contrast, this Court is in a unique position: the plaintiffs have already worked for three months with the proposed accommodation to prove that they successfully fulfilled the essential functions of their jobs. Klem and Miller have introduced evidence that the provision of a job coach, at no expense to Hertz, enabled them to perform the essential functions of their jobs. To date, Hertz has not produced evidence sufficient to sustain summary judgment that would permit a court to rule as a matter of law that Klem and Miller's accommodation would be inadequate or would eliminate an essential function of their jobs. As the reasonableness of the proposed accommodation is a material issue in this case, there remains a genuine issue of material fact in dispute.

B. Hertz Failed in Its Duty to Engage in Good Faith in the Interactive Process Required by the ADA's Implementing Regulations and Case Law.

By Hertz' own admission, it absolutely failed in its obligation to engage in the interactive process mandated by the ADA's implementing regulations and case law interpreting the meaning of that process. The deposition testimony of Mr. Lamb makes this proposition abundantly clear.

> Q: To the best of your knowledge, did the company make any effort to accommodate Mr. Klem and Mr. Miller after it decided to sever its relationship with Arkay?
>
> * * *
>
> A: No.

Lamb Dep. at 67.

The implementing regulations specifically address the role of the interactive process.

> Once a qualified individual with a disability has requested provision of a reasonable accommodation, the employer must make a reasonable effort to determine the appropriate accommodation. The appropriate reasonable accommodation is best determined through a *flexible, interactive process that involves both the employer and the qualified individual with a disability.*

29 C.F.R. pt. 1630, app. § 1630.9 (emphasis added). The regulations even set out an ideal framework within which this interactive process is to take place.

> When a qualified individual with a disability has requested a reasonable accommodation to assist in the performance of a job, the employer, using a problem solving approach, should:
>
> (1) Analyze the particular job involved and determine its purpose and essential functions;
>
> (2) Consult with the individual with a disability to ascertain the precise job-related limitations imposed by the individual's disability and how those limitations could be overcome with a reasonable accommodation;
>
> (3) In consultation with the individual to be accommodated, identify potential accommodations and assess the effectiveness each would have in enabling the individual to perform the essential functions of the position; and

(4) Consider the preference of the individual to be accommodated and select and implement the accommodation that is most appropriate for both the employee and the employer.

Id. Hertz admitted that it did absolutely nothing in the way of engaging in this interactive process, and has thereby not complied with their obligations under the regulations.

Applicable case law further demonstrates Hertz' failure. Courts have found that when an employer knows of an employee's disability and what would enable that employee to perform the essential functions of his job, that employer has an absolute duty to engage in the interactive process. *Bombard v. Fort Wayne Newspapers, Inc.*, 92 F.3d 560, 563 (7th Cir. 1996); *Bultemeyer,* 100 F.3d at 1285. There is no question that Hertz knew of Klem and Miller's disabilities. There is also no question that Hertz knew precisely what type of accommodation would enable Klem and Miller to perform the essential functions of their jobs. Thus, Hertz had an independent duty to engage in the interactive process. Moreover, even though they were under absolutely no obligation to do so, Klem and Miller (through Arkay, Inc.) actually *initiated* this interactive process. On June 13, 1994, the Executive Director of Arkay, Inc., Gregory Sundell, sent a letter to Hertz asking them to " reconsider your termination of employees Donald Klem and Ken Miller." 6/13/94 Sundell Letter to Hertz. Displaying a complete absence of good faith, Hertz failed to respond to this letter. As the Seventh Circuit explained,

> [C]ourts should look for signs of failure to participate in good faith or failure by one of the parties to help the other party determine what specific accommodations are necessary. A party that obstructs or delays the interactive process is not acting in good faith. *A party that fails to communicate, by way of initiation or response, may also be acting in bad faith. In essence, courts should attempt to isolate the cause of the breakdown and then assign responsibility.*

Beck v. University of Wisconsin Bd. of Regents, 75 F.3d 1130, 1135 (7th Cir. 1996) (emphasis added). The blame for the breakdown of the interactive process lies entirely upon Hertz. Hertz, however, denies any responsibility for the breakdown. As such, another genuine issue of material fact remains in dispute.

C. A Full-time Job Coach, Employed at No Expense to Hertz, Constitutes a Reasonable Accommodation

The newly approved EEOC guidelines for the application of Title I of the ADA to individuals with psychiatric disabilities, addresses this particular question:

> 27. Is it a reasonable accommodation to provide a job coach?
>
> *Yes.* An employer may be required to provide a temporary job coach to assist in the training of a qualified individual with a disability as a reasonable accommodation, barring undue hardship. An employer also may be required to allow a job coach paid by a public or private social service agency to accompany the employee at the job site as a reasonable accommodation.

EEOC Enforcement Guidance on the Americans with Disabilities Act and Psychiatric Disabilities, at 27 (citations omitted) (emphasis added). Thus, in the overwhelming number of situations, supported employment will constitute a reasonable accommodation. In adopting this regulation, the EEOC merely recognized the reality of the marketplace — supported employment works for both the employee and the employer. *See supra* § I. Employees using supported employment generally have lower absenteeism rates, have lower turnover rates, fill positions that many people consider "undesirable," and in many cases have lower salary requirements than those not using supported employment. It would be the rare occasion that supported employment might not constitute a reasonable accommodation. If that determination were made, it would necessarily be based on specific facts discerned at trial, not at the summary judgment stage.

The concept of reasonable accommodation is inextricably linked to an economic analysis; weighing the costs of the accommodation against the resources of the employer and the benefit received from employment. Notably, the statutorily enumerated defense of undue hardship is stated in economic terms. *See* 29 C.F.R. pt.1630, app. § 1630.15(d) ("to demonstrate that the cost of an accommodation poses an undue hardship, an employer would have to show that the cost is undue as compared to the employer's budget."). As the *Borkowski* court noted, "undue' hardship…looks not merely to the costs that the employer is asked to assume, but also to the benefits to others that will result." 63 F.3d at 139 (citation omitted). Hertz has made no claim of undue hardship. Even if it now asserts such a claim, that determination requires a highly fact-based analysis which Hertz has not equipped this Court to do at this stage of the litigation.

> [A]n employer cannot simply assert that a needed accommodation will cause it undue hardship, as defined in § 1630.2(p), and thereupon be relieved of the duty to provide a reasonable accommodation. Rather, an employer will have to present evidence and demonstrate that the accommodation will, in fact, cause it undue hardship. Whether a particular accommodation will impose an undue hardship for a particular employer is determined on a case by case basis. Consequently, an accommodation that poses an undue hardship for one employer at a particular time may not pose an undue hardship for another employer, or even for the same employer at another time.

29 C.F.R. pt. 1630, § 1630.15(d). However, a quick review of the current situation reveals that Hertz cannot possibly prevail in any such economic balancing analysis. Hertz is a large corporation with thousands of employees. Klem and Miller's job coaches were provided at *no cost* to Hertz. When balancing the benefit of Klem and Miller's contribution to the Airport Rental Operation location against the cost to Hertz (*ie.* zero), there can be no conclusion that accommodating Klem and Miller constitutes an undue hardship.

Hertz also misreads the applicable section of the EEOC regulations regarding the use of job coaches and supported employment. Hertz attempts to hang its hat on the sentence: "The term 'supported employment'... is not synonymous with reasonable accommodation." 29 C.F.R. pt. 1630, app. § 1630.9. Hertz attaches a different meaning to this sentence than is obviously intended. Simply put, this sentence means that the provision of a job coach is not *per se* a reasonable accommodation in every case. It hardly means that a job coach can *never* constitute a reasonable accommodation. Moreover, in light of the newly adopted regulations, such an interpretation cannot carry any weight.

V. The Termination of Employees with Disabilities Because of Conduct of a Third Party Which Is in No Way the Employees' Fault, Is a Violation of Both the ADA and Common Law Employment Concepts

There is one issue that remains absolutely *un*disputed: Klem and Miller were not terminated based on their conduct, but that of Arkay's job coaches.

In making this motion, Hertz asks the Court to endorse a concept that completely redefines the entire legal relationship between employers and employees. This redefinition also would thwart the entire meaning of the ADA as well as countless other state and federal statutes regulating the employer-employee relationship. Hertz terminated Klem and Miller because of the conduct of third parties. In totally disavowing any responsibility towards Klem and Miller, who are blameless, Hertz offends fundamental notions of justice and willfully ignores its obligations as defined by the ADA. A court endorsement of this action by Hertz would lead to immediate and absurd results. Should a deaf person be terminated for the misconduct of his or her sign language interpreter? Will an employer be permitted to fire a wheelchair using employee because a third party built a ramp incorrectly? The approach taken by Hertz not only offends traditional employer-employee relations, but it also defies the stated intent of the ADA: "[T]o provide clear, strong, consistent, enforceable standards addressing discrimination against individuals with disabilities." 42 U.S.C. § 12101(b)(1). Hertz attempts to rely on a defense of alleged misconduct of a third party which does not exist in the ADA.

VI. Conclusion

Hertz' concept and approach to this matter runs directly contrary to the stated purpose of the ADA. Further, the tenor of its brief evidences Hertz' fundamental misunderstanding of what this bipartisan federal statute requires. The ADA, legislation sponsored by Senators Dole and Kennedy and signed into law by President Bush, represents a decisive, nonpartisan statement of Congress that people with disabilities are not to be treated as objects of charity. Rather, people with disabilities are to be treated as individuals with all of the privileges of American citizenship. Hertz' brief opens with the statement "no good deed goes unpunished." Hertz is not governed by rules of charity; it is subject to statutory requirements. Hertz did not do a good deed here; Hertz violated federal law.

For all the foregoing reasons, Hertz' motion for summary judgment should be denied.

Respectfully submitted,

____

PETER DAVID BLANCK
(Mass. Bar No. 548686)
Professor of Law, Preventive Medicine, and Psychology, University of Iowa.
Director of Law, Health Policy and Disability Center.
(319) 335-9043

____

SID WOLINSKY
(Cal. Bar No. 33716)
Director of Litigation
Disability Rights Advocates
1999 Harrison Street; Suite 1760
Oakland, CA 94612
(510) 273-8644

DATED: October 16, 1997

APPENDIX D

EEOC v. Hertz, Amicus Brief in Support of Plaintiff EEOC

EASTERN DISTRICT OF MICHIGAN
SOUTHERN DIVISION

EQUAL EMPLOYMENT OPPORTUNITY COMMISSION,

Plaintiff,

v.

Case No. 96-CV-72421
Honorable John Feikens

DT
THE HERTZ CORPORATION,

Defendant,

and

THE HERTZ CORPORATION,

Third Party Plaintiff,

v.

ARKAY, INC.,

Third Party Defendant.

AMICUS CURIAE BRIEF IN SUPPORT OF PLAINTIFF

AMICUS CURIAE
Michigan Protection & Advocacy Service

STEWART R. HAKOLA (P37952)
Attorney for Amicus Curiae
Michigan Protection & Advocacy Service.
315 S. Front Street
Marquette, MI 49855
(906) 228-5910

TABLE OF CONTENTS

INDEX OF AUTHORITIES

OTHER

STATEMENT OF ISSUES

Amicus defers to the parties' presentation of the Statement of Issues.

STATEMENT OF CONTROLLING OR MOST APPROPRIATE AUTHORITY

Amicus defers to the parties' presentation of the Statement of Controlling or Most Appropriate Authority.

STATEMENT OF INTEREST OF AMICUS CURIAE

Michigan Protection & Advocacy Service (MPAS) is a private, non-profit organization which has been designated by three successive Michigan Governors to serve as Michigan's "protection and advocacy system" as required by federal law. Specifically, three separate federal statutes require each State to have in place a protection and advocacy (P & A) agency to enforce the legal rights of persons with disabilities. The three statutes mandate such an agency to serve, respectively, citizens with developmental disabilities such as mental retardation, 42 U.S.C. 6000 *et. seq.*, citizens with mental illness, 42 U.S.C. 10801 *et. seq.*, and citizens with disabilities other than developmental disabilities and mental illness, 29 U.S.C. 794e.

Under each of these statutes, the designated P & A agency has authority to "pursue legal, administrative, and other appropriate remedies." 42 U.S.C. 6042(a)(2)(A)(I); 42 U.S.C. 10805(a)(1)(B); and 29 U.S.C. 794e(f)(3). This authorization has been interpreted by the federal courts as conferring broad authority upon the P & A system, including the authority to file amicus briefs, intervene as a party in existing litigation, and bring actions in the name of the P & A system itself. *See, e.g., Larkin v. State of Michigan,* 883 F. Supp. 172 (E.D. Mich. 1994) (intervenor party status conferred upon MPAS), *Michigan Protection & Advocacy Service v. Babin,* 19 F.3d 1994 (6th Cir. 1994) (MPAS is appropriate plaintiff), and *Rubinstein v. Benedictine Hospital,* 790 F. Supp. 396 (N.D. N.Y. 1992) (noting that the federal law confers authority on "the system itself" and therefore enables the system to file litigation in its own name).

MPAS has been designated by Governor Engler to serve as Michigan's P & A system under all three federal statutes. Pursuant to its federal mandate, MPAS has participated in a wide variety of activities to enforce disability rights law, including the Americans with Disabilities Act (ADA). As a result, MPAS has acquired expertise in ADA issues and believes that its expertise may be helpful to the Court in its consideration of the present case.

Significantly, MPAS' expertise includes unique knowledge of the relationship between the accommodation duty of private employers and the availability of publicly-funded job assistance services, an issue which is critical in the present case. MPAS' unique ability to contribute on this issue is due to the fact that, in addition to serving as Michigan's designated P & A system, MPAS also serves as the State's designated "client assistance program" (CAP) responsible for advocating for the rights of persons with disabilities within the State vocational rehabilitation system. 29 U.S.C. 732. As Michigan's CAP, MPAS' advocacy is based on its federal enabling legislation, the Rehabilitation Act of 1973. Indeed, MPAS' authority as the CAP under the Rehabilitation Act expressly includes the duty to coordinate advocacy for vocational rehabilitation services from the State with advocacy under Title I of the ADA, as such are inherently intertwined. In this regard, the Rehabilitation Act states:

> (a) Establishment of grant program
>
> From funds appropriated under subsection (I) of this section, the Secretary shall, in accordance with this section, make grants to States to establish and carry out client assistance programs to provide assistance in informing and advising all clients and client applicants of all available benefits under this chapter, and, upon request of such clients or client appli-

cants, to assist and advocate for such clients or applicants in their relationships with projects, programs, and community rehabilitation programs providing services to them under this chapter, including assistance and advocacy in pursuing legal, administrative, or other appropriate remedies to ensure the protection of the rights of such individuals under this chapter and to facilitate access to the services funded under this chapter through individual and systemic advocacy. *The client assistance program shall provide information on the available services and benefits under this chapter and title I of the Americans with Disabilities Act of 1990* [42 U.S.C.A. § 12111 et seq.] to individuals with disabilities in the State, especially with regard to individuals with disabilities who have traditionally been unserved or underserved by vocational rehabilitation programs. In providing assistance and advocacy under this subsection with respect to services under this subchapter, *a client assistance program may provide the assistance and advocacy with respect to services that are directly related to facilitating the employment of the individual.*

29 U.S.C. 732(a) (emphases added).

Thus, MPAS' federal charter includes not just the authority to advocate for appropriate vocational rehabilitation services (such as job coaches) from the State but also to advocate for reasonable accommodation from private employers under Title I of the ADA, as these public and private sources of assistance are both "directly related to facilitating the employment of the individual." As with its activities under the three federal statutes vesting MPAS with authority to advocate for the rights of persons with various disabilities, MPAS' authority as the CAP program includes "the authority to pursue, legal, administrative, and other appropriate remedies" to protect the rights of persons receiving vocational rehabilitation services. 29 U.S.C. 732(b)(1).

Argument

I. Introduction and Summary of Argument

In light of its unique responsibility to coordinate individual rights to public vocational rehabilitation services and private employment accommodations, MPAS offers three principles for this Court's consideration.

First, MPAS believes that there is a significant overlap between a private employer's duty to provide reasonable accommodation and the availability of free job placement and retention services from public agencies, most notably agencies providing job coaches and other forms of assistance under the federal law mandating vocational rehabilitation services for persons with disabilities. Accordingly, MPAS asserts that an employer's duty to provide reasonable accommodation in order to avoid discrimination includes the duty to make a good faith effort to secure appropriate assistance from such service agencies.[1]

Second, such assistance from service agencies clearly includes the provision of government-funded job coaches. Specifically, federal law presumes that persons with mental retardation such as Mr. Klem and Mr. Miller are capable of competitive employment in integrated work settings if they receive appropriate training support and, accordingly, mandates that such persons are entitled to priority in receiving vocational rehabilitation services. In this regard, vocational rehabilitation services expressly include "supported employment," which is defined as including the assistance of a skilled job coach.

Third, MPAS, having reviewed Hertz's argument that Mr. Klem and Mr. Miller were not discharged "solely" because of disability, is concerned that employers not be allowed to transform disability-based decisions into "neutral" decisions. The ADA should not be read as authorizing a defense which, in the end, comes down to the assertion that the employees were fired not because of disability but because their accommodations were eliminated. Unlike other civil rights employment laws, the protected trait of disability is not irrelevant to job performance, thus requiring reasonable affirmative steps to accommodate individual employees. Because of the impact of disability upon the workplace, Congress expressly rejected a requirement that discrimination must be based "solely" on disability, choosing instead to reject such language in favor of adopting a "mixed motives" approach. Thus, as long as the employees' disability played a significant role in the decision, discrimination has been established even if other, non-discriminatory reasons (such as kissing job coaches) were also present.

II. An Employer's Duty to Provide Reasonable Accommodation Includes the Good Faith Effort to Utilize Government-Funded Assistance for Employees with Disabilities

An employer's duty to provide reasonable accommodation cannot be addressed in a vacuum. The ADA clearly requires a case-by-case approach in determining the factual issue of the reasonableness of a particular accommodation. An employee who loses her voice but who brings her own computer-generated voice synthesizer to her job at IBM is clearly in a different posture from an employee who demands that her mom-and-pop employer buy such a machine. Similarly, a small business may have no duty to provide a personal assistant to a worker with quadriplegia but would just as clearly have the duty to allow such a worker to bring an assistant funded by insurance benefits onto the worksite.

Perhaps the most important external source

---

[1] Title I of the ADA clearly establishes that a failure to provide reasonable accommodation to an employee with a disability is a distinct form of active discrimination, in addition to the standard civil rights frameworks for disparate treatment and disparate impact. 42 U.S.C. 12112(b)(5)(A)("discriminate" defined as including "not making reasonable accommodations").

of worksite assistance is the vocational rehabilitation system administered through a cooperative federal-State program. Specifically, the federal Rehabilitation Act of 1973 provides billions of dollars on an annual basis for States to provide job assistance to persons with disabilities. This vocational rehabilitation system is premised on the need to assist private employers, as demonstrated by the job placement and retention services it provides. For example, the State vocational rehabilitation system can provide subsidies to employers to offset the wages of workers with disabilities, can work with private employers to develop jobs across existing job categories for workers with disabilities, and can provide direct forms of assistance such as technology, communication devices, therapy, and job coaches to enable an employee with a disability to complete job requirements.[2] One indicator of the breadth of the State's responsibility in this area is that the services available from the State vocational rehabilitation system even include corrective surgery, dialysis, and prosthetic devices. 29 U.S.C. 723(a)(4).

In a particular case, the availability of specific services from external agencies can have critical importance with respect to the employer's claim that providing accommodation would impose an undue hardship. Volunteer readers may be available for employees who are blind, or a government program might provide the expensive protease inhibitors which can enable a worker who is HIV+ to retain his or her abilities. In the present case, for example, the State vocational rehabilitation system is explicitly charged with the duty to provide Mr. Klem and Mr. Miller with extensive services on a priority basis to facilitate their competitive employment. 29 U.S.C. 721(a)(5)(A) (vocational rehabilitation must first serve persons with severe disabilities such as mental retardation) and 29 U.S.C. 723 (scope of available services). This policy decision of Congress will be undermined if this Court endorses the employer's speculative and generalized assumption that Congress' objectives cannot be achieved, that Mr. Klem and Mr. Miller will *never* be able to perform real work.

III. The Federal Rehabilitation Act Recognizes that Persons with Mental Retardation Are Employable and Provides Extensive Services to Assist Employers in Learning This for Themselves

In 1992, the federal Rehabilitation Act of 1973 underwent extensive amendments. These amendments are often ignored in ADA employment disputes, which is unfortunate since they are among the most powerful entitlements in civil law. For example, the 1992 law imposes upon State vocational rehabilitation systems the duty to prove by "clear and convincing evidence" — the highest standard known in civil law — that a particular person with a disability is not capable of employment. 29 U.S.C. 722(a)(4)(A).

There is no doubt that the 1992 amendments spring from Congress' recognition that persons with mental retardation and other specific disabilities have been traditionally underserved and underutilized in the nation's workforce. The losses which accrue to both the individual and to society when persons are relegated to public benefits instead of productive work are obvious. Accordingly, Congress has clearly stated that persons with mental retardation are capable of competitive, integrated employment and are entitled to be afforded both vocational rehabilitation services and reasonable accommodations.

Overlap Between State Vocational Rehabilitation and Private Employment Accommodations

The amended Rehabilitation Act, for example, states:

> It is the policy of the United States that . . . [i]ndividuals with disabilities, including individuals with the most severe disabilities, are generally presumed to be capable of engaging in gainful employment and the provision of individualized vocational rehabilitation services can improve their ability to

---

[2] Such services fall within the available scope of legally-mandated vocational rehabilitation services. 29 U.S.C. 723(a)(2)(job placement and retention services), (a)(11)(technological aids and devices), and (a)(16)(supported employment).

> become gainfully employed.... Individuals with disabilities must be provided the opportunities to obtain gainful employment in integrated settings.

29 U.S.C. 720(a)(3)(A) and (B).

The express findings of Congress emphasize the untapped productivity of persons with disabilities and the need the align individualized services from State rehabilitation agencies with the duty of private employers to refrain from discrimination:

> Individuals with disabilities, including individuals with the most severe disabilities, have demonstrated their ability to achieve gainful employment in integrated settings if appropriate services and supports are provided...[T]he reasons for the significant number of individuals with disabilities not working... include... discrimination...[and] lack of education, training, and supports to meet job qualification standards.

29 U.S.C. 720(a)(1)(C) and (D).

Indeed, Congress' 1992 amendment of the Rehabilitation Act was designed to strengthen the overlap of the Rehabilitation Act and the ADA, as Congress found that "enforcement of [the Rehabilitation Act] and of the Americans with Disabilities Act of 1990 (42 U.S.C. 12101 et seq.) holds the promise of ending discrimination for individuals with disabilities." 29 U.S.C. 720(a)(1)(E). In short, Congress has repeatedly recognized that rehabilitation services and the end of discrimination are both essential:

> increased employment of individuals with disabilities can be achieved through the provision of individualized training, independent living services, educational and support services, and meaningful opportunities for employment in integrated work settings through the provision of reasonable accommodations... [I]ndividuals with disabilities continually encounter various forms of discrimination in such critical areas as employment.

29 U.S.C. 701(a)(4) and (5).

Available Vocational Rehabilitation Services

In order to assist employers in overcoming their history of discrimination, the Rehabilitation Act establishes a powerful range of publicly-funded services to assist individuals with disabilities in finding and retaining integrated employment. As mentioned earlier, such services include technology, medical care, counseling, college training, interpreters and readers, and transportation. 29 U.S.C. 723(a). The scope of vocational rehabilitation services also includes "supported employment services," which are defined as including "ongoing support services" to maintain individuals with severe disabilities such as mental retardation in employment. 29 U.S.C. 723(a)(16) and 29 U.S.C. 706(34). "Ongoing support services" are in turn defined as including "skilled job trainers who accompany the individual for intensive job skill training at the worksite," as well as "followup services such as regular contact with the employers" and "facilitation of natural supports at the worksite." 29 U.S.C. 706(33)(C).

These statutory provisions show that Congress' decision to direct vocational rehabilitation to persons such as Mr. Klem and Mr. Miller is not an empty promise. Instead, Congressional policy is implemented by concrete services such as job coaches, which are designed to enable the employee to learn the job in conjunction with regular communication with the employer and the use of natural supports in the work setting. Just as with the ADA, Congress employed some common sense, recognizing that *all* workers benefit from open communication with their employers and from the mentoring and training naturally provided by their colleagues. Because of their disabilities, Mr. Klem and Mr. Miller require more than standard orientation and training, and skilled job coaches are an important mechanism established by Congress to enable Mr. Klem and Mr. Miller to successfully learn their job requirements without imposing significant burdens on Hertz.

IV. Congress Expressly Rejected Incorporating a "Solely" Because of Handicap Requirement in the ADA

In its brief, Hertz suggests that the ADA employs a "solely" because of handicap standard. Although MPAS believes that this issue is not germane to the distinct discrimination standard of reasonable accommodation (see footnote 1), MPAS notes that Hertz' view is patently incorrect, as Congress explicitly rejected such a "solely" standard due to its recognition that disability discrimination can often be subtle.

Section 504 of the Rehabilitation Act, 29 U.S.C. 794, has, since 1973, prohibited discrimination because of handicap by any entity that receives federal financial assistance. In enacting the ADA, Congress drew heavily from the legal principles derived from almost twenty years of Section 504 enforcement. One element of Section 504, however, was flatly rejected by Congress when considering the ADA: Section 504's requirement that the discrimination occur "solely" because of handicap.

This is demonstrated by the plain language of the ADA, which does not use "solely" in any of its titles prohibiting discrimination because of disability in various areas. This omission was not an oversight, as evidenced by the ADA's legislative history:

> The Committee recognizes that the phrasing of ... this legislation differs from section 504 by virtue of the fact that the phrase "solely by reason of his or her handicap" has been deleted.... [T]he existence of non-disability related factors in the rejection decision does not immunize employers. The entire selection procedure must be reviewed to determine if the disability was improperly considered.

H.R. 101-485, 101st Cong., 2d Sess., pp. 85-86 (1990).

Congress' rejection of "solely" is not surprising, given the prevalence of "mixed motive" cases — in which both legitimate and illegitimate factors may influence a decision — in civil rights law. Indeed, during the same time period in which the ADA was being considered, Congress was also enacting legislation to overturn several Supreme Court decisions interpreting Title VII and other federal civil rights laws, including the Court's restrictive framework for mixed motive cases in *Price Waterhouse v. Hopkins*, 490 U.S. 228; 109 S. Ct.1775 (1989). This decision was ultimately overturned by Congress as part of the Civil Rights Act of 1991, in which Congress clarified:

> An unlawful employment practice is established when the complaining party demonstrates that race, color, religion, sex, or national origin was *a motivating factor* for any employment practice, even though other factors also motivated the practice.

42 U.S.C. 2000e-2(m)(emphasis added). *See also Laugesen v. Anacona Co.,* 510 F.2d 307, 317 (6th Cir. 1975) (in age discrimination suit, plaintiff need not prove that age was the sole factor in the termination decision).

Because employees with disabilities, by definition, have substantial limitations in major life activities, they may require additional services or modifications in the worksite. Accordingly, they are particularly susceptible to legal defenses sometimes employed in "mixed motives" cases, such as assertions that they were fired not because of their disability but because of their reliance on support services.

MPAS urges this Court to be skeptical of both Hertz's attempt to shift the focus to the job coaches and Hertz's argument that Mr. Klem's and Mr. Miller's disabilities were not the causal agent. In an analogous context, the Sixth Circuit confronted a fair housing case where persons with disabilities were denied a group home in the community. In that case, the defendants argued that the persons with mental retardation who were denied supported living in a group home were denied not because of handicap but because of their need for supervision. The Sixth Circuit flatly rejected this illusory distinction finding that "disabled individuals who wish to live in a community often have no choice but to live in [a supervised] facility." *Larkin, supra.*

In the present case, there is no doubt that Mr. Klem and Mr. Miller lost their jobs because of their use of supervised training to learn the job and that their disabilities were a motivating factor. Hertz's finger-pointing and its restricted view of the meaning of "discrimination" must therefore be rejected.

V. Conclusion and Relief Requested

A review of the case law decided since the ADA's enactment reveals that the broad remedial purposes of the ADA are not being realized, as persons with significant impairments — not just nicotine addicts, cross dressers, and migraine sufferers — are systematically being stripped of the ADA's protections. Mr. Klem and Mr. Miller are individuals with mental retardation who are not only within the core of the ADA but also the core of the federal law designed to provide vocational rehabilitation and assistance to private employers.

MPAS believes that a little common sense is needed in interpreting the ADA. How can an employer claim that publicly-funded job training assistance imposes an undue hardship? How can an employer justify not investing a little time to look into such assistance and engaging in a dialogue with an employee with a known disability? How will citizens with mental retardation ever find and learn real work if such minimal efforts are not required? Finally, how can an employer suggest that the loss of a job was not disability-based when the use of accommodation triggered the adverse employment action?

The ADA was written in a broad manner for a reason: to encompass the specific circumstances of specific cases so that the Congressional goal of overcoming the "various forms of discrimination" against persons with disabilities can be achieved. 42 U.S.C. 12101(a)(5). The present case shows that disability was undisputedly a critical factor in the decision or, at the least, raises sufficient issues of fact to warrant jury consideration. Accordingly, MPAS respectfully requests that the employer's motion for summary judgment be denied.

Respectfully submitted:

Dated: ______________________

By:______________________________
STEWART R. HAKOLA (P37952)
Attorney for Amicus Curiae
Michigan Protection & Advocacy Service
315 S. Front Street
Marquette, MI 49855
(906) 228-5910

APPENDIX E

EEOC v. Hertz, United States District Court Opinion

UNITED STATES DISTRICT COURT
EASTERN DISTRICT OF MICHIGAN
SOUTHERN DIVISION

EQUAL EMPLOYMENT OPPORTUNITY COMMISSION,

Plaintiff,

V.

Case No. 96-72421
Hon. John Feikens

HERTZ CORPORATION,

Defendant/Third-Party Plaintiff,

V.

ARKAY, INC.,

Third-Party Defendant.

______________________________/

Opinion and Order

I. Background

Chief Justice Earl Warren would often ask when judging a case: "Is it fair, Is it just?"

That question must be asked in this case. The Equal Employment Opportunity Commission (EEOC) and Arkay, Inc. (Arkay), a federally-funded entity which supplies job coaches to assist handicapped persons, have combined in this suit to seek sanctions against the Hertz Corporation (Hertz). They now have been joined by several groups, Disability Rights Advocates and Michigan Protection and Advisory Services, as amici, who support that effort.

With this array, one must ask what it is in this case that brings the EEOC and these rights advocate agencies together to pursue this matter.

One need not look far.

Arkay, Inc. is the motivator.

Arkay has an appealing approach. It seeks out employers, like Hertz, and makes a proposal: that if the employer will hire a handicapped person, it (Arkay) will provide a job coach, free of charge, to the employer, who will assist the handicapped person in doing some work for the employer. Arkay is paid for these efforts by federal government funding.

This is what happened in this case. In early 1994, Arkay went to Hertz and pointed out to it that at its rental car operations at Detroit Metropolitan Airport, it could hire two handicapped persons (mentally retarded) who could work a limited number of hours each day (approximately four hours—the record is not clear), and they would be trained and assisted by two job coaches provided by Arkay. It is clear in the record that these handicapped persons (Donald Klem and Kenneth Miller) would not be able to do the intended work, picking up trash in the Hertz parking lot, without training by and the actual supervision of the job coaches.

Hertz agreed, and the venture started. But it soon went awry. It appears that the job coaches furnished by Arkay had other distracting interests. One day (the record is not clear if this was the first time, or the only time), the job coaches had Mr. Klem and Mr. Miller seated in the back seat of a car while they, a man and a woman, according to current jargon, were "making out" in the front seat. It is not clear from the record just what was going on.[1] Hertz claims that four or five of its supervisors saw rather passionate lovemaking, while EEOC and Arkay claim the two were exchanging gifts and thanking each other with kisses.

When the event in the car was observed by the Hertz supervisors, the job coaches were ordered off the premises and the jobs of Messrs. Klem and Miller were terminated. What happened next is that Arkay went to the EEOC and claimed that a violation of the Americans With Disabilities Act (ADA) had occurred and EEOC had better do something about it.

This suit followed.

Plaintiff's major contention is that Hertz, having hired Messrs. Klem and Miller, now have a continuing duty to employ them, and that Hertz must provide reasonable accommodation to continue their training and employment. That reasonable accommodation, EEOC argues, would require Hertz to find other job coaches to train and supervise Mr. Klem and Mr. Miller.

When Arkay first approached Hertz, and asked it to hire Mr. Klem and Mr. Miller, Hertz had no legal obligation to do so. *See Reigel v. Kaisar Foundation Health Plan of N.C.*, 859 F.Supp. 963 (E.D.N.C. 1994).

When it did hire these men, it was essential that they be accompanied, while being trained and working on Hertz's premises, to be supervised by competent job coaches. Arkay committed itself to provide this important accommodation; it was the essential element, the consideration for the contract. That employment contract was breached by Arkay because of the conduct of its incompetent job coaches.

In this bizarre situation, EEOC, Arkay and the amici now seek to impose a legal obligation on

[1] The female participant is still employed with Arkay. The male participant was apparently married at the time. The female participant downplayed the incident, saying that she and her paramour were merely engaged in a "prolonged hug." The male participant was apparently never deposed.

Hertz that they say is compelled by 42 U.S.C. §12112 (ADA). Their complaint "relates solely to Hertz's failure to reasonably accommodate Klem and Miller...." This alleged failure to so accommodate, they claim, is discrimination.

Now to the facts that are not in dispute.

This case has its origins in defendant Hertz's April 1994 decision to contract with Arkay, Inc., for an employment service for individuals with developmental disabilities.[2] Arkay representative Susan Skibo contacted Hertz as to the possibility of employing Arkay personnel. Ms. Skibo eventually contacted Keith Lamb, one of Hertz's senior station managers at its Detroit Metropolitan Airport location, and outlined to him the arrangement that Arkay wanted to structure with Hertz: In exchange for Hertz's provision of menial tasks for Arkay's developmentally handicapped individuals, Arkay promised to provide job coaches to train them, to closely supervise them and, if necessary, tend to any of their medical needs. If Hertz would agree to employ and pay the handicapped individuals, Arkay would provide and pay the job coaches.

Mr. Lamb expressed some misgivings, but promised to speak to his supervisor, Gary Wellman, about Arkay's proposal. Mr. Lamb spoke with Mr. Wellman and told him that, in light of litter problems Hertz had on its premises, Arkay's proposal "might be something that would be good to try." (Lamb dep. At 15). Mr. Wellman, in turn, took the matter to his supervisor, Michael Kieleszewski, who sought and then obtained permission from Hertz Headquarters to accept Arkay's offer.[3]

Arkay is funded by Medicaid in an arrangement that it has with Wayne Community Living Services (WCLS), and that entity works with and through Arkay to provide supported employment for mentally retarded persons. The record indicates on behalf of WCLS, Arkay entered into this employment agreement with Hertz, which Arkay states in its Answer to Hertz's Third-Party Complaint against it, Para. 9, would be on a trial basis.

The term " 'supported employment,' which has been applied to a wide variety of programs to assist individuals with severe disabilities in both competitive and non-competitive employment, is not synonymous with reasonable accommodation." The *Interpretative Guidance* to Reg. 29 CFR 1630.9 states that an example of supported employment might include providing "a temporary job coach to assist in the training of a qualified individual with a disability...."

Before Messrs. Klem and Miller could be hired, however, Hertz had to make additional accommodations. First, Hertz agreed to waive its usual application and interview process. Hertz also allowed Messrs. Klem and Miller to take a paid half-hour break, even though their shift lasted only four hours. Most important, Hertz allowed Messrs. Klem and Miller to have supportive "job coaches."

The record also indicates that Hertz did not hold Messrs. Klem and Miller to the higher standards of its other employees. On one occasion, Mr. Lamb saw Mr. Klem spit on the floor inside Hertz's car return building, and area used by Hertz customers. Mr. Lamb did not discipline Mr. Klem; he wanted to give Mr. Klem an opportunity to adjust to his new environment. Mr. Miller and Mr. Klem also were not held to the attendance standards of other employees. Mr. Lamb testified that the pair missed work without penalty. Deposition testimony also raises serious questions whether, even with a job coach, Mr. Klem could perform the essential functions of his job. Both Mr. Lamb and one of Mr. Klem's job coaches testified as to incidents in which Mr. Klem spent part of a workday staring at airplanes overhead and refused orders from his job coach to do his job.

Hertz did accommodate to this. Hertz claims, however, that it could not tolerate problems created by the job coaches assigned to Messrs. Klem and Miller. The first job coach that Arkay sent was "mean" to Messrs. Klem and Miller. Hertz requested that this coach be replaced. Arkay granted this request and, for a time, provided a job coach that met Hertz's expectations. This second job coach was subsequently replaced by another coach who, on June 7,

---

[2] Arkay is funded, at least in part, by Medicaid.

[3] Prior to accepting Arkay's offer, Hertz had no employees assigned specifically to cleaning the parking lot. Hertz created positions for Messrs. Klem and Miller to do this. The positions have not been filled since Mr. Klem's and Mr. Miller's employment was terminated.

[4] Two Hertz managers, Gary Wellman and Michael Kieleszewski, testified that, had Arkay made such an offer, they would have considered extending the employment of Messrs. Klem and Miller.

1994, was involved in the incident which precipitated the termination of Hertz's relationship with Arkay.

To this incident, Hertz's response was swift. One of its managers confronted the job coaches and promptly told them to leave Hertz property. Hertz then contacted Arkay and severed its relationship with that company. Even though, at that point, it could have easily have done so, Arkay refused to turn Messrs. Klem and Miller over to another job agency performing the same function that Arkay performed.[4] Instead, Arkay threatened to, and eventually did, contact EEOC and induced it to institute this acation. The record is not clear that Arkay ever informed Wayne Community Living Services, of this situation, or that Arkay received WCLS's consent to secure other job coaches, i.e., organizations that, like Arkay, could have provided this type of employment support to Messrs. Klem and Miller.

II. Analysis

The comment of Judge Richard Posner in *Vande Zande v. State of Wisc. Dept. of Admin.*, 44 F.3d 538 (7th Cir. 1995), is instructive:

> [I]f the employer… bends over backwards to accommodate a disabled worker— goes farther than the law requires— …it must not be punished for its generosity by being deemed to have conceded the reasonableness of so far reaching an accommodation. That would hurt rather than help disabled workers.

While, as is pointed out hereinafter, EEOC cannot even come close to establishing a prima facie case of disability discrimination against Hertz, this is a case in which there is no discrimination whatever.[5] The teaching of the ancient fable is instructive: It took a child to point out to the crowd admiring what they thought was an ornately dressed emperor riding a horse, that the emperor had no clothes on at all. EEOC's position fits that fable. One wonders why that agency is unable to see clearly what it is attempting to claim. Hertz should be complimented for what it tried to do here—not sued. How does EEOC expect to further the goal of assisting handicapped persons that employers will hire if it seeks to punish them for their generosity?

Putting that aside for the moment, and taking on EEOC's argument that it has here a prima facie case, EEOC cannot and does not establish a prima facie case of discrimination required by ADA.

Monette v. Electronic Data Systems Corp., 90 F.3d 1173 (6th Cir. 1996), teaches that, to establish a prima facie case, a plaintiff must show that

> 1) he or she is disabled, 2) is otherwise qualified for the job, with or without "reasonable" accommodation, 3) suffered an adverse employment decision, 4) the employer knew or had reason to know of his or her disability, and 5) after rejection or termination the position remained open, or the disabled individual was replaced. (Citations omitted)

It is clear that plaintiff does not and cannot establish factor 2). Messrs. Klem and Miller are not qualified for the job because accommodation to permit them to function was not provided by Arkay (or anyone else). It is not the duty, obligation or responsibility of Hertz to provide job coaches, either on a temporary basis or on a permanent basis, to train and supervise these handicapped individuals.

It is also clear that after Messrs. Klem and Miller were terminated due to Arkay's breach of the trial arrangement, that these positions [Klem's and Miller's] did not remain open. These positions ceased when the arrangement failed. It is also clear that they [Klem and Miller] were not replaced.

The result in this case was not brought about by Hertz. Arkay and, perhaps, Wayne Community Living Services had a responsibility for "picking up the pieces", and should have initiated are opening of the arrangement with Hertz. The record indicates that had Arkay "made such an offer, Hertz would have seriously considered extending the employment" of Mr. Klem and Mr. Miller.

But, even more important, the position of the

---

[5] In cases brought under Title VII of the Civil Rights Act of 1964 (*see* 42 U.S.C. § 2000e-2 (a)(1)), once an employer proffers a legitimate, nondiscriminatory reason for a challenged employment decision, as Hertz has done in this case, the *McDonnell-Douglas* burden shifting framework becomes irrelevant, the only thing left to be decided is the ultimate question: whether defendant engaged in discrimination. *See St. Mary's Honor Society v. Hicks,* 509 U.S. 502, 510–512, 113 S.Ct. 2742, 2748–2750, 125 L.Ed.2d 407 (1993). The same reasoning applies to claims of discrimination brought under ADA.

EEOC is troublesome. This case should not have been brought against Hertz; EEOC's focus was misplaced. EEOC should have advised Arkay that this was not a case of discrimination against handicapped persons but rather a breakdown in Arkay's procedures in affording assistance to handicapped people.

Even EEOC's *Interpretative Guidance* stands in its way. The guidelines provide at 29 CFR 1630.9 that:

> The term "supported employment," which has been applied to a wide variety of programs to assist individuals with severe disabilities in both competitive and non-competitive employment is not synonymous with reasonable accommodation. Examples of supported employment include modified training materials, restructuring essential functions to enable an individual to perform a job, or hiring an outside professional ("job coach") to assist in job training. Whether a particular form of assistance would be required as a reasonable accommodation must be determined on an individualized, case by case basis without regard to whether that assistance is referred to as "supported employment." For example, an employer, under certain circumstances, may be required to provide modified training materials or a temporary "job coach" to assist in the training of a qualified individual with a disability as a reasonable accommodation."[6] (Emphasis added)

If a temporary job coach providing job training to a qualified individual may be a reasonable accommodation, the clear implication is that a full-time job coach providing more than training to unqualified individuals is not. Caselaw supports this view. *Ricks v. Xerox Corp.*, 877 F. Supp. 1468 (D.Kan. 1995), is on point. In that case, the district court ruled that an employee's request for a full-time "helper" to assist in the performance of the essential functions of his job was unreasonable as a matter of law. A similar result was reached in *Gilbert v. Frank,* 949 F.2d 637 (CA 2 1991), in which the U.S. Court of Appeals for the Second Circuit held that it was unreasonable to have two people performing the same tasks normally performed by one. Insisting that Messrs. Miller and Klem have a full-time job coach to assist in the performance of job duties on a permanent basis is, likewise, unreasonable.

Neither party disputes that Hertz had no initial obligation to hire Messrs. Klem and Miller. *See Reigel,* supra, at 963, 973: "[The ADA] cannot be construed to require an employer to make fundamental or substantial modifications in its operations to assure every disabled individual the benefit of employment."

EEOC, in the face of this precedent and in spite of its inability to point to any case mandating that a full-time job coach is a reasonable accommodation, advances the incredible argument that, because Hertz could have obtained a job coach for Messrs. Klem and Miller at no cost to itself, the provision of a job coach is a per se reasonable accommodation, and must be provided.

Plaintiff seeks to establish an expanded liability for putative employers who consider hiring handicapped persons, i.e., that once an employer evidences an intent to and does provide employment for a handicapped person with support for that person of a job coach, it is obligated to continue that relationship in perpetuity and without regard to any event(s) that make that employment relationship untenable. The ADA does not require this.

III. Conclusion

The motion brought by Hertz for summary judgment is GRANTED.

IT IS SO ORDERED.

/s/

John Feikens
United States District Judge

Dated: January 6, 1998

---

[6] The underlined portions deserve special attention. To begin with, there is no dispute here that the role of the job coaches in this case went far beyond that of "job training." The record reflects that the coaches supervised, disciplined, and assisted in the performance of work. In addition, Arkay representative Susan Skibo testified that neither Mr. Klem or Mr. Miller had ever worked without the full-time assistance of a job coach. Ms. Skibo further testified that they would always need this full-time assistance. Finally, while there is an issue of fact with regard to whether Messrs. Klem and Miller were qualified individuals, the fact that they required full-time assistance for more than job training moots, for purposes of summary judgment, the factual dispute.

APPENDIX F

EEOC Enforcement Guidance on the Americans with Disabilities Act and Psychiatric Disabilities

EEOC	NOTICE	Number 915.002
		Date 3-25-97

1. **SUBJECT:** EEOC Enforcement Guidance on the Americans with Disabilities Act and Psychiatric Disabilities

2. **PURPOSE:** This enforcement guidance sets forth the Commission's position on the application of Title I of the Americans with Disabilities Act of 1990 to individuals with psychiatric disabilities.

3. **EFFECTIVE DATE:** Upon receipt.

4. **EXPIRATION DATE:** As an exception to EEOC Order 205.001, Appendix B, Attachment 4, § a(5), this Notice will remain in effect until rescinded or superseded.

5. **ORIGINATOR:** ADA Division, Office of Legal Counsel.

6. **INSTRUCTIONS:** File after Section 902 of Volume II of the Compliance Manual.

3-25-97
Date

/S/
Gilbert F. Casellas
Chairman

DISTRIBUTION: CM Holders

REVISED EEOC FORM 106 (6/91) PREVIOUS EDITIONS OF THIS FORM ARE OBSOLETE AND MUST NOT BE USED

TABLE OF CONTENTS

Introduction

The workforce includes many individuals with psychiatric disabilities who face employment discrimination because their disabilities are stigmatized or misunderstood. Congress intended Title I of the Americans with Disabilities Act (ADA)[1] to combat such employment discrimination as well as the myths, fears, and stereotypes upon which it is based.[2]

The Equal Employment Opportunity Commission ("EEOC" or "Commission") receives a large number of charges under the ADA alleging employment discrimination based on psychiatric disability.[3] These charges raise a wide array of legal issues including, for example, whether an individual has a psychiatric disability as defined by the ADA and whether an employer may ask about an individual's psychiatric disability. People with psychiatric disabilities and employers also have posed numerous questions to the EEOC about this topic.

This guidance is designed to:

- facilitate the full enforcement of the ADA with respect to individuals alleging employment discrimination based on psychiatric disability;
- respond to questions and concerns expressed by individuals with psychiatric disabilities regarding the ADA; and
- answer questions posed by employers about how principles of ADA analysis apply in the context of psychiatric disabilities.[4]

What Is a Psychiatric Disability Under the ADA?

Under the ADA, the term "disability" means: "(a) A physical or mental impairment that substantially limits one or more of the major life activities of [an] individual; (b) a record of such an impairment; or (c) being regarded as having such an impairment."[5]

This guidance focuses on the first prong of the ADA's definition of "disability" because of the great number of questions about how it is applied in the context of psychiatric conditions.

Impairment

1. What is a **"mental impairment"** under the ADA?

   The ADA rule defines "mental impairment" to include "[a]ny mental or psychological disorder, such as... emotional or mental illness."[6] Examples of "emotional or mental illness[es]" include major depression, bipolar disorder, anxiety disorders (which include panic disorder, obsessive compulsive disorder, and post-traumatic stress disorder), schizophrenia, and personality disorders. The current edition of the American Psychiatric Association's *Diagnostic and Statistical Manual of Mental Disorders* (now the fourth edition, DSM-IV) is relevant for identifying these disorders. The DSM-IV has been recognized as an important reference by courts[7] and is widely used by American mental health professionals for diagnostic

---

[1] 42 U.S.C. §§ 12101–12117, 12201–12213 (1994) (codified as amended).

[2] H.R. Rep. No. 101-485, pt. 3, at 31–32 (1990) [hereinafter House Judiciary Report].

[3] Between July 26, 1992, and September 30, 1996, approximately 12.7% of ADA charges filed with EEOC were based on emotional or psychiatric impairment. These included charges based on anxiety disorders, depression, bipolar disorder (manic depression), schizophrenia, and other psychiatric impairments.

[4] The analysis in this guidance applies to federal sector complaints of non-affirmative action employment discrimination arising under section 501 of the Rehabilitation Act of 1973. 29 U.S.C. § 791(g) (1994). It also applies to complaints of non-affirmative action employment discrimination arising under section 503 and employment discrimination under section 504 of the Rehabilitation Act. 29 U.S.C. §§ 793(d), 794(d) (1994).

[5] 42 U.S.C. § 12102(2) (1994); 29 C.F.R. § 1630.2(g) (1996). *See generally* EEOC Compliance Manual § 902, Definition of the Term "Disability," 8 FEP Manual (BNA) 405:7251 (1995).

[6] 29 C.F.R. § 1630.2(h)(2) (1996). This ADA regulatory definition also refers to mental retardation, organic brain syndrome, and specific learning disabilities. These additional mental conditions, as well as other neurological disorders such as Alzheimer's disease, are not the primary focus of this guidance.

[7] *See, e.g., Boldini v. Postmaster Gen.,* 928 F. Supp. 125, 130, 5 AD Cas. (BNA) 11, 14 (D.N.H. 1995) (stating, under section 501 of the Rehabilitation Act, that "in circumstances of mental impairment, a court may give weight to a diagnosis of mental impairment which is described in the Diagnostic and Statistical Manual of Mental Disorders of the American Psychiatric Association ...").

and insurance reimbursement purposes.

Not all conditions listed in the DSM-IV, however, are disabilities, or even impairments, for purposes of the ADA. For example, the DSM-IV lists several conditions that Congress expressly excluded from the ADA's definition of "disability."[8] While DSM-IV covers conditions involving drug abuse, the ADA provides that the term "individual with a disability" does not include an individual who is currently engaging in the illegal use of drugs, when the covered entity acts on the basis of that use.[9] The DSM-IV also includes conditions that are not mental disorders but for which people may seek treatment (for example, problems with a spouse or child).[10] Because these conditions are not disorders, they are not impairments under the ADA.[11]

Even if a condition is an impairment, it is not automatically a "disability." To rise to the level of a "disability," an impairment must "substantially limit" one or more major life activities of the individual.[12]

2. Are traits or behaviors in themselves mental impairments?

   No. Traits or behaviors are not, in themselves, mental impairments. For example, **stress,** in itself, is not automatically a mental impairment. Stress, however, may be shown to be related to a mental or physical impairment. Similarly, traits like **irritability, chronic lateness,** and **poor judgment** are not, in themselves, mental impairments, although they may be linked to mental impairments.[13]

Major Life Activities

An impairment must substantially limit one or more **major life activities** to rise to the level of a "disability" under the ADA.[14]

3. What **major life activities** are limited by mental impairments?

   The major life activities limited by mental impairments **differ from person to person.** There is no exhaustive list of major life activities. For some people, mental impairments restrict major life activities such as learning, thinking, concentrating, interacting with others,[15] caring for oneself, speaking, performing manual tasks, or working. Sleeping is also a major life activity that may be limited by mental impairments.[16]

---

[8] These include various sexual behavior disorders, compulsive gambling, kleptomania, pyromania, and psychoactive substance use disorders resulting from current illegal use of drugs. 42 U.S.C. § 12211(b) (1994); 29 C.F.R. § 1630.3(d) (1996).

[9] 42 U.S.C. § 12210(a) (1994). However, individuals who are not currently engaging in the illegal use of drugs and who are participating in, or have successfully completed, a supervised drug rehabilitation program (or who have otherwise been successfully rehabilitated) may be covered by the ADA. Individuals who are erroneously regarded as engaging in the current illegal use of drugs, but who are not engaging in such use, also may be covered. *Id.* at § 12210(b).

Individuals with psychiatric disabilities may, either as part of their condition or separate from their condition, engage in the illegal use of drugs. In such cases, EEOC investigators may need to make a factual determination about whether an employer treated an individual adversely because of his/her psychiatric disability or because of his/her illegal use of drugs.

[10] *See* DSM-IV chapter "Other Conditions That May Be a Focus of Clinical Attention."

[11] Individuals who do not have a mental impairment but are treated by their employers as having a substantially limiting impairment have a disability as defined by the ADA because they are regarded as having a substantially limiting impairment. *See* EEOC Compliance Manual § 902.8, Definition of the Term "Disability," 8 FEP Manual (BNA) 405:7282 (1995).

[12] This discussion refers to the terms "impairment" and "substantially limit" in the present tense. These references are not meant to imply that the determinations of whether a condition is an impairment, or of whether there is substantial limitation, are relevant only to whether an individual meets the first part of the definition of "disability," *i.e.*, actually has a physical or mental impairment that substantially limits a major life activity. These determinations also are relevant to whether an individual has a record of a substantially limiting impairment or is regarded as having a substantially limiting impairment. *See id.* §§ 902.7, 902.8, Definition of the Term "Disability," 8 FEP Manual (BNA) 405:7276–78, 7281 (1995).

[13] *Id.* § 902.2(c)(4), Definition of the Term "Disability," 8 FEP Manual (BNA) 405:7258 (1995).

[14] 42 U.S.C. § 12102(2)(A) (1994); 29 C.F.R. § 1630.2(g)(1) (1996). *See also* EEOC Compliance Manual § 902.3, Definition of the Term "Disability," 8 FEP Manual (BNA) 405:7261 (1995).

[15] Interacting with others, as a major life activity, is not substantially limited just because an individual is irritable or has some trouble getting along with a supervisor or coworker.

4. To establish a psychiatric disability, must an individual always show that s/he is substantially limited in **working?**

   No. The first question is whether an individual is substantially limited in a major life activity **other than working** (*e.g.*, sleeping, concentrating, caring for oneself). **Working** should be analyzed only if **no other major life activity** is substantially limited by an impairment.[17]

Substantial Limitation

Under the ADA, an impairment rises to the level of a disability if it substantially limits a major life activity.[18] "Substantial limitation" is evaluated in terms of the **severity** of the limitation and the **length of time** it restricts a major life activity.[19]

The determination that a particular individual has a substantially limiting impairment should be based on information about how the impairment affects that individual and not on generalizations about the condition. Relevant evidence for EEOC investigators includes descriptions of an individual's typical level of functioning at home, at work, and in other settings, as well as evidence showing that the individual's functional limitations are linked to his/her impairment. Expert testimony about substantial limitation is not necessarily required. Credible testimony from the individual with a disability and his/her family members, friends, or coworkers may suffice.

5. When is an impairment sufficiently **severe** to substantially limit a major life activity?

   An impairment is sufficiently severe to substantially limit a major life activity if it **prevents** an individual from performing a major life activity or **significantly restricts the condition, manner, or duration** under which an individual can perform a major life activity, as compared to **the average person in the general population.**[20] An impairment **does not significantly restrict** major life activities if it results in only **mild limitations.**

6. Should the corrective effects of **medications** be considered when deciding if an impairment is so severe that it substantially limits a major life activity?

   No. The ADA legislative history unequivocally states that the extent to which an impairment limits performance of a major life activity is assessed without regard to mitigating measures, including medications.[21] Thus, an individual who is taking medication for a mental impairment has an ADA disability if there is evidence that the mental impairment, when left untreated, substantially limits a major life activity.[22]

---

[16] Sleeping is not substantially limited just because an individual has some trouble getting to sleep or occasionally sleeps fitfully.

[17] *See* 29 C.F.R. pt. 1630 app. § 1630.2(j) (1996) ("[i]f an individual is not substantially limited with respect to any other major life activity, the individual's ability to perform the major life activity of working should be considered…");

see also EEOC Compliance Manual § 902.4(c)(2), Definition of the Term "Disability," 8 FEP Manual (BNA) 405:7266 (1995).

[18] 42 U.S.C. § 12102(2) (1994).

[19] *See generally* EEOC Compliance Manual § 902.4, Definition of the Term "Disability," 8 FEP Manual (BNA) 405:7262 (1995).

[20] *See* 29 C.F.R. § 1630.2(j) (1996).

[21] S. Rep. No. 101-116, at 23 (1989); H.R. Rep. No. 101-485, pt. 2, at 52 (1990); House Judiciary Report, **supra n.2,** at 28–29. *See also* 29 C.F.R.

pt. 1630 app. § 1630.2(j) (1996).

[22] ADA cases in which courts have disregarded the positive effects of medications or other treatment in the determination of disability include *Canon v. Clark*, 883 F. Supp. 718, 4 AD Cas. (BNA) 734 (S.D. Fla. 1995) (finding that individual with insulin-dependent diabetes stated an ADA claim), and *Sarsycki v. United Parcel Ser.*, 862 F. Supp. 336, 340, 3 AD Cas. (BNA) 1039 (W.D. Okla. 1994) (stating that substantial limitation should be evaluated without regard to medication and finding that an individual with insulin-dependent diabetes had a disability under the ADA). Pertinent Rehabilitation Act cases in which courts have made similar determinations include *Liff v. Secretary of Transp.*, 1994 WL 579912, at *3–*4 (D.D.C. 1994) (deciding under the Rehabilitation Act, after acknowledging pertinent ADA guidance, that depression controlled by medication is a disability), and *Gilbert v. Frank*, 949 F.2d 637, 641, 2 AD Cas. (BNA) 60 (2d Cir. 1991) (determining under the Rehabilitation Act that an individual who could not function without kidney dialysis had a substantially limiting impairment).

Cases in which courts have found that individuals are *not* substantially limited after considering the positive effects of medication are, in the Commission's view, incorrectly decided. *See, e.g.*, *Mackie v. Runyon*, 804 F. Supp. 1508, 1510–11, 2 AD Cas. (BNA) 260 (M.D. Fla. 1992) (holding under sec-

Relevant evidence for EEOC investigators includes, for example, a description of how an individual's condition changed when s/he went off medication[23] or needed to have dosages adjusted, or a description of his/her condition before starting medication.[24]

7. How long does a mental impairment have to last to be substantially limiting?

   An impairment is substantially limiting if it lasts for more than several months and significantly restricts the performance of one or more major life activities during that time. It is not substantially limiting if it lasts for only a brief time or does not significantly restrict an individual's ability to perform a major life activity.[25] Whether the impairment is substantially limiting is assessed without regard to mitigating measures such as medication.

   Example A: An employee has had major depression for almost a year. He has been intensely sad and socially withdrawn (except for going to work), has developed serious insomnia, and has had severe problems concentrating. This employee has an impairment (major depression) that significantly restricts his ability to interact with others, sleep, and concentrate. The effects of this impairment are severe and have lasted long enough to be substantially limiting.

   In addition, some conditions may be long-term, or potentially long-term, in that their duration is indefinite and unknowable or is expected to be at least several months. Such conditions, if severe, may constitute disabilities.[26]

   Example B: An employee has taken medication for bipolar disorder for a few months. For some time before starting medication, he experienced increasingly severe and frequent cycles of depression and mania; at times, he became extremely withdrawn socially or had difficulty caring for himself. His symptoms have abated with medication, but his doctor says that the duration and course of his bipolar disorder is indefinite, although it is potentially long-term. This employee's impairment (bipolar disorder) significantly restricts his major life activities of interacting with others and caring for himself, when considered without medication. The effects of his impairment are severe, and their duration is indefinite and potentially long-term.

   However, conditions that are temporary and have no permanent or long-term effects on an individual's major life activities are not substantially limiting.

   Example C: An employee was distressed by the end of a romantic relationship. Although he continued his daily routine, he sometimes became agitated at work. He was most distressed for about a month during and immediately after the breakup. He sought counseling and his mood improved within weeks. His counselor gave him a diagnosis of "adjustment disorder" and stated that he was not expected to experience any long-term problems associated with this event. While he has an impairment (adjustment disorder), his impairment was short-term, did not significantly restrict major life activities during that time, and was not expected to have permanent or long-term effects. This employee does not have a disability for purposes of the ADA.

8. Can **chronic, episodic disorders** be substantially limiting?

---

tion 501 of the Rehabilitation Act that bipolar disorder stabilized by medication is not substantially limiting); *Chandler v. City of Dallas*, 2 F.3d 1385, 1390–91, 2 AD Cas. (BNA) 1326 (5th Cir. 1993) (holding under section 504 of the Rehabilitation Act that an individual with insulin-dependent diabetes did not have a disability), *cert. denied*,

114 S. Ct. 1386, 3 AD Cas. (BNA) 512 (1994).

[23] Some individuals do not experience renewed symptoms when they stop taking medication. These individuals are still covered by the ADA, however, if they have a record of a substantially limiting impairment (*i.e.*, if their psychiatric impairment was sufficiently severe and long-lasting to be substantially limiting).

[24] If medications cause negative side effects, these side effects should be considered in assessing whether the individual is substantially limited. *See, e.g., Guice-Mills v. Derwinski*, 967 F.2d 794, 2 AD Cas. (BNA) 187 (2d Cir. 1992).

[25] EEOC Compliance Manual § 902.4(d), Definition of the Term "Disability," 8 FEP Manual (BNA) 405:7273 (1995).

[26] *Id.*, 8 FEP Manual (BNA) 405:7271.

Yes. Chronic, episodic conditions may constitute substantially limiting impairments if they are substantially limiting when active or have a high likelihood of recurrence in substantially limiting forms. For some individuals, psychiatric impairments such as bipolar disorder, major depression, and schizophrenia may remit and intensify, sometimes repeatedly, over the course of several months or several years.[27]

9. When does an impairment substantially limit an individual's ability to **interact with others?**

   An impairment substantially limits an individual's ability to interact with others if, due to the impairment, s/he is **significantly restricted as compared to the average person in the general population.** Some unfriendliness with coworkers or a supervisor would not, standing alone, be sufficient to establish a **substantial limitation** in interacting with others. An individual would be substantially limited, however, if his/ her relations with others were characterized **on a regular basis** by **severe** problems, for example, consistently high levels of hostility, social withdrawal, or failure to communicate when necessary.

   These limitations must be long-term or potentially long-term, as opposed to temporary, to justify a finding of ADA disability.

   Example: An individual diagnosed with schizophrenia now works successfully as a computer programmer for a large company. Before finding an effective medication, however, he stayed in his room at home for several months, usually refusing to talk to family and close friends. After finding an effective medication, he was able to return to school, graduate, and start his career. This individual has a mental impairment, schizophrenia, which substantially limits his ability to interact with others when evaluated without medication. Accordingly, he is an individual with a disability as defined by the ADA.

10. When does an impairment substantially limit an individual's ability to **concentrate?**

    An impairment substantially limits an individual's ability to concentrate if, due to the impairment, s/he is **significantly restricted as compared to the average person in the general population.**[28] For example, an individual would be substantially limited if s/he was easily and frequently distracted, meaning that his/her attention was frequently drawn to irrelevant sights or sounds or to intrusive thoughts; or if s/he experienced his/her "mind going blank" on a frequent basis.

    Such limitations must be long-term or potentially long-term, as opposed to temporary, to justify a finding of ADA disability.[29]

    Example A: An employee who has an anxiety disorder says that his mind wanders frequently and that he is often distracted by irrelevant thoughts. As a result, he makes repeated errors at work on detailed or complex tasks, even after being reprimanded. His doctor says that the errors are caused by his anxiety disorder and may last indefinitely. This individual has a disability because, as a result of an anxiety disorder, his ability to concentrate is significantly restricted as compared to the average person in the general population.

    Example B: An employee states that he has trouble concentrating when he is tired or during long meetings. He attributes this to his chronic depression. Although his ability to concentrate may be slightly limited due to depression (a mental impairment), it is not significantly restricted as compared to the average person in the general population. Many

---

[27] *See, e.g., Clark v. Virginia Bd. of Bar Exam'rs*, 861 F. Supp. 512, 3 AD Cas. (BNA) 1066 (E.D. Va. 1994) (vacating its earlier ruling (at 3 AD Cas. (BNA) 780) that plaintiff's recurrent major depression did not constitute a "disability" under the ADA).

[28] 29 C.F.R. § 1630.2(j)(ii) (1996); EEOC Compliance Manual § 902.3(b), Definition of the Term "Disability," 8 FEP Manual (BNA) 405:7261 (1995).

[29] Substantial limitation in concentrating also may be associated with learning disabilities, neurological disorders, and physical trauma to the brain (*e.g.*, stroke, brain tumor, or head injury in a car accident). Although this guidance does not focus on these particular impairments, the analysis of basic ADA issues is consistent regardless of the nature of the condition.

people in the general population have difficulty concentrating when they are tired or during long meetings.

11. When does an impairment substantially limit an individual's ability to **sleep?**

An impairment substantially limits an individual's ability to sleep if, due to the impairment, his/her sleep is **significantly restricted as compared to the average person in the general population.** These limitations must be long-term or potentially long-term as opposed to temporary to justify a finding of ADA disability.

For example, an individual who sleeps only a negligible amount without medication for many months, due to post-traumatic stress disorder, would be significantly restricted as compared to the average person in the general population and therefore would be substantially limited in sleeping.[30] Similarly, an individual who for several months typically slept about two to three hours per night without medication, due to depression, also would be substantially limited in sleeping.

By contrast, an individual would not be substantially limited in sleeping if s/he had some trouble getting to sleep or sometimes slept fitfully because of a mental impairment. Although this individual may be slightly restricted in sleeping, s/he is not significantly restricted as compared to the average person in the general population.

12. When does an impairment substantially limit an individual's ability to **care for him/herself?**

An impairment substantially limits an individual's ability to care for him/herself if, due to the impairment, an individual is **significantly restricted as compared to the average person in the general population** in performing basic activities such as getting up in the morning, bathing, dressing, and preparing or obtaining food. These limitations must be long-term or potentially long-term as opposed to temporary to justify a finding of ADA disability.

Some psychiatric impairments, for example major depression, may result in an individual sleeping too much. In such cases, an individual may be substantially limited if, as a result of the impairment, s/he sleeps so much that s/he does not effectively care for him/herself. Alternatively, the individual may be substantially limited in working.

Disclosure of Disability

Individuals with psychiatric disabilities may have questions about whether and when they must disclose their disability to their employer under the ADA. They may have concerns about the potential negative consequences of disclosing a psychiatric disability in the workplace, and about the confidentiality of information that they do disclose.

13. May an employer ask **questions on a job application** about history of treatment of mental illness, hospitalization, or the existence of mental or emotional illness or psychiatric disability?

No. An employer may not ask questions that are likely to elicit information about a disability before making an offer of employment.[31] Questions on a job application about psychiatric disability or mental or emotional illness or about treatment are likely to elicit information about a psychiatric disability and therefore are prohibited before an offer of employment is made.

14. **When** may an employer lawfully ask an individual about **a psychiatric disability** under the ADA?

An employer may ask for disability-related information, including information about psychiatric disability, only in the following limited circumstances:

- **Application Stage.** Employers are prohibited from asking disability-related questions before making an offer of employment. An exception, however, is if an applicant asks for **reasonable**

[30] A 1994 survey of 1,000 American adults reports that 71% averaged 5–8 hours of sleep a night on weeknights and that 55% averaged 5–8 hours a night on weekends (with 37% getting more than 8 hours a night on weekends). *See* **The Cutting Edge: Vital Statistics — America's Sleep Habits,** Washington Post, May 24, 1994, Health Section at 5.

[31] *See* 42 U.S.C. § 12112(d)(2) (1994); 29 C.F.R. § 1630.13(a) (1996). *See also* EEOC Enforcement Guidance: Preemployment Disability-Related Questions and Medical Examinations at 4, 8 FEP Manual (BNA) 405:7192 (1995).

accommodation for the hiring process. If the need for this accommodation is not obvious, an employer may ask an applicant for **reasonable** documentation about his/her disability. The employer may require the applicant to provide documentation from an appropriate professional concerning his/her disability and functional limitations.[32] A variety of health professionals may provide such documentation regarding psychiatric disabilities including primary health care professionals,[33] psychiatrists, psychologists, psychiatric nurses, and licensed mental health professionals such as licensed clinical social workers and licensed professional counselors.[34]

An employer should make clear to the applicant why it is requesting such information, *i.e.,* to verify the existence of a disability and the need for an accommodation. Furthermore, the employer may request only information necessary to accomplish these limited purposes.

Example A: An applicant for a secretarial job asks to take a typing test in a quiet location rather than in a busy reception area "because of a medical condition." The employer may make disability-related inquiries at this point because the applicant's need for reasonable accommodation under the ADA is not obvious based on the statement that an accommodation is needed "because of a medical condition." Specifically, the employer may ask the applicant to provide documentation showing that she has an impairment that substantially limits a major life activity and that she needs to take the typing test in a quiet location because of disability-related functional limitations.[35]

Although an employer may not ask an applicant if s/he will need reasonable accommodation **for the job,** there is an exception if the employer could **reasonably believe,** before making a job offer, that the applicant will need accommodation to perform the functions of the job. For an individual with a non-visible disability, this may occur if the individual voluntarily discloses his/her disability or if s/he voluntarily tells the employer that s/he needs reasonable accommodation to perform the job. The employer may then ask certain limited questions, specifically:

- whether the applicant needs reasonable accommodation; and
- what type of reasonable accommodation would be needed to perform the functions of the job.[36]
- **After making an offer of employment, if the employer requires a post- offer, preemployment medical examination or inquiry.** After an employer extends an offer of employment, the employer may require a medical examination (including a psychiatric examination) or ask questions related to disability (including questions about psychiatric disability) *if* the employer subjects *all* entering employees in the same job category to the same inquiries or examinations regardless of disability. The inquiries and examinations do not need to be related to the job.[37]

---

[32] Enforcement Guidance: Preemployment Disability-Related Questions and Medical Examinations at 6, 8 FEP Manual (BNA) 405:7193 (1995).

[33] When a primary health care professional supplies documentation about a psychiatric disability, his/her credibility depends on how well s/he knows the individual and on his/her knowledge about the psychiatric disability.

[34] Important information about an applicant's functional limitations also may be obtained from non-professionals, such as the applicant, his/her family members, and friends.

[35] In response to the employer's request for documentation, the applicant may elect to revoke the request for accommodation and to take the test in the reception area. In these circumstances, where the request for reasonable accommodation has been withdrawn, the employer cannot continue to insist on obtaining the documentation.

[36] EEOC Enforcement Guidance: Preemployment Disability-Related Questions and Medical Examinations at 6–7, 8 FEP Manual (BNA) 405:7193–94 (1995).

[37] If an employer uses the results of these inquiries or examinations to screen out an individual because of disability, the employer must prove that the exclusionary criteria are job-related and consistent with business necessity, and cannot be met with reasonable accommodation, in order to defend against a charge of employment discrimination. 42 U.S.C. § 12112(b)(6) (1994); 29 C.F.R. §§ 1630.10, 1630.14(b)(3), 1630.15(b) (1996).

- During employment, when a disability-related inquiry or medical examination of an employee is "job-related and consistent with business necessity."[38] This requirement may be met when an employer has a reasonable belief, based on objective evidence, that: (1) an employee's ability to perform essential job functions[39] will be impaired by a medical condition; or (2) an employee will pose a direct threat due to a medical condition. Thus, for example, inquiries or medical examinations are permitted if they follow-up on a request for reasonable accommodation when the need for accommodation is not obvious, or if they address reasonable concerns about whether an individual is fit to perform essential functions of his/her position. In addition, inquiries or examinations are permitted if they are required by another Federal law or regulation.[40] In these situations, the inquiries or examinations must not exceed the scope of the specific medical condition and its effect on the employee's ability, with or without reasonable accommodation, to perform essential job functions or to work without posing a direct threat.[41]

  Example B: A delivery person does not learn the route he is required to take when he makes deliveries in a particular neighborhood. He often does not deliver items at all or delivers them to the wrong address. He is not adequately performing his essential function of making deliveries. There is no indication, however, that his failure to learn his route is related in any way to a medical condition. Because the employer does not have a reason-able belief, **based on objective evidence,** that this individual's ability to perform his essential job function is impaired by a medical condition, a medical examination (including a psychiatric examination) or disability-related inquiries would not be job-related and consistent with business necessity.[42]

  Example C: A limousine service knows that one of its best drivers has bipolar disorder and had a manic episode last year, which started when he was driving a group of diplomats to around-the-clock meetings. During the manic episode, the chauffeur engaged in behavior that posed a direct threat to himself and others (he repeatedly drove a company limousine in a reckless manner). After a short leave of absence, he returned to work and to his usual high level of performance. The limousine service now wants to assign him to drive several business executives who may begin around-the-clock labor negotiations during the next several weeks. The employer is concerned, however, that this will trigger another manic episode and that, as a result, the employee will drive recklessly and pose a significant risk of substantial harm to himself and others. There is no indication that the employee's condition has changed in the last year, or that his manic episode last year was not precipitated by the assignment to drive to around-the-clock meetings. The employer may make disability-related inquiries, or require a medical examination, because it has a reasonable belief, based on objective evidence, that the employee will pose a direct threat to himself or others due to a medical condition.

---

[38] 42 U.S.C. § 12112(d)(4) (1994); 29 C.F.R. § 1630.14(c) (1996).

[39] A "qualified" individual with a disability is one who can perform the essential functions of a position with or without reasonable accommodation. 42 U.S.C. § 12111(8) (1994). An employer does not have to lower production standards, whether qualitative or quantitative, to enable an individual with a disability to perform an essential function. *See* 29 C.F.R. pt. 1630 app. § 1630.2(n) (1996).

[40] 29 C.F.R. § 1630.15(e) (1996) ("It may be a defense to a charge of discrimination… that a challenged action is required or necessitated by another Federal law or regulation…").

[41] There may be additional situations which could meet the "job-related and consistent with business necessity" standard. For example, periodic medical examinations for public safety positions that are narrowly tailored to address specific job-related concerns and are shown to be consistent with business necessity would be permissible.

[42] Of course, an employer would be justified in taking disciplinary action in these circumstances.

Example D: An employee with depression seeks to return to work after a leave of absence during which she was hospitalized and her medication was adjusted. Her employer may request a fitness-for-duty examination because it has a reasonable belief, based on the employee's hospitalization and medication adjustment, that her ability to perform essential job functions may continue to be impaired by a medical condition. This examination, however, must be limited to the effect of her depression on her ability, with or without reasonable accommodation, to perform essential job functions. Inquiries about her entire psychiatric history or about the details of her therapy sessions would, for example, exceed this limited scope.

15. Do ADA **confidentiality requirements** apply to information about a psychiatric disability disclosed to an employer?

Yes. Employers must keep all information concerning the medical condition or history of its applicants or employees, including information about psychiatric disability, confidential under the ADA. This includes medical information that an individual voluntarily tells his/her employer. Employers must collect and maintain such information on separate forms and in separate medical files, apart from the usual personnel files.[43] There are limited exceptions to the ADA confidentiality requirements:

- supervisors and managers may be told about necessary restrictions on the work or duties of the employee and about necessary accommodations;
- first aid and safety personnel may be told if the disability might require emergency treatment; and
- government officials investigating compliance with the ADA must be given relevant information on request.[44]

16. How can an employer respond **when employees ask questions about a coworker who has a disability?**

If employees ask questions about a coworker who has a disability, the employer must not disclose any medical information in response. Apart from the limited exceptions listed in Question 15, the ADA confidentiality provisions prohibit such disclosure.

An employer also may not tell employees whether it is providing a reasonable accommodation for a particular individual. A statement that an individual receives a reasonable accommodation discloses that the individual probably has a disability because only individuals with disabilities are entitled to reasonable accommodation under the ADA. In response to coworker questions, however, the employer may explain that it is acting for legitimate business reasons or in compliance with federal law.

As background information for all employees, an employer may find it helpful to explain the requirements of the ADA, including the obligation to provide reasonable accommodation, in its employee handbook or in its employee orientation or training.

Requesting Reasonable Accommodation

An employer must provide a reasonable accommodation to the known physical or mental limitations of a qualified individual with a disability unless it can show that the accommodation would impose an undue hardship.[45] An employee's decision about requesting reasonable accommodation may be influenced by his/her concerns about the potential negative

---

[43] For a discussion of other confidentiality issues, *see* EEOC Enforcement Guidance: Preemployment Disability-Related Questions and Medical Examinations at 21–23, 8 FEP Manual (BNA) 405:7201–02 (1995).

[44] 42 U.S.C. § 12112(d)(3)(B), (4)(C) (1994); 29 C.F.R. § 1630.14(b)(1) (1996). The Commission has interpreted the ADA to allow employers to disclose medical information to state workers' compensation offices, state second injury funds, or workers' compensation insurance carriers in accordance with state workers' compensation laws. 29 C.F.R. pt. 1630 app. § 1630.14(b) (1996). The Commission also has interpreted the ADA to permit employers to use medical information for insurance purposes. *Id. See also* EEOC Enforcement Guidance: Preemployment Disability-Related Questions and Medical Examinations at 21 nn.24, 25, 8 FEP Manual (BNA) 405:7201 nn.24, 25 (1995).

[45] *See* 42 U.S.C. §§ 12111(9), 12112(b)(5)(A) (1994); 29 C.F.R.

consequences of disclosing a psychiatric disability at work. Employees and employers alike have posed numerous questions about what constitutes a request for reasonable accommodation.

17. When an individual decides to **request reasonable accommodation,** what must s/he say to make the request and start the reasonable accommodation process?

When an individual decides to request accommodation, the individual or his/her representative must let the employer know that s/he needs an adjustment or change at work for a reason related to a medical condition. To request accommodation, an individual may use "plain English" and need not mention the ADA or use the phrase "reasonable accommodation."[46]

Example A: An employee asks for time off because he is "depressed and stressed." The employee has communicated a request for a change at work (time off) for a reason related to a medical condition (being "depressed and stressed" may be "plain English" for a medical condition). This statement is sufficient to put the employer on notice that the employee is requesting reasonable accommodation. However, if the employee's need for accommodation is not obvious, the employer may ask for reasonable documentation concerning the employee's disability and functional limitations.[47]

Example B: An employee submits a note from a health professional stating that he is having a stress reaction and needs one week off. Subsequently, his wife telephones the Human Resources department to say that the employee is disoriented and mentally falling apart and that the family is having him hospitalized. The wife asks about procedures for extending the employee's leave and states that she will provide the necessary information as soon as possible but that she may need a little extra time. The wife's statement is sufficient to constitute a request for reasonable accommodation. The wife has asked for changes at work (an exception to the procedures for requesting leave and more time off) for a reason related to a medical condition (her husband had a stress reaction and is so mentally disoriented that he is being hospitalized). As in the previous example, if the need for accommodation is not obvious, the employer may request documentation of disability and clarification of the need for accommodation.[48]

Example C: An employee asks to take a few days off to rest after the completion of a major project. The employee does not link her need for a few days off to a medical condition. Thus, even though she has requested a change at work (time off), her statement is not sufficient to put the employer on notice that she is requesting reasonable accommodation.

18. May someone **other than the employee request a reasonable accommodation** on behalf of an individual with a disability?

Yes, a family member, friend, health professional, or other representative may request a reasonable accommodation on behalf of an individual with a disability.[49] Of course, an employee may refuse to accept an accommodation that is not needed.

---

§ 1630.2(o), .9 (1996); 29 C.F.R. pt. 1630 app. § 1630.9 (1996).

[46] *Schmidt v. Safeway, Inc.*, 864 F. Supp. 991, 3 AD Cas. (BNA) 1141 (D. Or. 1994) (an employee's request for reasonable accommodation need not use "magic words" and can be in plain English). *See Bultemeyer v. Ft. Wayne Community Schs.*, 6 AD Cas. (BNA) 67 (7th Cir. 1996) (an employee with a known psychiatric disability requested reasonable accommodation by stating that he could not do a particular job and by submitting a note from his psychiatrist).

[47] *See* Question 21 *infra* about employers requesting documentation after receiving a request for reasonable accommodation.

[48] In the Commission's view, *Miller v. Nat'l Cas. Co.*, 61 F.3d 627, 4 AD Cas. (BNA) 1089 (8th Cir. 1995) was incorrectly decided. The court in *Miller* held that the employer was not alerted to Miller's disability and need for accommodation despite the fact that Miller's sister phoned the employer repeatedly and informed it that Miller was falling apart mentally and that the family was trying to get her into a hospital. *See also Taylor v. Principal Financial Group*, 5 AD Cas. (BNA) 1653 (5th Cir. 1996).

[49] *Cf. Beck v. Univ. of Wis.*, 75 F.3d 1130, 5 AD Cas. (BNA) 304 (7th Cir. 1996) (assuming, without discussion, that a doctor's note requesting reasonable accommodation on behalf of his patient triggered the reasonable accommodation process); *Schmidt v.*

19. Do requests for reasonable accommodation need to be **in writing?**

No. Requests for reasonable accommodation do not need to be in writing. Employees may request accommodations in conversation or may use any other mode of communication.[50]

20. **When** should an individual with a disability **request a reasonable accommodation** to do the job?

An individual with a disability is not required to request a reasonable accommodation at the beginning of employment. S/he may request a reasonable accommodation at any time during employment.[51]

21. May an employer ask an employee for **documentation** when the employee requests reasonable accommodation for the job?

Yes. When the **need for accommodation is not obvious,** an employer may ask an employee for **reasonable** documentation about his/her disability and functional limitations. The employer is entitled to know that the employee has a covered disability for which s/he needs a reasonable accommodation.[52] A variety of health professionals may provide such documentation with regard to psychiatric disabilities.[53]

Example A: An employee asks for time off because he is "depressed and stressed." Although this statement is sufficient to put the employer on notice that he is requesting accommodation,[54] the employee's need for accommodation is not obvious based on this statement alone. Accordingly, the employer may require **reasonable** documentation that the employee has a disability within the meaning of the ADA and, if he has such a disability, that the functional limitations of the disability necessitate time off.

Example B: Same as Example A, except that the employer requires the employee to submit **all** of the records from his health professional regarding his mental health history, including materials that are not relevant to disability and reasonable accommodation under the ADA. This is not a request for **reasonable** documentation. All of these records are not required to determine if the employee has a disability as defined by the ADA and needs the requested reasonable accommodation because of his disability-related functional limitations. As one alternative, in order to determine the scope of its ADA obligations, the employer may ask the employee to sign a limited release allowing the employer to submit a list of specific questions to the employee's health care professional about his condition and need for reasonable accommodation.

22. May an employer require an employee to go to a health care professional of the **employer's (rather than the employee's)**

Safeway, Inc., 864 F. Supp. 991, 3 AD Cas. (BNA) 1141 (D. Or. 1994) (stating that a doctor need not be expressly authorized to request accommodation on behalf of an employee in order to make a valid request).

In addition, because the reasonable accommodation process presumes open communication between the employer and the employee with the disability, the employer should be receptive to any relevant information or requests it receives from a third party acting on the employee's behalf. 29 C.F.R. pt. 1630 app. § 1630.9 (1996).

[50] Although individuals with disabilities are not required to keep records, they may find it useful to document requests for reasonable accommodation in the event there is a dispute about whether or when they requested accommodation. Of course, employers must keep all employment records, including records of requests for reasonable accommodation, for one year from the making of the record or the personnel action involved, whichever occurs later. 29 C.F.R. § 1602.14 (1996).

[51] As a practical matter, it may be in the employee's interest to request a reasonable accommodation **before** performance suffers or conduct problems occur.

[52] EEOC Enforcement Guidance: Preemployment Disability-Related Questions and Medical Examinations at 6, 8 FEP Manual (BNA) 405:7193 (1995).

[53] *See supra* nn.32–34 and accompanying text. *See also Bultemeyer v. Ft. Wayne Community Schs.*, 6 AD Cas. (BNA) 67 (7th Cir. 1996) (stating that, if employer found the precise meaning of employee's request for reasonable accommodation unclear, employer should have spoken to the employee or his psychiatrist, thus properly engaging in the interactive process).

[54] *See* Question 17, Example A, *supra.*

choice for purposes of documenting need for accommodation and disability?

The ADA does not prevent an employer from requiring an employee to go to an appropriate health professional of the employer's choice if the employee initially provides insufficient information to substantiate that s/he has an ADA disability and needs a reasonable accommodation. Of course, any examination must be job-related and consistent with business necessity.[55] If an employer requires an employee to go to a health professional of the employer's choice, the employer must pay all costs associated with the visit(s).

Selected Types of Reasonable Accommodation

Reasonable accommodations for individuals with disabilities must be determined on a case-by-case basis because workplaces and jobs vary, as do people with disabilities. Accommodations for individuals with psychiatric disabilities may involve changes to workplace policies, procedures, or practices. Physical changes to the workplace or extra equipment also may be effective reasonable accommodations for some people.

In some instances, the precise nature of an effective accommodation for an individual may not be immediately apparent. Mental health professionals, including psychiatric rehabilitation counselors, may be able to make suggestions about particular accommodations and, of equal importance, help employers and employees communicate effectively about reasonable accommodation.[56] The questions below discuss selected types of reasonable accommodation that may be effective for certain individuals with psychiatric disabilities.[57]

23. Does reasonable accommodation include giving an individual with a disability **time off** from work or a **modified work schedule?**

Yes. Permitting the use of accrued paid leave or providing additional unpaid leave for treatment or recovery related to a disability is a reasonable accommodation, unless (or until) the employee's absence imposes an undue hardship on the operation of the employer's business.[58] This includes leaves of absence, occasional leave (*e.g.*, a few hours at a time), and part-time scheduling.

A related reasonable accommodation is to allow an individual with a disability to change his/her regularly scheduled working hours, for example, to work 10 AM to 6 PM rather than 9 AM to 5 PM, barring undue hardship. Some medications taken for psychiatric disabilities cause extreme grogginess and lack of concentration in the morning. Depending on the job, a later schedule can enable the employee to perform essential job functions.

24. What types of **physical changes to the workplace** or **equipment** can serve as accommodations for people with psychiatric disabilities?

Simple physical changes to the workplace may be effective accommodations for some

---

[55] Employers also may consider alternatives like having their health professional consult with the employee's health professional, with the employee's consent.

[56] The Job Accommodation Network (JAN) also provides advice free-of- charge to employers and employees contemplating reasonable accommodation. JAN is a service of the President's Committee on Employment of People with Disabilities which, in turn, is funded by the U.S. Department of Labor. JAN can be reached at 1-800-ADA-WORK.

[57] Some of the accommodations discussed in this section also may prove effective for individuals with traumatic brain injuries, stroke, and other mental disabilities. As a general matter, a covered employer must provide reasonable accommodation to the known physical or mental limitations of an otherwise qualified individual with a disability, barring undue hardship. 42 U.S.C. § 12112(b)(5)(A) (1994).

[58] 29 C.F.R. pt. 1630 app. § 1630.2(o) (1996). Courts have recognized leave as a reasonable accommodation. *See, e.g., Vande Zande v. Wis. Dep't of Admin.*, 44 F.3d 538, 3 AD Cas. (BNA) 1636 (7th Cir. 1995) (defendant had duty to accommodate plaintiff's pressure ulcers resulting from her paralysis which required her to stay home for several weeks); *Vializ v. New York City Bd. of Educ.*, 1995 WL 110112, 4 AD Cas. (BNA) 345 (S.D.N.Y. 1995) (plaintiff stated claim under ADA where she alleged that she would be able to return to work after back injury if defendant granted her a temporary leave of absence); *Schmidt v. Safeway, Inc.*, 864 F. Supp. 991, 3 AD Cas. (BNA) 1141 (D. Or. 1994) ("[A] leave of absence to obtain medical treatment is a reasonable accommodation if it is likely that, following treatment, [the employee] would have been able to safely perform his duties...").

individuals with psychiatric disabilities. For example, room dividers, partitions, or other soundproofing or visual barriers between workspaces may accommodate individuals who have disability-related limitations in concentration. Moving an individual away from noisy machinery or reducing other workplace noise that can be adjusted (*e.g.*, lowering the volume or pitch of telephones) are similar reasonable accommodations. Permitting an individual to wear headphones to block out noisy distractions also may be effective.

Some individuals who have disability-related limitations in concentration may benefit from access to equipment like a tape recorder for reviewing events such as training sessions or meetings.

25. Is it a reasonable accommodation to **modify a workplace policy?**

Yes. It is a reasonable accommodation to modify a workplace policy when necessitated by an individual's disability-related limitations, barring undue hardship.[59] For example, it would be a reasonable accommodation to allow an individual with a disability, who has difficulty concentrating due to the disability, to take detailed notes during client presentations even though company policy discourages employees from taking extensive notes during such sessions.

> *Example:* A retail employer does not allow individuals working as cashiers to drink beverages at checkout stations. The retailer also limits cashiers to two 15-minute breaks during an eight-hour shift, in addition to a meal break. An individual with a psychiatric disability needs to drink beverages approximately once an hour in order to combat dry mouth, a side-effect of his psychiatric medication. This individual requests reasonable accommodation. In this example, the employer should consider either modifying its policy against drinking beverages at checkout stations or modifying its policy limiting cashiers to two 15-minute breaks each day plus a meal break, barring undue hardship.

Granting an employee time off from work or an adjusted work schedule as a reasonable accommodation may involve modifying leave or attendance procedures or policies. As an example, it would be a reasonable accommodation to modify a policy requiring employees to schedule vacation time in advance if an otherwise qualified individual with a disability needed to use accrued vacation time on an unscheduled basis because of disability-related medical problems, barring undue hardship.[60] In addition, an employer, in spite of a "no-leave" policy, may, in appropriate circumstances, be required to provide leave to an employee with a disability as a reasonable accommodation, unless the provision of leave would impose an undue hardship.[61]

26. Is adjusting **supervisory methods** a form of reasonable accommodation?

Yes. Supervisors play a central role in achieving effective reasonable accommodations for their employees. In some circumstances, supervisors may be able to adjust their methods as a reasonable accommodation by, for example, communicating assignments, instructions, or training by the medium that is most effective for a particular individual (*e.g.*, in writing, in conversation, or by electronic mail). Supervisors also may provide or arrange additional training or modified training materials.

Adjusting the level of supervision or structure sometimes may enable an otherwise qualified individual with a disability to perform essential job functions. For example, an otherwise qualified individual with a disability who experiences limitations in concentration may request more detailed

---

[59] 42 U.S.C. § 12111(9)(B) (1994); 29 C.F.R. § 1630.2(o)(2)(ii) (1996).

[60] *See Dutton v. Johnson County Bd.*, 1995 WL 337588, 3 AD Cas. (BNA) 1614 (D. Kan. 1995) (it was a reasonable accommodation to permit an individual with a disability to use unscheduled vacation time to cover absence for migraine headaches, where that did not pose an undue hardship and employer knew about the migraine headaches and the need for accommodation).

[61] *See* 29 C.F.R. pt. 1630 app. § 1630.15(b), (c) (1996).

day-to-day guidance, feedback, or structure in order to perform his job.[62]

Example: An employee requests more daily guidance and feedback as a reasonable accommodation for limitations associated with a psychiatric disability. In response to his request, the employer consults with the employee, his health care professional, and his supervisor about how his limitations are manifested in the office (the employee is unable to stay focused on the steps necessary to complete large projects) and how to make effective and practical changes to provide the structure he needs. As a result of these consultations, the supervisor and employee work out a long-term plan to initiate weekly meetings to review the status of large projects and identify which steps need to be taken next.

27. Is it a reasonable accommodation to provide a **job coach?**

Yes. An employer may be required to provide a temporary job coach to assist in the training of a qualified individual with a disability as a reasonable accommodation, barring undue hardship.[63] An employer also may be required to allow a job coach paid by a public or private social service agency to accompany the employee at the job site as a reasonable accommodation.

28. Is it a reasonable accommodation to make sure that an individual takes **medication** as prescribed?

No. Medication monitoring is not a reasonable accommodation. Employers have no obligation to monitor medication because doing so does not remove a barrier that is unique to the workplace. When people do not take medication as prescribed, it affects them on and off the job.

29. When is **reassignment** to a different position required as a reasonable accommodation?

In general, reassignment **must** be considered as a reasonable accommodation when accommodation in the present job would cause undue hardship[64] or would not be possible.[65] Reassignment **may** be considered if there are circumstances under which **both** the employer and employee **voluntarily agree** that it is preferable to accommodation in the present position.[66]

Reassignment should be made to an equivalent position that is vacant or will become vacant within a reasonable amount of time.

---

[62] Reasonable accommodation, however, does not require lowering standards or removing essential functions of the job. *Bolstein v. Reich*, 1995 WL 46387, 3 AD Cas. (BNA) 1761 (D.D.C. 1995) (attorney with chronic depression and severe personality disturbance was not a qualified individual with a disability because his requested accommodations of more supervision, less complex assignments, and the exclusion of appellate work would free him of the very duties that justified his GS-14 grade), *motion for summary affirmance granted*, 1995 WL 686236 (D.C. Cir. 1995). The court in *Bolstein* noted that the plaintiff objected to a reassignment to a lower grade in which he could have performed the essential functions of the position. 1995 WL 46387, * 4, 3 AD Cas. (BNA) 1761, 1764 (D.D.C. 1995).

[63] *See* 29 C.F.R. pt. 1630 app. § 1630.9 (1996) (discussing supported employment); U.S. Equal Employment Opportunity Commission, "A Technical Assistance Manual on the Employment Provisions (Title I) of the Americans with Disabilities Act," at 3.4, 8 FEP Manual (BNA) 405:7001 (1992) [hereinafter Technical Assistance Manual]. A job coach is a professional who assists individuals with severe disabilities with job placement and job training.

[64] For example, it may be an undue hardship to provide extra supervision as a reasonable accommodation in the present job if the employee's current supervisor is already very busy supervising several other individuals and providing direct service to the public.

[65] 42 U.S.C. § 12111(9)(B) (1994). For example, it may not be possible to accommodate an employee in his present position if he works as a salesperson on the busy first floor of a major department store and needs a reduction in visual distractions and ambient noise as a reasonable accommodation.

See EEOC Enforcement Guidance: Workers' Compensation and the ADA at 17, 8 FEP Manual (BNA) 405:7399–7400 (1996) (where an employee can no longer perform the essential functions of his/her original position, with or without a reasonable accommodation, because of a disability, an employer must reassign him/her to an equivalent vacant position for which s/he is qualified, absent undue hardship).

[66] Technical Assistance Manual, *supra* note 63, at 3.10(5), 8 FEP Manual (BNA) 405:7011–12 (reassignment to a vacant position as a reasonable accommodation); *see also* 42 U.S.C. § 12111(9)(B) (1994); 29 C.F.R. § 1630.2(o)(2)(ii) (1996).

If an equivalent position is not available, the employer must look for a vacant position at a lower level for which the employee is qualified. Reassignment is not required if a vacant position at a lower level is also unavailable.

Conduct

Maintaining satisfactory conduct and performance typically is not a problem for individuals with psychiatric disabilities. Nonetheless, circumstances arise when employers need to discipline individuals with such disabilities for misconduct.

30. May an employer **discipline** an individual with a disability for **violating a workplace conduct standard** if the misconduct **resulted from a disability?**

    Yes, provided that the workplace conduct standard is job-related for the position in question and is consistent with business necessity.[67] For example, nothing in the ADA prevents an employer from maintaining a workplace free of violence or threats of violence, or from disciplining an employee who steals or destroys property. Thus, an employer may discipline an employee with a disability for engaging in such misconduct if it would impose the same discipline on an employee without a disability.[68] Other conduct standards, however, may not be job-related for the position in question and consistent with business necessity. If they are not, imposing discipline under them could violate the ADA.

    Example A: An employee steals money from his employer. Even if he asserts that his misconduct was caused by a disability, the employer may discipline him consistent with its uniform disciplinary policies because the individual violated a conduct standard — a prohibition against employee theft — that is job-related for the position in question and consistent with business necessity.

    Example B: An employee at a clinic tampers with and incapacitates medical equipment. Even if the employee explains that she did this because of her disability, the employer may discipline her consistent with its uniform disciplinary policies because she violated a conduct standard — a rule prohibiting intentional damage to equipment — that is job-related for the position in question and consistent with business necessity. However, if the employer disciplines her even though it has not disciplined people without disabilities for the same misconduct, the employer would be treating her differently because of disability in violation of the ADA.

    Example C: An employee with a psychiatric disability works in a warehouse loading boxes onto pallets for shipment. He has no customer contact and does not come into regular contact with other employees. Over the course of several weeks, he has come to work appearing increasingly disheveled. His clothes are ill-fitting and often have tears in them. He also has become increasingly anti-social. Coworkers have complained that when they try to engage him in casual conversation, he walks away or gives a curt reply. When he has to talk to a coworker, he is abrupt and rude. His work, however, has not suffered. The employer's company handbook states that employees should have a neat appearance at all times. The handbook also states that employees should be courteous to each other. When told that he is being disciplined for his appearance and treatment of coworkers, the employee explains that his appearance and demeanor have deteriorated because of his disability which was exacerbated during this time period.

---

[67] 42 U.S.C. § 12112(b)(6) (1994); 29 C.F.R. § 1630.10, .15(c) (1996).

[68] *See* EEOC Compliance Manual § 902.2, n.11, Definition of the Term "Disability," 8 FEP Manual (BNA) 405:7259, n.11 (1995) (an employer "does not have to excuse . . . misconduct, even if the misconduct results from an impairment that rises to the level of a disability, if it does not excuse similar misconduct from its other employees"); *see* 56 Fed. Reg. 35,733 (1991) (referring to revisions to proposed ADA rule that "clarify that employers may hold all employees, disabled (including those disabled by alcoholism or drug addiction) and nondisabled, to the same performance and conduct standards").

The dress code and coworker courtesy rules are not job-related for the position in question and consistent with business necessity because this employee has no customer contact and does not come into regular contact with other employees. Therefore, rigid application of these rules to this employee would violate the ADA.

31. Must an employer make reasonable accommodation for an individual with a disability who violated a conduct rule that is job-related for the position in question and consistent with business necessity?

An employer must make reasonable accommodation to enable **an otherwise qualified individual with a disability** to meet such a conduct standard **in the future,** barring undue hardship.[69] Because reasonable accommodation is always prospective, however, an employer is not required to excuse past misconduct.[70]

Example A: A reference librarian frequently loses her temper at work, disrupting the library atmosphere by shouting at patrons and coworkers. After receiving a suspension as the second step in uniform, progressive discipline, she discloses her disability, states that it causes her behavior, and requests a leave of absence for treatment. The employer may discipline her because she violated a conduct standard — a rule prohibiting disruptive behavior towards patrons and coworkers — that is job-related for the position in question and consistent with business necessity. The employer, however, must grant her request for a leave of absence as a reasonable accommodation, barring undue hardship, to enable her to meet this conduct standard in the future.

Example B: An employee with major depression is often late for work because of medication side-effects that make him extremely groggy in the morning. His scheduled hours are 9:00 AM to 5:30 PM, but he arrives at 9:00, 9:30, 10:00 or even 10:30 on any given day. His job responsibilities involve telephone contact with the company's traveling sales representatives, who depend on him to answer urgent marketing questions and expedite special orders. The employer disciplines him for tardiness, stating that continued failure to arrive promptly during the next month will result in termination of his employment. The individual then explains that he was late because of a disability and needs to work on a later schedule. In this situation, the employer may discipline the employee because he violated a conduct standard addressing tardiness that is job-related for the position in question and consistent with business necessity. The employer, however, must consider reasonable accommodation, barring undue hardship, to enable this individual to meet this standard in the future. For example, if this individual can serve the company's sales representatives by regularly working a schedule of 10:00 AM to 6:30 PM, a reasonable accommodation would be to modify his schedule so that he is not required to report for work until 10:00 AM.

Example C: An employee has a hostile altercation with his supervisor and threatens the supervisor with physical harm. The employer immediately terminates the individual's employment, consistent with its policy of immediately terminating the employment of anyone who threatens a supervisor. When he learns that his employment has been terminated, the employee asks the employer to put the termination on hold and to give him a month off for treatment instead. This is the employee's first request for accommodation and also the first time the employer learns about the employee's disability. The employer is not required to rescind the discharge under these circumstances, because the employee violated a conduct standard — a rule prohibiting threats of physical harm against supervisors — that is job-related for the position in question and

---

[69] *See* 29 C.F.R. § 1630.15(d) (1996).

[70] Therefore, it may be in the employee's interest to request a reasonable accommodation **before** performance suffers or conduct problems occur. *See* Question 20 *supra.*

consistent with business necessity. The employer also is not required to offer reasonable accommodation for the future because this individual is no longer a qualified individual with a disability. His employment was terminated under a uniformly applied conduct standard that is job-related for the position in question and consistent with business necessity.[71]

32. How should an employer deal with an employee with a disability who is engaging in misconduct because s/he is **not taking his/her medication?**

The employer should focus on the employee's conduct and explain to the employee the consequences of continued misconduct in terms of uniform disciplinary procedures. It is the **employee's** responsibility to decide about medication and to consider the consequences of not taking medication.[72]

Direct Threat

Under the ADA, an employer may lawfully exclude an individual from employment for safety reasons only if the employer can show that employment of the individual would pose a "direct threat."[73] Employers must apply the "direct threat" standard uniformly and may not use safety concerns to justify exclusion of persons with disabilities when persons without disabilities would not be excluded in similar circumstances.[74]

The EEOC's ADA regulations explain that "direct threat" means "a significant risk of substantial harm to the health or safety of the individual or others that cannot be eliminated or reduced by reasonable accommodation."[75] A "significant" risk is a high, and not just a slightly increased, risk.[76] The determination that an individual poses a "direct threat" must be based on an individualized assessment of the individual's present ability to safely perform the functions of the job, considering a reasonable medical judgment relying on the most current medical knowledge and/or the best available objective evidence.[77] With respect to the employment of individuals with psychiatric disabilities, the employer must identify the specific behavior that would pose a direct threat.[78] An individual does not pose a "direct threat" simply by virtue of having a history of psychiatric disability or being treated for a psychiatric disability.[79]

33. Does an individual pose a direct threat in operating machinery solely because s/he takes **medication** that may as a side effect diminish concentration and/or coordination for some people?

No. An individual does not pose a direct threat solely because s/he takes a medication that may diminish coordination or concentration for some people as a side effect. Whether such an individual poses a direct threat must be determined on a case-by-case basis, based on a reasonable medical judgment relying on the most current medical knowledge and/or on the best available objective evidence. Therefore, an employer must determine the nature and severity of this individual's side effects, how those side effects influence his/her ability to safely operate the machinery, and whether s/he has had safety problems in the past when operating the same or similar machinery while taking the medication. If a significant risk of substantial harm exists, then an employer must determine if there is a reasonable accommodation that will reduce or eliminate the risk.

Example: An individual receives an offer for a job in which she will operate an

---

[71] Regardless of misconduct, an individual with a disability must be allowed to file a grievance or appeal challenging his/her termination when that is a right normally available to other employees.

[72] If the employee requests reasonable accommodation in order to address the misconduct, the employer must grant the request, subject to undue hardship.

[73] *See* 42 U.S.C. § 12113(b) (1994).

[74] 29 C.F.R. pt. 1630 app. § 1630.2(r) (1996).

[75] 29 C.F.R. § 1630.2(r) (1996). To determine whether an individual would pose a direct threat, the factors to be considered include: (1) duration of the risk; (2) nature and severity of the potential harm; (3) likelihood that the potential harm will occur; and (4) imminence of the potential harm. *Id.*

[76] 29 C.F.R. pt. 1630 app. § 1630.2(r) (1996).

[77] 29 C.F.R. § 1630.2(r) (1996).

[78] 29 C.F.R. pt. 1630 app. § 1630.2(r) (1996).

[79] House Judiciary Report, *supra* n.2, at 45.

electric saw, conditioned on a post-offer medical examination. In response to questions at this medical examination, the individual discloses her psychiatric disability and states that she takes a medication to control it. This medication is known to sometimes affect coordination and concentration. The company doctor determines that the individual experiences negligible side effects from the medication because she takes a relatively low dosage. She also had an excellent safety record at a previous job, where she operated similar machinery while taking the same medication. This individual does not pose a direct threat.

34. When can an employer refuse to hire someone based on his/her **history of violence or threats of violence?**
An employer may refuse to hire someone based on his/her history of violence or threats of violence if it can show that the individual poses a direct threat. A determination of "direct threat" must be based on an individualized assessment of the individual's present ability to safely perform the functions of the job, considering the most current medical knowledge and/or the best available objective evidence. To find that an individual with a psychiatric disability poses a direct threat, the employer must identify the specific behavior on the part of the individual that would pose the direct threat. This includes an assessment of the likelihood and imminence of future violence.

Example: An individual applies for a position with Employer X. When Employer X checks his employment background, she learns that he was terminated two weeks ago by Employer Y, after he told a coworker that he would get a gun and "get his supervisor if he tries anything again." Employer X also learns that these statements followed three months of escalating incidents in which this individual had had several altercations in the workplace, including one in which he had to be restrained from fighting with a coworker. He then revealed his disability to Employer Y. After being given time off for medical treatment, he continued to have trouble controlling his temper and was seen punching the wall outside his supervisor's office. Finally, he made the threat against the supervisor and was terminated. Employer X learns that, since then, he has not received any further medical treatment. Employer X does not hire him, stating that this history indicates that he poses a direct threat.

This individual poses a direct threat as a result of his disability because his recent overt acts and statements (including an attempted fight with a coworker, punching the wall, and making a threatening statement about the supervisor) support the conclusion that he poses a "significant risk of substantial harm." Furthermore, his prior treatment had no effect on his behavior, he had received no subsequent treatment, and only two weeks had elapsed since his termination, all supporting a finding of direct threat.

35. Does an individual who has attempted **suicide** pose a direct threat when s/he seeks to return to work?
No, in most circumstances. As with other questions of direct threat, an employer must base its determination on an individualized assessment of the person's ability to safely perform job functions when s/he returns to work. Attempting suicide does not mean that an individual poses an imminent risk of harm to him/herself when s/he returns to work. In analyzing direct threat (including the likelihood and imminence of any potential harm), the employer must seek reasonable medical judgments relying on the most current medical knowledge and/or the best available factual evidence concerning the employee.

Example: An employee with a known psychiatric disability was hospitalized for two suicide attempts, which occurred within several weeks of each other. When the employee asked to return to work, the employer allowed him to return pending an evaluation of medical reports to determine his ability to safely perform his job. The individual's therapist and psychiatrist both submitted documentation stating that he could safely perform all of his job functions. Moreover, the employee performed his job safely after his return, without reasonable accommodation. The employer, however, terminated the individual's employment after evaluating the doctor's and therapist's reports, without citing any contradictory medical or factual evidence concerning the employee's recovery. Without more evidence, this employer cannot support its determination that this individual poses a direct threat.[80]

Professional Licensing

Individuals may have difficulty obtaining state-issued professional licenses if they have, or have a record of, a psychiatric disability. When a psychiatric disability results in denial or delay of a professional license, people may lose employment opportunities.

36. Would an individual have grounds for filing an ADA charge if an employer refused to hire him/her (or revoked a job offer) because s/he did not have a professional license due to a psychiatric disability?

If an individual filed a charge on these grounds, EEOC would investigate to determine whether the professional license was required by law for the position at issue, and whether the employer in fact did not hire the individual because s/he lacked the license. If the employer did not hire the individual because s/he lacked a legally-required professional license, and the individual claims that the licensing process discriminates against individuals with psychiatric disabilities, EEOC would coordinate with the Department of Justice, Civil Rights Division, Disability Rights Section, which enforces Title II of the ADA covering state licensing requirements.

---

[80] *Cf. Ofat v. Ohio Civ. Rights Comm'n*, 1995 WL 310051, 4 AD Cas. (BNA) 753 (Ohio Ct. App. 1995) (finding against employer, under state law, on issue of whether employee who had panic disorder with agoraphobia could safely return to her job after disability-related leave, where employer presented no expert evidence about employee's disability or its effect on her ability to safely perform her job but only provided copies of pages from a medical text generally discussing the employee's illness).

Subject Index

F

G

S

T

U

W

Table of Cases

Cases are referenced to chapter and corresponding section(s) in the book.
For instance, **IV § 4.2** indicates that the case is cited in Chapter Four, Section Two.

About the Author

Peter David Blanck is a professor of law, of preventive medicine, and of psychology at the University of Iowa. He received his Ph.D. in psychology from Harvard University and his J.D. from Stanford Law School, where he served as president of the Stanford Law Review.

Blanck is the director of the Law, Health Policy, and Disability Center at the Iowa College of Law. He is a member of the President's Committee on the Employment of People with Disabilities, and he has been a senior fellow of the Annenberg Washington Program, in which capacity he explored the implementation of the Americans with Disabilities Act (ADA). He has written many articles on the ADA, has received grants to study the law's implementation, and his work has received national and international attention.

Blanck has been president of the American Association on Mental Retardation's (AAMR) Legal Process and Advocacy Division and chair of AAMR's Legislative and Social Issues (LASI) Committee. He has been a commissioner on the American Bar Association Commission on Mental and Physical Disability Law, chair of the American Psychological Association's Committee on Standards in Research, and a fellow at Princeton University's Woodrow Wilson School, Domestic Policy Institute.

Prior to teaching at Iowa, Blanck practiced law at the Washington, D.C., firm Covington & Burling, and served as a law clerk to the late Honorable Carl McGowan of the United States Court of Appeals for the D.C. Circuit.